REFUGE NEW ZEALAND

Refuge New Zealand

A nation's response to refugees and asylum seekers

Ann Beaglehole

First published 2013
Text copyright © Ann Beaglehole
Volume copyright © Otago University Press

The moral rights of the author have been asserted.
ISBN 978-1-877578-50-2

A catalogue record for this book is available from the National Library of New Zealand. This book is copyright. Except for the purpose of fair review, no part may be stored or transmitted in any form or by any means, electronic or mechanical, including recording or storage in any information retrieval system, without permission in writing from the publishers. No reproduction may be made, whether by photocopying or by any other means, unless a licence has been obtained from the publisher.

Publisher: Rachel Scott
Editor: Anna Rogers
Design/layout: Fiona Moffat
Index: Diane Lowther

Printed in New Zealand by Printstop Ltd, Wellington

Contents

	Acknowledgements	7
	Introduction	9
CHAPTER ONE	The first refugees	19
CHAPTER TWO	Escaping from Europe and Asia	30
CHAPTER THREE	Choosing the 'best' refugees	43
CHAPTER FOUR	A change of direction	63
CHAPTER FIVE	Refugees from South East Asia	79
CHAPTER SIX	From refugee to new settler	96
CHAPTER SEVEN	'The children are a triumph'	117
CHAPTER EIGHT	An inconvenient obligation?	129
CHAPTER NINE	'Integration takes time'	163
CONCLUSION	A fine record?	188
	Notes	192
	Bibliography	231
	Index	253

Acknowledgements

Many people have helped with the researching and writing of this book. I am grateful to the Waitangi Tribunal Unit, particularly to Richard Moorsom, who played a crucial part in arranging the leave that enabled me to write the first draft. My greatest debt is to Klaus Neumann, of Swinburne University of Technology, who instigated the project, obtained funding for it from the Australian Research Council and made useful comments on my early drafts. Without his collaboration the book could never have been written. I am most grateful to the Australian Research Council for their support. I am grateful too for the support of Swinburne's Institute for Social Research (now called The Swinburne Institute). Without the support of both the Institute for Social Research and Swinburne University the project would not have gone ahead. Thanks also to Tony Haas, who made helpful suggestions on an early draft, and to Anthony Hubbard for his comments. The Ministry of Foreign Affairs and Trade and the Department of Labour gave me permission to use their records. Thanks to Neil Robertson and Wendy Searle for their timely responses to my requests. I am also indebted to Lillian Loftus at the Faculty of Humanities and Social Sciences of Victoria University of Wellington for administration support and Lydia Wevers at the Stout Research Centre for a space in which to work.

A number of people gave useful information. I would especially like to thank Mary Boyce, Peter Cotton, Lianne Dalziel, Roya Jazbani, Rachel Kidd, Don McKinnon, Aussie Malcolm, Dr Nagalingam Rasalingam, Theresa Sawicka-Brockie, Keith Taylor, Kevin Third and Conrad Wright. Colleagues at the Waitangi Tribunal Unit gave valuable feedback on the section of the book about Maori as refugees. The Asia 2000 Foundation pointed me on the right path regarding files associated with the project. Heartfelt thanks to Catherine Falconer-Gray who helped with the checking and the cutting of the manuscript. I would especially like to thank Joe Beaglehole, Malcolm McKinnon (as so often before), Steven Price and Teresa Shreves most sincerely for crucial advice and support. Thanks are also owed to staff at the Alexander Turnbull Library for their help with sourcing and ordering images and to the New Zealand Red Cross for permission to use their images. I am most grateful to Keith Taylor for the images he made available for the book from his archives.

A big thank you to Wendy Harrex of Otago University Press for helping to launch the book in a new direction, and to publisher Rachel Scott and editor Anna Rogers for their help in bringing the book to completion. Finally, I am grateful to David Beaglehole, who a few years ago said, 'Don't delay. Get on with your writing.'

Ann Beaglehole

Introduction

Refugee and asylum seeker policies are controversial in many parts of the world, and New Zealand is no exception. *Refuge New Zealand* looks at the history of this country's response to refugees and asylum seekers in order to shed light on its present refugee policy. It explores New Zealand's unique approach to refugees and asylum seekers and tells the story of the involvement of the state and ordinary people in helping the victims of wars and conflicts by offering them a chance to start a new life.

Since 1944, when refugees were first distinguished from other migrants in official statistics, New Zealand has accepted more than 30,000 refugees.[1] Although that total is not large relative to the many millions of refugees and displaced people in the world, it is high for a country of this size. New Zealand is ranked as fifth in the world in terms of the numbers of refugees accepted and settled since World War II.[2] Fewer than 20 countries have refugee resettlement programmes. New Zealand is one of only a small number of nations to accept refugees considered hard to settle, such as women at risk, medical/disabled and emergency protection cases.[3] New Zealanders are justly proud of the country's record of refugee settlement. From the perspectives of some refugees and asylum seekers, however, New Zealand's policies have been harsh. Which groups and categories have been chosen and why? Who has been kept out and why? How has public policy governing refugees and asylum seekers changed over time?

Unlike migrants who choose to migrate in search of new opportunities, refugees are forced to leave their homeland, typically to escape persecution because of their ethnicity, their religion or their political beliefs, or because they have been displaced by wars and other conflicts. Asylum seekers are people without United Nations High Commissioner for Refugees (UNHCR)-mandated refugee status; they seek to establish this after they have reached a country of asylum. Their claims are assessed under the 1951 United Nations Convention, the 1967 Protocol Relating to the Status of Refugees and other conventions relating to torture and civil and political rights.

These international agreements came about because, soon after the end of World War II, there was need for a general definition, replacing previous ad hoc agreements, of who was to be considered a refugee. The United Nations Convention relating to the Status of Refugees was adopted on 28 July 1951. Signatories could stipulate that their commitment related only to people who had become refugees as a result of events taking place in Europe before 1951. The 1967 protocol made the 1951 provisions applicable to refugee situations after 1951 and worldwide. New Zealand is a signatory to both the convention and the protocol.[4] Another agreement signed by New Zealand is the Agenda for Protection 2002, which covers a range of measures relating to the status of refugees not addressed in 1951 and 1967.[5]

The 1951 convention defines a 'refugee' as any person who:

owing to well-founded fear of being persecuted for reasons of race, religion, nationality, membership of a particular social group or political opinion, is outside the country of his nationality and is unable, or owing to such fear, is unwilling to avail himself of the protection of that country; or who, not having a nationality and being outside the country of his former habitual residence as a result of such events, is unable or, owing to such fear, is unwilling to return to it ...[6]

The distinction between migrants and refugees and between refugees and asylum seekers may become blurred at times. Members of the New Zealand public, especially those opposed to the arrival of dark-skinned strangers or people who chatter loudly in foreign languages, have not always differentiated between immigrants, refugees and asylum seekers. For the refugees themselves, there may be a degree of stigma attached to the label 'refugee'. 'In the first place, we don't like to be called "refugees." We ourselves call each other "newcomers" or "immigrants",' wrote German Jewish refugee Hannah Arendt in 1943 after fleeing Nazi Germany for the United States. 'We declared that we had departed of our own free will to countries of our choice … we were immigrants or newcomers who had left our country because one fine day it no longer suited us to stay … we wanted to rebuild our lives, that was all.'[7]

More than 60 years later, in New Zealand, Somali refugee Hassan Adam, a Muslim, expressed similar feelings. 'I never planned to be a refugee. It is a stigma, a title that goes with you for the rest of your life.' Adam and his wife Fowzia Mohamed fled the war lords in Somalia, finding temporary refuge in Malaysia before coming to New Zealand. For seven years Adam was unable to find work in New Zealand that matched his skills. The label of refugee was 'a curse'.[8] For asylum seekers, however, refugee status is the sought-after passport to a new life, bringing the hope of permanent settlement in the country that has given them temporary asylum.

Another term, which may be more suited to the plight of nineteenth-century Maori alienated by war and land loss, is 'displaced person' or 'internally displaced person'. An internally displaced person (IDP) is someone who is forced to flee his or her home country but who remains within its borders. IDPs are often referred to as refugees, although they do not fall within the legal definition. The term 'refugee' is preferred in this book, however, because, as it argues, some fugitive Maori did cross borders in the nineteenth century.

Small numbers of people who were in effect refugees – though, like some Maori, they do not meet the legal definition – arrived in New Zealand in the nineteenth and early twentieth centuries. They included Danes fleeing suppression of their language and culture under Prussian occupation in the 1870s, and Jews escaping persecution in Tsarist Russia and Poland from the 1880s.

By the early 1900s, however, refugees could no longer merge 'into the general stream of immigration', without requiring passports or visas, as they had done earlier. The imposition of tight controls by sovereign nation states and the closing of their frontiers to entry by migrants resulted in refugees being 'shunted from border to border'.[9] The displacement of people caused by World War I was mostly temporary, and the first large-scale refugee movement of the twentieth century is considered to have been caused by the Russian Revolution in 1917. Significant refugee movements during the 1920s occurred in the aftermath of the collapse of the Ottoman Empire. Many thousands of Armenian refugees, for example, fled to different parts of Europe and the Middle East in 1923. From the early 1930s huge refugee movements were created by the policies of Nazi Germany, the dictatorship in Italy and the Spanish Civil War. World War II, which started in 1939 and ended in 1945, caused the uprooting of 40 million people in Europe. The majority were repatriated by 1945 but approximately one million so-called displaced persons (DPs) were left in European camps.[10]

The first sizable groups of people to be granted refuge in New Zealand arrived in the years before, during and immediately after World War II. They included Jews escaping Nazi Europe, Chinese women and children fleeing the advance of the Japanese, Polish children brought to New Zealand from Persia (Iran) in 1944 and European DPs who were accepted between 1949 and 1952.

The establishment of communist-backed regimes after 1945 in Europe and Asia created waves of refugees fleeing oppression and lack of economic opportunities in their countries. If they were white and had the skills needed in New Zealand they received a warm welcome. Several groups of refugees from communism settled in New Zealand between the mid-1950s and the end of the 1980s, including Hungarians, Czechs, Slovaks and Poles. Refugees from Africa, Asia and the Middle East arrived from the 1970s and in greater numbers in the 1980s. Vietnamese, Cambodian and Laotian refugees were accepted in significant numbers in the aftermath of the Vietnam War.

Forced migration, including refugee flows, asylum seeker arrivals, internal displacement and development-induced displacement, has increased considerably 'in volume and political significance' since the ending of the Cold War in the late 1980s and early 1990s. According to sociologist Stephen Castles, it has become 'an integral part of North-South relationships' and is a crucial dimension of globalisation.[11] The most recent groups of refugees considered in the book have arrived since the end of the Cold War from diverse places in Africa: Somalia, Burundi, Ethiopia, Rwanda and the Sudan.

The scale of the refugee problem in the early twentieth century led to the beginning of international action on behalf of refugees who had nowhere to go owing to the closed frontiers of many countries that had previously received immigrants. The League of Nations appointed Dr Fridtjof Nansen as the first High Commissioner for Refugees in 1921. After his death in 1930, the league created the International Nansen Office, which functioned from 1931 to 1938. In the 1920s and early 1930s, New Zealand, as a member of the League of Nations, contributed to the administrative costs of various refugee offices and committees. The Inter-governmental Committee on Refugees (IGCR), mainly concerned with Jewish refugees, was set up in 1938 and remained in operation until 1947. The United Nations Relief and Rehabilitation Administration (UNRRA) started in 1943 to deal with refugee problems during the war. Both the UNRRA and the IGCR were replaced by the International Refugee Organisation (IRO) when it was established in 1947. In 1950, the IRO was in turn replaced by the Office of the United Nations High Commissioner for Refugees (UNHCR), an agency that New Zealand has supported since its inception. Another agency that has had considerable New Zealand support is the United Nations Relief and Works Agency for Palestine Refugees (UNRWA), set up in 1949. New Zealand played a dominant role in its foundation and has supported it with financial contributions, though not by settling Palestinian refugees here.[12]

New Zealand's commitment to international refugee work in the mid-twentieth century reflected 'the New Zealand Labour government's international idealism ... and a strong sense of moral obligation and humanitarianism'.[13] As George Laking, Secretary of Foreign Affairs from 1967 to 1972, observed, 'New Zealand may have little power to influence the outcome of many of the great problems that beset the world. But ... where it can, it must join in the efforts to solve them.'[14]

Refuge New Zealand focuses on New Zealand's efforts in the area of refugee settlement, not on New Zealand's role in and financial support of international organisations such as the IRO, the UNHCR and the International Committee of the Red Cross. Nor does the book examine New Zealand's response to refugee emergencies and appeals when the outcome was the giving of monetary aid or food (refugee relief work), or New Zealand's overseas aid programmes.

Economic, political and humanitarian considerations have all played a part in the selection and admission to New Zealand of refugees from overseas, with one or other dominating at different times. Refugee intakes have been larger where there were clear economic benefits to New Zealand and the particular refugee group was regarded as suitable for settlement. When only humanitarian considerations were involved, intakes have tended to be smaller.

'Oh, we had such dreams of New Zealand! What a clean, healthy, good, beautiful, smiling country it must be with only clean, beautiful, smiling, good, healthy people. It sounded like Paradise,' says a former Hungarian refugee in Janet Frame's novel, *Living in the Maniototo*. He also remembers his elation when learning that a New Zealand selection officer had deemed his family 'spotless', because it meant that they would be offered resettlement – New Zealand wanted 'people who would "fit in", readily and painlessly (painless for those already here). Like invisible mending. Or like an insect that moves to another tree and is given new camouflage and told, stay on that bough, blend, and all will be well.'[15]

The careful selection of refugee settlers to ensure they would 'fit in' has been an important theme in refugee policy over the years, particularly until the late 1980s. Some refugees and asylum seekers have been more welcome than others, and children, especially orphaned ones, were often preferred.

Refugee policy, especially the selection of refugees, has had close links to immigration policy, and to New Zealand's foreign relations. The book discusses New Zealand's changing response to the pressure from Britain, the United States and the UNHCR to accept refugees as settlers. It also touches on the contribution refugee policy makes to New Zealand's reputation as a generous and compassionate country, active on the world stage.

Also investigated is the humanitarian impulse in refugee policy. *Refuge New Zealand* suggests that in some cases, where intentions have not been primarily humanitarian, outcomes have nonetheless been beneficial (in relation to the acceptance of displaced people, for example). Sometimes the opposite has been the case, with intentions humanitarian but the effect not entirely beneficial (in relation to unaccompanied minors from Cambodia).

Over the years, government ministers, in announcing the most recent intake of refugees, have sometimes prefaced their speeches with a reference to New Zealand's fine record of humanitarian assistance. *Refuge New Zealand* examines New Zealand's actual record to reveal the gap that has sometimes existed between reality and rhetoric. It also highlights some of the ways New Zealand's so-called humanitarian tradition or record has been used to legitimate current policy and to reassure sceptics that present policies did not cut across secure and honourable traditions.

But although New Zealand's refugee policy has had significant pragmatic aspects, the genuinely humanitarian impulse behind the country's refugee work must not be underestimated. Some refugees have been chosen simply to meet their own needs for safety and new homes, rather than New Zealand's labour market requirements or foreign policy objectives. The 'handicapped' refugee programme, which began in the late 1950s, provides an example of the purely humanitarian aspect of refugee policy, with New Zealand leading the world in the acceptance of refugee families with 'handicapped' members.

Refuge New Zealand asks, too, why New Zealanders, located so far away from world trouble spots, would want to become involved in the rescue of the victims of violence and persecution in distant places. The role and values of religious organisations and churches are discussed. Except in relation to Jewish refugees in the 1930s, churches have played a crucial role in influencing refugee immigration policy towards a more humanitarian direction and in helping settle refugees. An important theme touched on here is the absolutely vital part played in New Zealand's refugee programme by people at all levels of society – from Labour Prime Minister Norman Kirk in the late 1960s and early 1970s to hundreds of community volunteers working with refugees in 2012. They have believed that they live in a lucky country and therefore should take some responsibility for the less fortunate in the world.

Although the book focuses on the selection and acceptance of refugees, it also touches on aspects of their integration and settlement after their arrival, particularly on the provision of assistance services. (It does not, however, deal with such topics as the financial support given to refugees in the form of benefits and grants, or the refugees' own efforts, through their associations or in other ways, to make new lives in the country.)

How adequately did the system of pepper-potting refugees (spreading them around the country for resettlement purposes), practised until the mid-1980s, meet the needs of refugees? From the government's point of view, dispersed refugees were expected to assimilate more easily. In mid-twentieth-century New Zealand, this approach was also thought to be a means of avoiding the formation of alien enclaves. The essential role in resettlement of a critical mass of refugees in their own communities, supporting each other and helping newcomers, was not recognised by the Department of Labour until around the late 1990s.

Unlike Australia, with its vast array of specialist services for immigrants and refugees, New Zealand's model of resettlement has involved the use of volunteers to help refugees, particularly with their initial housing and employment needs. Until the 1990s, mainstream services were responsible for providing assistance for refugees on the same basis as any other New Zealand resident and citizen. The availability of specialist services, such as Refugees as Survivors (RAS) centres for refugees who had survived traumatic situations, has been a fairly recent development.

Public opinion has been a significant player in New Zealand's refugee policy. Refugee advocates have sometimes criticised governments for a lack of generosity, for example in the number of refugees accepted, but the exercise of a certain amount of caution before bringing new settlers to New Zealand, particularly in substantial numbers, is perfectly understandable. Governments would be negligent if they did not consider deeply rooted fears of strangers, or concerns about unemployment and housing shortages. It is in no one's interest – neither local New Zealanders nor prospective newcomers – if refugees arrive without the backing of adequate community support. The issue of community acceptance and support for the refugee programme is discussed in relation to the work of New Zealand's main refugee resettlement agency – Refugee Services Aotearoa – which combined with the New Zealand Red Cross in December 2012.

Governments have both led public opinion on refugee admission and responded to public pressure for or against the admission of specific groups. In the case of the acceptance of Asian refugees from Uganda in the early 1970s, for example, the government tried to generate public support by referring to New Zealand's previously generous refugee track record. With Indo-Chinese refugees, the government eventually responded to public opinion, which seemed to favour a more generous response.

The pressure on governments over the years to accept refugees has come from a range of groups. Most effective have been those with international connections and credentials, such as Amnesty International and the Red Cross. Churches have played a significant advocacy role through the National Council of Churches and the Inter-Church Commission on Immigration and Refugee Resettlement (since 1975), which went through a number of name changes (including RMS Refugee Resettlement) before becoming Refugee Services Aotearoa in 2012. Several other organisations have also been involved, such as the Hebrew Immigrant Aid Society, the Islamic Association, the Polish Association and various other ethnic groups.

The book also explores the extent and type of community support received by different groups of refugees. Jewish refugees in the mid- and late 1930s encountered a mixed reception. Every Polish child who arrived in 1944 was given a flower to welcome him/her to New Zealand. Southlanders in Invercargill in 1965 went to huge lengths to give the Old Believers, Russian Christians from China, a remarkable reception. Some of the Indo-Chinese refugees who came in the 1980s encountered considerable warmth from their sponsors, leading to the formation of lifelong friendships. The reception of some more recent arrivals has not been so positive.

Asylum seekers, who have not been chosen by New Zealand for settlement in the country, have been a subject of much public debate in recent years. They are viewed by many governments as an inconvenient obligation largely because their unheralded arrival has been seen to conflict with the rights of sovereign nations to protect their borders and choose their settlers.

Because of its location, New Zealand has not been threatened by the prospect of the arrival of unmanageable numbers of asylum seekers and refugees. It is currently regarded by the UNHCR as having one of the fairest, the most thorough and the most efficient refugee determination procedures in the world. The book asks whether the praise is justified. The case of Algerian asylum seeker Ahmed Zaoui has been a test of aspects of the process, with government and the courts struggling to find an appropriate balance between individual rights, humanitarian considerations and the needs of national security.

The historical perspective is, by and large, missing in current New Zealand debates about refugees and asylum seekers, and *Refuge New Zealand* aims to fill this gap. It responds to the recent significant public interest in refugees and asylum seekers and tries to look beneath the stereotypes that bedevil refugee immigration. It questions, too, the widely held perception/myth that New Zealand is a small country with a long tradition of compassionate policies towards refugees. As Tom Shand, Minister of Immigration in Keith Holyoake's National government, noted in 1962:

> *Although our contribution may seem very small to those who are cognisant both of our high standard of living and of the poverty and misery which is so common in the world, I think it is fair to say in defence of what successive Governments have done that we are regarded in international circles as a country which has shown exceptional generosity in assisting people who are less fortunate than we are, and which, at the same time, has had an exceptional success in achieving a considerable degree of racial amity among peoples of divergent races within our borders.*[16]

While acknowledging New Zealand's significant contribution at different times, *Refuge New Zealand* examines the country's actual record, focusing on major shifts in refugee and asylum seeker policy.

CHAPTER ONE

The first refugees

During the invasion of the Waikato, wrote John Gorst in 1864, 'the refugees from Pukaki, Mangere' and other Maori villages near Auckland, a number of them 'old, infirm people', were driven from their homes and their lands confiscated.[1] Gorst, who was the first resident magistrate in the Waikato from 1861 to 1863, went on to tell how the refugees – men and women who had refused to give up their weapons and take the oath of allegiance to the Queen – 'showed the most intense grief at leaving a place where they had so long lived in peace and happiness … The scene, as described to me by an eye-witness, was most pitiable.'

> The fugitives were, of course, unable to carry all their goods with them. What remained behind was looted by the colonial forces and the neighbouring settlers. Canoes were broken to pieces and burnt, cattle seized, houses ransacked, and horses brought into Auckland and sold by the spoilers in the public market. Such robbery was of course unsanctioned by the government, but the authorities were unable to check the greediness of the settlers.[2]

The word 'refugee' was in fairly common use by the mid-nineteenth century to describe people escaping religious and political strife.[3] Government records include numerous references to Maori as refugees. In 1867, for example, the *Appendix to the Journals of the House of Representatives (AJHR)*, refers to

'Waikato refugees', expelled from one district and able, or at times not able, to settle in another.[4] A 1910 *AJHR* report speaks of 'a refugee tribe' hospitably received by iwi, or turned away.[5] Newspaper reports, too, contain many references to 'Waikato refugees' and to 'Maori refugees'.[6]

Much more recently, various Waitangi Tribunal reports have described Maori as refugees. The report on the Orakei Claim, for example, states that dispossessed Ngati Whatua were 'made virtual refugees, a disillusioned, scattered and landless people'.[7] The Te Urewera report refers on several occasions to Maori refugees, for example to 'refugees from Waikaremoana' at Ruatahuna placing 'an unbearable strain on the resources of the community'. In the second part of this report some Maori are described as fleeing, being pursued and fighting in response to events in Te Urewera.[8] Among the main themes of the tribunal's three-volume *Wairarapa ki Tararua Report* – in which Maori are described as refugees on a number of occasions – are powerlessness and displacement.[9]

'Refugee' is an apt word to describe the Maori experience under colonialism for several decades of the nineteenth century and in the early twentieth century. Maori were a sovereign people before colonisation, with title to the land;[10] after colonial subjugation some did become refugees.

Applying the word to Maori does invite comparisons with contemporary international law and norms in relation to refugees under United Nations conventions. Because Maori do not fit these definitions of refugees, some may argue that 'internally displaced person' – someone forced to escape from his or her home but remaining within his or her country's borders[11] – is a more appropriate term. However, it is possible to argue, as historian James Belich does, that two national zones existed in large parts of New Zealand in the nineteenth and early twentieth centuries, with fugitive Maori crossing borders from one to the other. The zones were 'politically independent of each other', though social, cultural, legal and administrative interactions between them were common.[12]

The period 1863–69 was the point where the tide of Maori independence began to turn, 'but that tide ran out very slowly'. Maori independence persisted long after the New Zealand Wars, in part because of remaining 'centres of resistance'. The largest of these was the King Movement, whose territory came to be known as the King Country. In 1884, this 'encompassed 7,000 square miles, nearly one-sixth of the North Island ... Thus, in the late nineteenth century, an independent Maori state nearly two-thirds the size of Belgium existed in the middle of the North Island.' At least until this time, the King

Country was 'making and enforcing its own laws, conducting its own affairs, sheltering fugitives from Pakeha justice and killing Europeans who crossed its borders without permission'.[13]

Maori experienced colonialism and European settlement in a variety of ways. Kupapa Maori, who were friendly to the Crown, and often prospered after the wars, viewed their situation differently from Maori badly affected by the wars and land confiscations.[14] The impact of land losses was incalculable for a people who had regarded themselves as 'politically lords of the land as well as landlords'.[15] The loss of land was associated with loss of mana and consequent demoralisation. There was no Maori word for 'refugee' in the nineteenth century, but the word 'whakarau', meaning 'exiles' or 'unhomed' was used. Te Kooti applied it to the prisoners from the East Coast who had been transported to the Chatham Islands in 1865–66.[16]

The research of historians Judith Binney and Bronwyn Elsmore shows that some Maori identified strongly with the Israelites or Hebrews of the Old Testament. Like Maori, they had lost their land and become fugitives under foreign rule. Identification with the plight of dispossessed ancient Hebrews to some extent shaped religious movements like Pai Marire, Ringatu and Ratana.[17] 'We are like wandering Israelites without a home; we are living on the branch of the tree,' Chief Reihana Te Aroha is reported to have said at a meeting at Orahiri in 1869. Asking that confiscated land in the Waikato be returned to iwi in exchange for peace, he said: 'Give back the soil, give back Waikato, give back Tamaki (i.e. Pukaki, Mangere, &c). Although I am living on the branch of the tree I still cling to the soil (I will not give up my right to it).'[18]

In his 2011 novel, *The Parihaka Woman*, contemporary Maori writer Witi Ihimaera explores the connection between Old Testament Israelites and Maori. In the book, three sisters, described as 'refugees', have fled from Parihaka and take refuge with other Maori in Wellington, arriving at Kaiwharawhara marae just as night is falling:

> *Some people, recognising the feathers in Ripeka and Meri's hair, came to greet them. 'Aue, we are all refugees', they said. 'Even here in Wellington, ever since the Pakeha came in 1840 with his deed of purchase, we have been gradually forced out. His is the great white tribe who owns Whanganui-a-Tara now.'*[19]

One of the sisters voices her fears about what the future may hold for 'the iwi katoa of all Aotearoa':

> *To be herded onto and live the rest of their lives in reserves ... or at the edges of the land, the fringes of the sea, the tops of mountains, offshore islands ... or to scrabble with others for scraps and pieces of unwanted broken biscuit, in the*

great cities of the Pakeha ... If Maori continued to fight against the Pakeha ... would Maori be erased all together?[20]

But how useful is it to apply the term 'refugee' to Maori? In Belich's words, 'Facing the facts' about our history contributes to our growing understanding of New Zealand's past, moving from the once generally held Pakeha view, that colonisation benefited indigenous people by bringing progress, civilisation and introducing modern systems of land ownership and government.[21] Evidence suggests that while a minority benefited, many Maori became impoverished and landless.

Some former refugees from overseas embrace the term; others are indifferent or resent its application to their own situation. Some Maori, too, may disapprove of the word, perhaps because it appears to focus more on how Maori society was damaged by colonisation, than on how it survived. But refugees everywhere are survivors, not just victims. Some Pakeha may disapprove of calling Maori refugees. But the question has to be this: Despite effective resistance and resilience in dealing with negative Crown policies, did some Maori end up in a refugee-like situation? This chapter argues that they did.

Inter-tribal warfare

Before the arrival of Europeans, inter-tribal conflict among Maori created refugees. There were occupation disputes and battles between iwi over contested land. Some ended with the expulsion of hapu, who fled from traditional homelands, leaving the victors in possession. When one iwi displaced another, complex situations arose related to differing lines of descent from the ancestral iwi of a particular region and those derived from the replacement of the original iwi by more recent migrants. 'Some groups migrated as refugees, or as allies in war, and the nature of the ensuing relationship between the migrant group and the resident group varied accordingly.'[22]

The Musket Wars of the 1810s, 1820s and 1830s changed the nature of inter-tribal warfare and inflicted significant casualties on Maori – precise estimates of the number of people killed vary – causing thousands to flee from their traditional lands.[23] From 1921, for example, Ngapuhi leader Hongi Hika took revenge on Tamaki iwi by attacking two Ngati Paoa pa. Hundreds were killed and captured as slaves. He repeated his assaults on other iwi: Ngati Maru near Thames, and Ngati Whatua. The latter undertook several journeys of exile to escape attacks from Ngapuhi and other tribes. They eventually settled in Te Horo in 1831 but returned to Tamaki later in the decade.[24]

The use of muskets resulted in unprecedented population movements and displacement, as the *Wairarapa ki Tararua Report* points out. The worst casualties resulted 'not from the battles themselves but from the redistribution and concentration of the population as people fled the fighting and became refugees'. And what followed was 'economic disruption, the loss of crops and access to food sites, starvation, and disease as a result of overcrowding and unsanitary conditions'.[25]

The invasion of the Chatham Islands by Taranaki Maori in 1835, and the ensuing mass killing and enslavement of the Moriori population, including many women and children, is another example of inter-tribal conflict creating refugees. Those Moriori not killed or enslaved in 1835–36 are said to have died subsequently of 'despair'.[26]

Refugees of the New Zealand Wars

From 1845 to 1872 the wars between the British and Maori tribes of the North Island, marked by fierce and brutal fighting, produced refugees. In 1928, the Sim Commission, set up to inquire into the justice of the confiscations of Maori land, concluded, in relation to the Taranaki war, that Wiremu Kingi and his people were 'driven from the land, their pas destroyed, their houses set fire to, and their cultivations laid waste'. The commission painted a devastating picture of the colonists' greed, 'impatience' and 'clamour' for land, leading to the 1860 Waitara purchase, 'the spark which set all ablaze'. Regarding 'the Parihaka expedition in 1881', the commission concluded that, though the prophet Te Whiti was 'pacific' and the villagers were unarmed, the government 'took the extreme step of pouring into his village of Parihaka an overwhelming armed force. Then, after reading the Riot Act to a passive and orderly crowd of men, women and children, they proceeded to make wholesale arrests, to evict the villagers, and to destroy houses and crops.'[27]

Waitangi Tribunal reports, too, speak of the war refugees. The report on Central North Island claims, for example, discusses the fate of the Waikato refugees after their displacement – whether they were given refuge by other iwi, whether some iwi had an obligation to support Waikato refugees and whether the refugees sought reconciliation with Pakeha. 'After the end of the Waikato war, Tuwharetoa accepted refugees from Waikato, Pai Marire, and at the same time sought to enter into a relationship with the Crown.'[28]

There are numerous contemporary newspaper references to 'Waikato refugees' attending, or not attending, large 'Native meetings'. Some accounts suggest that they were seen as causes of tension in the districts to which they had fled.[29] Refugees were often seen as 'welcome guests' at first, but problems arose if they stayed for many years. Several newspapers reported tensions between Waikato refugees and Ngati Maniapoto. On 8 June 1869, for example, the *Daily Southern Cross* described a meeting between a group of Pakeha and the King Party:

> They (Ngati Maniapoto) would ... gladly get rid of the Waikatos altogether if the latter could be induced to settle on portions of the Waikato. They are annoyed at the obstinacy of the Waikatos, and already a suspicion is gaining ground that these people whom the Ngatimaniapotos have received as guests and refugees desire to remain in permanent possession of the land on which they have been provided with an asylum on sufferance.

As the same paper noted the following January,

> Long residence on the Ngatimaniapoto land would, according to native custom, confer a kind of proprietary right upon the refugees, and it may be presumed that the Ngatimaniapoto are anxious to see the refugees again located in Waikato before they have lived sufficiently long in the Ngatimaniapoto country to acquire a vestige of title. This supposition would account for a great deal of the jealousy that has been known to exist for some time past between these two great tribes.[30]

As fighting in the Waikato was winding down, 'virtual civil war' between Maori on the East Coast created more refugees.[31] Between 1864 and 1872 factions of Ngati Porou fought each other with government-supplied guns. One group supported Pai Marire, a messianic religious movement; the other tried to resist them. Ngati Porou's aim was to maintain its own sovereignty; the government's was to try to stop the spread of Pai Marire, which aimed to drive Pakeha from Maori land and supported the Kingitanga, the movement to create a Maori nation under a Maori King.

Maori in Turanga had remained neutral during the wars in Taranaki and Waikato, refusing to support either the Crown or the Maori King. In 1865 members of Pai Marire arrived in Turanga and the majority of Turanga Maori converted to the new faith, which promised to protect their lands and independence. The government 'decided to grasp the opportunity to use the Ngati Porou and colonial forces then in the district to destroy the Pai Marire influence along the East Coast and, in the process, break the independence of the Turanga tribes'. In November Crown forces attacked and besieged Pai Marire at Waerenga-a-Hika, just inland from modern-day Gisborne. Around 800 Maori, including 300 women and older children, were in the pa at the time: almost the entire population of Turanga. The pa fell after five days and inhabitants either escaped or surrendered. Seventy-one were killed.[32]

After the surrender of the pa, the Crown imprisoned 113 men and transported them to the Chatham Islands, later sending 10 more. The prisoners were to be held for an indeterminate period and Turanga Maori land was confiscated as punishment. There was also pressure to give up more of their land to the Crown as 'reparations'. Conditions on the Chathams were harsh, particularly for people unused to a cold climate. The prisoners were required to build their own accommodation and grow their own food; around 22 men and some women and children died from illness. One of the prisoners was Te Kooti Arikirangi Te Turuki, who began to build up the principles of a new faith – the Ringatu – and planned their escape back to the mainland in 1868.[33] There they sought refuge in the Urewera. As the *Evening Post* of May 1870, for example, reported, Te Kooti and his supporters were 'still hiding in the Wai-o-eka gorge, with a few followers, and destitute of food, except fern-root, and what they can pick up. It seems that honey is much depended on by these refugees in the country they are now in.'[34] When Te Kooti sought refuge with Tuhoe, who agreed to hide him, British troops 'unleashed their wrath', destroying Tuhoe crops and buildings and taking the only remaining arable land, including access way to their fishing grounds.[35] Such scorched earth tactics were also used in Tauranga, with devastating effects on Ngati Ranginui.[36]

Refugees were also created by violent retaliation to non-violent resistance by Maori to European occupation. The best-known instance of this was at Parihaka in 1881. Less well known is the earlier situation of a community driven off their land in the Waitaki Valley on the South Island in 1879. Under the leadership of Ngai Tahu prophet Hipa Te Maiharoa, in 1877 they had reoccupied 'old tribal grazing land', but two years later their 'peaceable community ... was dismantled and its inhabitants evicted forcibly by police'.[37] In Buddy Mikaere's account, 'on a bitterly cold day', some 150 men, women and children 'marched slowly out into the snow. Turning their backs on the little village they had raised in the tussock, they began the long trek back to the coast.' The sad procession included 30 drays and wagons, 100 horses and a similar number of dogs. 'As the people marched, a column of smoke rose in the sky behind them: the police were burning their homes.'[38] During the journey down the Waitaki Valley on bad roads in appalling winter weather, several old people and young children perished.

Displaced Pakeha

Fearing threat to their lives and homes from Maori, especially when the colonial forces were defeated or had suffered a setback, Pakeha were also forced to take refuge from time to time during the wars. In 1860, as the *Wellington Independent* reported on 14 August, 'Taranaki refugees' sought refuge in Wellington, but the 'southern provinces' were regarded as safer, so some of the women were provided 'an asylum' in Nelson. On the 21st, the paper stated:

> *The exodus to Nelson of all the women and children is fast taking place. The steamers* Fawn *and* Cordelia, *have before now, perhaps, landed nearly all of them there. It is gratifying to observe how cheerfully the burden is borne, and with what facility accommodation is provided. Buildings are being rapidly prepared. Fifty workmen in government employ have voluntarily given a couple of days' work to expedite them ... So that for any number of refugees who may come ... shelter can be found.*

Money and clothing were also collected. Pakeha New Zealand pulled together to help the refugees. As the *Independent* concluded, 'While we earnestly desire that the occasion for such efforts may soon cease, we shall the less regret the necessity that now exists, as it has the effect of thus drawing the several settlements together, and uniting them in the bond of common brotherhood.' Because Nelson was regarded as having 'received more than her share' of refugees, refuge and funding for the refugees was also sought elsewhere.[39]

By 1861, as the *Lyttelton Times* reported, a fund had been set up 'for the relief of the Taranaki sufferers' in the 'Maori war', with a 'large sum of money' collected. The fund, though 'very far short of the losses sustained by the settlers', was intended to help those made 'destitute' by helping them 'to resume their farming operations'.

> *Besides the entire destruction of more than three-fourths of the homesteads in the country, and the injury the farms have sustained in the destruction of fences, the growth of thistles, &c., the greater part of the stock on which the mass of the farmers exclusively relied has disappeared. For months past the insurgents have been living on our cattle and sheep, and have wantonly destroyed more than they have consumed.*[40]

By August 1864, most of the refugees who had sought refuge in Nelson had returned to Taranaki.[41] After the Taranaki refugee situation seemed to be over, reports appeared in 1868 of Pakeha settlers attacked by Pai Marire in Poverty Bay. The women and children, described as 'refugees', or as 'seeking refuge', were evacuated from the Wairoa settlement and area to the north of Napier.[42] The *Star* described settlers escaping 'barefooted in their night clothes', and the *Wellington Independent* wrote of fundraising efforts for 'the relief of the survivors of the late horrible massacre'.[43]

Land loss

Increasing Maori landlessness from the 1860s meant more refugees. Land loss resulted from confiscations, compulsory acquisitions of land and land sales, and from Maori agreeing to long-term leases in an attempt to gain some income from remaining land. Severance from traditional lands led to economic marginalisation and widespread poverty. Several Waitangi Tribunal reports describe the dire consequences suffered by landless Maori.

The government confiscated substantial areas of Maori land after the wars of the early 1860s. Both tribes who had 'rebelled' against the Crown, and those who had supported it, suffered. Under the New Zealand Settlements Act 1863 and its amendments, land was confiscated in South Auckland, Waikato, Tauranga, Opotiki-Whakatane, Taranaki and the Mohaka-Waikare district of Hawke's Bay. The largest confiscations were in Waikato and Taranaki. Under separate legislation, land was confiscated also in Poverty Bay. The consequences differed from region to region but were extremely severe for the Waikato-Tainui and Taranaki tribes, for Ngai Te Rangi in Tauranga and for Ngati Awa, Whakatohea and Tuhoe in the eastern Bay of Plenty. Some of the confiscated land was eventually returned to Maori, though not necessarily to the original owners. Some 'returned' areas were then bought by the Crown. This happened in Tauranga between 1864 and 1868.[44]

Taranaki Maori, as the Waitangi Tribunal noted in 1996,

were dispossessed of their land, leadership, means of livelihood, personal freedom, and social structure and values. As Maori, they were denied their rights of autonomy, and as British subjects, their civil rights were removed ... All were affected, even non-combatants, because everyone's land was taken, people were relocated, land tenure was changed, and a whole new social order was imposed. The losses were physical, cultural, and spiritual.[45]

In Tauranga, the scale of Maori land loss through Crown purchasing and other means was so extensive, and so little land remained, that Maori were unable to develop the little they had left.[46]

Growing Maori landlessness was also caused by the government's unjust land-purchasing policies and practices, particularly the failure to leave sufficient reserves of land for Maori to survive, let alone thrive, in the future. The focus was on the acquisition of Maori land for Pakeha settlement. The bulk of the South Island was bought in the Kemp purchase of 1848 and by 1891 Maori retained only 11 million of the North Island's 28 million acres. A substantial minority of this land was leased, or held in small blocks scattered through Pakeha areas.[47] By 1900 Maori had lost most of their land.

Land purchasing officers increasingly dealt only 'with sellers of a tribe, though they were but a few, ignoring chiefs and others as though the few were solely entitled'.[48] Pre-purchase payments were sometimes used to exert pressure on chiefs to sell. The tactic took advantage of Maori poverty and debt and was intended 'to lock Maori into a process from which they could not retreat'.[49] Another unfair tactic was to pay a nominal price for land that had the potential for a very early substantial rise in value. For example, Ngai Tahu were paid only £2000 for 20 million acres, 'a substantial part of the South Island and almost a third of the total area of the country', and were left with 'totally inadequate land'.[50] The inadequacy of the purchase price was particularly problematical if Maori had insufficient land.

Maori were pressured to sell their land without the government fulfilling its side of the agreement to set aside adequate amounts of land to enable them to participate in the new economy. With significant cultural differences between Maori and settlers wanting land, there was considerable chance of misunderstanding. Where Maori seemed to agree to sales, they understood and expected that they were contracting to share their resources. Ngai Tahu, in return for the sale of much of the South Island, expected to 'participate in and enjoy the benefits that would flow from the settlement of their land. As part of that expectation they wished to retain sufficient land to protect their food resources. They expected to be provided with, or to have excluded from the sale, adequate endowments that would enable them to engage in the new developing pastoral and commercial economy.' However the Crown 'left Ngai Tahu only sufficient land for bare subsistence, with no opportunity to turn, as European settlers soon did, to pastoral farming'.[51]

Practices of the Maori Land Court contributed to landlessness. The court was charged by parliament to convert tribal titles to titles held in individual ownership. Lands owned by many people were vested by the court in 10 or fewer persons, who came to be regarded as absolute owners, able to sell the land if they chose. Tribal authority and control were lost and further land was able to be sold.[52]

There were many circumstances that forced Maori to sell land: poverty, and getting into debt due to the high cost of obtaining titles; the need for capital to develop land; the cost of attending government land purchase meetings; and having to pay taxes, for example a levy for roadworks. There was, as the Waitangi Tribunal has suggested, no free choice in such cases and Maori could not 'step out of the poverty cycle they were caught in'.[53] The compulsory acquisition of land against the wishes of Maori, for public works and for defence purposes, also led to land losses.

Once were refugees?

Maori displaced by the wars and by land sale and confiscation had become refugees. They suffered from poverty, homelessness and poor health. Loss of economic resources and mana contributed to demoralisation. Social dislocation, as families separated and went in search of work elsewhere, caused low morale.[54]

There was also a lingering sense of injustice. For Tuhoe, as late as 2012, 'the confiscation line where the Crown had pushed Maori off their land over a century before held a central place in the consciousness of iwi'. As Tuhoe chief Treaty of Waitangi settlement negotiator Tamati Kruger recalled, 'I remember like any other Tuhoe of my age going to town [as a child] and my parents and great-grandmother would tell me, "This is your stolen land. You need to get this back."'[55]

By the 1930s the deprived social and economic circumstances of many Maori were gradually becoming a matter of concern to Pakeha society. An exceptionally clear-eyed view of the impact of the past came from a Methodist leader in 1936. He believed that 'the wars and land confiscations had left a septic wound in the hearts of the Maoris'.[56] The difficulties of Maori were not, however, generally attributed to the colonial experience, but were seen largely as a failure to adapt.

The government's obligations to help Maori adapt better were sometimes used as a justification for limiting refugee intakes from overseas. In a 1962 letter to Alan Brash of the National Council of Churches, who was advocating for New Zealand to open doors to refugees from Hong Kong, Tom Shand, Minister of Immigration in the ruling National government, wrote:

> We have an average of 1600 to 2000 rural Maoris, unskilled and inadequately educated for city life, to absorb each year into our industrial structure. Added to this we have a responsibility to take increasing numbers of our own island peoples and the people of Samoa. Every Chinese refugee of the type available from Hong Kong aggravates this problem with which we are scarcely coping adequately as I am sure you will agree.[57]

Similar arguments were used on other occasions. Later chapters touch on Maori and Pakeha responses to refugee arrivals from overseas. In the mid-twentieth century, some Maori welcomed refugees but attitudes to immigration hardened by the millennium. As for Pakeha, good-hearted people wanted to open doors to refugees from abroad, perhaps unaware, or perhaps because they were aware, that New Zealand had once had home-grown refugees.

CHAPTER TWO

Escaping from Europe and Asia

In the 1930s and 1940s non-Maori New Zealanders were isolated from the rest of the world, except Britain, in a way difficult to imagine today. They were proud of their mostly British heritage and took for granted that the most desirable immigrants to New Zealand would be British. Jews and Chinese were considered to be among the least desirable settlers, yet, in the late 1930s, Jews escaping Nazi Europe and Chinese women and children fleeing the advance of the Japanese, comprised the first two sizable groups of refugees accepted by New Zealand.

Jewish refugees

Anti-Jewish campaigns began in Germany in 1933, with the introduction in April of discriminatory laws, the first of around 400 pieces of anti-Semitic legislation passed between 1933 and 1939. By 1938, Nazi anti-Semitic polices were being applied with increasing ruthlessness within Germany and in Austria, which was annexed that year. Austria had accommodated a significant number of Jews emigrating from other countries whose governments pursued anti-Semitic policies. On 9 November 1938, the German government used the pretext of the murder of a German diplomat by a young Polish Jew to initiate Kristallnacht, a series of pogroms against Jews throughout Germany. Thousands of synagogues, businesses and homes were burnt down and many Jewish men were imprisoned in concentration camps.

The victims of Nazi persecution did not usually try to emigrate until it was beyond question that their future was imperilled.[1] When they decided to leave, they tried to obtain entry permits from several countries and migrated to wherever a permit was available, and sometimes even if it was not. As they searched the world for new homes they found that most doors, including New Zealand's, were closed, or almost closed, to them. Their hasty departure meant they were unable to meet New Zealand immigration criteria before their arrival. One woman left Germany in the face of immediate threats: 'If you're not out within twenty-four hours, you'll be in a concentration camp.' Refugees 'clutched at straws to find a way into a country'.[2]

Gerty Gilbert, who came to New Zealand from Brno in Czechoslovakia in 1939 at the age of 16, recalled the desperate search for a country to escape to. Her parents, unable to get visas and entry permits, stayed behind and perished in a concentration camp.

> *Nobody wanted us. You had to be very clever and to have contacts of an important sort to be able to get out and to get in anywhere. People tried desperately hard. For us, it was a mixture of luck, coincidences and a fair amount of machinations and skill. You also had to have a certain amount of money. It was my mother who was determined to get us out. 'The sooner the better,' she said. New Zealand was one of the prize places to go to, but it was incredibly difficult to get in. New Zealand didn't want us; nor did anyone else really.*[3]

In the 1930s New Zealand did not accept applicants for entry because they were refugees. Rather, like any other migrants, refugees were subject to the restrictions of the 1931 Immigration Restriction Amendment Act. This legislation, which gave the Minister of Customs and his officials the discretion to decide who was suitable to enter New Zealand, prevented non-British subjects, so-called aliens, from entering New Zealand unless they had guaranteed employment, a considerable amount of capital or 'possessed knowledge or skills which would enable them to rehabilitate readily, but without detriment to any resident of New Zealand'.[4]

A Jewish refugee, enquiring about migration to New Zealand in 1938, was told by the New Zealand High Commissioner's Office in London:

> *The New Zealand Government is not at present encouraging immigration ... In the case of persons not of British birth and parentage, it is necessary for*

such persons to obtain permits from the Minister of Customs at Wellington before they may proceed to the Dominion. The High Commissioner has received advice from his Government that it has recently been found necessary to discontinue the issuing of such permits except in very special cases.[5]

It was, therefore, hardly worthwhile making an application.

A historian of the Jewish community in New Zealand has dismissed New Zealand's efforts to rescue the victims of Nazi persecution as 'insignificant paltriness',[6] but such harsh judgements do not take sufficient account of the circumstances of the time. They included New Zealand's long-standing opposition to non-British immigration, post-Depression fear of unemployment and support for restriction from influential professional associations and unions. Attitudes prevalent in the Labour government also contributed to the restrictive policy.

The immigration authorities' selectors' first consideration was whether an applicant could be readily absorbed into the dominion's population. Edwin Dudley Good, Comptroller of Customs in the mid-1930s, was explicit: 'Non-Jewish applicants are regarded as a more suitable type of immigrant.'[7] Walter Nash, Minister of Customs in New Zealand's first Labour government, which took office in 1935, held the same view: 'There is a major difficulty of absorbing these people in our cultural life without raising a feeling of antipathy to them.'[8]

Jewish refugees were also considered unsuitable on occupational grounds. Many of them were professional or business people and New Zealanders of the same type were anxious to keep out possible rivals. As the refugee advocate F.A. de la Mare noted after meeting with Nash and fellow Labour Party minister Mark Fagan in December 1938, the government's justification for restricting the entry of refugee business people was that 'anti-Semitism, never far from the surface, was very apt to emerge in the case of the talented race whose members can often beat us at our own game, especially the game of money making'.[9] On another occasion, Nash, whose views at this time are of particular interest because of his subsequent humanitarian position on the acceptance of refugee families with 'handicapped' members (see Chapter Six), argued that such refugees should be refused entry because they lacked the skills that were needed in New Zealand.

No-one would wish to add to the mass of unskilled workers looking for jobs, and by unskilled I would include those whose skill does not fit them for work in New Zealand. Among the applicants who wish to come there are many more of the clerical type than of the building operative type and it is the latter that New Zealand needs.[10]

Labourers or skilled tradespeople were not acceptable either, however, particularly to the trade union movement, because they might put New Zealanders out of work. In the aftermath of the Depression of the 1920s and early 1930s, New Zealanders remained afraid of the prospect of unemployment. In March 1939 the Christchurch Refugees Emergency Committee, which lobbied the government for the admission of refugees in greater numbers, sent the Department of Industries and Commerce a list of refugees who wanted to come to New Zealand and who had skills that would benefit the country. Rather than stressing humanitarian arguments for admitting the applicants, the committee emphasised that those on the list were employable without displacing New Zealanders and could make a particular contribution to the country's economic development. Their list included applications from textile workers, iron workers and manufacturers of stationery, leather, knitted goods, timber goods, battery accumulators, and brake and clutch linings. There were applications from chemists, mechanical and electrical engineers, textile engineers, locksmiths and printers, to name just a few. Most of the applications were declined.[11]

Some refugees were lucky. One young woman had fled Vienna in September 1938. Of the time before her departure, she recalled: 'They treated Jews like animals. We lived in fear. You never went out on the street without a toothbrush in case you were picked up.' Arriving in trepidation on a four-week visitors' permit, she was impressed by the friendliness of the officials she first encountered in New Zealand. The customs officer who examined her arrival papers said, 'You can't see our wonderful country in four weeks' and stamped six months on the permit. That temporary residence eventually turned into permanent residence and citizenship.[12]

For applicants and their sponsors, it was very hard to tell in advance how the rules governing entry would be interpreted. The regulations were extremely restrictive and the restrictions seemed to be applied arbitrarily. Having the right work skills did not necessarily help in obtaining the sought-after permits. Contacts and money sometimes did. Often the new arrivals were unable to explain how they had succeeded in entering New Zealand while many others had been prevented from doing so. Without exception they put it down to good luck.[13]

The influential trade union movement played an ambiguous role. Traditionally unions were opposed to immigration, especially of racial minorities, but many unionists believed there should be solidarity between New Zealand workers and the victims of fascism.[14] However, both the Federation of Labour (FOL) and the government preferred non-Jewish victims. The government in fact agreed to resettle 200 non-Jewish political refugees from the Sudetenland, which had been annexed by Germany – and where many of Hitler's opponents, such as trade unionists and Social Democrats, had fled in 1933 – but only a handful of these refugees arrived.[15]

Although there was ambivalence about and opposition to the acceptance of the refugees from such powerful groups as the FOL, the Dominion Settlement Association and the Five Million Club (the two latter organisations favoured New Zealand increasing its population, though not with Jewish refugees), the refugees did have some support in the community. Pressure on the government to accept Jewish refugees came from individual academics such as historian John Beaglehole and from groups such as the Christchurch Refugees Emergency Committee. Similar committees, formed in other main centres, urged the government to do more to help the refugees. Groups such as the Peace Pledge Union and the League of Nations Union also argued for a more humanitarian immigration policy.[16] Thomas Bloodworth, a member of the Legislative Council, New Zealand's upper house of parliament, urged the government to 'accelerate the rate of admission' of 'suitable refugees' in order to meet 'the urgent need' for a larger population in New Zealand for commercial, industrial, social, defence and general development purposes.[17]

The response of the churches to the plight of Jewish refugees was, like that of the trade union movement, ambivalent. This is particularly interesting in view of the churches' great devotion to numerous, and predominantly non-Jewish, refugee causes in the years to come and their strenuous efforts to influence government policy in favour of refugee settlement. Although church leaders generally favoured letting in more refugees, guarantors for refugees among church people were scarce and churches were dubious about taking responsibility for individual families. Only the Society of Friends (the Quakers) actively tried to influence government policy and later helped refugees who came to New Zealand.[18]

The government was also under some pressure from Britain to accept refugees to ease the flow of refugees to Britain and to Palestine. Pressure came, too, from the Intergovernmental Committee on Political Refugees, set up by the Evian Conference, a conference on refugees arranged in July 1938 on the initiative of United States President Franklin D. Roosevelt. New Zealand was represented by Cyril Burdekin from the New Zealand High Commission in London. He expressed his government's sympathy for 'those unfortunates who were compelled to seek new homes' and indicated that New Zealand was prepared to consider applications, but the number accepted would be governed by economic conditions.[19]

Most people in New Zealand probably supported the position put by Burdekin – the country could do no more than express sympathy. However, a writer in the left-leaning publication *Tomorrow* noted that New Zealand had lost an opportunity to make a significant contribution. 'An official pronouncement that New Zealand was to receive a definite and generous number of refugees might have changed the whole tenor of the Evian Conference.' The writer also commented that New Zealand had been willing to make principled statements on the international stage in the past. 'During the Abyssinian crisis the courageous pronouncement of the New Zealand representative at Geneva appealed to the imagination of the democratic peoples of the world.'[20] New Zealand governments would make such statements and generous and innovative offers in relation to refugees in the future. On the question of Jewish refugees from Nazism, however, the country was unwilling to take a stronger stand.

About 1100 refugees fleeing persecution in Nazi Europe were eventually accepted for settlement in New Zealand before the outbreak of World War II. Thousands of others were declined entry. New Zealand's restrictive polices do need to be seen in the context of the policies of national exclusiveness and closed frontiers of other countries that could have given refuge. The Australian government, for example, undertook in 1938 to admit 15,000 refugees over three years but only about 7000 arrived before the war started.[21]

New Zealand's reluctance to take a significant number of refugees seemed to be justified by the strength of public opinion against the small number who did gain admittance. Resentment against the refugees, many of whom were classified as enemy aliens during the war, became particularly marked in the last two years of the war and in the immediate postwar period. In 1945, the Otago Division of the British Medical Association requested 'all refugee doctors in New Zealand to be returned to their own countries to help in reconstruction now that the war was over'. This proposal was not prompted by New Zealand doctors' deep concern for reconstruction in Europe but by their desire to remove their unwelcome competitors from the country.[22]

The Returned Servicemen's Association (RSA) passed a similar resolution at its annual conference in July 1945:

> *Any person or persons who arrived in New Zealand from Germany, Austria, Hungary or Italy since 1939 must return to their own countries within two years after hostilities with Germany have ceased and they should be allowed to take out of New Zealand the same amount of money or property or both*

that they declared to the Customs Department on entering New Zealand; any further money or property that they possess to be realised and the proceeds handed to the New Zealand Government for distribution among needy wives and dependents of those who fought while the enemy aliens enjoyed peace and plenty in New Zealand.[23]

Leaving behind relatives had been the sad experience of many of the Jewish refugees who fled Nazi Europe before war broke out. Former refugees, when interviewed 50 years on, still remembered mothers, fathers, brothers, sisters standing on the platform as the train pulled away from the station. Many of these relatives did not survive. Those who did had spent the war in hiding or in concentration camps. Their families had done what little they could to help them from New Zealand. While it was still possible to leave Europe, they had tried to obtain New Zealand entry permits for their relatives. The success or failure of these attempts depended on a combination of luck, contacts and money – and on their knowing enough English to set the appropriate procedures in motion. Eva Brent (not her real name), despite her poor English, 'tried and tried' to make the arrangements, but 'it was hopeless, absolutely hopeless. New Zealand wouldn't accept old people and my father was seventy. We corresponded through the Red Cross for some time and then my parents disappeared.' Later she found out that they had been killed in Auschwitz.[24]

German refugee Helmut Einhorn's attempt to rescue his parents failed because he was not wealthy enough to pay their fares, or to guarantee their 'support and abode', as the regulations required, nor did he have the wealthy contacts who could have made these commitments on his behalf. When war broke out, he lost contact with his parents. They were taken to concentration camps in about 1940 or 1941, where they died. Paul Oestreicher's father, also from Germany, had every intention of bringing his mother to New Zealand, but after the war began all contact was cut off. 'My grandmother left behind in Meiningen was rounded up and eventually committed suicide. She was a strong woman; she sat down and wrote farewell letters to members of the family. We have the record of her suicide.'[25]

Fred Turnovsky's attempt to rescue his parents by arranging their emigration from Czechoslovakia to the United States, before the United States entered the war, also failed. In order to achieve this, he needed to remit £3000 to the United States. Getting together such a large sum of money was in itself a big problem, but the main difficulty was that the Reserve Bank declined his application to remit the money. Many years later, at a social function, Turnovsky met the chief cashier who had turned down his application: 'I asked him if he remembered me and my request to remit £3,000 and he said, "Yes, it was very unfortunate."

"It may interest you to know," I said to him, "that my parents were killed by the Nazis."[26]

Just before the war in Europe ended, about mid-April 1945, the newspapers began to publish photographs and eyewitness accounts of the concentration camps. People had already known that these camps existed, though some had been doubtful. In mid-May 1945, the newspapers published accounts by New Zealanders who served with the British Army and had visited the camps and were able to verify that earlier accounts had not been exaggerated.[27] After visiting Majdanek death camp in Poland, New Zealand diplomat and intelligence officer Paddy Costello, in a detailed report to Prime Minister Peter Fraser and the External Affairs Department on 26 March 1945, provided details of the gas chambers and other facts about the way the extermination was carried out.[28] The fact that New Zealanders and the New Zealand government were well aware of the atrocities is significant in the light of this country's restrictive postwar Jewish immigration policy.

The Jewish Welfare Society set up a search bureau to help Jews living in New Zealand trace missing family members,[29] and an immigration bureau to 'assist people who are settled here to bring out their relatives'. The columnist in the *Jewish Chronicle*, who described the bureau's role, did not believe this could readily be achieved, and warned that 'tangible results cannot be expected quickly'.[30] This certainly proved to be the case, for those who were able to identify surviving relatives could not simply sponsor their migration to New Zealand. To some extent, shipping problems and the priority given to the more than 9000 servicemen and other New Zealanders in Britain who had applied to return home accounted for the delays and the reluctance to bring Holocaust survivors to New Zealand.[31]

But the main impediment to the reunion of families, which the Intergovernmental Committee on Refugees (IGCR) had expected New Zealand to facilitate, was 'the question of policy'.[32] A statement by the New Zealand Delegation to the United Nations Special Committee on Refugees and Displaced Persons on 10 May 1946 opened with the obligatory expressions of sympathy about the plight of refugees, but went on to say that the New Zealand government did 'not favour mass or group immigration of refugees' and that the immigration of aliens would continue to be restricted under the Immigration Act.[33] Replying to the request from the IGCR, R.M. Campbell, Official Secretary to the New Zealand High Commission in London, stated that each case was dealt with 'in a sympathetic manner'.[34] Yet only 120 permits were granted out of 588 requests from close relatives.[35]

By contrast, between August and October 1945, Australia, with similar shipping problems and pressures to give priority to repatriating Australian service personnel, undertook to 'give favourable consideration to persons in Australia who wish to bring out to that country close relatives who had survived in Europe'.[36] By March 1946, 2000 landing permits had been issued and, in spite of the shipping shortage, Jewish refugees began arriving in September of that year.[37] Australia's policy of granting permits on humanitarian grounds alone continued until early 1947. It owed much to the Labour Prime Minister, Ben Chifley, and his Minister for Immigration, Arthur Calwell. Both men stressed Australia's humanitarian obligations and were willing to take political risks to retain their policy for 18 crucial months after the war. They did this in spite of a great deal of criticism that the needs of aliens were taking precedence over those of Australian servicemen, and in spite of opposition to the immigration of aliens in general and Jews in particular.[38] Eventually 35,000 Holocaust survivors found haven in Australia.[39]

New Zealand's restrictions contrasted not only with Australian policy, but also with the increasing national consensus, which originated before the war, that New Zealand needed to increase its population.[40] In December 1945, a parliamentary select committee was set up 'to consider the ways and means of increasing the population of the Dominion', and immigration was one of the issues discussed. Seventy individuals and organisations made submissions,[41] among them the four New Zealand Jewish communities. The reasons they offered in support of the migration of the relatives of Jews living in New Zealand included 'the saving of the remnants of European Jewry' and 'the stabilising effect' that the reunion of families would have on the lives of those already here. 'The Jew who has suffered agonies about the fate of his nearest and dearest in Hitler-dominated Europe, has never been able to enjoy wholeheartedly the freedom and the plenty which were denied to those he loved.'[42]

Their memorandum also pointed out the potential benefits to New Zealand: 'We fully realise that New Zealand must consider the question of immigration solely from the viewpoint of her own requirements of people who will help her solve population problems such as defence, labour and the establishment of secondary industries.' The communities emphasised that the prospective migrants would be carefully selected to make good New Zealand citizens. If elderly, they would be supported by their New Zealand families and would not become a burden on the state. All the newcomers would 'bring a wealth of cultural knowledge or industrial experience from which New Zealand is bound to benefit'.[43] Detailed information was provided: 340 of the applicants were close relatives of New Zealand Jews; the majority were young, youngish or middle-aged; they included tradesmen, engineers, mechanics, applicants with horticultural skills, office workers, dressmakers or milliners, domestic workers and nurses.[44] Importantly, in view of the housing shortage, the Jewish community offered to take responsibility for housing any newcomers.[45]

The select committee's conclusions were not encouraging:

> *No person who has followed the trials of the Jewish race over the past decade can but feel considerable sympathy for them ... [but] in view of the fact that matters of high government policy are involved and that the government has, over the years, particularly prior to the war, accepted a number of such Jewish refugees, we think that we will have fulfilled our responsibilities in this regard if we bring this matter to the notice of the government. In view of the housing situation and the demand at the present time for special types of workers, we doubt whether it is advisable to recommend preferential treatment to any particular type of immigrant.*[46]

In fact, the committee repeatedly recommended preferential treatment, but for people of 'British stock'. If sufficient numbers of this most desirable type of immigrant were not available, then immigrants from Northern European countries were preferred.[47] In its report, the committee outlined the approach to refugee policy to be followed in the years ahead. A key component was the careful selection of prospective refugee migrants to provide useful skills for New Zealand and to preserve the status of New Zealanders. A 1946 report from the Director of Employment made the same point:

> *It is considered that New Zealanders and British immigrants should obtain preference in filling the more attractive jobs in the community. If we are obliged to accept a number of refugees, these people would be more easily assimilated if the selection is largely restricted to the unskilled types who are prepared to accept employment in heavy industries. It is felt that professionals and highly skilled technical personnel are more likely to prove difficult to assimilate in that before long they would desire to embark on their own account as employers of labour.*[48]

The writer was echoing the views already expressed by professional and business organisations and by the RSA, and in 1951 senior public servant Reuel Lochore made a similar point – that the very success of the refugees' adjustment was a cause of resentment against them:

> *There was the feeling that nothing was known nor could be firmly ascertained about these fugitives from enemy territory; unless, of course, one chose to believe the highly-coloured stories which a few of them told concerning their experiences. And, most significant of all: instead of congregating in little*

unobtrusive alien cells, like the Italians or the Yugoslavs, the refugees were to be found everywhere: buying taxis, taking trades examinations, knocking at the door of the professions, starting new industries, taking over farms.[49]

Lochore stressed the extent to which the Jewish refugees stuck out in the monocultural New Zealand of the 1930s and 1940s, noting their 'peculiarities of dress, manner and speech, their breaches of all our little undiscussable conventions'. He was particularly critical of their social behaviour:

> They lack discretion and tact. They revel in displays of emotionalism and self-pity, and fail to realize how we despise such lack of self-control. On social occasions, and other occasions too, they talk loudly and untiringly about their own affairs. Being bad listeners they cannot take a hint, nor sense an attitude from what we prefer to leave unsaid.

If the refugees were unpopular, he decided, it was 'no doubt' because their success had aroused jealousy, 'but it is in far greater measure because so many of them … do not know how to behave themselves'. Their failure was no doubt because the standard of acceptable British behaviour was high indeed: 'We British are a very great people. We have a particularly high standard of social culture; a consciousness of the feelings and needs of our brother man is always present in us … A Central European has much to learn in this respect if he is to become one of us.'[50]

Lochore concluded by noting that his critical comments applied only to the refugee adults – the children were the 'real success of this migration … completely accepted by their own generation, happy and successful, they are New Zealanders … who have shown a real genius of adaptation'.[51] The preference for refugee children, especially orphans, is a recurring theme in the history of refugee migration to New Zealand (see Chapter Seven).

Refugees from China

The Chinese originally came to work in Otago's goldfields; by 1869 there were about 2000 Chinese men in New Zealand. Between 1879 and 1888, 21 separate bills responded to fears about the growing number of Chinese in the country. The 1881 Chinese Immigrants Act was the first piece of legislation passed in New Zealand to restrict the entry of a specific group of people. The number of Chinese who could be landed from one ship was limited to one for every 10 tons of the vessel's weight, and a poll tax of £10 was imposed on each Chinese person entering the country. In 1888 the ratio of immigrants to ship tonnage was cut to one Chinese person per 100 tons. In 1896, the ratio of immigrants to ship tonnage was halved to one per 200, and the poll tax increased to £100 (about 10 years' earnings).[52]

From 1920 until 1974 the key piece of legislation determining who would and who would not be allowed to enter New Zealand was the Immigration Restriction Act of 1920 and its amendments. Chinese migrants were one of the main targets of the Act. Prime Minister William Massey (Liberal Prime Minister from 1912 to 1925) said that it was 'the result of a deep seated sentiment on the part of the large majority of the people of this country that this Dominion shall be what is often called a "white" New Zealand.'[53] Special provisions prevented the entry of wives and families of Chinese men in New Zealand to ensure that the Chinese would not 'multiply.'[54]

According to James Ng, historian of the Chinese in New Zealand, anti-Chinese prejudice in the nineteenth century, which was pervasive and openly espoused by Prime Minister Richard Seddon, was 'intense and … deeply degrading to all the participants, tormentor and tormented alike'. And the persecution continued, affecting the 'diminished number of New Zealand-Chinese as they hung on after the gold mining to establish small businesses.'[55] In 1905 an elderly Chinese man was murdered in Wellington by Lionel Terry, an Englishman angered by Chinese immigration and obsessed with what was then commonly called the 'yellow peril'.[56]

Yet, shortly before World War II the New Zealand government, surprisingly, offered temporary permits to Chinese women and children, a concession that arguably provided the foundation for New Zealand's first refugee settlement programme. It had been prompted by the escalation of the Sino–Japanese War. China was under Japanese attack from 1931, with Beijing occupied in 1937. The advancing Japanese armies overran Canton; by 1938 its surrounding villages, many of them the homes of Chinese in New Zealand, were under threat.[57] The Presbyterian church acted as an enthusiastic advocate, lobbying the government on behalf of the Chinese living in New Zealand.[58]

In February 1939, the government decided to accept applications for a two-year visa from the wives, and children aged up to 16, of Chinese men who had permanent resident status. Various conditions were imposed to ensure the refugees would not be a charge on the state and would leave New Zealand at the appropriate time. Husbands had to pay a bond of £500 'guaranteeing that the wife would take all children born to her in this country away from New Zealand, and that the husband would "give all necessary consents for this".' Permits were granted on the condition that the sum of £200 was deposited with Customs on arrival. The money would be forfeited if the conditions of the permit were not complied with. Various other precautionary measures to ensure the temporary refugees did not overstay, and to exclude any babies who might be born to them in New Zealand, were also set in place in May 1939. The first permits were granted in June 1939 but the government ended the scheme early in 1940 owing to concern that Chinese families were taking over fruit shops vacated by New Zealand fruiterers who had joined the armed forces. Altogether 240 women and 244 children under 16 entered the country while it was possible to do so.[59] Their permits were renewable, and most of them remained in New Zealand beyond the initial two years. As happened to many of New Zealand's refugees in the years to come, the Chinese families were dispersed throughout New Zealand.[60]

According to historian Manying Ip, 'The 1939 concession was to become a milestone in the history of Chinese settlement in New Zealand: an unintentional outcome of a hesitant open-door policy.'[61] During World War II, China's fight against the Japanese helped to soften New Zealanders' attitudes towards the Chinese. Their contribution to market gardening was acknowledged: this was classified as an essential industry.[62] In 1944, the poll tax and tonnage restrictions were abolished and three years later 1323 Chinese who were in New Zealand on temporary visas were granted permanent residence. They included 249 of the wives permitted temporary entry in 1939 and their New Zealand-born children.[63]

The small number of Jews and Chinese who entered New Zealand immediately before and during the war encountered prejudice and suspicion. Given how much New Zealanders then distrusted people who were culturally different, it is perhaps remarkable that New Zealand accepted any Jewish or Chinese refugees at all. Their admission contributed in a small way to changing New Zealand society and New Zealanders' perspectives on immigrants who did not share an Anglo-Celtic heritage. More such immigrants were to come in the postwar period, not least as a result of New Zealand's decision to resettle other refugees, albeit in small numbers.

CHAPTER THREE

Choosing the 'best' refugees

At the end of World War II, more than a million people were stranded – mainly in Germany, Austria or Italy – and could not, or did not want to, return home. The organisations set up to care for these displaced persons, or DPs as they came to be known, asked New Zealand, Australia and various other countries to resettle some of the refugees.[1]

DPs from World War II

In 1946, when asked to make a contribution to the resettlement of displaced people, New Zealand told the United Nations Special Committee on Refugees and Displaced Persons that the government did not 'favour mass or group immigration of refugees'.[2] External Affairs Minister Peter Fraser thought it would be at least 'the autumn of 1947 before present congestion of New Zealand residents in [sic] United Kingdom is cleared, and until this has been done it is not possible to say how many refugees New Zealand may be able to accept as settlers'. New Zealand was prepared to play its part in solving the DP problem, but only after fulfilling its obligations to its own citizens. This meant ensuring there was adequate housing for the rehabilitation of returned servicemen.[3]

By late 1947, the International Refugee Organisation (IRO), the forerunner of the United Nations High Commissioner for Refugees (UNHCR), became concerned that some countries 'were skimming off the better immigrants' and asked for 'mass resettlement schemes' to be urgently implemented.[4] But the New Zealand government continued to delay making a decision. It wanted to increase the country's population but was concerned about the types of DPs available. 'New Zealand was not anxious to admit Jews or undemocratic elements,' the New Zealand Parliamentary Under-Secretary, Harry Combs, told the director of the Displaced Persons Centre in Senigallia, on Italy's Adriatic coast. His response was that the longer New Zealand waited, the greater was the risk that the 'cream of the crop' of the DPs would be taken by other countries, with only the 'less desirable' remaining.[5] The reluctance to accept DPs must also be seen in the context of contemporary immigration policy. Assisted British immigration had resumed by mid-1947. In May that year the Labour government had announced that 9600 British immigrants would enter the country in the next three years.[6]

By mid-1948 some groups in the community considered that the government was taking unnecessarily long to decide about accepting DPs. Members of a deputation to Walter Nash, the Minister of Customs, said that New Zealand was unfairly leaving Britain and the other dominions to shoulder the burden. The Reverend Gladstone Hughes, who represented the Presbyterian church, 'appealed for a declaration of policy ... which would show that New Zealand was not behind in the matter of sympathising with the people for whom we are responsible'. Nash replied that the government had not shirked the question from a monetary point of view but because '[t]here was something in the argument too that we cannot find accommodation for our own people'.[7]

By September 1948 several resettlement countries, including Canada and Australia, had indicated to the IRO that they would increase their intakes of DPs. On 24 September the government agreed to accept a very limited number of DPs, stipulating that the intake should include orphans and single women, family groups and some elderly. The specific number and type would be determined later.[8]

The process of DP selection highlights the strength of racial prejudice and stereotyping in postwar New Zealand. There was a bias in favour of some ethnic groups (northern Europeans) and against other groups (Jews and Slavs). This was justified by the assumption that a small community such as New Zealand could not afford to have 'alien groups who are not at one with ourselves'.[9] In 1947 Herbert Leslie Bockett, New Zealand's Director of Employment, was unapologetic about discriminating against some groups and favouring others. New Zealand was perfectly within its rights in selecting 'the persons whom we regard as desirable future citizens'. It was not a fundamental human right of any alien to enter New Zealand but a privilege.[10]

A 1954 Department of Labour report on immigration policy justified the discriminatory policy on different grounds. New Zealand required migrants to be assimilated to avoid unassimilable migrants congregating in 'alien enclaves', as had happened in some other countries.

> *The idea of groups of aliens cornering large slices of New Zealand farming areas or establishing 'foreign quarters' in our cities and towns is anathema to most New Zealanders. We give to all alien permanent residents the unrestricted right to acquire and occupy freehold property but we do not want whole areas to be pegged out by them. This outlook, which calls for new settlers to be assimilated, and not merely integrated, may possibly be explained largely by the difference between the physical size of New Zealand and the areas of other countries referred to.*[11]

Ministerial correspondence regarding New Zealand's intake of DPs contains many references to the types of refugees considered desirable or undesirable on the basis of their ethnicity. For example, the Director of Employment advised that 'Preference should be given to racial types which are likely to be easily assimilated into New Zealand industries … It is considered that the most suitable types are likely to be found amongst races other than Jews or Slavs.'[12]

Considerations that had influenced the government's policy regarding the prewar refugees from Nazism continued to determine policy after 1945. Central to these were assumptions about the unsuitability of refugees of Jewish origin. Experience with the prewar refugees, though considered relatively satisfactory regarding assimilation, showed that the government's concerns about the prevalence of anti-Semitism, often fuelled by economic and professional rivalries, were justified. By restricting the immigration of Jewish DPs, the government could expect to avoid the more extreme manifestations of such social tensions.

After 1948 such restrictions could more easily be justified on the grounds that the applicants of Jewish origin had a national home in Israel.[13] In September 1947 Foss Shanahan, the Acting Permanent Head of the Prime Minister's Department, told the Prime Minister that there were an estimated 1,375,000 DPs in Europe, 'of whom a large number are Jews'. He also noted that 'The proposals for the future of Palestine provided inter alia for the immediate entry of some 100,000 Jews, and for continuing Jewish immigration after these are absorbed. But the plans were not fully approved by both governments and remain tentative.'[14]

Official papers from the period June 1947 to May 1948 suggest that New Zealand supported proposals to enable Jewish refugees to go to Palestine (about to become Israel).[15] In any case, the decision to avoid as much as possible the selection of Jewish refugees seemed to be made in anticipation of Israel's establishment. After that, the problem of Jewish DPs had a ready solution. Balts, as they were called, from Estonia, Lithuania and Latvia, were regarded as the most desirable DPs because they were thought to be the most assimilable, closest to the Scandinavian peoples who were considered, after the British, the best immigrants.[16] There was, however, a stumbling block: an IRO requirement that DP selection be carried out without discrimination against specific groups. There were, however, ways to get around such an obstacle. 'Although officially there is to be no discrimination as to race or religion, the selection team will be instructed in confidence as to how selection is to be made in this respect,' the New Zealand High Commission reported to the Department of External Affairs in 1948.[17] A paper written by the department for the guidance of the officers selecting the DPs suggested ways by which New Zealand could circumvent IRO stipulations against ethnic bias:

> It is usual to require receiving countries to agree that selection will be carried out without discrimination to race and religion. The final responsibility for selection rests, however, with the receiving countries and any difficulties that might present themselves in this respect can be overcome by selection officers taking care to ensure that the people selected can reasonably be assimilated into the life of the community. In this respect, Jewish refugees are likely to be difficult to assimilate. Nationals of the Baltic States would be most suitable for settlement in New Zealand and should be given preference.[18]

New Zealand's intention to pursue a discriminatory selection process was also justified on the grounds that it was in line with Australia's.

> The Australian selection mission is apparently still confining its selection to Balts and Poles. On being questioned as to their policy in regard to the acceptance of Polish Jews we are advised that, although there was no decision to discriminate against Jewish applicants, they were accepted only upon giving an undertaking to accept and remain in manual work in remote locations. No further comment seems necessary.[19]

New Zealand, like Australia, wanted DPs who were manual workers. Ideal candidates were 'unskilled' young people who were willing to work on farms, on hydro schemes, on logging operations, as domestic workers, and in hospitals.[20] 'What was wanted was the "he" type of man who could rough it and do a day's work,' said prominent Labour politician and former Minister of Public Works, Bob Semple, expressing his concern in parliament that the wrong type of refugees were being selected. 'The country wanted the type of men who built the Empire.'[21] The desired 'type' was young – the upper age limit was 55 years – but those who were not quite of working age were sought after too, with 'unaccompanied youth' of 15–17 years of age wanted for placement as trainees in various trades.[22]

'Intellectuals' were definitely not wanted, Neither were specialists and professional people.[23] Nurses were welcomed, but not doctors or dentists. The Medical Council recommended strongly to the government that New Zealand should not admit foreign doctors because of the 'large number' already allowed in during the past 10 years. (The 'large number' referred to was the 34 Jewish medical practitioners admitted in the mid- to late 1930s.) The Dental Council also anticipated difficulties if overseas dentists were permitted to come to New Zealand.[24] The Department of Labour and Employment justified not selecting skilled professionals on the ground that they could not practise in New Zealand without obtaining some form of New Zealand qualification. 'Even if they could obtain such qualification, and lack of finance would prevent this in the case of displaced persons, their employment opportunities are not great if they exist at all. To a slightly lesser degree the same applies to most occupations calling for a high degree of skill or experience …' The few professionals chosen had all agreed to accept unskilled work. They were 'reasonably contented and settled', but they had been the hardest to place, 'and it would be idle to pretend that there is scope for any number of them'.[25]

'Unskilled types' of refugees were preferred over specialists because they were 'prepared to accept employment in heavy industries' and would be more easily assimilated.[26]

Single people were preferred to family groups because they would not compete with New Zealand families for housing. Women were preferred over men, 'in the proportion of one male for every two females', but children not attached to family groups were New Zealand's first priority (see Chapter Seven).[27] Security issues also had to be considered. Selectors were urged to take particular care with security screening to try to prevent war criminals, Nazi collaborators and traitors from entering New Zealand.[28] 'There will be Nazi sympathizers and communists amongst those offering. We want neither. We have our home bred dissidents without importing them …' They could not afford to rely on Allied military screening. At its best, it would be good, but 'at its worst it might be poorer than can be accomplished here with our own means'. After all, the authorities in charge of the camps wanted New Zealand to take as many immigrants as possible. 'We must recognise the danger of their overlooking the security aspect.'[29]

The selectors were instructed to give priority to people of 'long standing displacement' over recent refugees. This was not on humanitarian grounds, but on the basis that 'their reason for displacement is better established by the military authorities'.[30] The concern was the communist, and to a lesser extent the fascist, sympathies of some DPs. According to the authorities, the possibility of a 'Fuchs case' in New Zealand could not be disregarded.[31] (In 1950, Klaus Fuchs, a German immigrant, was tried under the British Official Secrets Act for giving atomic research information to the Soviet Union.) Historian Bill Sutch considered that the screening for left-wing views was so effective that the DPs who came here 'tended to have more reactionary political and economic views than the New Zealand average'.[32]

Despite New Zealand's vigilance, some former Nazis were resettled in New Zealand. A 1953 Internal Affairs report noted: 'For some time it has been fairly clear that the wartime activities of a certain number (probably not a large number) of displaced persons in New Zealand were highly dubious.' It recommended that those concerned should not be naturalised and should be threatened with deportation. The report also noted the existence of files containing information about genuine refugees who had suffered mental breakdown as a consequence of fearing Nazi persecution in New Zealand.[33]

In 1990, Anthony Hubbard reported in the *NZ Listener* that new evidence from the Simon Wiesenthal Centre, based in Los Angeles, suggested that 'people implicated in war crimes' had settled in New Zealand.[34] In the second of a two-part investigation Hubbard focused on how 'flawed immigration screening by the Western allies after World War II let war criminals slip through their fingers and into their countries'. He revealed how this had happened, showing that New Zealand's processes 'were as inadequate as those anywhere'. Former DP selection team member Clive Cameron, interviewed by Hubbard, recalled that one of the difficulties the selection team had faced was that few applicants possessed original documents, only papers from the refugee camp. Selection depended a great deal on the applicant's personal plausibility. Hubbard noted that while 'the myth' was that 'pro-Axis personnel were automatically barred', this was by no means the case. The policy 'of shutting the door to anyone who had fought in the pro-Axis forces … was relaxed in the later stages of the selection process'.[35] New Zealand's policy of selecting strongly anti-communistic young Baltic applicants made the entry of DPs with pro-Nazi views, including war criminals, more likely.

In 1992 the Simon Wiesenthal Centre gave the New Zealand government a list of 47 DPs who were thought to be suspected war criminals. When Detective Senior Sergeant Wayne Stringer tracked them down he found that many had already died; others he was able to strike off his list. He narrowed his focus to one man, Jonas Pukas, who had been a member of the 12th Lithuanian Police Battalion, which massacred Jews during the war. Pukas insisted that he had only witnessed the killing of Jews, and not taken part. After an investigation, the National government decided there was not enough evidence to charge Pukas, who died in 1994 aged 80.[36]

The kind of DPs chosen was also determined by the availability of 'suitable types' of refugees. Orphans and children not attached to family groups were simply unavailable. There were insufficient suitable single women to fill New Zealand's quota and married people and families had to be included in greater numbers than anticipated. The number of Balts who met New Zealand's selection criteria was smaller than required. 'A large proportion of the displaced persons of Baltic origin presented for selection were intellectuals of various grades' and hence unsuitable. Also, 20 per cent of the male Balts had to be ruled out because they had served with the Axis forces,[37] though this rule was later relaxed. Competition with other British Commonwealth countries, all selecting the same kind of immigrants, made it increasingly difficult for New Zealand to fill its quota without deviating from the established criteria.[38] As a result the selectors were allowed some flexibility: 'To the extent that people of Baltic origin may not be available, it is recommended that other types who are likely to be easily assimilated into New Zealand conditions be included, with the possible exclusion of Jews and Slavs.'[39]

In later intakes the criteria became more liberal concerning the ethnicity, age and occupations of the refugees. In later drafts, too, family groups were accepted since there were 'practically no single people in the IRO camps remaining'.[40]

By 1951, Greek Roumanians, Bulgars and Albanians were being considered for selection. L.E. (Ted) Ellison, head of the selection team, noted that they seemed 'by and large' to be 'a decent crowd', and though 'a couple of them may be a bit on the swarthy or olive side … in the main they would not look out of place in a New Zealand crowd'. The pre-selection officer had already 'rejected those whose colouring would create too great a contrast'.[41] To fill the established quota a number of refugees who did not meet the original criteria were selected. Included among them were 100 'elderly' DPs, chosen on a humanitarian rather than an employment basis, as well as Hungarians, Russians, Poles, Yugoslavs, Czechs and some Jewish refugees.⁴²

The government's initially cautious approach to accepting DPs, and its careful attitude to selection, was perhaps partly justified by the negative public response to the arrival of the 'foreigners'. In July 1951 the *Southland Daily News* reported that workers were concerned about Europeans entering 'industry': 'Will the arrival of thousands of European displaced persons in New Zealand threaten the present standard of living?' According to the Southland Trades Council, 'it was not the British immigrants who were causing the trouble but the European displaced persons'; it had had 'many complaints about the unsuitability of many of these people. It was not the fault of the employers but the fault of those people who were representing New Zealand in the selection of the displaced persons overseas.'⁴³

Between 1949 and 1952, more than 4500 refugees came to New Zealand under the auspices of the IRO. They arrived in four intakes, with 941 accepted in 1949–50, 978 in 1950–51 and 2663 in 1951–52.⁴⁴ An article about the arrival of the first group in the June 1949 issue of the Department of Labour's *Monthly Review of Employment* reassured readers that the 'European settlers' on board the ship had been 'specially selected in Europe by a New Zealand Mission'. All of them were of 'good physique' and the department expected 'to be able to place in employment all but a few of the more elderly'. They were described in glowing terms:

> First, despite the terrible war-time experiences endured by many of them, they were all of upright and courageous bearing, and looked fit and strong. Second, they ... are astonishingly keen to become New Zealanders, to learn our language, and become acquainted with our customs as fully and as quickly as possible. Third, they are keen to start work ... Finally, they have been very greatly impressed by the friendly welcome given them and they like very much what they have seen of this Country and our people.

No one expected, the article continued, 'people so courteous and intelligent, so well-ordered, clean and quiet. Nor people so ready to laugh and be jolly. Nor such lovely children.' There was, though, 'a gap to be bridged', as became evident when the 'new citizens' arrived at the Pahiatua Camp, where all refugees were first sent. '"Scouts" sent out from the men's dormitories were quickly back, breathless with astounding information: "There are no guards at the gates!" Unbelievable freedom at last! To sum up, New Zealand's humanitarian gesture seems likely to reap a rich and not entirely expected reward.'⁴⁵

The article also quoted a newcomer from Latvia: 'We are people who have lost everything, even our beloved native land, but we have not lost our self-dignity and hope that somewhere in the world a place will be found for us where we will no longer be obliged to live in camps and receive charity.'[46]

Lore Bobic arrived in New Zealand on the *Hellenic Prince* in 1950. She and her husband were housed first at Pahiatua and then assigned their first workplaces and an apartment in Wellington. 'For a few years I had my meals on an upturned fruit crate with a towel over it so that I wouldn't tear my stockings on it. And then we slowly saved, bought some furniture and in 1958, a house.' One of her early impressions of New Zealand was of the 'appalling poverty … The general style and standards maintained in life were much plainer and simpler than in Germany.' The biggest problem for the government and for the new arrivals was to find accommodation. By contrast, 'there was so much work … that employers stood in queues at the Labour Department because they were desperate to find workers'.[47]

Cold War refugees

From the 1950s to the 1970s New Zealand was a land of peace and plenty, at least for much of the non-Maori population. Yorkshireman Austin Mitchell's popular 1972 book, *The Half Gallon Quarter Acre Pavlova Paradise*,[48] struck the right chord with New Zealanders in portraying the country as a kind of heaven on earth. Many people would also have agreed with the later observation of Robert Muldoon, prime minister from 1975 to 1984, that in the 1950s New Zealanders had avoided most of the troubles of the world beyond their shores.[49] In 1952 New Zealand had a population of two million people; by 1970 it was almost three million with Maori numbering 227,090.[50] The vast majority of the non-Maori population was of British/European origin. Mid-twentieth-century New Zealand was characterised by labour shortages and a relatively young population.[51]

During the Cold War years, the world was divided into communist and non-communist spheres of influence. European refugees, fleeing from communism, were generally welcomed in New Zealand. The country competed with other resettlement countries, first for Hungarians and later for Czechs, Slovaks and Poles, also escaping communist regimes.

Hungarians, 1956–59

Like the rest of the Western world, New Zealand responded swiftly to the refugee crisis following the Hungarian Revolution of October–November

1956. The government would accept 500 refugees in order to 'avoid the more awkward, and, in the long run, more expensive course of offering to take a larger number of refugees'. On 19 November, Ronald Algie, the Acting Minister of External Affairs, reported to Cabinet that this offer was 'probably as much as we can readily manage',[52] but by the end of the month, the number had doubled. Eventually, 1117 of the 200,000 or so people who had fled from Hungary settled in New Zealand between 1956 and 1959.[53]

The welcome given to the Hungarian refugees may be seen as part of the Cold War politics of the 1950s.[54] By accepting refugees New Zealand showed that it was aligned with the West against communism. As Alistair McIntosh, Secretary of External Affairs, observed in November 1956, the acceptance of the refugees was 'fortunately ... a case in which political and humanitarian considerations go hand in hand'.[55] The fact that the refugees were white and generally regarded as an economic asset – they were mainly younger and had work skills needed by New Zealand – contributed to the government's positive response.[56] In contrast with the late 1940s and early 1950s, when the refugees in demand were unskilled manual workers, by this time migration from Pacific Island countries was meeting the demand for manual workers for industry and service sectors and New Zealand wanted mainly skilled workers.[57]

Not long after the decision was made to accept 500 Hungarian refugees a New Zealand selection officer, attached to the New Zealand Migration Office in London, was sent to Austria to select the first draft. New Zealand acted promptly, considering it 'desirable to make an early start' in order to gain 'the maximum benefit and publicity value'. The government also thought that if the initiative was 'to be made a worthwhile gesture', it would 'be necessary to modify our usual selection criteria to some extent', and proposed

> *that we should offer to include up to twenty-five family groups with not more than two children and also that the inclusion of a limited number of aged parents should be agreed to subject to the condition that they will be accompanied by a son or daughter capable of accepting ultimate responsibility for the parent's maintenance.*[58]

In early November, the government suggested that 'established occupational criteria be applied as far as possible', with the inclusion of the 'maximum possible number of single women'.[59] Though, as Minister of Immigration Ralph Hanan noted later in the month, 'the selection of people not likely to be happy in their new surroundings was to be avoided'.[60] He was keen to emphasise, however, that 'no rigid conditions' were attached to New Zealand's offer: 'The policy followed in selecting refugees would largely depend on the needs of the situation and the wishes of the refugees themselves.' Although New Zealand was willing to accept a number of family groups, 'together with aged persons who wished to accompany their sons and daughters',

> it should also be realised that many – perhaps most – of the refugees had left behind them in Hungary their nearest relatives ... A moment's reflection would show that it might be a mistaken kindness to bring half-way round the world lonely old people who were entirely separated from their relatives and who retained their ties of personal affection with Hungary. There was every indication that homes were being found for these people in Western European countries within easy reach of Hungary.[61]

As with the DPs, children, especially orphans, were thought to adapt most readily to New Zealand conditions.

The officer appointed to choose Hungarian refugees remarked on the 'chaotic conditions' of the selection mission. The 'type of refugees' on offer ranged from 'the professional to the labouring categories' and 'several doctors of medicine registered, despite the fact that I impressed on them that their qualifications would not be recognised in New Zealand'.[62] Among the 'remarkably young' refugees – most were aged between 14 and 30 – there was 'a preponderance of single men ... from all walks of life'.[63]

There were difficulties with refugees making false declarations. In the light of security concerns in the age of the War on Terror (see Chapter Eight), it is interesting to note attitudes when the Cold War was at its height. There was, the officer reported, 'still no means of obtaining any security information about the refugees'. There were even rumours in Austria that communist agents were 'being filtered through the refugee channels', but when the timing was so urgent, only a short interrogation was possible.

> We asked such questions as reasons for leaving Hungary, whether ever a member of the Communist Party, attitude towards communism ... and other similar questions. It should be realised, however, that the intelligent refugee knew what answers we expected to our questions and the value of his answers was therefore obviously prejudiced by his desire to get to New Zealand. My own impression was that about 99% of them are likely to be genuine anti-communists ... I feel however that the security organizations in New Zealand should be warned to be on their toes to watch closely for any refugees with communist leanings ...[64]

Concerns about Communist Party membership and affiliation resurfaced after the refugees arrived in New Zealand. The welfare officer assigned to the Hungarian refugees said that, in his view, they were politically harmless, *even if some of them do happen to be, or have been, members of the Communist Party. I have been told that rumours have been spread according to which I am ... merely a paid agent of the government to spy on their political beliefs. Some of the refugees do not approach me with confidence. The rumours as far as I can ascertain originate with a certain clique of the 'old Hungarians'.*[65]

The officer selecting the Hungarian refugees noted that many 'stated that their desire to go to New Zealand was prompted by the fact that it was as far as possible from the communist regime'. He was struck by 'the courage of these people', many of them only teenagers, with 'stories of capture, escape, throwing Molotov cocktails'. He noticed that 'the women appear to work on equal footing with men'. For instance, one of the girls had 'worked in the building industry and one, who was an engine driver, at a coal mine'. On the whole, he was 'deeply impressed by the quality of the Hungarian refugees as future settlers in New Zealand'. In his opinion, the 'vast majority' would 'make first class citizens'.[66]

The response to the Hungarians showed what could 'be achieved in terms of international cooperation in an emergency situation of great political interest'.[67] The response of the West, including New Zealand, also had a wider significance in that it helped to shape the way humanitarian organisations, such as the UNHCR, would deal with refugees for decades to come.[68] According to the UNHCR, assisting Hungarian refugees 'was the first modern relief effort, and, after an understandably chaotic start, it proceeded remarkably smoothly'. In responding to the Hungarians, various matters of refugee law needed to be resolved. Were the fleeing Hungarians to be classified as refugees? Did the UNHCR have the mandate to deal with them? Under the 1951 United Nations Refugee Convention, refugees were the product only of events that had occurred before 1951. Another important development was the granting of refugee status to the Hungarians as a group. Until then refugee status had been conferred only on individuals.[69]

The first 66 Hungarians reached Auckland on 13 December 1956. Department of Labour officials reported that 'A weary, bewildered and white faced group of people disembarked, facing the ordeal of landing, unknown, in a new country with strange customs, different laws, and above all a foreign language.'[70] Ian W. Fraser, a Presbyterian minister from Lower Hutt who witnessed the arrival of the 'victims of the revolution', was so moved that a few years later he established the Nansen Home for elderly refugees (see Chapter Six). Fraser recalled that the first Hungarian to emerge from the plane stood on the top step, flung up both his arms and, holding his head high in the air, shouted in Hungarian, 'Praise be to God! He has brought us to a free country.'[71]

Immigration Minister Hanan greeted the new arrivals:

> *Above all I want you to know that you are among friends, and that you will be given all possible help to make you feel at home in New Zealand. This is a free country. Its people are happy and fortunate. They have been very deeply moved by the sufferings of Hungary, and they are full of admiration for the courage and heroism of the Hungarian people.*[72]

Fraser remembered the refugees' surprise at the absence of police, surely an indictment on the situation that had made them flee Hungary.[73]

Each new arrival was provided with £5 in cash and an English–Hungarian dictionary. (One former refugee recalled the children being given £2.) Temporary reception centres for the refugees were set up at Mangere in Auckland and at Trentham and Woburn near Wellington.[74] The welcome was warm at both the official and the community level. The New Zealand Red Cross reported on several fundraising efforts by Junior Red Cross members, including a cake and sweet stall, a pet's day and a collection at a mothers' afternoon tea party. One little boy emptied his money box of his whole year's savings, amounting to 19s 11d, and handed it in to the Red Cross office to help Hungarian children.[75]

Although the government intended to disperse the refugees throughout New Zealand, in 1957 and 1958 most were in the main centres, the largest numbers in Wellington followed by Auckland and Christchurch.[76] Voluntary agencies worked with officers from the Employment and Immigration Division of the Department of Labour to help the new arrivals find accommodation and employment.[77] Offers of housing and work for Hungarian refugees came from all over New Zealand and English language classes were made available. The Department of Internal Affairs provided interpreters and distributed pamphlets in Hungarian.[78] This was the heyday of the welfare state, when the government was expected to have an active role in people's lives, including new citizens.

Despite the welcome, and the help, adjustment was hard for some of the refugees, especially for young men on their own who knew little English. Many, Internal Affairs reported, 'do not appreciate the advantages of attending the classes provided for them'. The Department of Labour remarked on instances of vagrancy and drunkenness among Hungarians in the late 1950s.[79]

The department also had concerns about the refugees' social and psychological adaptation. Although well housed, employed and doing a good job, 'naturally they will not lose in a few days the fears, prejudices and suspicions their old life has created in them. They have to learn different standards of behaviour and convention and acquire familiarity with customs that are strange to them.' They also had to learn to understand New Zealand's very different culture, to realise

> that a policeman is a respected servant of the public; that our Courts administer justice, not politics; that Government officers are not party agents; that where they work there is nobody to spy on them and report to a political boss; that our trade unions are democratic organisations and not agencies of the state; and that the rights of the individual is not just a hollow phrase.

Agencies and individuals assisting the refugees were advised that they needed careful handling: 'The fact of being a refugee … results often in behaviour which arouses resentment among the people in the country of asylum.' Refugees could 'estimate too highly the possibilities of the country and the qualities of the people offering asylum. The longed-for country of asylum and resettlement becomes the subject of wishful thinking, conjuring up many illusions which the unstable, insecure present denies …' A new arrival could be anxious and tense, 'with a strong desire for self preservation', and not behave according to 'the established norms of the society in which he is placed. He needs sympathetic understanding and careful handling to help him to become adjusted to his new environment.'[80]

Adjustment was easier for Hungarians who came to New Zealand with members of their families, or with a spouse, as Louis Toth did. At that time, he 'knew as much about New Zealand as New Zealanders probably know about Hungary' and spoke little English. Although a librarian by training, his first job was in a saw mill in Southland. Later he moved to Wellington, did a library course and became a university librarian.[81]

Another Hungarian refugee resettled by New Zealand was my mother, Eva Szegoe. She had gone to the British Council in Vienna to get books to read about New Zealand. 'Everything sounded so perfect. You see we came from a communist country where you had health [care], school, everything free. New Zealand was a happy medium.' Our family – Eva, my father and I – left Hungary on 9 December 1956, taking the train towards the west and getting off at a village close to the Hungarian border. As Eva remembered,

> *In a peasant house we stayed until darkness. We only started off after darkness. That was very important because there were still watchtowers. They were patrolling all the time. My husband had two big bottles of vodka in case we met Russians. We had a guide who took us over the minefields. We really needed the guides. I wasn't sure I wanted to continue and started to cry. The future was just a big question mark.*

After reaching Austria and spending several months in a refugee camp, we were interviewed and accepted by New Zealand. We sailed on the ship *Sibajak* and arrived in Wellington in August 1957. After landing, we were taken to the Trentham immigration camp in the Hutt Valley. 'My husband had a job the next day.' Before long Eva had a job too.

> We were happy that from our pay we could straight away replace things which we left behind. That was a great thing – now we had spare money. Right from the first week we put money aside ... I was very happy because we could work and the people were very nice. We liked the people – the honesty. And freedom; you could say what you think.

The Szegoe family took out New Zealand citizenship in 1962. 'We were waiting [for] the day. We were very, very proud of getting the citizenship.'[82]

Czechs and Slovaks, 1968–71

Another group to receive a positive welcome were refugees from Czechoslovakia who came to New Zealand between 1968 and 1971. Around 35,000 Czechs and Slovaks escaped to Western Europe in the refugee crisis created by the Warsaw Pact invasion of Czechoslovakia in 1968.[83] New Zealand was keen to accept a small number of the refugees as a further gesture against communism in the Cold War. Like the Hungarians, the Czechoslovaks were white, which in the 1960s added to their desirability as immigrants. The National government did not delay making a decision. As Prime Minister Keith Holyoake observed,

> New Zealand will accept them. There are good reasons why it should. First, there is the humanitarian aspect. Second, a significant proportion of these people are likely to be in the professional and technician classes and, thirdly, New Zealand in its own interests and reputation should demonstrate that it is prepared to assist in this problem.[84]

The first group of eight of the 100 refugees the government had agreed to accept arrived in November 1968. The occupations of the five men give a further clue about the reasons for the prompt decision to accept the refugees: each had specialist skills highly sought after in New Zealand.[85] As David Thomson, Acting Minister of Labour, said, 'While our primary purpose is to offer a new life to these displaced people, it is confidently expected that many will bring with them skills which are in short supply in New Zealand.'[86]

The acceptance of the Czech refugees, whose travel costs would be met by the New Zealand government and who would receive landing grants of $10 on arrival, was made subject to various conditions. Those accepted had to have professional, technical or other qualifications 'for which there was a demand in New Zealand', though 'a proportion of lesser skilled people may be accepted for humanitarian reasons'. The refugees were to be informed before their departure that 'while every effort will be made to find them permanent jobs and accommodation on their arrival, they must be prepared to face the prospect of having to accept temporary accommodation and of having to wait for a suitable job'.[87]

As had happened with the Hungarian refugees, there was a scramble among refugee-receiving countries to accept the best people on offer. Despite acting swiftly, New Zealand had some trouble obtaining the number of skilled people it wanted.[88] The selection process seemed more akin to the recruitment of skilled migrants than the selection of needy refugees on mainly humanitarian grounds. The selection officer, who seemed to find his task rather challenging, reported that, based on what he had seen, 'there is no real refugee problem as far as we understand it. However, there is no doubt a political problem in respect to refugees, but this is a different matter.' One of his main difficulties was that the refugees had so many choices open to them. 'Most of the refugees with any ability could quite easily be absorbed either in Austria, Germany or surrounding countries as all these countries are short of skilled or semi-skilled labour.' Some, however, 'mainly for political reasons', preferred to leave Europe and start a new life in Canada, the United States, Australia or New Zealand.[89]

New Zealand, facing stiff competition from other countries, needed to find ways to attract the refugees.

> *What we must realise is that the majority of these people with any skill, who wish to go to these countries, are not going to go just for the sake of leaving Europe, or earn a livelihood as they can do that in Austria if they desire. These people want to know what type of country they are going to, what the life is like, and what are their prospects and so on. Canada, Australia, USA realise this and have information evenings and film evenings in the refugee camps to stimulate interest. This of course is something we did not do.*[90]

One of New Zealand's main attractions, and the reason why it received a large number of initial applications, was that the selected applicants expected to be leaving Austria before the winter. When the applicants were told that New Zealand was expecting to take its quota of 100 people in groups of 25 and that the first group would not be leaving Traiskirchen Camp until February, the refugees complained 'bitterly to the camp officers' and a number withdrew their applications. Eventually 24 were chosen for the first draft. The whole business had been 'challenging … While we have not obtained the numbers we would have liked, I think we have been fortunate in the standard of the persons we have selected.'[91]

Like the Hungarian refugees 10 years earlier, the Czechoslovakians underwent security screening. At first the Department of Labour considered that Communist Party membership in itself should not debar refugees from being considered, provided they could get a clearance from the New Zealand Security Intelligence Service (SIS). But eventually, as the United States and other countries rejected all refugees with previous records of party membership, New Zealand did the same – or tried to.[92] In fact, excluding such refugees proved a major headache, with the SIS considering that there might be 'some difficulty' in doing so. Although the selection officer had declined a number of the applicants because they belonged to the Communist Party, other refugees who may also have been involved in the party were perhaps accepted.[93]

In addition to the 100 refugees who came in 1968–69, a further 25 people came in 1970–71. Subsequent small intakes of refugees from Czechoslovakia, with the technical skills needed by New Zealand, arrived in the early 1970s.[94]

Poles, after 1981

As with earlier groups of East European refugees, New Zealand's response to the plight of Poles escaping political turmoil in their country between 1981 and 1982 was rapid. On 27 July 1981 Cabinet approved the entry of 100 of the refugees who had sought political asylum in Austria.[95] Martial law was imposed in Poland on 13 December and by early January 1982 New Zealand had decided that 'Any Polish national with skills in the Occupational Priority List who can meet normal immigration requirements … will be favourably considered for permanent residence.'[96]

The relative ease with which East European refugees had settled probably accounted for the speedy government decision 'to take a sympathetic view of applications' from Poles.[97] That Polish refugees had skills New Zealand needed and were fleeing from communism were also important factors. Although New Zealand was much more open to ethnic diversity in the early 1980s than it had been earlier, the fact that the refugees were white also contributed to the ease of their acceptance. Eventually, around 290 Poles came to New Zealand between 1981 and 1983.[98] A number of them had the characteristics of economic rather than political refugees, though the distinction had become increasingly blurred in the later years of the Cold War.

As had been the case with earlier refugees and DPs, the brief for the officer selecting Polish refugees had, in some respects, the tone and contents of a human resources instruction manual for choosing company employees. In choosing the first 100 refugees, preference was to be given to those who had relatives or friends in New Zealand and to single people or married couples without children 'who have skills that would assist with placement in New Zealand'. Selection officers were required to record specific details about applicants' work experience, ensuring that there were no significant gaps between jobs. Although the ability to speak English was desirable, the lack of this would not rule someone out.[99]

The Poles had to have been granted refugee status, or to have lodged an application for this. Each person's fare would be paid by the New Zealand government as a loan, which refugees were expected to repay within three years of their arrival.[100] New Zealand did not accept any 'broken families' and was also reluctant to accept engaged couples unless both people were considered suitable. 'Separated and divorced persons should be avoided unless clear evidence is seen of an absolute divorce and no maintenance commitments.'[101]

The first 25 Polish refugees arrived in Auckland in September 1981. Polish communities in the main centres had agreed to find sponsors and to look after the new arrivals. 'There is a variety of occupations [among the refugees] and we do not think there will be any problems regarding employment,' reported the Department of Labour in September 1981.[102]

Further small groups of Polish refugees came in the mid- and late 1980s. Anna Reutt-Marciszewski arrived in 1987. She was at university when the workers' protests began in 1980:

> [In] September that year they formed a movement called Solidarity. But the formation of Solidarity couldn't change the living conditions of the Polish people. The strikes continued and spread ... My university was closed when some students occupied it. At the end of 1981 the situation was very difficult economically and politically ... There were severe shortages of food ... I and my boyfriend planned to leave and go to West Germany, because we couldn't see any chance for improvement in our country ... We had passports, and everything was booked ... Then the government introduced Martial Law. The border was closed. We couldn't go anywhere.

It took Anna and her husband until 1987 to get passports to leave the country. 'Officially' they travelled as tourists, which meant taking a minimum of luggage and leaving behind important documents, such as their marriage and education certificates. They had only vague ideas about New Zealand. 'We knew so little about what we were coming to. In Poland everyone has a dream about living in a capitalist country – that you can get a good job, your own house, earn a good salary. Before we left Poland we thought we were going to Paradise.' Anna and her husband, both economists, found it hard to get work in their former professions. Anna missed her parents, her country, the beautiful old buildings of the city where she used to live, small cafes, theatres with Polish plays and 'cabarets with humour about our reality'. Gradually, life in New Zealand became a little easier and, in spite of the losses and difficulties, Anna did not regret leaving Poland. 'I'm very grateful to this country that has allowed me to stay.'[103]

Not all the newcomers felt the same way. Some had unrealistic expectations of New Zealand, believing, for example, that they should immediately be given a house, a car and a job. This was partly because 'their only idea of the West was what they had seen in American cowboy films on TV'. Not surprisingly New Zealand disappointed them.[104]

Some of the Polish refugees were critical of the selection process and keen to make suggestions on 'improving the quality of [subsequent] intakes'. They felt it was 'very important to have a good interpreter'; one used by the New Zealand government in Austria 'was very friendly with privileged Poles'. They also proposed a list of questions for prospective migrants – questions that were more intrusive and searching than New Zealand officials would have been prepared to ask. These included 'Why did you leave Poland?', 'What is your opinion of the communist system?', 'How much did you earn in Poland?' and 'What was your standard of living?' Such questions, they believed, would help to determine whether 'a person has had privileges in Poland [these people have been very unsettled since arriving in NZ]'. The refugees also thought that applicants should be asked if they had attended English classes at Traiskirchen Camp, since this 'should show good motivation if a person intended settling in the West'.[105] The Polish refugees also thought they should have been given more information about New Zealand before they came. A number of them had left their winter clothes in Austria because they thought they were coming to a tropical climate.[106]

These suggestions highlight the kind of resettlement difficulties they were experiencing as new settlers in New Zealand in the 1980s. One of these, unemployment, was not a significant issue for refugees who came in the 1950s and 1960s. The somewhat different outlook of late Cold War refugees is apparent too. They differ from some earlier groups of more 'grateful' newcomers who would not have been brazen enough to offer suggestions to the host so soon after their arrival. In fact, the Department of Labour eventually adopted aspects of the recommendations made by the Polish refugees. Ethnic community members were sometimes included in later selection teams and, from the 1990s, the government improved the settlement information it gave to prospective and new migrants.

Refugees from the Soviet Union and other East European countries

Refugees from the Soviet Union and East Europe with skills needed in New Zealand, whose refugee situations fitted well with Cold War politics, continued to be accepted between the 1970s and the downfall of communist governments in 1991. The first quota for East European refugees was established in 1974 and from 1979 it was steadily filled with refugee families from Romania, Poland, Czechoslovakia and Bulgaria, 'who have presented few resettlement problems in the long run'.[107]

By 1990, however, the Department of Labour was concerned that increasing numbers of applicants under the quota appeared to have the characteristics of economic migrants rather than those of political refugees. Five hundred and seven refugees had eventually come under the East European quota by the time it ended in 1991.[108] Around 335 Soviet Jews settled in New Zealand between the 1970s and the end of the Cold War. Assisted by the Hebrew Immigrants' Aid Society (HIAS), they came in several quotas of 25 or 50 people.[109]

New Zealand tried to choose the 'best' of the displaced people needing resettlement after World War II and then the 'best' among the Cold War refugees on offer. Humanitarian considerations and international obligations played a smaller part in the selection process than obtaining settlers with the right skills and acceptable ethnic backgrounds. However, in the face of strong competition from other countries, and despite assumptions that refugees with the wrong ethnicity, such as Jews and Slavs, would be difficult to assimilate, New Zealand eventually accepted a wider group of displaced people purely on humanitarian grounds.

CHAPTER FOUR

A change of direction

Until the late 1960s, New Zealand's refugee intakes had by and large reflected the European bias applied to immigration policy. Increased tolerance of ethnic diversity emerged gradually in the 1970s under the leadership of Labour's Norman Kirk, who became prime minister in 1972. His view was that New Zealand's future lay with Asia and the Pacific and that the country needed an immigration policy which ignored applicants' race, colour and religion. A 1974 review began the process of removing ethnic bias from immigration policy. After that, British and Irish migrants, like others, were required to obtain a permit before they left their home countries. In practice, however, migrants from traditional source countries such as Britain and northern Europe continued to be favoured.[1] The even more significant policy shift, reflected in immigration policy changes which came in 1986–87, is discussed in Chapter Nine.

Asians from Uganda, 1972–73

In 1971–72, 42 Chinese refugees facing racial and religious persecution came to New Zealand.[2] Then between 1972 and 1973 New Zealand accepted 244 Ugandan Asians, as members of Uganda's Indian community were known, of the 60,000 expelled in the course of President Idi Amin's 'Africanisation' policy. As with the Cold War refugees, New Zealand's relatively quick response was probably because the government could see potential benefits of accepting well-educated, professional and business people as settlers. Despite assurances from the government that the small number of refugees possessed the skills the country needed, there were concerns in the community about the prospect of Asian settlers. The lively debate occasioned by the acceptance of the Ugandan Asian refugees is discussed later in the chapter.

Like the Chinese, Indians came originally as sojourners, not intending to settle permanently in New Zealand. Moreover, as James Ng notes, from 1900 to 1950 'white' New Zealand policy resulted in enforced sojournism.[3] Before 1920, Gujaratis came to New Zealand, either en route to or on their way back from periods as indentured labourers on plantations in Fiji. Indian migration was very small until after World War I. There were around 100 Gujaratis in New Zealand in 1916; by 1921 there were 539, and 200 Punjabis.[4]

As their numbers grew, Indian settlers experienced racism, with numerous instances of politicians and members of the public speaking out against 'Hindoos'. Although Indians were disliked just as much as the Chinese, it was harder to legislate against them. As early as 1892 Richard Seddon tried and failed to have an act passed that would prevent Indians from hawking, and successive governments tried unsuccessfully to have the poll tax and tonnage restrictions already imposed on the Chinese extended to all Asians, including Indians.[5] Unlike the Chinese, most Indians were British subjects and after 1840 free to enter New Zealand. As a British colony, New Zealand was unable to legislate freely on areas of policy that affected imperial interests. The British government, though sympathetic to the objectives the colony was trying to achieve in restricting Asian immigration, disapproved of the explicit racism of the legislation proposed in the 1890s. The British had rejected several bills, for example the 1896 Asiatic Restriction Bill, on the grounds that it was the imperial tradition to make no distinction in favour of or against any race or colour. New Zealand's 1899 Immigration Restriction Act was eventually passed because it restricted the entry of Asians, including Indians, obliquely only rather than explicitly and was therefore acceptable to the British.[6] The legislation prohibited the entry of immigrants who were not of British or Irish parentage and who could not fill out an application form 'in any European language' – which in practice meant English.[7]

These rules remained in place until the Immigration Restriction Amendment Act of 1920 introduced further bars to Asian immigration. There were some tentative steps towards non-discriminatory immigration policy in 1961 with the passing of the Immigration Amendment Act, according to which non-New Zealand citizens – other than Australians and including Britons and Irish of European descent – were required to have a permit before entering New Zealand. Although this practice was a formality, it marked the beginning of the move to equalising regulations governing the entry of Britons and non-Britons.[8]

The Ugandan Asian community originated from pre-colonial times in a network of South Asian traders, and grew with the importation by the British of Indian farmers, soldiers and coolies. Ugandan Asians, who occupied a middle position between the British and the Ugandans, were excluded from political life but had considerable economic influence. Even those who had lived in East Africa for two generations or more had kept up their links with India. When Uganda became independent from Britain in 1962 not many Ugandan Asians chose at first to participate in the political process. By 1968 thousands who had applied for Ugandan citizenship were either unsuccessful in their applications or did not have their applications processed because they had delayed making them.[9]

In 1969 Uganda's President Milton Obote introduced legislation restricting further immigration from South Asia and the right of non-citizens to hold trade licences. He also intended to force the departure of Asians who held British passports, but before he could do so his regime was toppled by a military coup in January 1971. On 4 August 1972 Idi Amin, Obote's successor as president, announced that all Asians holding British passports, then thought to number 80,000, were sabotaging the country's economy and must leave Uganda.[10] The next day Amin issued an ultimatum: all residents of Asian ancestry had to depart within three months or face imprisonment in detention camps.[11] He later set midnight of 8 November as the final deadline. On 9 August he confirmed that the expulsion order also included residents who were nationals of India, Pakistan and Bangladesh.[12]

New Zealand teacher Heather Benson, who was living in Uganda with her Ugandan husband and children between 1969 and 1975, recalled how the Asian community was bullied: they were accused of smuggling, tax evasion, currency racketeering, undercutting African businessmen and supporting only their own charities. 'Worst of all, in Amin's eyes, was the refusal of Asians to allow their daughters to marry Africans.' The accusations aroused hatred. Benson witnessed the intimidation of the Asian community. 'The army made a point of humiliating Asians in the streets and in their workplaces. Asian parents told me of girls being molested, cars being taken at gunpoint, merchants being intimidated into giving away their goods to army personnel.'

Like some Jewish refugees in Nazi Germany who did not want to emigrate until they were certain their future was in peril, some Ugandan Asians could not, at first, see the writing on the wall. The parents of two of Benson's pupils were divided about the wisdom of leaving Uganda. Mrs Patel was desperate to flee the country but Mr Patel did not want to leave the family business and his comfortable home in Uganda. 'I was born here. I belong here. We'll stay here,' he said. He thought his wife was overreacting to Amin. 'Yesterday he hated Tanzanians, today he hates Asians, tomorrow he will hate the British … It won't last. You'll see.'[13]

Before long, the tensions increased: 'Carloads of Asians heading for the borders or for the airport were flagged down, robbed and beaten. One family fleeing to Kenya were stopped and forced at gunpoint to consume a bag of chillis they were carrying with them.' Benson learned that the two younger children later died of asphyxiation when their burnt throats swelled up.[14]

Asians began to descend on Kampala from all corners of Uganda to line up in front of foreign embassies, ready to migrate to any country in the world that would take them. New Zealand's acceptance of Ugandan refugees was in response to appeals from the UNHCR and from Britain, whose approach took the form of a request for consultation.[15] Initially Prime Minister John Marshall and his National government argued the need for a concerted Commonwealth effort to change Uganda's policy,[16] but by September 1972 the government had changed its mind, not least because of pressures from the churches and other groups in the community.[17] On 12 September the Foreign Affairs Minister, Keith Holyoake, announced New Zealand's decision to accept up to 200 Asians from Uganda who possessed British passports and held professional and technical qualifications in demand in New Zealand. The British welcomed this 'generous gesture'.[18]

Holyoake was reputed to be a 'consensus politician', a 'pragmatic, intuitive conservative', and Marshall's strong Christian beliefs and liberal leaning may have played a part in the government's decision.[19] The agreement to take a number of Asians – not too many – from Uganda was a pragmatic decision and less controversial than not accepting any refugees.

In making his offer, Holyoake drew on New Zealand's 'fine record of humanitarian assistance in situations of this sort' and cited the acceptance of refugees from Hungary and Czechoslovakia.[20] This use of the past to justify a present policy suggests that Holyoake may not have been convinced that there was enough public sympathy for the refugees. Future governments would make the same link. Holyoake also stated that New Zealand 'could possibly take' more Asian refugees from Uganda, though such a decision 'would depend on the standard of people involved and the manner in which they would fit into the New Zealand society. It would also depend on the professional demand for them without jeopardising chances for New Zealanders.'[21]

He was trying to placate both those who wanted a more generous policy towards refugees and those who had concerns about the harmful social impact of Asian refugee migration. His statement highlights the contentious nature of the decision to accept even a relatively small number of Asian refugees. As the Minister of Immigration noted in April 1973, there had been 'a mixed reception' to Holyoake's announcement. 'Some, mainly church groups, have requested that more should be accepted; others, mainly private citizens, have argued for less or even none.' The government had decided to proceed, 'notwithstanding the opposition in some quarters'.[22]

It would be surprising if there had not been considerable debate in a period when Asian migrants were still generally regarded as unsuitable and unassimilable. An *Evening Post* article of 26 August 1972 had highlighted several of the more contentious issues and pointed out: 'With the pending expulsion of thousands of Asians from Uganda, citizenship qualifications and immigration policies around the world are coming in for increasing scrutiny.' One of the chief arguments already advanced against New Zealand accepting a significant number of displaced Asians was the increasing problems being experienced 'in coping with the in-flow of Polynesians'. (This aspect is discussed later in the chapter.) There was also the matter of worsening unemployment.

But against these arguments were 'humanitarian considerations', and the policy of successive New Zealand governments to allow in 'reasonable numbers of people who could make a worthwhile economic or cultural contribution to the community, who would be readily assimilated and who would be accepted and welcomed by the community in general'. But there must be no 'serious upset to the racial balance' in the country. 'Inevitably', concluded the columnist, 'whatever steps the government takes will be interpreted against the emotion-charged backdrop of race relations.' New Zealand's international reputation was also a vital consideration – 'the effect on New Zealand's image as a country which boasts that its immigration policies are not influenced by race or national considerations'.[23]

As we shall see, New Zealand's independent and ethical role on the world stage was even more evident in the initiatives of the Labour government that came into power at the end of 1972. Prime Minister Norman Kirk's foreign policy initiatives, which reflected his neutralist/non-aligned approach, included recognising the People's Republic of China; forming strong ties with black Africa, Asia and the Pacific; withdrawing New Zealand troops from Vietnam; and canning military conscription in New Zealand. A *Dominion* editorial of 15 September 1972 thought that the government had 'settled for a middle course' on accepting Asians from Uganda.

> *The National Council of Churches is probably right when it claims the government's decision … is about the least New Zealand can offer and save face in the international community. Caught between the fire of the Federation of Labour, nervous over threats to job security, and the churches, which wanted a warmer humanitarian response, the government settled for a middle course which pleases neither. Still, it has made a gesture and … the 200, representing only about 3 per cent of the total Asian-Indian community here ought to be quickly and without much grating on either side absorbed into New Zealand society. The adjustment should be facilitated by the fact that the arrivals will be middle-class and not ghetto-prone.*[24]

The Tai Tokerau District Maori Council held similar views. As the *Evening Post* had reported on 5 September, the council decided to recommend that immigration applications for the next year be deferred 'to allow selection of a limited number of Asian-Ugandans'. However, 'because of the high unskilled and poorly educated employment figures, many of whom were Maori, in New Zealand at present, preference should be given to professional and specialist refugees'.[25]

Comment about the government's decision also took the form of letters to newspapers from a range of groups and individuals. A correspondent to the *Dominion* objected to the 'racist immigration policy' implicit in the token numbers to be accepted:

> *The New Zealand government seems unduly fond of token numbers of various kinds, from forces in Vietnam to kill and maim, to Indians' and other groups' admission to this country. We in New Zealand congratulate ourselves on our 'harmonious multiracial society' yet the tone and substance of Sir Keith Holyoake's statements on the possible entry of displaced Ugandan Asians into N.Z. reveals the selectivity which protects this Polynesian-European haven. Is there any reason to doubt that Indian immigrants will be at least as worthy as any other groups in NZ? Why is it necessary to restrict entry to so very few and to 'a group possessing mainly professional and technical qualifications in demand in N.Z.'?*[26]

But other correspondents opposed the decision to take even 'token' numbers. FOL president Tom Skinner was against the migration of Asians from Uganda because unemployment meant 'No room existed in New Zealand for imported labour'. There was space for more people – 'but only when growth and development is faster'. Although he had sympathy for the refugees, he did not want them put into a position where there were no 'fruitful jobs'.[27]

A measured *Evening Post* editorial of 27 September 1972 backed the concerns expressed by the FOL and others, such as the mayor of Christchurch, about the possible risk to New Zealand's 'vulnerable employment situation'. The FOL's stance was not 'insensitive', but 'merely realistic'. The government had responded to such concerns by selecting refugees with skills needed by New Zealand and not in fields in which there was 'already local unemployment'.[28]

The views of Sidney Wood, president of the New Zealand League of Rights, a Pro-Christian, anti-communist and pro-British organisation with a number of branches throughout the country, were less measured. He believed the problems that had arisen in places such as Fiji, 'where the indigenous people are now a minority', could easily arise in other places. 'We here in New Zealand have already received a great number of Polynesians – far too many, some of us think.' Whatever the government decided, 'it must provide a basis for our Western culture to continue its development'; Wood was concerned that immigrants 'of the calibre now being pressed upon us will quickly become the majority'.[29]

Some of the letters opposing the acceptance of Asian refugees, despite their often racist views, raised important issues about New Zealand's refugee policy. A correspondent writing under the pseudonym 'Charity Begins at Home' wrote: 'I feel that New Zealand has no moral obligation whatever to come to the aid of holders of British passports if they are expelled from Uganda. It is up to Britain, or perhaps India and Pakistan, to take them in. I contend that this country already contains sufficient coloured immigrants.'[30] Several correspondents asked why New Zealand was prepared to help refugees when local people were in need,[31] and others were not so much opposed to New Zealand accepting Asian refugees as upset that the government had not helped them. As 'Mother of Two' asked, 'Why bring people to New Zealand from other countries when there aren't enough houses for our own people? Why should we have to suffer for or feel sorry for those people … I've had to manage on relief with two children and no help.'[32] And 'Pioneer Stock' wanted Maori to be helped first: 'We don't want to be in the position of England with all the problems associated with her large coloured citizenship … I love my Maori brothers and sisters … I would support any movement to give them a better deal in what is, after all, their own country.'[33]

One matter that came up repeatedly in the debate was New Zealand's responsibility to its Polynesian neighbours. The number of Pacific Island migrants in New Zealand had increased in leaps and bounds in response to New Zealand's labour market needs. In 1936 Pacific Island people in New Zealand had numbered fewer than 1000. At the end of World War II, New Zealand's Pacific Island population was 2000; in 1956 it was 8000. When there was a downturn in the economy in the mid- and late 1960s the government introduced regulations to control immigration from Samoa,[34] but Pacific Island people who were New Zealand citizens – Cook Islanders, Niueans and Tokelauans – continued to have freedom of entry. By 1971 New Zealand's Pacific Island population had reached around 44,000.[35] In the early 1970s, arrivals from Western Samoa numbered around 1500 a year, with about the same number from other Pacific Islands.[36] Finding ways of regulating the flow and determining the status of Pacific Island migrants in New Zealand was a significant public policy issue just as the need of Ugandan Asians for refuge became urgent.

New Zealand's 'continuing obligation to Pacific Island immigrants' was used as an argument for limiting the size of refugee immigration – for example, in an *Evening Post* editorial of 13 September 1972[37] – and Holyoake made the same point: 'Because New Zealand's primary responsibility is to the peoples of the Pacific Islands, large numbers of whom are admitted to New Zealand every year, there are limits on the numbers we can accept from Uganda.'[38]

The *Dominion* editorial quoted earlier noted that while the public was 'likely to accept sympathetically the government's decision', allowing the arrival of the refugees raised 'the wider question of New Zealand's immigration policies as well as consideration of developing ethnic patterns'. The writer suggested that many would 'find disquieting' the dramatic growth in the number of Pacific Islanders living in New Zealand. The impact of the 'broadly Polynesian influence' on 'the New Zealand identity' was 'substantial'. Although the Minister of Maori and Island Affairs had emphasised the rewarding cultural contribution of this contact, and spoken against the 'drab sameness' of the predominating Anglo-Saxon characteristics of the country,

> *the pace of transformation, and the socio-economic and indeed racial pressures inevitably associated with it, promote uneasiness. It will be of more value to the Islanders generally that New Zealand help them improve their conditions and opportunities at home than accept them in embarrassing numbers here.*[39]

In offering to accept Asians from Uganda, New Zealand expected to be able to select refugees who were British citizens, had already made their way to Britain and possessed professional, technical and trade qualifications in demand in New Zealand.[40] The refugees must also 'have sufficient competence in English to allow practice of their skills upon arrival in New Zealand'. Preference was also to be given to those 'with small numbers of relatives and to those with relatives already resident in New Zealand'.[41]

As was the case with previous criteria set for selecting refugees, New Zealand had trouble filling the Ugandan Asian quota within the conditions set.[42] For example, the stipulation that the refugees had to be selected from those who had arrived in Britain limited the numbers available because the requirement made the promise of New Zealand 'illusory' and most Ugandan Asians 'took their chances and went to Australia or Canada'.[43] The majority of applicants failed to meet at least one of New Zealand's occupational criteria.[44]

By the end of November 1972, the government, concerned about the slow progress of the selection of Asians from Uganda – 'the exercise could drag on interminably with continuing strains on administration both here and in London' – proposed to broaden the category.[45] In doing so, it was responding to public pressure in favour of more liberal admission. According to an early November government report, there was a degree of 'public agitation' from church groups to increase the numbers, to lower the qualification for admittance and to speed up the selection process. The churches were particularly concerned about helping 'Asians of undetermined nationality' in Uganda who were not covered by New Zealand's criteria.[46] Before the government could act, however, the National Party lost the 1972 election to Labour.

As early as January 1973 Kirk announced a review of Ugandan Asian immigration to see what more should be done. The new government was willing to consider accepting stateless Asians and to consider easing the professional qualification requirements.[47]

Like the previous administration, Labour was responding to 'public agitation' in favour of more liberal criteria. Some of the pressure came from the Inter-Church Committee on Immigration, representing the National Council of Churches, the Catholic Church and the Jewish communities, and founded in 1969. The committee's February 1973 submission to the Minister of Immigration referred to several newspaper articles critical of the previous government's 'meagre response' and suggesting that New Zealand could afford to be more charitable. The Roman Catholic *Tablet*, for example, said that New Zealand's criteria for accepting refugees showed 'a shallow, sickening, unchristian attitude … what about those who lack skills and qualifications?'[48]

The committee's submission was, however, also revealing about the organisation's own doubts concerning Asian immigration: ' In view of the fact that ... coloured immigration, and especially Asian immigration, will become an increasingly debated question in New Zealand, we think it would be important to keep track of the families who come to New Zealand, and to attempt to do some general research which will give us some facts for the future.'[49]

The committee's cautious approach is unlikely to have found much favour with the new government. Kirk, determined on an ethical approach to foreign policy and an end to discrimination against Asian migrants, wanted a policy on refugees that prioritised their needs, not New Zealand's labour market requirements. As Leader of the Opposition, he had already signalled that he favoured building goodwill in Asia towards New Zealand. In June 1971 he had told the Auckland Branch of the Institute of International Affairs that there was 'no thornier subject' than Asian immigration, 'no topic more open to misinterpretation for political purposes'. But, he continued, 'we ought not to shirk this problem because it is vitally important in establishing our sincerity in the eyes of Asians and because it is important to us to develop the population of our own country and to enjoy the diversity that can come to it'. The stumbling block to a good relationship with Asia was an immigration policy that 'spells out to the Asian, "All migrants are welcome but not coloured."' If New Zealand wanted to win acceptability in Asian countries, it had 'to accept as well as seek acceptability'. Kirk suggested that 'a small country like New Zealand' should be 'thinking about how we can come to terms with Asian immigration in a realistic way and develop policies which show our preparedness to accept Asians as individuals'. In its handling of immigration policy, New Zealand should demonstrate its 'certain desire that each individual should be admitted to this country on the basis of his worth as a person and not excluded or included because of the colour of his skin, his race or his religion'.[50]

In the words of his biographer Margaret Hayward, Kirk 'saw politics not as an end' but as a way to work for a better world.[51] Not long after taking office, he issued a lengthy policy statement entitled 'New Zealand in the world of the 1970s':

> We want New Zealand's foreign policy to express New Zealand's national ideals as well as to reflect our national interests. We cannot promise perfection but we shall strive to relate what we say and do abroad to the values that govern our policies at home ... We believe in the individual human worth and dignity of every man, woman and child regardless of race or colour ... Believing as we do in the dignity and equality of all human beings, we totally reject all doctrines of racial superiority ... Every action

a people takes in international affairs is an announcement of the kind of people they really are.[52]

On 16 April 1973, Cabinet approved the entry, at the government's expense, of 50 cases of stateless Ugandan Asian refugees in addition to those approved earlier – in effect between 150 and 200 people. They would be accepted from transit camps in Europe. One fifth of the cases included family members with a disability.[53] Announcing the decision at a press conference, Kirk explained that 'New Zealand should not say it wanted only "the best apples in the barrel"'. He was sure most New Zealanders would agree that 'these [families] were the people who needed help most'.[54] (New Zealand's response to 'handicapped' refugees is discussed further in Chapter Six.)

In the course of a conversation on 30 March 1973 between Kirk and Ole Volfing, the UNHCR representative, the Prime Minister's personal commitment was clear. When Kirk asked Volfing what 'classes' of handicapped people remained in camps in Europe, he replied that they were mostly the elderly (this usually meant over 45) 'but that some were blind or crippled in some way'. He added that his office would not submit for entry to New Zealand an elderly couple without a breadwinner. When Kirk asked why not, Volfing said that the UNHCR would prefer New Zealand to take increased numbers of people rather than concentrate on the handicapped.

> *The Prime Minister commented that it may be the handicapped who need New Zealand's help more than the others. He hoped New Zealand would not turn people down merely because they were old. We would certainly take some of the refugees who were handicapped because their need was greater. We would also, of course, like to have some breadwinners, but in any determination the degree of need must be the most important consideration. Both the elderly and children who were crippled and might be rehabilitated were in great need.*

Kirk then told Volfing that he felt the Cabinet would be sympathetic to accepting more than 50 cases: 'He would not like New Zealand to be a country which did not take on its share of such international responsibilities.'[55] Secretary of Foreign Affairs Frank Corner, who was also at the meeting, as was David McDowell, responsible for New Zealand's United Nations obligations and for the refugee area, recalled Kirk's invariably positive, decent and humanitarian approach.[56]

By comparison, Australia's response was 'miserly'. It approved 383 Ugandan Asians for entry, selecting the refugees on the basis of Australia's need, not that of the refugees.[57] That New Zealand's policy was significantly more generous was in no small measure due to the contribution made by Norman Kirk. His period in office, however, was cut short by his sudden death in 1974 at the age of 51. Wallace (Bill) Rowling became the next Labour Prime Minister.

The extent of community support for the Ugandan refugees was evident in the numerous letters to the government from firms and employers of all types, wishing to provide work and other help.[58] The offers, particularly of jobs, suggested that, alongside the suspicion and hostility discussed earlier, there was abundant goodwill towards the refugees, and that skilled workers – from scrub cutters and machinists to lawyers and doctors – were in great demand in early 1970s New Zealand.

'First Ugandan Asian family to arrive here is now counting its blessings' ran the *Evening Post* headline on 8 November 1972.

> Eight suitcases, two hold-alls, a push chair, and just over $100 in cash – these were the total possessions of the first Ugandan Asian family to arrive in Auckland today ... Not much with which to start a new life ... but 36-year-old Mr Avi-nash Ganesh Deobhakta was counting his blessings.

A barrister with relatives in New Zealand, he arrived in the country with his wife Kanan and two small children. He had a job and accommodation awaiting him.[59] A later story was headed 'Ugandan family finds life without servants is different':

> Minus their Ugandan houseboy, nanny, gardener, and guard, the first Ugandan Asian family to arrive in Auckland under the government's immigration quota is gradually coming to terms with life in a new country ... Cutting the grass, cleaning the windows, and minding the children on a regular basis are new experiences for the Deobhaktas, who also had a guard in Uganda – to protect their property.[60]

The family's house had been taken over by the Ugandan government – Deobhakta, formerly a state attorney and chief magistrate, now employed as a legal executive in Auckland, doubted whether he would ever see the proceeds from the sale. The family was renting a house and looking forward to starting a new life in New Zealand.

Like the Jewish arrivals in the 1930s, Asians from Uganda probably confused New Zealanders. Poor and uneducated refugees were more comfortable to deal with than those who were highly educated and, formerly at least, well-to-do. Hence the ambiguous tone of the second newspaper report. It is not entirely sympathetic to a family previously accustomed to a comfortable and sophisticated lifestyle.

Fifteen years later, *More* magazine published an article on the Deobhakta family, focusing on Kanan Deobhakta. The photos of the family's arrival, showing her with her two small children, standing beside her husband, now lay 'tattered and yellowing' in a bottom drawer in the Deobhaktas' Epsom home. In the intervening years Kanan Deobhakta had become a dancer. The circumstances that had caused a professional Indian family to flee their homeland were rarely discussed. 'Kanan looks again at the picture of herself smiling broadly and grimaces. "I was not so happy in reality."' Life in New Zealand had worked out well for the family, with Avinash Deobhakta doing well in the legal profession and the children succeeding in school; but despite the kindness of New Zealanders, the early years had been hard and lonely. 'At Christmas the Deobhaktas would receive a charity box. Kanan knew it was meant as a genuinely caring and concerned gesture and had tried hard not to be humiliated.' But although settlement went smoothly, she felt that the family was destroyed. Like many refugees she grieved over the hard fact that, in spite of her concerted efforts, she was not able to bring her parents to New Zealand.[61]

Chilean refugees, 1974–82

New Zealand accepted 354 refugees – 92 families – who fled Chile after the democratically elected left-leaning Popular Unity government of Salvador Allende was replaced by the military dictatorship of General Augusto Pinochet in 1973. Approximately 35,000 people left the country.[62] These Chilean refugees were the first Latin Americans to enter New Zealand in significant numbers. They arrived in small groups of 20 and 30 between 1974 and 1982, when the quota for Chilean families was closed.[63] This intake of refugees was also the first to be assisted by the Inter-Church Commission on Immigration and Refugee Resettlement (ICCI), founded in 1975 to work with government on refugee resettlement. (The ICCI grew out of the earlier Inter-Church Committee on Immigration.)[64]

Unlike some of the refugees discussed so far, those from Chile were not fleeing communism or a left-wing dictatorship. In fact, some former Chilean refugees played an important role in left-wing activism in New Zealand during the late twentieth century.[65] Somewhat surprisingly, and in contrast with the swift acceptance of refugees escaping communism, the Kirk government was initially reluctant to accept refugees from Chile, possibly because it feared the political fallout from welcoming the settlement of refugees with strong left-wing affiliations.

During Allende's presidency, the country had become 'something of a haven for political activists of left-wing persuasion from other Latin American countries'. A large number of Bolivians, Uruguayans, Colombians and

Brazilians settled in Chile, some out of sympathy for the economic and social reform programmes of the Popular Unity government, others because they were sought by their own governments for questioning about their political activities.[66] When the Allende government was overthrown, the new regime made it clear that left-wing foreigners were no longer welcome in Chile. Around 2000 such people had registered as refugees with the UNHCR by the end of 1973.

The UNHCR's appeal to New Zealand to accept refugees who could not be placed in their country of first choice came in November 1973. It was hardly surprising that none of the refugees had expressed a first preference to settle in New Zealand. There was no established Spanish-speaking community in the country and, in Latin America, New Zealand was not known as a country of immigration.[67]

The churches and some private individuals, concerned about the plight of refugees in Chile, had also been urging the government to act. The National Council of Churches offered to help with processing applications in Chile and with resettling the refugees in New Zealand. The government was initially cautious. One concern seemed to be that the 'police and security checks might present some difficulty'.[68] In the end, the offers of assistance in the community combined with the request for assistance from the UNHCR led to government agreement to 'allow a number of refugees in Chile to settle in this country'. That number was 20. The matter of security was resolved by the SIS advising the government that for 'this type of refugee' security checks should be carried out before permanent entry status was accorded.[69] New Zealand had prior experience on which to draw. The Associate Minister of Foreign Affairs, Joe Walding, announced the decision to accept the Chilean refugees: 'The Government has been deeply concerned about events in Chile and we welcome this opportunity to do something constructive for those who are unable to remain in Chile.'[70] As historian Anton Binzegger would later comment, 'There was little internal reaction to the refugee issue as such, and the government appeared to have the tacit approval of the public.' He also noted that the FOL had imposed a ban on trade with Chile because of suppression of trade unions in that country. 'It can be taken, therefore, that sympathies lay with the refugees.'[71]

Of the first 20 families, four came from the large group of foreign refugees 'deprived of their haven in Chile by the Coup'. The remaining 16 were from the several thousands of citizens who had fled to Peru.[72] The ICCI was reported to be pleased 'with the success and calibre of the initial groups'.[73] As more offers of assistance came from individuals and organisations, the government agreed to take a further group of 20 families from Chile.

In making a case to the Prime Minister for the acceptance of more refugees, Secretary of Foreign Affairs Frank Corner gave a mixture of humanitarian and pragmatic reasons:

> *The acceptance of a further group of Chilean refugees would accord with New Zealand's traditional policies towards political refugees. As a further practical mark of the government's continuing concern with the humanitarian aspects of events in Chile it could help to assuage domestic opinion in New Zealand which could be sensitive to moves – such as a Ministerial visit – which could indicate a return to a more normal diplomatic relationship with Chile. Finally, the humanitarian need is as great as ever, and could indeed increase.*[74]

Two of the points in Corner's report are of particular interest. First, as noted earlier, 'traditional policies' were used to justify current practice, and to persuade those in doubt about the rightness of a particular course of action. The reference also shows the existence of political amnesia or at least of a limited term of reference. Corner appeared to have conveniently forgotten the racial bias pervasive in New Zealand's policy approach to refugees from Nazism in the 1930s, DPs in the 1940s and Chinese refugees in every decade before the 1970s. Second, there is the reference to the need to 'assuage domestic opinion', which 'could be sensitive to moves' to return as soon as possible to normal relations with the new administration in Chile The emphasis accorded re-establishing relations with new governments despite concerns about humanitarian issues highlights another ongoing thread in foreign policy, namely a reluctance to cut diplomatic ties and disrupt existing relationships. These issues are discussed further in Chapter Eight.

More small groups of refugees from Chile entered New Zealand in the late 1970s and in the 1980s.[75] Disquiet that refugees with left-wing or even communist political sympathies had been allowed into the country continued to trouble some members of the public.[76] Chilean refugees, interviewed several years after their arrival in New Zealand, believed that 'efforts were made' to ensure that refugees coming to New Zealand would not be 'trouble makers'. A workshop on Chilean refugees held in the mid-1980s came to a similar conclusion – that New Zealand had put great emphasis on selecting politically moderate refugees out of a fear 'of ideas'.[77]

The political activism of Latin American refugees, especially Chileans, concerned about political prisoners in their home countries, led to pressure to admit further refugees from Nicaragua, El Salvador, Columbia and Peru. Small numbers came from these countries and helped to build the Latin American community in New Zealand in the 1980s.[78] However, a number of the Chileans who arrived in the 1970s and 1980s have left. In contrast with other refugee groups, some Chileans have regarded New Zealand as a place of exile, not a new home. They considered returning to Chile, especially once the political situation had eased after the first 'summer of democracy' in 1989.[79] Others moved to Australia, where the community was considerably larger.[80]

CHAPTER FIVE

Refugees from South East Asia

In the aftermath of the Vietnam War, over 1.5 million people fled Vietnam, Laos and Cambodia because they feared or experienced persecution. New Zealand became reluctantly involved in the international efforts to resettle Indo-Chinese refugees.[1] The complexity of their settlement in New Zealand was unprecedented because of New Zealanders' long-standing opposition to Asian immigration and because, until the mid-1980s, New Zealand had no policies and administrative structures to respond to larger numbers of culturally diverse refugees.

After Vietnam

According to several historians, the Vietnam War was the most significant foreign policy issue confronting New Zealand in the 1960s.[2] In 1964 the National government, under Keith Holyoake, committed troops to the conflict. The decision was justified on the grounds of New Zealand's obligations under the South East Asia Treaty Organisation (SEATO) and the country's own future security needs: the government feared that New Zealand would not be assisted by its allies if it did not come to their assistance in Vietnam. Although the military commitment was modest, it was highly controversial.

Norman Kirk's Labour government withdrew the last remaining New Zealand troops from Vietnam – most of them had in fact been brought home by the time of the 1972 election – and in 1973 recognised the Hanoi government.³ The victory of the combined Vietcong and North Vietnamese forces in 1975 reinforced the position of those who had felt that New Zealand's part in the war had been morally wrong and unjustified. Attitudes about New Zealand's obligations to Indo-Chinese refugees reflected earlier divisions over involvement in Vietnam, though there was not a neat division along these lines. For example, on 24 April 1975 National Party MP David Thomson asked the Prime Minister: 'Is the policy of a welcome which New Zealand gave in respect of Polish and Hungarian refugees from communist aggression in Europe to be followed in respect of Vietnamese refugees from communist aggression in Indo-China; and, if not, what is the reason for the discrimination?'⁴

Rowling's government wished to avoid offending North Vietnam, 'which did not look too kindly on the evacuation of South Vietnamese refugees during the last days of the former Saigon Government'. North Vietnam saw the flight of refugees as forced evacuation by the United States and wanted these people to be repatriated as Vietnamese citizens.⁵ Labour in turn blamed National for having helped to create the refugees because of its military policies while in office. New Zealand, argued Labour, had an obligation to help Indo-Chinese refugees in order 'to atone' for 'past sins in Vietnam'.⁶ As Labour MP Michael Bassett said on 8 April 1975,

> We must help where we can with orphans and refugees, however much some may feel that most refugees would be wiser to recognise the inevitable instead of fleeing from it … the blood is on National's hands and on National's conscience … Every orphan here is partly their creation, every maimed child their responsibility.⁷

New Zealand's initial reluctance to get involved in resettling Indo-Chinese refugees needs to be seen partly in the light of the divisions over the Vietnam War. As had been the case when New Zealand was called on to resettle DPs after World War II, the government was also unwilling to resettle people who were not British or Northern European. The cautious response to accepting refugees from Indo-China also reflected New Zealand's foreign policy approach. An important part of this was the adoption of an increasingly independent stance, which took the form of resisting pressure from the United States and Britain for a joint response. Another was the gradual shift in focus from Europe to the Asia–Pacific region since 1945. By the 1970s, the country's foreign policy interest was seen as best served by the maintenance of peace and prosperity closer to home.⁸ Greater tolerance of Asian immigration and a contribution to the refugee problems in the area came to be seen as a requirement to promote New Zealand's regional interests.

Despite this gradual policy shift there was still, in the mid-1970s, considerable ambivalence in some sections of the New Zealand community towards settlers from Asia. To some extent this was because New Zealand had accepted few such migrants and was unaccustomed to, and suspicious of, non-British settlers. In 1974–75 close to 40 per cent of all immigrants came from Britain; less than 4 per cent were from Asia.⁹

As we shall see in Chapter Seven, New Zealand's first involvement with Indo-Chinese refugee resettlement was as part of Operation Babylift, which sent Vietnamese orphans to Western countries. Another early response by New Zealand to the plight of Indo-Chinese refugees was to grant political asylum to some 24 Colombo Plan students from Vietnam studying at Auckland University.¹⁰ The plan was set up in 1950 to contribute to the economic development of countries in South and South East Asia. New Zealand was a founding member, along with Australia, Canada, Ceylon, India, Pakistan and Britain. By the early 1970s, over 900 trainees from South, North and South East Asia had come to New Zealand to study engineering, agriculture, health sciences and a range of arts and science subjects.¹¹

The decision to give asylum to Colombo Plan students from Vietnam who were in New Zealand when the war ended, was controversial. Although it was well accepted by the 1970s that some South East Asian students would come to New Zealand for their education under the plan, they were invariably expected to return home afterwards. With pressure on New Zealand to respond to the growing Indo-Chinese refugee crisis in 1975, the Labour government was divided over how the Colombo Plan student problem was best addressed. The Ministry of Foreign Affairs was primarily concerned to ensure that New Zealand's relationship with the new Vietnamese government was not jeopardised. The minister also thought it inappropriate to give political asylum to students who were not in any danger and should go home to rebuild their country. Immigration Minister Fraser Coleman, on the other hand, said publicly that Vietnamese students would not be sent home.¹²

The issue came up in parliament on 28 May 1975 when R.J. Harrison, MP for Hawke's Bay, asked how many Vietnamese were in the country, how many of them were students, how many requests for asylum had been made and how many would be declined. Coleman supplied the figures. Out of 94 students, a quarter had applied to remain permanently and they would be allowed to do so: there would be 'no question of anyone being sent home at the present time'.[13] In 1976, 41 Cambodian students who had arrived in New Zealand on Colombo Plan and Ford Foundation scholarships during the early 1970s were also granted permanent residency.[14]

New Zealand, under pressure from the United States and the UNHCR to take refugees, hoped to 'get some mileage with UNHCR' over accepting the Indo-Chinese students for permanent residence.[15] But the mileage gained must have been insufficient since by May 1975 the government was considering admitting a small number of Vietnamese families under ordinary immigration programmes. On 19 May 1975 Rowling told the UNHCR that the government would look sympathetically at applications from those who could demonstrate close personal connections to New Zealand. New Zealand had decided on this course of action because of past experience. This had shown that 'where there were linguistic and cultural difficulties, these problems could prove to be insuperable in preventing the absorption of such persons into the community'. As a result, New Zealand 'would not be able to indicate the number it would accept until the number with direct connections had been established'.[16]

On 3 June the first of many meetings to discuss the admission of Vietnamese families was held between Foreign Affairs, the Department of Labour (Immigration Division) and the ICCI. By this time, a productive working relationship had developed between the ICCI and the Immigration Division.[17] At a meeting on 10 June, ICCI Director the Reverend Keith Taylor said that the agency was at a loss over what action to take on the government's suggestion that the ICCI settle families from Vietnam. Although public support was strong, with many people contacting the ICCI and offering to help, the agency did not know how many refugees were to be accepted and whether this group was going to be the first of others. At this stage the numbers to be resettled seemed to be up to the ICCI to determine, though the government would set the criteria for selection. People would not be accepted on a first come first served basis, which would favour those who were able to pay their way out.

Foreign Affairs, as with Colombo Plan student applicants for political asylum, considered that the Indo-Chinese refugee problem had to be addressed in a way that would not jeopardise New Zealand's relationship with the new Vietnamese government.[18] A further meeting on 2 July focused on how many refugee families from Indo-China could be resettled. Taylor was even more cautious than the government about New Zealand's capacity to resettle and absorb the refugees. While the Department of Labour thought it a good idea to consider taking 'handicapped' cases, Taylor preferred Vietnamese refugees with strong family connections in New Zealand. The meeting decided that the number should be kept to approximately 10 families.[19]

As Taylor recalled 30 years later, those meetings reflected the pressure New Zealand was under from the United States to take refugees. The ICCI favoured a political solution to the refugee problem and considered that New Zealand should not be asked to pick up 'the casualties of United States Vietnamese policy'. But he and the World Council of Churches were being pushed 'to come to the party'.[20] Reluctantly they did, still very concerned about possible negative public reaction to the Indo-Chinese refugees.

By the end of 1975, when a National government had been formed under Robert Muldoon, New Zealand had agreed to accept 135 Vietnamese refugees. This was in addition to 114 Indo-Chinese students who were also granted indefinite extensions to stay in the country. But the new government was as reluctant as its predecessor to get involved in a more significant resettlement programme. At the same time, public concern about South East Asian refugees was growing.[21]

In May 1977 Ole Volfing, the UNHCR Director of External Affairs, and Gilberto Rizzo, the UNHCR representative for Australia and New Zealand, met Foreign Affairs and Department of Labour officials to ask for a more active response from the New Zealand government to the increasingly serious refugee situation. The UNHCR representatives outlined the severe dangers faced by refugees in Thailand which, along with Malaysia, was under growing pressure from the arrival of refugees. There had been several reports of the Thai military forcing Cambodian refugees back over the border, and reports of '"boat people" sinking themselves in the sight of ships in a desperate bid to be brought on board to assure refugee status'.[22] New Zealand's contribution was needed not just because of the token number of refugees the country could take but also because the presence of New Zealand and other small nations could give momentum to the UNHCR programme, since the United States did not want to continue taking refugees when few other countries were doing so. The 'cooperative response to taking refugees' would also be helpful as it would 'soften' the attitude of the countries of first asylum towards the refugees. If New Zealand and other countries did not help with resettling the refugees, then Malaysia, Thailand and Indonesia would turn the refugee boats away, 'reprovision them and point them in the direction of Australia and New Zealand'.[23]

A slow reaction

The government was slow to commit to resettling larger numbers of South East Asian refugees partly because British immigration in the years before the Indo-Chinese refugee crisis had resulted in strain on New Zealand's 'absorptive capacity',[24] in other words the limit the country had set on the number of immigrants it would accept before it began to feel overwhelmed culturally or its citizens were displaced from jobs. To a much larger extent, though, the reluctance came from concerns about the refugees' ability to integrate into New Zealand society. Although the Immigration Act of 1974 had involved a shift away from explicitly racist criteria for admitting immigrants, British and Northern European migrants continued to be favoured.[25] Before May 1977 there was a widely held belief among Department of Labour and Foreign Affairs officials and the ICCI that most boat people were illiterate peasants or fishermen. Information showing that the refugees were educated and potentially useful seems to have had a positive effect on the ICCI. The label 'middle class' seemed particularly reassuring and changed the agency's perceptions about how the refugees would fit into New Zealand society.[26]

Until 1977, the government and the ICCI also agreed that Indo-Chinese refugees should not be moved from the South East Asia region. This view had 'a crippling effect' on the initial decision-making process and was a major factor in New Zealand's delay in responding to the UNHCR call to assist South East Asian refugees.[27] Government indecision and ICCI caution were eventually overcome by the weight of public support for settling refugees. On 8 July 1977 the ICCI, noting the increased number of approaches about assisting refugees, 'timidly ventured into the unknown and made a submission to Government on the possible number it could comfortably resettle'. The number suggested was 420.[28]

In his analysis of the lead-up to this submission, Robin Gallienne appears critical of the ICCI's overly cautious approach, but it is not hard to understand the agency's stance. Estimating how many refugees New Zealand could take, based on the degree of goodwill in the community, was no mean feat. If the goodwill was judged insufficient, how was the ICCI to engender more? Yet adequate community support was crucial because although the ICCI received a small grant from the government, it depended on the efforts of voluntary workers and donations collected from churches around the country. New Zealand's lack of recent experience of settling larger groups of refugees, let alone refugees from South East Asia, was also a good reason for caution. The agency was used to coping only with small numbers of refugees. As an ICCI coordinator recalled,

'We didn't have any resources at all, my office was … a box, to carry round with me … using the telephone in the hallway … that was the office desk … any writing that had to be done, letters sent off, that was all done at home.'[29]

The ICCI's submission drew on the experience of Australia, which had made the commitment to settle significant numbers of Indo-Chinese refugees considerably sooner than New Zealand. Between 1975 and 1977 it had accepted 2420 Vietnamese boat people; New Zealand took 414 during the same period.[30] Indo-Chinese refugees were settling well in Australia with apparently few or no employment problems, and estate agents and owners regarded them as good tenants.[31] Keith Taylor also recalled that, owing to the 'huge sensitivity' to bringing in South East Asian refugees, the ICCI was monitoring the negative reaction to them in Australia, trying to ensure the same did not happen in New Zealand.[32]

In some respects the Australian experience was not particularly relevant. Unlike Australia, New Zealand did not have administrative structures set up to settle refugees. Refugee immigration in New Zealand was dealt with by part of the permanent entry section of the Department of Labour. One senior official did the refugee work as well as other tasks: 'It wasn't a very onerous duty at that stage … we didn't really appreciate … what it was going to develop into.'[33]

New Zealand's commitment to accepting South East Asian refugees began to firm up in July 1977 in response to continuing domestic and international pressure. The government sought to maintain a balance between two main imperatives: presenting a good image for the international community and managing domestic public opinion for and against the refugees. A telex to diplomatic posts on 27 July 1977 announced that the government 'had accepted the "grass roots" desire to assist Indo-Chinese "boat" refugees in Malaysian and Thai camps.'[34]

New Zealand's intake would consist of up to 70 refugee families, numbering about 420 people (the number submitted by ICCI) who had fled from Vietnam, Laos and Cambodia. The refugees had to meet various criteria: they had to hold UNHCR refugee status; they had to 'generally' have not more than four dependent children under the age of 18; and ideally those accepted should be literate, have an occupational background adaptable to New Zealand and include, in each family, a breadwinner no older than 45.[35] The refugees also had to meet health requirements: applications from people suffering tuberculosis, leprosy or syphilis were rejected.[36]

Before the decision was made public, the ICCI arranged a meeting on 23 July to plan the reception and settlement of the refugees. Representatives from the

National Council of Churches, the Departments of Health, Labour and Social Welfare, the Wellington Polytechnic School of Languages, the Red Cross, the YWCA, the St Vincent de Paul Society, members of the Vietnamese, Cambodian and Laotian communities and ICCI staff all attended. It seems the meeting was pervaded by a strong spirit of Kiwi 'do it yourself' and improvisation. Everyone was willing to pitch in. Various agencies offered goods and services such as accommodation, blankets, clothing, meals and interpreters. A similar meeting was held in Auckland. The government seemed just as willing to improvise solutions. But everyone felt they had a lot to learn about settling Indo-Chinese refugees.[37]

The decision is made

The first selection team comprised a senior immigration officer, the ICCI's Keith Taylor and a doctor. The selection mission was thought of as 'a one-off affair', and refugees were selected with possible negative reaction in New Zealand in mind.[38] This perhaps explains the preference for choosing refugees with middle-class attributes and the skills and ability to fit into Western society.

As had happened with the post-World War II DPs and Cold War refugees, changing circumstances in South East Asia meant that New Zealand's selection criteria had to be changed to fit reality. There was some flexibility in the policy to allow for this. Gallienne suggests there was considerable behind-the-scenes activity at this stage, indicating a shift in government policy from one of grudging acceptance to a more flexible approach 'where policy would not be so remote from the realities in South East Asia'. For example, Wellington told the New Zealand Embassy in Bangkok that the Minister of Immigration 'intends to approve requests to accept refugees other than boat people'. But there were strict limits: refugees who were not boat people could be chosen only if they had friends or relatives in New Zealand willing to pay the fare and provide sponsorship.[39]

New Zealand's lack of reliable information and expert knowledge about the refugee situation meant that it was dependent on the UNHCR and on other countries, particularly Australia, to provide essential information. As the medical officer on the selection team noted: 'It is also essential to have knowledge of the people, their habits, customs, and if possible some of their languages.'[40] This expertise was missing.

Gallienne writes of the 'theatrical aspect' of the selection process. New Zealand had to make up for being a latecomer on the scene and convince the world at large – and the UNHCR and South East Asians in particular – that it wanted to be part of the regional response and do its bit to help. The selectors acted rather like tourists, with New Zealand officials and UNHCR staff trooping 'up and down the coasts of West and East Malaysia' and Thailand, visiting nine refugee camps. This involved extensive travelling by air, in hired cars and even in a New Zealand Air Force helicopter. The work was arduous and the long hours and tropical climate took their toll. The team's adventures included near drowning when travelling in a small boat and 'hair-raising' drives.[41]

Because other countries had already carried out selections, New Zealand's choice of refugees was more restricted. As had happened in the past, New Zealand selectors faced competition from other countries for the same category of refugee. For example, a number of resettlement countries also wanted professional and tradespeople. Moreover, by the time New Zealand selectors arrived in the camps, the UNHCR was focusing on 'hard core' refugees – those who had been turned down by other countries. As Gallienne notes, larger countries were willing to take greater numbers of refugees provided the people were of 'high quality'. Because New Zealand could take only a small number, it had to accept refugees other countries had declined.[42] This apparently generous and humanitarian act of compassion was to a degree forced on New Zealand (see Chapter Six).

The New Zealand team seemed somewhat surprised that, in Thailand, selection was not just a matter of picking out a group of very grateful refugees. Although camp life was hard and conditions Spartan, the refugees 'were not inspired with a strong desire to come to New Zealand'.[43] Going to an unfamiliar country scared them more than the harsh conditions of the camp. The New Zealanders' selection methods were low key and humane in comparison with those of some other countries, particularly the United States, whose selectors seemed to find it 'necessary to humiliate the potential migrants in the course of the selection process'. But this was probably because the UNHCR had pre-selected refugees destined for New Zealand and the team simply had to verify information already provided on the forms. Eventually they selected 210 refugees in Thai camps who met New Zealand's criteria and were willing to emigrate. They chose well-educated professional people and ethnicity was not a factor. Chinese refugees – first and second generation Cantonese who were Vietnamese citizens – comprised more than 50 per cent of the camp population, and were selected on the same basis as ethnic Vietnamese. This lack of ethnic bias is noteworthy in view of past strong prejudice against Chinese settlers in New Zealand.[44]

When the first group arrived in Auckland on 22 September 1977 the Customs Department and the Ministry of Agriculture and Fisheries undertook a full baggage search and the refugees were kept away from the public until they had been medically cleared. A planned official welcome to be attended by the Minister of Immigration, Frank Gill, and held in the customs hall away from the media and the public, did not take place because of last-minute changes in the refugees' travel schedule. Instead a message of welcome was read to the refugees.

> We realise you have been through difficult, indeed, hazardous times during which your very survival, in many cases, may have been uncertain. Those times are now over and you have the opportunity of starting your lives anew. We hope that, with the help that will be available to you from New Zealanders, you will all be successful in adjusting to and settling in this, your new home.[45]

The government went to some lengths to manage possible adverse public reactions to the refugees. The Minister of Immigration emphasised that they would not be a burden on taxpayers because sponsors were available for all the families who had been accepted. Transporting the refugees was at minimum cost – the total was not substantial and, in terms of the pressing human need, not more than New Zealand could afford.[46]

Australia was in a good position to advise New Zealand on how to deal with any political fallout. For example, the public perception that refugees were 'taking our jobs' could be quickly dealt with by explaining that they were moving into work that Australians or New Zealanders did not want.[47] As the ICCI had done earlier, the government also used Australian experience to reassure the public about how successfully the refugees would be integrated into Western culture. The Minister of Immigration emphasised that the boat people came from backgrounds 'that would enable them to resettle well in a country such as ours'. This had been the case in Australia.[48]

More refugees after 1977

At the end of 1977, after the initial selection mission was completed and the first groups of refugees had arrived, the New Zealand government seemed to feel that it had done its duty. A humanitarian gesture had been made and, although help for Indo-Chinese refugees would continue, it would be at a reduced rate. There was no plan to accept further significant numbers of refugees. But the refugee problem and the numbers, especially of Vietnamese, needing help grew from 1978 and New Zealand was obliged to respond to growing international pressure. This took many forms and came from the UNHCR, from South East Asian countries and from the United States. Australia's example made New Zealand's efforts seem 'feeble'. By June 1978 Australia had accepted 11,000 Indo-Chinese refugees and was receiving international praise for its efforts.[49]

During 1978, before making any further commitment, New Zealand was waiting for an assessment report conducted by the ICCI of the resettlement process so far. This was clearly a convenient excuse for delaying further commitment, and was used to justify the government's 'frozen stance',[50] but it became increasingly difficult for the government to continue postponing a commitment and to follow an independent policy.

One reason for the delay was fear of a backlash against the refugees who were already in the country. There were occasional letters to the government complaining that too many scarce resources were being spent on refugees at the expense of their own communities. These included the Samoan community, who wrote to the government asking for equivalent resources to be spent on their own people.[51]

Keith Taylor recalled some negative reaction to the refugees when they first arrived, despite the small numbers and the fact that they were spread around the country to help ensure acceptance in the community,[52] but it is hard to find significant evidence of a backlash. This may be because, in the face of wide publicity about the desperate plight of the refugees, negative reactions took place out of the public eye. Gallienne cites the example of a conversation between the UNHCR's Volfing and a highly placed member of the New Zealand government who commented that New Zealand would prefer to take refugees from Northern Ireland rather than Indo-China as there would be fewer problems of assimilation.[53]

The ICCI assessment, based on separate reports by the various agencies involved, finally went to the government in October 1978.[54] The ICCI concluded that the Indo-Chinese refugee settlement programme had, on the whole, been successful. Their conclusion paved the way for New Zealand to at last respond to requests to take more refugees. In December New Zealand agreed to take a quota of 600 Indo-Chinese refugees for 1979,[55] but still more was expected. Australia, with a commitment for 1979 to resettling 10,500 refugees, complimented New Zealand on its quota but said that it was only a beginning. They felt that 'every contribution helped build up international momentum and helped also to reassure Malaysia and Thailand'. Australia was also increasing its financial contributions to UN for refugee activities.[56]

New Zealand responded by agreeing to accept 900 refugees during 1979.

In addition to the 600 government-selected refugees, 100 could be admitted under an emergency quota that enabled New Zealand to respond quickly to immediate need. New Zealand would also accept refugees under its family reunification policy.[57] (These still-contentious policies have both helped and hindered the ability of refugees settled in New Zealand to bring in members of their families. Chapter Nine discusses the various family reunion policies adopted by New Zealand over the years.) By 1979 there were increasing signs of 'compassion fatigue' among countries of first asylum and countries of refugee settlement. Burdened by the continuing influx of refugees, South East Asian countries had begun trying to stem the flow by refusing entry to large shiploads.[58] At the same time they so increased the pressure on the international community that there was a marked change of attitude around the world. By mid-1979 New Zealand, too, found itself pushed into taking further action. At first it cited its obligations to Pacific Island immigrants (a justification used to good effect in the past) and its already large immigration population, but before long it was forced to act.[59]

In 1979, New Zealand took part in a United Nations conference on Indo-Chinese refugees held in Geneva. The most important outcome of the conference was the Orderly Departure Programme (ODP), under which Vietnam agreed to stop encouraging departures in large numbers.[60] In return, resettlement countries undertook to provide material support and resettlement opportunities to ease the burden on South East Asian countries. They also agreed that refugees already in camps in the region were to be resettled in various countries around the world.[61]

First as Under-Secretary to the Minister of Immigration, and then as Minister, Aussie Malcolm was the very hands-on and involved member of the National government dealing with the settlement of Indo-Chinese refugees from 1976 to 1984. He played a key role, though then unreported, as facilitator of the agreement to set up the ODP.[62] New Zealand diplomat Gerald Hensley, who was New Zealand High Commissioner for Singapore, worked with him at the Geneva Conference to broker 'the multi-national agreement known as "Orderly Departure" that ended the Indo-China refugee crisis. To make it work it had to be seen as a Vietnamese/Cambodian initiative, and that is how it was projected, but it was us that did it!'[63]

An outcome of the ODP agreement was New Zealand's decision in July 1979 that it would not accept as refugees people who left Vietnam with the consent of the Vietnamese government. However, a limited number of those who no longer qualified as refugees would be able to enter New Zealand under family reunification policies.⁶⁴ That month the government also agreed to accept 1800 Indo-Chinese refugees to arrive by mid-1981.⁶⁵

In contrast with 1977, the selection of refugees in 1979 was done with more appreciation of their plight and less emphasis on New Zealand's needs, despite the difference between New Zealand's ideal selection criteria and the actual characteristics of the refugees available widening each year.⁶⁶ One of the requirements for selection was, as before, suitability to settle in New Zealand.⁶⁷ But what precisely did 'suitable' mean? Ministry of Foreign Affairs and Department of Labour officials disagreed over interpretation, the former considering that the latter, which had control over selection, was being too restrictive. Selectors also aimed to choose a mixture of ethnicities. In response to approaches from members of the Cambodian and Lao communities, they tried to help fledgling ethnic communities by choosing appropriate refugees, though not at the expense of being 'even-handed' about ethnicity.⁶⁸ As in 1977, New Zealand took some pride in choosing refugees as humanely and considerately as possible. 'We didn't interview anyone we weren't going to accept,' recalled Malcolm's private secretary. 'We always held the belief that it was totally wrong to interview someone, thereby give them hope, and then say no, we don't want you.'⁶⁹

Malcolm also stressed that New Zealand, unlike other countries, chose purely on the basis of humanitarian factors and the needs of the refugees:

> *I rejected the Australian, Canadian and US approach of only taking the healthy and skilled and instead took the ones no one else would accept ... When I found myself both Minister of Immigration and Minister of Health [I was] able to respond within hours to medical crises in refugee camps in South East Asia by directing people to be flown direct to operating theatres all over New Zealand.*⁷⁰

He regarded as pointless the effort some countries put into selecting refugees with education and qualifications. In his view, previous qualifications did not really matter since without local language skills and local qualifications, refugees would find it difficult to pursue their former occupations.

What was really important, however, was managing the numbers accepted and ensuring that New Zealand did not select at any one time more refugees than the community could cope with:

> *If you try to push resettlement at a faster rate, then you are setting up refugees for failure. As a refugee would say, better to stay in the camp than fail in the country of resettlement. If the refugee was going to face racial prejudice and lack of opportunity in New Zealand, it is better for the refugee to stay in the*

camp. The purpose of resettlement is to give a better life to a refugee. If a country can't offer that, it is better not to offer resettlement.[71]

The management of community attitudes was essential. Those involved had to be aware when compassion fatigue was setting in, to ensure that every refugee came to a welcoming community. This required strong ministerial involvement, not a refugee settlement programme driven largely by officials and the UNHCR. But Malcolm acknowledged that the Indo-Chinese refugee resettlement programme reflected the 1970s and 1980s and was a facet of a more interventionist government. It was also easier then to gauge the public mood because New Zealand was more homogenous.

The refugees selected in March 1979 were followed by an almost continuous flow throughout the 1980s and mid-1990s. Many were family members of refugees already in New Zealand.[72]

About 4600 of the refugees chosen to come to New Zealand between 1979 and 1992 were from Cambodia. Although the magnitude of the Cambodian refugee crisis did not become evident until after the collapse of Pol Pot's Khmer Rouge regime in 1979, about 16,000 Cambodians had managed to cross the border into Thailand in 1975. The communist Khmer Rouge had destroyed the country's economic and social infrastructure by abolishing money, schools and private property. The country's population had been driven from Cambodia's towns to labour camps in the provinces, where approximately 1.7 million Cambodians died from starvation, exhaustion and malnutrition. Many had been tortured or killed for opposing the regime. The numbers of Cambodian refugees reached a peak in 1979, when around 270,000 people sought refuge in Thailand.[73]

Borany Kanal, who came to New Zealand in 1980, experienced many of the horrific events in Cambodia. In 1975 when New Zealand was cautiously deliberating over whether or not to accept a small number of Indo-Chinese refugees, she was seven years old. Her family's ordeal began after the capture of Phnom Penh when they, like more than two million other residents of that city, were forced to move to a rural area.

> *By then, we had been living under the Khmer Rouge for nearly four years. When the country was first taken over in 1975, there were about thirty members of my family all living in Phnom Penh. By the time the Vietnamese came, there were only five of us still alive, and we were split up, all living in different places around the province of Pursat.*

After the Vietnamese invasion, Borany and her family walked to Thailand where they lived in the Khao-i-Dang refugee camp.

> *Every day in the camp, lists of names would be put up. They were the names of those who had been accepted to go to other countries. Finally, one day, our name was on the list. We were going to New Zealand! My family arrived … in September 1980. We came as official refugees, brought by the New Zealand government. As we got off the plane at Auckland Airport, I felt the coldness of the wind on my eyes and on the skin of my face. I remember thinking, 'Is it this cold in New Zealand?' … We had medical examinations and blood tests, and for the first time in my life I had a bath. In Phnom Penh we had always had showers. When I first saw the bath I thought, 'What do they do with that container?' … Later we went to a marae. The people there sang to us, to welcome us, and one person in our group sang a song in Khmer to reply.*

The Kanals were then taken by their sponsor to a house in Porirua, near Wellington. 'I thought that it must be his house, because it all looked so nice. There was even a bowl of apples on the table. It was only after he had left that I realised that the house was for us. I couldn't believe it. It was a proper house!'[74]

By the end of March 1980 a total of 1977 Indo-Chinese refugees had been resettled in New Zealand.[75] Indo-Chinese refugee arrivals continued during the 1980s. In the middle of the decade the refugee programme, comprising an annual intake of 650 people, consisted almost exclusively of Indo-Chinese refugees.[76]

By 1980, the government had come to regard 'the admission and resettlement of refugees' as 'an important humanitarian priority in New Zealand's immigration policy'. The procedures that had 'evolved' to deal with refugees accepted under the Indo-Chinese quota differed from those followed for other programmes in a number of ways. Most of the refugees were selected by immigration officers who travelled to the camps.

> *They are then transported to New Zealand in groups, and their arrival is phased over a period of time to ensure that each group has access to the full range of medical and orientation facilities on arrival and can begin the process of being absorbed into the community before the next group arrives.*[77]

These systems would be further developed in the years ahead to support the settlement of more Indo-Chinese refugees and, from the 1990s, the arrival of refugees from Africa and the Middle East.

By 1982, in selecting Indo-Chinese refugees for settlement, New Zealand was giving priority to refugees with immediate family in New Zealand.[78] Government officials tried to ensure that refugees who were 'pepper-potted' or dispersed throughout New Zealand were settled in the same towns as their relatives. This very worthy and humanitarian objective of reuniting families showed how much more humane refugee resettlement had become since

Holocaust survivors had been refused entry to New Zealand.[79] There were, however, other considerations. The Ministry of Foreign Affairs saw 'advantages' in selecting refugees for the 1985–86 intake 'from camps in ASEAN countries' (Association of South East Asian Nations, formed in 1967) 'rather than helping out, say, Vietnam'. Giving 'greater priority to assisting friendly countries in the region, that is the ASEAN countries and Hong Kong', as Foreign Affairs preferred, meant 'taking a lower number of only the most deserving family reunification cases from camps in Vietnam'.[80]

Prioritising friendly ASEAN countries also meant compromises in relation to Cambodian refugees, who probably needed the most help. Although the Ministry of Foreign Affairs accepted 'that those Kampucheans who sought refuge from the Pol Pot regime with the communist Vietnamese rather than with pro-western ASEAN countries are no less deserving in humanitarian terms … as the "eligible" supply of refugees exceeds the quota NZ can accept in any year', New Zealand should concentrate on 'assisting friendly countries in the region rather than Vietnam'.[81]

The fourth Labour government, with David Lange as Prime Minister and Minister of Foreign Affairs, had taken office in July 1984. The pragmatic thinking of the Ministry of Foreign Affairs in mid-1985 possibly fitted better with the priorities of the former National government. The thinking certainly contrasted markedly with the previous Labour government's stance on Vietnam.

Community attitudes

As will be discussed in the next chapter, the resettlement programme was greatly dependent on community acceptance of the refugees. On the whole, this seemed to be adequate. Some people were critical of the government, lobbying the Minister of Immigration to take more refugees and to help more than it was already doing.[82] Two high-profile public figures, Hugo and Bill Manson, urged the government to admit more refugees on the grounds that New Zealand, by its involvement in the Vietnam War, was part of the refugee calamity.[83]

Among the critics were those who felt that the refugees were being treated as potential immigrants, with selection based on skills that would benefit New Zealand rather than on the needs of the refugees. Aussie Malcolm denied this was the case. In his view, New Zealand had a liberal selection policy: 'Age or youth is not a barrier to selection and we do not only seek skilled people. Our selection methods and criteria are praised by the United Nations as being far closer to the ideal than most other countries.' He also emphasised that quality of resettlement came before quantity. A major limitation was human and community resources. One could not simply bring in refugees and dump them at the airports. 'We are dealing with a tragic, human problem and it requires an approach that is mature and balanced as well as being humanitarian and heartfelt.'[84]

Around 20–30 per cent of the letters and phone calls received by the government were bigoted, racist or simply opposed to New Zealand's involvement. Disgruntled people wrote to tell the government that these 'yellow, slit-eyed' people should not be let into New Zealand.[85] By late 1979, Malcolm clearly felt confident that such critics were in the minority. In response to a concerned correspondent who thought the government was letting in too many Vietnamese refugees, he wrote: 'While I respect your right to hold personal views about the government's involvement in helping to resettle Indo-Chinese refugees, I cannot accept them as being representative of those held by the majority of New Zealanders.' Furthermore, he was not prepared to make 'apologies for accepting into New Zealand on humanitarian grounds people who come within the mandate of the United Nations High Commissioner for Refugees'. It was also a matter of maintaining New Zealand's humanitarian reputation, built up in previous decades.[86]

In view of New Zealanders' past attitudes to racial minorities, why was the public response to Indo-Chinese refugees generally so positive? The media attention given to boat people in 1978 had probably contributed a great deal to arousing public sympathy for the refugees, as did publicity from 1979 about the cruelty of the Pol Pot regime. This attitude was certainly helpful in harnessing community support for the new arrivals as they settled into the community. Approaches from the public offering sponsorship and jobs flooded into the Department of Labour. As was the case with earlier groups of refugees, offers of homes for refugee children were also plentiful.[87] But according to an opinion poll conducted in 1980, 34 per cent of those surveyed wanted either fewer Indo-Chinese refugees or none at all.[88]

CHAPTER SIX

From refugee to new settler

The 1930s and early 1940s were characterised by a 'sink or swim' approach to refugee settlement. Jewish refugees, who in fact entered the country as migrants, were assisted by Jewish welfare societies in the main centres or left to their own devices to manage as best they could. In the same way, new arrivals from China were supported by members of the Chinese community already in New Zealand. After 1948 the Department of Labour provided some settlement services such as introductory classes in New Zealand life, customs and language, for DPs who were placed for six weeks at the Reception and Training Centre in Pahiatua.[1]

But helping the newcomers to learn about New Zealand life and conditions was not enough. The government's explicit intention in the 1940s and 1950s was 'to ensure that the alien was exposed to the forces of assimilation', and 'to assist the alien to adjust himself to society' (not that resources were ever put into actually doing this). All refugees needed help, it was thought, to prevent them feeling 'overpowered by the new environment'. This was especially necessary for 'some well-educated aliens' who might 'feel a contemptuous intellectual superiority towards cultural standards in New Zealand'.[2]

Settlement services

Various arms of the welfare state combined with the voluntary efforts of church workers and ethnic communities to provide orientation and a range of other services for Cold War refugees in the 1950s and 1960s. By the early 1970s New Zealand's model of resettlement was at work in embryonic form. In settling Asian refugees from Uganda in 1972 the government worked with the Indian Association and with churches,[3] which had received a considerable number of offers of jobs, accommodation and sponsors for individual refugees and families.[4] In 1972 there were approximately 6000 people of Indian origin in New Zealand and the government was expecting them, through their association, to be involved with the churches in the resettlement of the newcomers. A coordinating committee was formed to help the refugees, particularly those with no family connections in New Zealand.[5]

On 25 September 1972 External Affairs and Department of Labour officials, the Wellington Indian Association, churches and the Jewish Relief and Welfare Organisation attended a meeting of the committee in Wellington. The model of resettlement exemplified by the cooperation between the meeting's attendees would be modified over the years but has remained fundamentally unchanged to this day. In brief, the government's role has been to set the broad policy and to administer regulations. The daily work of resettlement has been left to community groups, particularly church and ethnic organisations. The burden of resettlement, including financial costs, has been shared between the government and the community. In the case of Asians from Uganda, the government agreed to pay the refugees' fares. Responsibility for paying the travel costs of refugees shifted over years between the government and refugees themselves, with the refugees sometimes offered loans to cover travel costs.

This refugee settlement model accorded a crucial role to the main agency coordinating the various churches and other voluntary groups working with government to settle refugees. The 1970s and 1980s were years of increasing importance for the Inter-Church Committee on Immigration, founded in 1969 by the National Council of Churches and the Catholic Immigration Committee to represent the interests of the churches on immigration.[6] In 1975 the Inter-Church Commission on Immigration and Refugee Resettlement (ICCI) was formed by the National Council of Churches, the Catholic Church and the United Hebrew Immigration Society (HIAS), which represented the Jewish welfare agencies in New Zealand.

Chilean refugees were the first group assisted by the ICCI. The agency's next challenge, which came between the late 1970s and the late 1980s, was the resettlement of Indo-Chinese refugees. As Aussie Malcolm put it, 'In the end we got what we wanted, a brilliant settlement programme. Our refugee resettlement programme in my view was simply the best in the world.'[7] Malcolm's glowing view of New Zealand's refugee resettlement programme echoed that of the UNHCR representative for New Zealand, Paul Hartling, who regarded New Zealand's resettlement programme as 'a good model for the rest of the world' and thought the country had done 'a remarkable job' in integrating Indo-Chinese refugees.[8] Malcolm believed that the New Zealand model succeeded because it was a concerted effort between politicians, bureaucrats and members of the community. 'While I may have been "conductor", or perhaps "first violinist", the performance was of an orchestra.'[9]

The New Zealand model worked relatively well thanks to the ICCI and its network of church volunteers. In 1979 the Department of Labour took over the provision of reception and orientation as it did not consider the ICCI could cope with the arrival of much larger groups, but the agency was left with more than enough on its hands and a pivotal role. It was responsible for placing refugees in the community, for finding accommodation and jobs and, above all, for generating public support. The ICCI had two key related tasks: to mobilise its nationwide networks to assist refugee resettlement and to arrange sponsorship for the refugees.[10]

The basis of the Indo-Chinese resettlement programme was the partnership between government and the community. The government was responsible for setting up refugee resettlement committees, drawing together organisations active in the community already working with refugees and government agencies. The committees' main role was to coordinate the resettlement programme in the various areas. They also had a liaison role to ensure that sponsors met their obligations. The committees were disbanded after 1980 with the administrative network of the ICCI taking over the resettlement programme – at least in theory.[11]

As Keith Taylor noted in the mid-1980s, the work of refugee resettlement in New Zealand was largely done by volunteers:

> These sponsors – churches, service clubs, community groups etc. – are coordinated by the Inter-Church Commission on Refugee Resettlement, which works in close co-operation with the government and international agencies … The volunteers provide household goods, find housing and jobs and are involved with counselling, English tutoring and countless other tasks for as long as the refugees need them. The Government provides social welfare benefits, English courses, medical and dental care …[12]

New Zealand's first Refugee Day, organised by the ICCI and celebrated on 1 August 1983, was planned to further build public support for the refugee programme. Its various objectives included drawing 'attention to the cultural diversity and benefits which accompany refugee resettlement', and it was also intended 'to build greater awareness of refugee problems on a national and international level; to highlight national resettlement and sponsorship programmes' and 'to focus on the ongoing financial needs of the ICCI'.[13]

Officially the ICCI became the Refugee and Migrant Service (RMS) in 1990;[14] between 2005 and 2008 it was known as RMS Refugee Resettlement. From 2008 until 2012, when the agency combined with the New Zealand Red Cross, it was known as Refugee Services Aotearoa New Zealand.[15] Changes in name and structure notwithstanding, the main role has remained substantially the same – mobilising community involvement in refugee resettlement and finding sponsors in the community for refugees accepted under various refugee quotas and, after 1987, the annual global refugee quota.

Two key features of New Zealand's model of resettlement require further discussion. The first of these is the somewhat controversial aspect of the refugee programme known as 'pepper-potting' or distributing refugees around New Zealand. This was a particular feature of the years 1975–80, and was done either to ensure that refugees were resettled in places where their labour was required, or to prevent the creation of 'alien enclaves': the DPs were dispersed to jobs found by the Department of Labour, for example in forestry. The Old Believers from China had wanted to be settled as a group, but were dispersed in order to prevent the formation of alien enclaves and to encourage assimilation (see p. 110); the government had also dispersed Hungarian refugees around the country for similar reasons.

As we saw in Chapter Five, officials tried to mitigate the effects of pepper-potting by ensuring that newly arriving members of Indo-Chinese refugee families were able to settle in the same towns as their relatives. Taylor recalled that in the days when the ICCI felt it was 'walking a tightrope' in helping Indo-Chinese refugees gain community acceptance, they were spread around the country 'to help ensure their acceptance in the community'.[16] Pepper-potting of Indo-Chinese refugees was also done in accordance with the availability of refugee sponsors in different locations, but the system had little regard for new arrivals' need to be close to each other for support. After 1980, although some refugees continued to be settled where sponsors were available, both the government and the ICCI took greater account of refugees' needs for ethnic community support. Before 1980 refugees had been spread from one end of

New Zealand to another,[17] often stuck in areas where they felt isolated from other refugees, had little chance to learn English, develop other work skills or even have access to Asian foods.[18]

Pepper-potting was also a challenge for small New Zealand communities where suitable accommodation, employment and language classes were harder to find than in main centres. Soon after 1980 refugees in provincial New Zealand started to migrate to the main centres, particularly to Auckland and sometimes to Australia, to be part of larger ethnic communities. By 1986, 50 per cent of new settlers were placed in Auckland after their orientation programme at the Mangere Reception Centre.[19]

While acknowledging the problems caused by pepper-potting, Malcolm considered that the mobility of refugees after settlement was not necessarily a measure of failure or that the practice had not been somewhat justified in the circumstances. He acknowledged that settling refugees in small communities was probably not ideal, 'but if it occurred with high degree of support from the local community, the initial settlement may be successful'. The fact that the refugees eventually moved to Auckland did not mean the refugee programme had not worked.[20]

The second aspect of New Zealand's model of resettlement that warrants further comment is the strong voluntary input through the sponsorship system. Its origins lay in the mid-twentieth century, when church groups were involved in sponsoring the settlement of elderly White Russian refugees and Russian Christians from China. The shape and methods of New Zealand's resettlement programme were subsequently influenced by the mixture of government and voluntary input involved in settling Asian refugees from Uganda. The direction of New Zealand's developing resettlement programme, which already included considerable input from voluntary agencies and a variety of government departments, was reinforced by Australian experience with settling Indo-Chinese refugees. The Australians thought that the input of strong voluntary agencies combined with considerable government support had worked well for them.[21]

By the mid-1980s New Zealand's resettlement programme relied on the ICCI to find sponsors for the refugees and to provide reception for them. As Taylor recalled, volunteers obtained through ICCI's extensive networks of churches provided a 24-hour resettlement service, with the government contributing only a small amount of funding. But the extensive use of church volunteers had a downside for refugees: 'Some tried to convert refugees, or get them to go to Church.'[22] Houmpheng Rattanong, who came to New Zealand in

1980 from Laos, noted that refugees sometimes went to church solely to please their sponsors, even if they did not understand the service, and were adherents of a non-Christian faith.

Some refugees feel they have sinned by going to church. I have one friend in Auckland who goes to church on Sundays. He then returns home and prays to Buddha for forgiveness for sinning by going to church ... Our people have been Buddhists for thousands of years. It is difficult to change it. We have lost everything. Buddhism is the only thing we can bring with us; the only thing that can support us is on the inside.[23]

Sponsors were seen as playing a vital role in helping refugees to settle into the local community and assisting them with the many small problems of day-to-day living in a new country. Sponsors helped refugees to place their children in schools, enrol with the local doctor, find English classes, access social welfare benefits (refugees were entitled to receive the emergency unemployment benefit until the 'breadwinner' began working) and, above all, offered 'encouragement and friendship'.[24]

Many refugees have been grateful for the help they received from their sponsors and many sponsors have appreciated the chance to make a difference to the lives of new settlers. Lifelong friendships have been formed. Sometimes, however, the sponsor–refugee relationship has been fraught with problems. Houmpheng Rattanong described some of the difficulties: 'We came to New Zealand for freedom, not for an improved material life. We need help to stand on our own feet and become independent. We know that is a big task and realise that sponsors are volunteers. We do not want to ask too much of them but there is no one else to ask.' He felt there was a need for more ex-refugee social workers and community workers. When he first came to New Zealand, his sponsors tried to prevent him from taking the bus from Christchurch to Blenheim in case he got lost.

I helped my brothers swim across the river and come to New Zealand. I did not think I would become lost. I am not a child ... when do we stop being refugees? We want to be independent as soon as possible. If sponsors are 'too good' as sponsors we will use their help as sponsors for a long time. Sometimes the person who is there to solve our problems becomes our problem. Sometimes the helper needs us for a longer period of time then we need him/her. We do not need second hand clothes forever. The best sponsors are those who eventually become our friends because friends are equal.[25]

Similarly, Anna Reutt-Marciszewski, who arrived from Poland in 1987 and lived at first with her sponsor in Pahiatua, remembered: 'It's a large and generous thing, to offer to be a sponsor, but I think it's very difficult being responsible for a family in a new country.' Though she and her husband had plenty of help, Anna often felt like packing her bags and going back to Poland. One of the things she found particularly hard was to be the recipient of so much help from people. It made her feel 'such a small person, with no pride'.[26]

A letter from a former refugee to a relative, written in 1982 and found by chance in a refugee processing centre in Indonesia, gives a rare, frank view of one Vietnamese refugee's early impressions of settling in New Zealand.

> We arrived at a very big Airport but there were very few people about ... Those who came to meet us were very friendly and we soon felt welcome and they helped us with our bags as we got through the Customs baggage inspection. We then got into buses and drove a short distance to an old Army Camp. The barracks here, however, are very neat and clean and well laid out not like the refugee camps ... The rooms inside were very small with only two people to a room ... Everything is nice and clean and tidy and most of the sheets and towels and that all of which are provided, appear to have never been used before ... The Centre itself is very good and clean, there are plenty of books and magazines and there is even television and games such as ping-pong and billiards which you can play. The food is very good ... You can eat as much as you like and there is milk every day and cream.

The letter goes on to say the food and material were cheap, though electricity and labour seemed very expensive. In terms of employment, there seemed to be plenty of jobs available. 'New Zealand people are very idle and don't work hard, and don't work very long hours. Many New Zealanders also live off welfare. The life here is very comfortable for them. Life is very comfortable and very peaceful and democratic.'[27]

Little mention has so far been made of the role played by the other partner – the government – in the provision of settlement services. By March 1987 a total of 7546 Indo-Chinese refugees had settled in New Zealand.[28] During a conference on Indo-Chinese refugees held in Geneva in June 1989 and attended by New Zealand, a Comprehensive Plan of Action (CPA) was developed to identify solutions to the ongoing problem of refugees in the region. The CPA, which focused primarily on Vietnamese asylum seekers, contained a range of measures to control the flow of refugees, including a cut-off date for refugees arriving in camps who would be processed for resettlement. Those declined refugee status would be offered voluntary repatriation. Resettlement countries, including New Zealand, made a commitment under the CPA to help deal with the backlog of refugees, estimated in 1989 to be around 70,000.[29] The New Zealand government agreed to accept 1000 refugees over the following three years as part of the annual quota of 800, subject to sponsorship being available.

The numbers accepted would include a 'fair share of hard core cases'.[30]

Despite the relatively large numbers of refugees arriving under the refugee programme, including those considered hard to settle and some with special health needs,[31] government-provided specialist settlement assistance was meagre in the 1980s. After on-arrival orientation services for varying periods up to 12 weeks at the Mangere Refugee Reception Centre, refugees were catered for by mainstream social, education and health services on the same basis as other New Zealanders, and their sponsors gave them continued help.

By the late 1980s there was growing awareness that some refugees were experiencing significant difficulties in establishing themselves, partly because of a lack of adequate settlement services. There was no comprehensive social services policy regarding the refugees and immigrants entering the country. A conference on refugee mental health held in May 1988 concluded that New Zealand's health and welfare services were 'poorly equipped to handle the special needs of ethnic minority members'.[32]

Shortly after the conference, the government's Social Equity Committee charged the Department of Social Welfare with developing such a comprehensive policy in conjunction with other agencies involved with refugees and immigrants.[33] As an official in the Department of Social Welfare, I was part of this process. After several months of fairly intensive activity – there were enthusiastic meetings with other agencies and excellent papers were written – the initiative fizzled out. There seemed to be no real will by the government to provide specialist settlement services for refugees. These, including the introduction of ethnic community workers as suggested by Houmpheng Rattanong, had to wait until the 1990s.

The 'hard core'

In the 1940s, 1950s and 1960s, policy-makers used the labels 'handicapped' and 'hard core' to categorise refugees regarded as potential liabilities for a variety of reasons such as ill health, disability, advanced age, having large numbers of dependent children, lacking the required work skills or any other characteristic that might make them a potential financial and social burden. For many years such refugees had languished in refugee camps, thus making them even less attractive to resettlement countries.

In 1949, when facing problems in finding enough applicants to meet its target, New Zealand first considered accepting some 'hard core' refugees who were being left behind in the DP camps. Because the types New Zealand had most wanted were unavailable, it accepted a number of people who would not be 'economically self-supporting'. The Department of Labour had made a virtue out of necessity, reporting on the 'uniqueness of New Zealand's offer', 'a contribution toward the great humanitarian work of [the] IRO' (see Chapter Three).[34] New Zealand continued to take small numbers of 'handicapped', 'hard core' refugees and 'humanitarian cases' as part of later DP groups.[35] Planning for the acceptance of a further 10 'hard core' refugee cases was under way from around 1954. Correspondence between the Inter-Church Council on Public Affairs (a forerunner of the ICCI) and the UNHCR suggests that in February 1956 the latter was hopeful that New Zealand might take 10 refugees suffering from tuberculosis, together with their families. They 'might be permitted to enter this country for placement in institutions. Apparently, there are a number of vacancies in Sanatoria due to the great advances made in recent years in the treatment of TB.'[36] As the UNHCR explained to the council,

> the young and healthy refugees are welcomed by those countries needing manpower, while the aged and sick who are of no economic value to the receiving country, are generally passed over. Many of these refugees who are classified by our office as 'difficult cases' have been existing in camps since the end of the last war and are still waiting for the chance to be given a permanent home.[37]

Alarm bells seem to have rung for the government over the prospect of TB cases entering New Zealand for the letter to the Inter-Church Council contains a hand-written 'No!' in heavy black ink on the left-hand margin beside the words 'refugees suffering from tuberculosis', which are underlined.[38] In 1956, though overall mortality from tuberculosis was falling, there were 1806 newly notified cases of the disease in New Zealand.[39] A letter from the Department of Labour to the council in April 1956 refers to 'some misunderstanding' over the proposal to arrange for the admission of refugees suffering from TB. The government, in discussions with the UNHCR, had made 'no offer to consider tubercular cases submitted by the High Commissioner for Refugees subject to satisfactory accommodation arrangements being made by church organizations'.[40] Since active TB cases would have to be placed in appropriate institutions, and the churches did not operate such places, refugees with TB could not be accommodated. In any case, the department added, it was doubtful that the health authorities would agree to the acceptance of TB cases.[41] (See Chapter Nine for New Zealand's response to refugees with TB in 2012–13.)

By mid-1956 the possibility of accepting refugees with TB had been replaced by discussions about 'ten deserving cases', and these focused on who would be responsible for the costs of settling the new arrivals. Although the churches would be responsible for the accommodation and 'welfare' of the refugees, the government understood that 'church authorities could not be expected to meet the full cost of looking after these people'. As Ralph Hanan, Minister of Immigration, told a deputation from the Inter-Church Council in June 1956, 'it could become a question of some emergency benefits being paid from the Social Security Fund'.[42]

New Zealand's pioneering initiative regarding refugee families with handicapped members came during World Refugee Year (WRY). The year had been the idea of private individuals in Britain who wished to raise public awareness of the plight of the approximately 1.5 million refugees in the Middle East, in Europe and in Asia. The initiative eventually received the support of the United Nations, which launched the year in 1959.[43]

WRY provided the framework for a major intensification of effort by the UNHCR to promote the resettlement of the 32,000 refugees still in camps in Europe,[44] many of whom had been there since 1945. One-third of these families included a person with a disability.[45] New Zealand made a financial contribution to WRY and accepted the first 20 of such families.[46]

One of the new arrivals was two-year-old Ferdinand from Hungary, who was in urgent need of medical attention.[47] The H family, who had been living in a camp in Austria for 14 years, were also part of the first intake. The family was regarded as hard to settle because Mr H had lost a leg and no country was willing to accept him. His 12-year-old son had been born in the camp and had lived there all his life.[48]

New Zealand's acceptance of these families was pioneering for two reasons. First, New Zealand helped to lead a new international emphasis on the resettlement of 'handicapped' refugees in family units. In the 1950s, international practice among countries outside Europe was to consider 'handicapped' refugees on an individual basis, without necessarily including their families. Often when a 'handicapped' refugee was accepted for resettlement by a country, the family would be split up. Refugees were forced to choose between the offer of a new life and being able to continue to care for a dependent relative. In such circumstances most people chose to give up their chance to migrate.[49]

Second, New Zealand did not require the disabled person to be sponsored by a private individual who would guarantee they would not be a burden on the state. The government assumed full financial responsibility for the refugee families accepted, with the Inter-Church Council on Public Affairs taking on the role of finding sponsors to help the families settle in the community.[50]

The arrangement marked the beginning of New Zealand's model of refugee resettlement.

In 1959, when the first group of refugees had left Europe, the UNHCR, August Lindt, cabled New Zealand's Labour Prime Minister, Walter Nash: 'I fervently believe that other governments will be influenced by this example and it will result in new doors being opened to refugees.'[51] Economic criteria had determined the acceptance of prewar refugees from Europe, and the selection of postwar DPs and of Hungarian refugees. New Zealand's policy regarding 'handicapped' refugees was the beginning of a new stage in the evolution of refugee policy.

New Zealand made an outstanding contribution to WRY. Circumstances had changed since New Zealand had selected Hungarian refugees for resettlement. The main influences were no longer Cold War rivalries. What now mattered was publicity on the world stage. Another imperative was the need to respond to public sympathy for refugees.[52] The Labour government responded to strong domestic pressures from individuals, churches and organisations such as the United Nations Association. It was a case of the community leading the way, not the government taking the initiative and subsequently trying to obtain support. As Nash observed, 'The extent to which any country can receive refugees depends upon the goodwill and assistance which the residents of that country are prepared to offer.'[53] His own 'great passion' at this stage in his life for international affairs may also have been a factor.[54]

After WRY, perhaps to forestall possible criticism that New Zealand had been too generous, the government promoted the idea that accepting 'handicapped' refugees had been beneficial for all concerned. A Department of Labour report to the National Council of Churches provided details of how well the 80 families from Europe with 'handicapped' members were settling and emphasised the goodwill and support of the community:

> Not only have the churches made a splendid contribution to this work, but also non-religious organisations such as Rotary Clubs, Girl Guides Associations, Junior Chambers of Commerce, and the like. You will also be interested to know that in some districts, inter-denominational committees have been established for the purpose of sponsoring refugee groups. Some members of the families we have received have been very severely handicapped, but with the co-operation and goodwill of the local committees, their resettlement has been made possible. For example, one district has accepted a family, the head of which is deaf and dumb. This, too, has been a successful resettlement.[55]

An External Affairs report also stressed the positive aspects of New Zealand's 'handicapped' refugee programme. Contrary to accepted opinion, the 'handicapped' families had not proved burdensome but had settled well and before long 'were making a contribution to the national economy'.[56]

Probably because the programme had succeeded, in 1962 the National government, which had taken office after the 1960 election, agreed to accept 200 'handicapped' European refugee families as part of the country's further contribution to WRY.[57] By 1963 New Zealand had resettled over 200 families with 'handicapped' members, most of whom had been rejected by other countries.[58] New Zealand continued to receive high praise from the UNHCR, and other countries followed suit by resettling 'handicapped' refugees in family units.

In 1967 New Zealand announced its willingness to accept 20 more cases.[59] The gesture was in response to the UNHCR's 'final drive' to resettle World War II refugees still in camps in Europe, the Middle East and Asia. The largest number for whom resettlement was envisaged was in Italy. 'It is shocking – and a reflection on the whole system of international refugee work,' wrote the UNHCR, Sadruddin Aga Khan, 'that in 1967 [UN]HCR and the international community should still be seeking solutions for European refugees … men and women have been waiting ten or fifteen years for the chance to start a new life'.[60]

The Nansen Home

Elderly refugees were among those regarded as hard to settle. The Nansen Home, which opened in Lower Hutt in 1963, was established to provide a home for elderly White Russian refugees who had fled the Soviet Union after the Russian Revolution of 1917. The home was the idea of the Reverend Ian W. Fraser, who had been moved by the plight of refugees after a tour of Europe in 1958. During his travels, he had become aware of the work for refugees undertaken by the Waldensian church in Italy. In particular, he was impressed that the church did not select refugees who would be useful to their community – healthy, able-bodied people with the skills they needed.

> *I have always felt that refugees should be taken without selection. That is the way to receive them on compassionate grounds, as we claim to be doing. When they cross the border and claim asylum, the receiving country of first asylum has no choice as to who comes or what their skills may be. They [the Waldensian Church] take all who are genuine refugees and that is the way they should be helped – simply because they are refugees. When they are carefully selected, it shows that we are wanting to help ourselves first and foremost, not considering their needs as refugees.*[61]

And so the seeds for the home, which Fraser decided to name after Fridtjof Nansen, who worked on behalf of refugees after World War I, were sown.[62] Years of lobbying, persuading, discussing and proposal development followed. Fraser prepared the ground for the scheme, bringing on board the National Council of Churches, and gaining the support of the UNHCR and finally the government.[63] As Alan Brash, General Secretary of the National Council of Churches, told Prime Minister Walter Nash, the White Russian refugees had been 'driven out of China' and 'could be brought to New Zealand'. They were old, their need was 'urgent' and 'their plight pitiable'.[64]

The government, concerned about accepting elderly refugees who would not become self-supporting, was at first reluctant about the scheme. The Department of Labour told the National Council of Churches that New Zealand preferred to bring in groups of 'handicapped' refugee families as its contribution to WRY.[65] Eventually, however, the government succumbed. As Nash told the Cabinet, 'it would clearly be a worthwhile scheme from the humanitarian point of view, and would add to New Zealand's reputation as a country willing to do its utmost to assist in the solution of world refugee problems'.[66]

Financing the project required extensive fundraising and public appeals. The level of government financial support needed was estimated to be about £16,575 a year.[67] At first, though, the government agreed to issue entry permits for the refugees but declined any financial assistance, only later agreeing to make a special grant for each resident admitted to the Nansen Home that was equal to the age benefit – at that time £4 5s per week.[68]

The first three refugees arrived three days before opening day, 30 May 1963. When the 'huge Qantas Electra taxied up to the terminal building and the passengers began to disembark', the reporters wondered if they would be able to recognise the refugees. But there was no mistaking them. 'After everyone else was out there came three small ladies, wearing scarves over their heads, with drab clothes, helped to the building by hostesses and air crew.'[69]

When the refugees were shown their new home, one woman 'could not believe her eyes'.

> *They were all firmly convinced that they were going to be set to work, with the threat, 'No work; no food'. Although the arrangements were carefully explained to them in their own language they did not really believe it. They thought that after the initial welcome the tough side would be uncovered ... One wonders what has been the treatment of a woman of eighty-six who expected to be set to work?*[70]

It was hard to get used to the idea that in the middle of Lower Hutt there was a home for elderly Russian refugees, wrote the Reverend A. Quigley in the *Hutt News* after the home's opening. His examination of the notion of extending charity beyond New Zealand is revealing. The Nansen Home was 'of special significance', he decided, because it brought 'no obvious return to our country'. It was simply 'disinterested concern which receives these aged refugees'. One would not be surprised to find an institution like the Nansen Home in 'the countries nearer the centre of the political upheavals of our time', but it was a novelty in New Zealand, 'where we have seemed so far, in terms of distance and knowledge, from the troubles of men of other nations'. The project would be easier to understand, he thought, 'if the refugees were going to contribute to the community by their labour', but they would 'need looking after in the same way as the elderly people in any eventide home'. In setting up the Nansen Home, New Zealand had simply 'shown compassion and recognised a duty towards people of another race':

> I don't write this so that we may be pleased with ourselves! But I think we may see the Nansen Home as a further sign that we may be growing up into some kind of maturity as a nation. In the modern world the mature nation is the nation which recognises that the world is one community, and tries to act as a responsible member of that community.[71]

The notion of extending charity to people in faraway places seemed to appeal to ordinary New Zealanders. Many people now in their late sixties can recall extensive bouts of fundraising for CORSO (the Council of Organisations for Relief Services Overseas) during their childhood in the 1950s. Fraser's account in *The Story of Nansen Home* shows local groups hard at work to make the refugees feel at home by providing entertainment and recreational activities, taking refugees out for afternoon drives and inviting them to play bowls or chess. An effort was made to teach them English – a brave idea in view of their advanced years – and a psychologist was consulted about the refugees' adjustment problems.[72] The enthusiasm of people in the Hutt Valley seems remarkable because the Nansen Home (and other refugee resettlement projects) involved New Zealanders who had probably never travelled outside the country but rose above the prevailing social climate of suspicion of difference to welcome strangers from distant shores. The plight of refugees, so different from 'us', which could have aroused suspicion and intolerance, instead prompted the generosity and energy of ordinary people.

Like most refugees, the Nansen Home's first three residents had been scarred by the times they had lived through. Irina Vanteeva, aged 86 when she arrived in New Zealand, was born in the small village of Nalisova in Russia near the Ural Mountains. She had received little education as a child but trained as a nurse when she was 14. After nursing for many years, in 1917 when she was 40 she moved to Harbin in China to escape persecution in her homeland. She married but had no children; by the time her husband died she was 79. She received a small pension from the Chinese authorities but had to beg in the streets of Harbin to supplement her meagre income. In 1962 she left for Hong Kong and from there moved on to New Zealand and the Nansen Home.[73]

Sixty-eight-year-old Natalia Kozutina was born in the village of Iliinka in Russia, east of the Urals. Her parents were peasants; she had little schooling and remained illiterate. She married at the age of 18, just before the start of World War I, and had a son; her husband was killed in 1915. When news of the revolution reached them in 1917, Natalia and her son fled to Harbin where she worked as a nurse and as a domestic. Because of her illiteracy she was unable to keep in touch with her son and they lost contact; she never found out what had become of him. She was described as a 'cheerful person, who enjoyed all that was done for her, and joined in the activities of the Home'.[74]

The Nansen Home completed its task of caring for the refugees in September 1984 and the trust that had administered it was wound up. The building was taken over by the Presbyterian Support Services (PSSA) as an old people's home for non-refugee New Zealanders. The six remaining refugees were looked after by the PSSA for as long as required.[75] The need for such a home had lessened gradually by the late 1960s as elderly refugees were able to be accepted for resettlement with their families. Eventually most countries adopted this policy.

Old Believers

Another example of the humanitarian impulse and practical Christianity working hand in hand is the story of the Russian Christians from China, known as Old Believers. Like the elderly White Russian refugees, they were supporters of the Tsarist government. Fundamentalist Christians, they first challenged, and subsequently broke away from, the Russian Orthodox Church after the introduction of reforms in the seventeenth century. Persecuted, they became scattered throughout Russia; many escaped to Siberia. They resisted collectivisation of the Russian Revolution of 1917 and fled to China where an estimated 2000 Old Believers settled in Sinkiang or near Harbin. From 1952 as the Chinese authorities increased their demands for taxes, some Old Believers departed for Hong Kong. Others remained trapped in China in trying conditions until 1964 when the Chinese finally allowed them to leave for Hong Kong. From there, international agencies tried to find them countries of resettlement around the world.[76]

Australia eventually agreed to accept 110 Old Believers. As a result of pressure from the National Council of Churches, with Ron O'Grady in charge of the refugee work, the National government agreed to accept 88. In his book about the refugees O'Grady commented that New Zealand 'showed a particularly generous spirit' by agreeing to resettle the families with handicapped members. Prime Minister Keith Holyoake and Minister of Labour Tom Shand wrote to the National Council of Churches, assuring support and offering good wishes for the venture.[77]

The first major decision was where the Old Believers were to live: eventually Invercargill was chosen. Another question was whether they were to live together as a community, as they had done in Brazil. Although this possibility was investigated, and the decision was not easy, they were resettled 'as separate family units, making some provision for them to meet together as they desired'.[78] There were various reasons. One was the high price of land: 'The financial resources of the Church would be stretched to even make a deposit on a sufficiently large tract of land.' Another important factor was 'the sophistication of New Zealand farming methods', although what this meant was not clear. Were the methods too sophisticated for the Old Believers to learn? The main difficulties, though, were 'sociological': 'How would New Zealanders react to the establishment of such a community?'[79]

In the end the government made the decision for the church. Shand 'would not sanction the establishment of an exclusive religious community'. His view was that, after the Old Believers had lived in New Zealand for a few years and then chose to live together in a community on one block of land, that would be their right, 'but at the outset it was in their own interest that they should at least learn the type of country to which they had come'.[80] This position was consistent with past government policies. Alien enclaves were not wanted in New Zealand. Successive governments would take a similar stand.

The first group of 16 Old Believers from Sinkiang Province arrived in Christchurch on 14 July 1965. Although all foreigners were conspicuous in mid-twentieth century New Zealand, the Old Believers stood out more than others,[81] as O'Grady recalled:

> The incongruity of a group of people who had travelled mainly by horse and cart being suddenly whisked across the sky at 500 mph was not lost on the reception party. The scream of jets faded and the usual stream of passengers

emerged from the plane ... The press photographer whistled. 'Good God,' he said, 'look at that.' The old man who emerged was an impressive figure. A weather-beaten face and a long beard gave him the appearance of an Old Testament patriarch. Thigh-length leather boots and a peasant smock tied at the waist with string completed the picture of the first of the Old Believers.[82]

The 'patriarch' was 70-year-old Avdei, who acted as spokesman. The disembarking women looked odd too, in their boots and long skirts and with scarves tied round their heads. The children were dressed like their parents. 'It was hard to believe that this was happening in New Zealand.'[83]

O'Grady also noticed that, in contrast with their 'worn-out looking clothes', several of the men had 'expensive cameras' slung over their shoulders. He supposed that they had bought these in Hong Kong where some of the refugees had obtained work. These items did not fit the stereotype of refugees as plucky and dignified but also poor and pitiable. One man had with him a large packet of seeds, which was impounded by the Department of Agriculture inspector. The next day the refugees flew to Invercargill to 'a remarkable reception'. As they crossed the tarmac, they were identified by their sponsors who greeted them with a few words in Russian. Each of the girls was given a doll and the boys a small toy. A light meal of 'peeroshkas' (piroshkis – pasties filled with cabbage, rice and eggs or mince) had been prepared by local Russians, 'followed by the appropriate New Zealand supplement, a cup of tea ... Big New Zealand mouths took a tentative bite at the pasties, and quickly decided that Russian cooking wasn't too bad.' Welcoming them, the Chairman of the Southland Branch of the National Council of Churches said, 'Your character has been tested by the fire of persecution and suffering – here you will have freedom to work and worship.' The following day's editorial in the *Southland Times* noted that New Zealand was limited in what it could do internationally, but in the refugee field its role could be significant. 'The job is not done for prestige. It is a matter of conscience.'[84] Local farmers went to enormous lengths to make the refugees welcome. 'Over 1500 Southlanders donated money, clothes, houses.' Some Southland farmers even tried to learn Russian.[85]

As one of the Southland farmers involved in the project said, helping refugees 'is what the churches ought to be doing more often. This is real Christianity.'[86] New Zealanders' generous impulses were readily awakened by the Russian refugees because with their tattered clothes and seventeenth-century way of life they seemed so obviously needy. Jewish refugees, who did not look obviously needy, had not so readily aroused the humanitarian impulse in the 1930s and 1940s. They were seen as competitors for jobs, or as suspect 'enemy aliens', and

Eating bananas in Vienna, December 1956. The author (Ann Szegoe, left) and friends eating their first bananas in Vienna after crossing the border from Hungary to Austria (you couldn't get bananas in Hungary at that time). From Vienna they went to live in the refugee camp at Korneuburg to await selection for a country of settlement.
(Above right) Mother and child: Eva Szegoe and daughter Ann on board the ship *Sibajak* sailing to New Zealand, August 1957.

A group of Hungarian refugees celebrating their first New Year's Eve in Wellington, having escaped from Hungary after the uprising in 1956. Photograph: Dénes Siklosi

A nurse, her daughter and another child, among the 4500 Displaced Persons from Europe accepted by New Zealand after World War II, arrive by train at the Pahiatua refugee resettlement camp, 1949.

Photograph: W. Walker, National Publicity Studios, Alexander Turnbull Library, ¼-016793

Newly arrived refugees from Czechoslovakia, fleeing communism, about to start English language classes, 1970.

Evening Post, 18 November 1970, Alexander Turnbull Library, EP/1970/4977

The first group of Asian refugees from Uganda, expelled under President Idi Amin's 'Africanisation' policy, arrive in Wellington, 1972.

Evening Post, 8 November 1972, Alexander Turnbull Library, EP/1972/5327/5

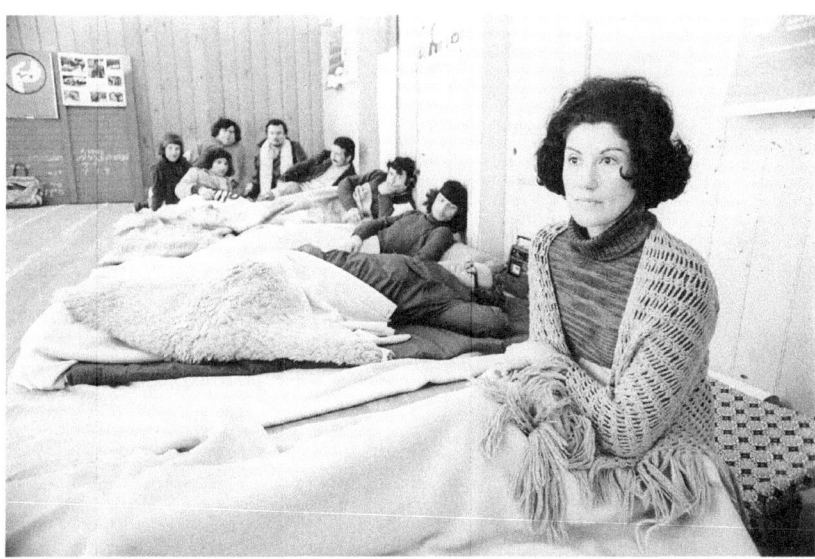

Chilean refugees of the 1973 military coup against the government of Salvador Allende begin a protest vigil at Wesley Church in Taranaki Street, Wellington, to draw attention to the plight of political prisoners being held without trial in Chile. Similar vigils were planned in Christchurch and Auckland, 1978.

Evening Post, 3 June 1978, Alexander Turnbull Library, EP/1978/1980

This young girl from Chile resettled in New Zealand in the mid-1970s.

Photograph: Keith Taylor

Refugees from Laos, who arrived in New Zealand in 1985, still facing the battle to learn English and find suitable work three years later.

Evening Post, 12 October 1988, Alexander Turnbull Library, EP/1988/3942

This Vietnamese family, pictured at the Mangere Refugee Reception Centre, in Auckland, made New Zealand home in 1979.

Photograph: Keith Taylor

Three Vietnamese refugee families, sponsored by churches in the Porirua/Plimmerton area, arrive from a refugee camp in Hong Kong, 1982. Several thousand Indo-Chinese refugees (from Vietnam, Cambodia and Laos) came to New Zealand in the aftermath of the Vietnam War.

Evening Post, 26 March 1982, Alexander Turnbull Library, EP/1982/0915

Three students from Cambodia about to begin their studies at Victoria University in Wellington, 1974.

Evening Post, 22 February 1974, Alexander Turnbull Library, EP-Politics-Immigration-Refugees-06

Children from Cambodia who arrived in Wellington in 1980 pictured two years later. *Evening Post*, 8 March 1982, Alexander Turnbull Library, EP/1982/0709

This Cambodian family still have mixed feelings: their new life in New Zealand has not wiped the memories of life in Cambodia under Pol Pot. *Evening Post*, 26 June 1997, Alexander Turnbull Library, EP/1997/1825

The rapid growth in the number of Cambodian students prompted a Porirua school to add a South East Asian flavour to its multicultural concert in 1993. *Evening Post*, 25 August 1993, Alexander Turnbull Library, EP/1993/2982

Hutt Valley Rotarians begin a community project in Waterloo Road, Lower Hutt: cleaning and painting the Nansen Home for elderly refugees from the former Soviet Union ('White Russian' refugees), 1973. *Evening Post*, 3 November 1973, Alexander Turnbull Library, EP/1973/4811

Some of the Polish children, of the over 700 given asylum in New Zealand in 1944, pictured in the dining room of the Polish children's camp at Pahiatua, about 1945. The Polish children were orphaned or had become separated from their families during World War II. Alexander Turnbull Library, ½-035132

Newly arrived Assyrian Christian refugees from Iraq, fleeing the Iran–Iraq war (1980–85), gather for breakfast in their new homeland, 1985. *Evening Post*, 26 October 1985, Alexander Turnbull Library, EP/1985/4810

Refugees from Iraq, 1998.
Evening Post, 1998, ATL reference: Iraq Group: EP – Ethnology – General, Ethnic Groups in NZ–O8

Somali refugees protest outside parliament to draw attention to the plight of Somalis in Kenya who want to join family members in New Zealand, 1995.

Evening Post, 1995, Alexander Turnbull Library, EP/1995/4812

Poring over immigration papers: three Somali families hoped to raise nearly $20,000 to bring family members (a woman and her two sons) to New Zealand, 1995. *Evening Post*, 1995, Alexander Turnbull Library, EP/1995/0346

A new life for Somali children reunited with their mothers in New Zealand, 1995. The families had fled their war-torn country for refugee camps in Kenya, where families often became separated.

Evening Post, 15 September 1995, Alexander Turnbull Library, EP/1995/3882-31

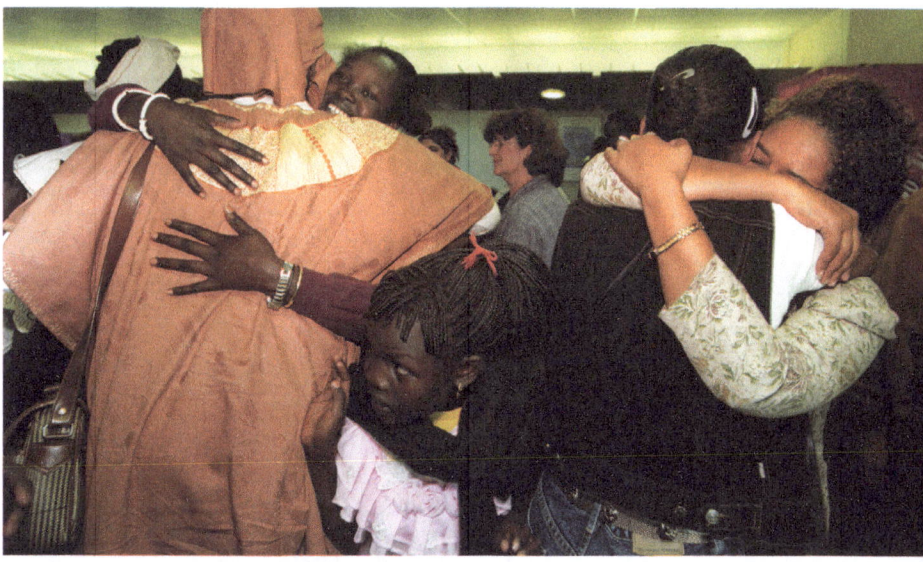

Refugees reunite at the airport with Ethiopian neighbours, 2000.

Evening Post, 23 March 2000, Alexander Turnbull Library, EP/2000/0980

A cartoon by Tom Scott published after New Zealand Prime Minister Helen Clark's decision to accept Afghani 'boat people' from the Norwegian freighter *Tampa*.
Tom Scott, *Evening Post*, 7 September 2001, Alexander Turnbull Library, H-652-024

Algerian asylum seeker Ahmed Zaoui was a test case for New Zealand's refugee determination process.
Garrick Tremain, *Otago Daily Times*, 14 December 2004, Alexander Turnbull Library, DX-022-140

Allan Hawkey, *Waikato Times*, 10 July 2007, Alexander Turnbull Library, DCDL-0003566

Tom Scott, *Dominion Post*, 15 September 2007, Alexander Turnbull Library, DCDL-0003928

Allan Hawkey, *Waikato Times*, 7 July 2010, Alexander Turnbull Library, DCDL-0014735

James Hubbard, Setford News Photo Agency, 12 April 2012, Alexander Turnbull Library, DCDL-0020896

Tom Scott, *Dominion Post*, 17 April 2012, Alexander Turnbull Library, DCDL-0020851

Malcolm Evans, Christchurch *Press*, 21 May 2012, Alexander Turnbull Library, DCDL-0021540

Malcolm Evans, Alexander Turnbull Library, DCDL-0025000

New Zealand Red Cross Disaster Welfare Support Team volunteer Andrew Tuck with Afghan interpreter Faisal Rezai at his new home in Hamilton. Nicola Inglis / New Zealand Red Cross

Dr Jenny McMahon, New Zealand Red Cross president, helping to unload the belongings of the Afghani interpreters.

Corinne Ambler / New Zealand Red Cross

Immigration Minister Michael Woodhouse welcoming Afghani families to New Zealand, 2013. New Zealand Defence Force

certainly as intruders bringing unwelcome cultural differences and old world tensions to New Zealand.[87]

According to O'Grady, writing in 1972, the resettlement of the Old Believers was 'the most ambitious programme of refugee resettlement attempted by the churches in New Zealand'.[88] (In the 1990s Gallienne made a similar claim, observing that the Indo-Chinese refugee resettlement 'was the most complex refugee experience ever faced by New Zealand'.[89]) The reason was not the number of Old Believers, which totalled 112 – that figure included babies born in New Zealand – but the fact that the refugees 'could be considered socially handicapped'. Most were illiterate or had received little schooling. Their religious beliefs had led to their distinctive dress, speech and customs, which had hardly changed since the seventeenth century. The Old Believers accepted by New Zealand also contained a number of refugees with physical disabilities.[90]

By the early 1980s, although the bulk of the community remained in Invercargill, some had moved to Christchurch and Gore. They were employed in factories, the railways, the Electricity Department and in the freezing works. Some of the women worked in the clothing industry; others in cooking.[91] With jobs in plentiful supply, finding employment was not the problem for the Old Believers that it would become for later refugees.

A number of the children left the faith and moved away to avoid the restrictive lifestyle; others left New Zealand to join bigger communities overseas. The Old Believers who stayed became New Zealand citizens.[92]

Refugees with special needs since the 1970s

New Zealand continued to accept refugees with special needs, though fewer came from Europe and more from other trouble spots in the world.[93] As Aussie Malcolm recalled, the New Zealand selection team was explicitly instructed to 'pick the refugees that no one else wants'. This policy was in stark contrast with that of countries such as Australia, which 'picked the eyes out of the refugee market'. Australia and Canada both saw the refugee programme in labour-market terms and selected the most intelligent and best trained refugees. In Malcolm's opinion, neither country was concerned about the needs of the refugees. 'New Zealand was.'

Australia 'ran extensive medical testing in the camps' and rejected refugees with special health needs. New Zealand decided not to do such testing; illness was not considered relevant. 'We preferred to put the refugees on a plane and bring them to New Zealand so that their health problems could be taken care of. New Zealand took pride in selecting refugees who were ill and not chosen by other countries.' Malcolm also believed in cutting through the red tape that prevented quick action. In one case, a refugee who urgently needed an operation to save her eyesight was accepted by New Zealand and brought to the country in 72 hours. 'We took pride in such missions.'[94]

In the 1990s the terminology changed from 'handicapped' or 'hard core' to 'medically disabled'. Don McKinnon, who was Minister of Foreign Affairs and Trade in the National government from 1990 to 1999, recalled that the previous policy of accepting refugees 'whose personal circumstances were in the "difficult category" posed a problem' since 'however admirable the sentiments, it came to include not just amputees but those with notifiable diseases'.[95]

Despite the problems associated with refugees suffering from notifiable diseases, those considered harder to settle, for whatever reason, have continued to be accepted as part of New Zealand's annual refugee quota of 750 people. In 2007 they entered the country under such categories as 'medical', 'emergency', 'women at risk' and 'protection'. Many had previously been declined by other countries. New Zealand has been one of the few countries in the world to accept refugees with HIV/Aids. Such refugees enter under the 'medical' category.[96] (The topic of refugees with special health needs returns in Chapter Nine.)

New Zealand's acceptance in 1959 of refugee families with special needs shows how a small country – the population was then just over two million[97] – can occasionally influence international action. A few months after August Lindt had praised New Zealand's initiative in accepting refugee families with handicapped members, the Australian government followed New Zealand's lead.[98]

Along with the resettlement of Polish children in 1944 (discussed in Chapter Seven), the resettlement of 'handicapped' and 'hard to settle' refugees from the late 1950s has become a crucial part of New Zealand's record of refugee assistance. Successive governments have referred to this record, using it to justify further refugee programmes and intakes. They have also used the historical record to excuse inaction or a meagre or tardy response.

According to Anton Binzegger, the generosity of New Zealand's overall settlement of refugees with disabilities should not be exaggerated because the total number of refugees accepted without economic motives predominating has been relatively small.[99] Also, 'where a handicapped refugee is a member of a family, the family as a whole can still be an economically viable unit, thereby reducing arguments about rejection on economic grounds'. He acknowledges that this did not apply to the acceptance of elderly refugees without families in 1963. In the late 1970s when Binzegger was writing his book, the government continued to contribute to the operating costs of the Nansen Home's 45 residents.

A remarkable aspect of New Zealand's refugee policy regarding 'hard to settle' refugees has been the influence of a small number of committed individuals – community and church leaders with a passion for humanitarian action. By forcing the government to act, and through their own efforts to fundraise and harness community support, people like Ron O'Grady and Alan Brash of the National Council of Churches, Ian Fraser and others working within church and community groups, have ensured that New Zealand's programme of refugee assistance has not simply been pragmatic and utilitarian. Typically, these idealistic people had their eyes opened to the misery in the world while overseas. They came back from wars and trips, where they had encountered refugees in camps, determined to make a better world.

Several government ministers also stand out. Walter Nash was Prime Minister during World Refugee Year when New Zealand undertook to accept refugee families with handicapped members. The 'activist side of Christianity still strongly appealed' to him. In talks and lay sermons he always stressed universal Christian love, which must not be exclusive but must extend to all men. As his biographer Keith Sinclair commented, all his life Nash had assumed the role of 'unpaid social worker', 'helping pensioners to get pensions, young couples to get mortgages, people with their troubles'.[100]

Norman Kirk was also committed to an ethical foreign policy. He believed that New Zealand should embrace the challenge of accepting refugees who were particularly hard to settle. Aussie Malcolm's commitment to resettling Indo-Chinese refugees stands out too. His special cause – bringing a group of unaccompanied minors to New Zealand – is discussed in the next chapter. More recently, there has been Prime Minister Helen Clark's decision that New Zealand would accept Afghan refugees from the Norwegian freighter *Tampa* (see Chapter Eight). The refugees had been turned away by Australia and accepting them seems to have been her personal decision.[101] The gesture was certainly in keeping with New Zealand's record of offering humanitarian assistance to refugees declined by other countries.

New Zealand's acceptance in 1959 of refugee families in which one or more members were 'handicapped' is justly regarded as an outstanding and pioneering endeavour in the area of refugee policy. The initiative, probably more than any other, gave rise to New Zealand's reputation as an independent and compassionate player on the world stage. Over the years several thousands of refugees have benefited from what is probably the most obvious manifestation of the internationalist ideal at the heart of refugee assistance programmes. It represents the purely humanitarian aspect of New Zealand's refugee resettlement policy.

CHAPTER SEVEN

'The children are a triumph'

When Reuel Lochore wrote those words in his 1951 book about European refugees in New Zealand he was referring to the children of Jewish families who had settled here in the late 1930s. He thought that the children, showing 'genius of adaptation', were 'the real success of this migration of people who were wholly unsuited to our conditions'.[1] As a previous writer had claimed in 1944, 'Children are the best type of immigrants. They are fresh and eager; willing to accept their adopted country as their own; to adopt its ways and to be in every way except by birth citizens of that country. Coming as children they have no great language problems to overcome and no foreign background to forget.'[2]

The Polish children, 1944

Among the victims of World War II were thousands of Polish children uprooted from their homes, who had lost one or both parents and who had known years of war, hunger, prison camp life and disease. New Zealand's formal refugee resettlement programme has often been considered to have begun in 1944 when a group of 834 mainly Catholic Poles arrived in New Zealand to spend the duration of the war here. They included 732 children, most of them orphaned in the war; the remainder were their caregivers.³ Owing to the political situation in Poland after 1945, the refugees were accepted for permanent settlement in New Zealand rather than returning to Europe as originally planned.⁴

After 1939, when Poland was invaded by both Germany and the Soviet Union, between 1.5 and 2 million Poles were deported to the Soviet Union. Many children were orphaned or became lost or separated from their families. After the German invasion of the Soviet Union in 1941 an amnesty was declared for captive Poles, in return for the formation of a Polish army to fight the Germans. Unable to return home because of the war, thousands of Polish children found refuge in orphanages set up in the southern Soviet Union by the Polish army. In 1942 about 20,000 Polish women and children, many of them orphans, were evacuated from the Soviet Union. Some found temporary refuge in Iran, where they spent the next three years in refugee camps.⁵

The idea of giving asylum to the Polish children came from Countess Wodzicka, the Polish Red Cross delegate in New Zealand and wife of Poland's Honorary Consul, Count Kazimierz Wodzicki, who suggested it to her friend Janet Fraser, the wife of Labour Prime Minister Peter Fraser. The latter wrote to the consul on 23 December 1943 offering the 'hospitality' of the New Zealand government to between 500 and 700 Polish refugees: 'Our whole conception of the scheme is that it should cater for the largest number of children.'⁶ The *Evening Post* quoted him as saying: 'It would be an act of Christian philanthropy and kindness, in which New Zealanders should be pleased to participate, to welcome these children, and a few of their parents and attendants, giving them a chance to recuperate.'⁷

The children were brought to New Zealand on board the American troopship the *General Randall*, which was also carrying about 3000 soldiers on their way back from the front for leave in Australia and New Zealand. The wartime journey was a risky one. Because of the ever-present danger of Japanese mines and the likelihood of encounters with Japanese submarines, the ship was escorted by two small warships and navigated a zig-zag course.⁸

In the account of the voyage given by Krystyna Skwarko, the *General Randall*, which the children and their caregivers had boarded at Bombay, struck the refugees as 'almost a luxury vessel in comparison with the merchant ship' that had transported them from Basra on the first part of their journey. On the *General Randall* were canvas bunks, plenty of wash basins and showers and abundant excellent food. Above all there was the kindness of the soldiers. 'They tried to break the monotony of the journey by entertaining the children with films and playing sports and games with them. It was a pleasure to see soldiers hardened by the experience of war turning skipping ropes for little girls. Few will forget "Uncle New Zealand" and many others whose names the children did not know but whose kindness they remember to this day.'[9]

The adults in the group were mainly women, many of them widows. 'Some of the children were so young and so traumatised by harrowing experiences of exile and war – including loss of their families – that they did not know who or how old they were, or where they came from.' When they had disembarked the refugees travelled to a former internment camp at Pahiatua, which became known as the Polish Children's Camp.[10] 'After the dry, barren and yellow countryside of Persia, New Zealand appeared a real fairyland.'[11]

Another refugee recalled how, after a month at sea, they sailed into Wellington Harbour on 1 November 1944.

> *The sun burst through the clouds and shone on the new country ... The following day there was a surprise awaiting us at the Wellington Railway Station. There were hundreds of smiling Wellington school children waving New Zealand and Polish flags as a gesture of welcome on the platform from which we were to leave for Pahiatua. The singing of the national anthems and gifts and flowers made the occasion even more moving.*[12]

Another of the children, Jan Wojciechowski, who came to New Zealand with his sisters, also remembered the intensity and warmth of that initial welcome.[13] As he climbed 'up the narrow steps into his assigned carriage' at Wellington Railway Station, he was handed a bottle of milk, a carton of ice cream and a boxed lunch, prepared by the Red Cross.

> *That first sweet taste of the creamy New Zealand ice-cream would stay with Jan and his sisters for many years; clothing and possessions were meaningless to a boy whose life had become conditioned by food and survival. The concept of New Zealand as a physical space, a nation, was similarly of no consequence to him. Life and home for him had become 'here', like his ancestors of the eastern Poland borderlands, whose image of homeland was simply of where they were, rather than some country with ever-shifting borders and rulers. Ice-cream, though, was real. It was food. It was nice. It was survival, the only reality he needed to know.*[14]

Not all refugees have been so warmly welcomed, so why did the Polish children have such a reception? One explanation is that they were invited by the government – hence the title of Skwarko's book, *The Invited*. Another explanation is that many of the children were orphans. Regardless of their ethnicity, orphaned children have been eagerly sought after in New Zealand. The archives of the Department of Labour contain numerous letters from members of the public and organisations wishing to adopt orphans. In most cases, none were available.

What is one to make of this eagerness to accept orphaned children? There was a mixture of motives and considerations at work: the humanitarian impulse to help poor children in need (it is easier for many people to feel compassion for orphaned children than for adults); the belief that New Zealand has something special to offer as the best place in the world to bring up children; and the view that orphaned children, whatever their cultural and ethnic backgrounds, can most easily be moulded into assimilated and useful citizens.

After the war the Pahiatua camp was gradually closed down and the children, who had completed a Polish primary education there, were sent away in small groups to receive their secondary education at Catholic boarding schools in different parts of New Zealand. The children and their caregivers did not want to be split up and would have preferred their Polish world at the camp to continue, but the government felt that since the refugees were going to stay permanently in New Zealand they had to be prepared for life in their new country. The refugees themselves acknowledged this – the children had to learn English and other necessary skills.[15]

From the government's point of view, the Polish camp was untenable on a permanent basis because it was an 'alien enclave'. The Polish children were, however, more fortunate than other pepper-potted refugees. They were lucky in having a period of time at a place where their Polish cultural identity was nurtured. This period of transition between their old and new worlds strengthened them for their exposure and assimilation to New Zealand.

The acceptance of the more than 700 Polish children was New Zealand's most prominent and generous response to refugee children, but it was not the first time that it had been open to accommodating such refugees. In sharp contrast to the thousands of Jewish adults declined permits to enter New Zealand in the 1930s, a small number of Polish Jewish orphaned children succeeded in gaining admittance. Max and Annie Deckston, themselves immigrants from Poland who had settled in Wellington in 1900,[16] saw anti-Semitism growing in Europe and decided to bring orphaned children to New Zealand. They obtained the sought-after visas and 20 children came in two groups between 1935 and 1937. 'Little victims of European savagery find refuge in New Zealand,' reported the *New Zealand Radio Record* on 26 May 1939. 'Arrangements are now being made to bring eight more friendless, homeless little sufferers from Europe.'[17] However, the Deckstons' attempt to bring a third group failed. By then the New Zealand government 'placed insurmountable obstacles in their way and these children were left to their fate in Poland'.[18]

In selecting DPs after the war, New Zealanders were keen to accept children, particularly orphans. Those between the ages of five and 12 were greatly desired, because 'from the point of view of assimilation, children present the least problems'.[19] The selectors were instructed to choose 200 orphans and unaccompanied children.[20]

After the Hungarian Revolution in 1956, the Department of Labour and the New Zealand Red Cross were inundated with offers to adopt Hungarian children. These people were told that although there were unaccompanied children among the refugees, they were not orphans.[21] Immigration Minister Ralph Hanan expressed 'his deep appreciation of the generous spirit' prompting the many offers and pointed out 'the extreme difficulty in determining whether an unaccompanied child arriving in Austria was an orphan'.

> *One could not neglect the possibility that a child might later be sought after by its family with resulting suffering for all concerned ... It was questionable in such circumstances [whether] we should be acting in the best interest of all concerned in bringing children to this country.*[22]

Chinese orphans, 1962

From the 1940s, large waves of Chinese refugees were triggered by the civil war (1927–50), the establishment of communist rule and the policies of the new government. The acceptance in 1962 of a small number of Chinese orphans from Hong Kong (and a few families with children later in the 1960s and early 1970s) needs to be seen in the context of the strong anti-Chinese sentiment of the time and the very strict controls on Chinese immigration. The reluctance to accept Chinese refugees in significant numbers contrasts with the readier acceptance of Hungarians, Czechoslovak refugees and European refugee families from Indonesia, Hong Kong and China in the 1950s and 1960s.[23]

New Zealand was not alone in having extremely restrictive policies on Chinese immigration in these decades. 'Investigation so far has shown a very great reluctance to accept Chinese immigrants anywhere in the world,' observed the UNHCR Chief of Mission in Hong Kong in a 1955 report.[24] Five years earlier a study group of the New Zealand Institute of International Affairs had noted: 'Encouragement of immigration from Asia is not recommended. It would be likely to create more problems than it would solve and it would fail to alleviate sensibly Asia's population problem.'[25]

In 1951 Lochore, who seems to have been considered an authority on immigration by the government because he had travelled widely and had worked as naturalisation officer with the Department of Internal Affairs, concluded that New Zealand's need for more population should ideally be met by British migrants. And if there were not enough British migrants, Continental European migrants, preferably from Western and Northern Europe, could be turned into 'new Britishers'. 'Suitable aliens,' he wrote, could become 'vectors of the British way of life that still has so much to give to the world.' Immigration from Asia, however, 'would not fulfil this purpose; Asia must solve her problem of living standards and population pressure in her own way.'[26]

With strong fears of floods of 'race aliens' entering New Zealand, it is hardly surprising that New Zealand's response to the plight of Chinese refugees, like that of other Western countries, was 'extremely slow'.[27] Eventually, in 1962 the government agreed to accept 50 Chinese orphans from Hong Kong for adoption by New Zealand families,[28] probably out of a wish to be seen as helping to solve the world's refugee problems and as a response to a certain amount of public pressure.[29] The acceptability of orphans would have made the decision politically feasible.

The conflicting imperatives influencing the government are evident in the lead-up to the acceptance of the Chinese orphans. A 1958 External Affairs Department report estimated that approximately 800,000 Chinese had fled from mainland China and were living in Hong Kong in 1958. The government of Hong Kong had so far borne alone the burden of helping the refugees but it was not apparent what assistance New Zealand might offer.[30] The possibility of New Zealand accepting Chinese orphans was first raised by Bob Sprackett, a Christchurch Presbyterian minister. Sprackett, who lived in Norman Kirk's electorate, had become aware, while travelling in Hong Kong, of the plight of some 2600 children who were either orphans or abandoned. In August 1960 he wrote to Kirk proposing that New Zealand accept 15–25 of the Hong Kong orphans. 'These children – fine looking children they are – could be integrated into New Zealand family and social life. They could become useful New Zealanders.'[31]

The Department of Labour expressed reservations:

> What would be the reaction of the Chinese community here? It is inevitable that once the Chinese community learned that we were accepting orphaned children we would receive representations from individual families and from the Chinese Consul-General for the government to extend this scheme, not only to orphaned relatives of Chinese here but also to so-called adult refugees. The Department could not recommend the extension of the scheme along these lines ...[32]

Kirk also took up the cause and wrote to Prime Minister Keith Holyoake in January 1961.[33] The following May the Department of Labour told Holyoake that it could not support Sprackett's proposal because of the likely reaction of the local Chinese community 'on whom restrictions have been placed in respect of the immigration of relatives and adopted children'. Nonetheless, the decision to accept 20 orphans was announced in June 1962.[34] The figure, decided on 'as a special humanitarian gesture', bore 'no direct relation to the number of orphan children available for adoption in Hong Kong'. In fact, External Affairs admitted, 'we do not know how many orphan children are available there for adoption'.[35]

'You might tell the Australians in confidence,' the Minister of External Affairs told the New Zealand High Commissioner in Canberra on 12 June, that 'this decision is not a result of recent influx of refugees to Hong Kong, nor of recent approach made to Prime Minister by Chinese Charge d'Affaires.' It was a gesture to the many church organisations and private individuals who had for some time been pressing the Minister of Labour to grant entry permits to Chinese orphans. The decision had been publicised because of press interest in the plight of refugees in Hong Kong and numerous representations to the Prime Minister.[36] The Australians, however, felt upstaged by New Zealand, though 'the token gesture arguably backfired when a visiting UNHCR representative told New Zealanders that the offer had been a "mistaken effort" because "adopted children usually grew up much happier and better adjusted if their foster parents were of the same race and background"'.[37]

The New Zealand Chinese Association wrote to Holyoake in June 1962 thanking the government for accepting the orphans, but also took the opportunity to point out that it was 'natural for the Chinese community here to be more immediately concerned with the welfare of relatives and former friends and their young families now in the refugee category' and expressed the hope that the government would 'see its way clear to make a more sympathetic appraisal of applications'.[38]

An increase to 50 Chinese orphans was announced on 3 July 1962. Holyoake said the government had been impressed by the warm response to the earlier decision, and the higher total was a response to numerous approaches from people wishing to adopt the orphans and asking for more to be admitted.[39]

> As a small country, we are not in a position to make a substantial contribution to the resettlement of large groups of Chinese refugees. We have, however, greatly appreciated the efforts of church organizations and others to help orphan children in Hong Kong, who, I think everyone will agree, are particularly worthy of any assistance that people in this country can offer.[40]

The thinking behind the government's new offer was portrayed in different terms in an External Affairs report to the New Zealand High Commissioner in Canberra: the decision had been made partly 'in effort to stave off pressure from National Council of Churches for admission of Chinese refugee families (they have suggested 100 families)'.[41]

Accepting families was clearly out of the question. The government could offend the local Chinese community, who were 'always' pressing the government to widen the categories of relatives who could be admitted. 'In addition, the refugees themselves would have relatives they would want to bring in. This problem would not arise with orphans.'[42] And as we have seen, even the orphans were thought to be a risk, albeit a smaller one.

Unaccompanied minors from Cambodia

In view of the negative attitudes to Asian migration and the widely held opinion that children, especially orphans, made the best migrants, it is not at all surprising that New Zealand's first involvement with Indo-Chinese refugee resettlement was a belated and token gesture as part of Operation Babylift. As North Vietnamese troops advanced on Saigon, the United States began evacuating tens of thousands of Vietnamese refugees. Early in April 1975 Operation Babylift began, flying Vietnamese orphans to various Western countries. Initially, New Zealand was not a Babylift destination, but in early May the government decided to admit three babies.[43]

This action caused considerable controversy, with some sections of the public urging the government to save more babies and others defending the minimalist approach. The debate hinged on whether it was right, on humanitarian and rational grounds, to accept orphans.[44] Those on the government's side argued that it was better to wait until 'the dust had settled' and then 'to reappraise the position', presumably because by then some 'orphans' would have been reunited with their families.[45] When New Zealand was resettling refugees from Indo-China, the Department of Labour received many offers of homes for refugee children.[46]

The Indo-Chinese refugee intake of 1984 (see Chapter Five) included a group of young Cambodian refugees who had lost their parents and other close family members while the Khmer Rouge ruled Cambodia (then Kampuchea) from 1976 to 1979, overseeing one of the worst genocides of the twentieth century. In the late 1970s and early 1980s, the UNHCR discouraged countries from selecting Cambodian minors for resettlement on the grounds that the children should not be resettled away from their own people.⁴⁷ The aim was for children and young people to be reunited with their families if at all possible. By the early 1980s as a result of a massive tracing exercise, most Cambodian children and young people were reunited with their relatives, and the Red Cross still hoped to find the families of more children.⁴⁸ By 1983, small groups of children and young people whose relatives had not been traced still remained in camps throughout Thailand. Addressing their plight became a personal crusade for then Minister of Immigration Aussie Malcolm, who had first become concerned about their situation following his visit to camps in Thailand in 1982.

He was keen to assist the groups of youngsters who 'congregated' in 'de facto foster families of about eight to twelve people which have been set up by the UNHCR and other aid agencies'.⁴⁹ He was convinced that it was time for the young people to be resettled elsewhere. But UNHCR policy did not favour this solution, not because there was any longer much chance of tracing the children's families but because the children would be too hard to settle. Some were former soldiers of Pol Pot and others had been without normal parental control for much of their formative years. The UNHCR was concerned that the difficulties of dealing with uncontrolled, 'unruly' children might deter resettlement countries from taking further refugees.⁵⁰

The New Zealand Department of Education had reservations about the project,⁵¹ as did New Zealand's resettlement agency – the ICCI. Its concerns were 'in the light of overseas experience', particularly in South Australia, which had been visited by Director Keith Taylor.⁵² The Australian decision to take up to 100 unaccompanied minors was expected to cause 'major debate' in the welfare community, with doubts expressed about whether bringing them to Australia was in the children's best interest.⁵³

Taylor was particularly worried that the project 'could backfire on the ICCI as the chances of successful settlement are not great'. The ICCI wanted to know who would pick up the pieces 'once the publicity and fanfare' were over and who would 'carry the responsibility for having brought them here'. The ICCI was also concerned about possible confusion of roles between volunteers and paid staff and lack of clarity about which agency was responsible for which task. Such a project should have 'a full-time government funded Khmer community New Zealander living in with the family … This is particularly important for male teenagers.'⁵⁴

To Malcolm, the UNHCR policy of not resettling unaccompanied minors in resettlement countries meant, in effect, sacrificing 'the children for the greater good of the whole resettlement programme',[55] and he refused to accept such a policy. 'The children were turning up injured in the camps. Couples were setting up as foster parents of these children, denying themselves resettlement opportunities.' Malcolm decided to try to bring some of the children to New Zealand 'because something had to be done – they couldn't be left to rot'.[56]

The scheme went ahead in spite of UNHCR reservations and the concerns of the ICCI and other agencies, largely because of Malcolm's determination. The involvement of some key church leaders helped. Malcolm's friendship with Paul Hartling of the UNHCR and with a senior member of the Thai Supreme Command also made it possible to proceed.[57]

The 12 unaccompanied minors and their caregivers arrived in New Zealand in February 1984. They looked to be in good health and appeared much younger than their actual ages because of years of malnutrition under Pol Pot. Several had just been turned down by Australia.[58] Typically, they had been separated from their parents at a young age and forced to join mobile teams of workers. They had not been able to attend school for several years. Later they had lost their parents and other family members, who were either killed or died as a result of illness, and they had fled to Thailand, often to avoid Vietnamese military conscription. They may have spent some time with foster parents until the arrangement broke down and/or lived in the children's centre in one of the camps.[59] The young people's tragic and traumatic lives before coming to New Zealand meant that the project required intensive community effort involving a large number of governmental and non-governmental agencies.[60] In this, the resettlement of Cambodian young people was not unlike earlier projects involving refugees with special health or other needs.

A review undertaken seven months after the young Cambodians' arrival emphasised both the challenges and the successes of the enterprise. It noted 'terrific advances in their personal maturity, their physical health, their confidence and their ability to speak English which clearly shows ... that for all the difficulties that have been had by the various groups who have been responsible for them, the resettlement of these children has in real terms been quite successful'.[61]

The 'difficulties' referred to included communication problems owing to the initial unavailability of Khmer/English dictionaries,[62] and confusion of roles between the local Cambodian community and all the other agencies involved in looking after the children. The review also pointed out that the children had not been medically cleared at Mangere before they entered the community.[63] A report five years after the children's arrival also showed the challenges of the enterprise.⁶⁴ Why was the project so tough for all involved? Both the troubled backgrounds of the young people and the inadequacy of the resources available to assist them in New Zealand were part of the reason – specialist services for traumatised children were not set up until the beginning of the twenty-first century. New Zealand's efforts to resettle and rehabilitate a number of the Pol Pot regime's casualties shows the humanitarian impulse by and large undiluted by the pragmatic considerations that had influenced the acceptance of the Chinese orphans. It also highlights that compassion and goodwill are not necessarily enough in cases of extremely troubled refugee children.

By contrast the resettlement of the far more numerous Polish children – many of whom had also lost most members of their families and had spent several years of their childhood in traumatic and deprived circumstances – is generally understood to have benefited both the refugees and the New Zealand community. Several factors help to explain the different outcomes, despite the fact that there were only 12 Cambodian children and several hundred Polish children. The Poles were younger than the Cambodians, which probably made their adjustment easier. They were also close to other people who had witnessed their hardships and understood their trauma. Also helpful was the fact that the Polish children formed a sizable group, which made it possible for their caregivers to create a safe, self-contained Polish world within the Pahiatua camp. When the children left the security of the camp for New Zealand boarding schools, they were better prepared than the Cambodians.

The problems associated with the Cambodian settlement experiences suggests that children and young people, especially those who have suffered trauma and are without parental and other family support, do not make the most suitable or the most successful migrants. Nonetheless, Lochore's conclusion, that children show a 'genius of adaptation', has validity. Anecdotal evidence suggests that, regardless of their countries of origin, many of the refugee children and young adults who have come to New Zealand have adjusted very well indeed. They have usually mastered English and New Zealand customs much more quickly than refugees who came as adults. This ability to integrate quickly largely accounts for the preference for child refugees, particularly orphaned ones, which characterised New Zealand's response between the 1930s and the 1980s.

Until recently, however, New Zealand has not been well prepared to deal with the significant problems of adjustment that children and young people typically confront problems of belonging: identity and intergenerational conflicts not faced by adult migrants. Furthermore, unlike adults, young refugees have often been disadvantaged by having had their education disrupted. Above all, the major losses and catastrophes of the past usually have wrenching and probably long-term consequences, however young the children were when the traumatic events took place.

CHAPTER EIGHT

An inconvenient obligation?

Asylum seekers, who in New Zealand are sometimes labelled 'spontaneous refugees', need to establish their refugee status after they arrive in the country of asylum. Many Western countries believe they pose, at best, an inconvenient obligation. This is partly because the processing of refugee status applications from genuine refugees and unsuccessful or bogus applicants can be both costly and time-consuming. Furthermore, although many countries including New Zealand recognise legal and moral obligations to accept refugees fleeing persecution, the unheralded arrival of asylum seekers conflicts with the long-standing right of sovereign nations to protect their borders and to choose their refugee settlers.

Refugees have spontaneously arrived in New Zealand since the nineteenth century. They included small groups of Danes fleeing South Jutland in 1876 and Jews fleeing pogroms in the Soviet Union and Eastern Europe; both groups found refuge in New Zealand in the late nineteenth and early twentieth centuries. By the early 1900s, in addition to restrictions on Chinese and Indians, there were restrictions on Germans and people with communist, socialist or radical nationalist beliefs entering New Zealand. Some of the Jewish refugees fleeing Nazi Europe arrived with temporary visitor permits, hoping to be given permanent asylum. Like the Danes before them these Jews were in effect refugees, though they were not recognised as such at the time.

A small number of people from the Soviet Union sought refuge in New Zealand during the Cold War. One of them was Svetlana Stalin, Joseph Stalin's 'blameless daughter', who tried to obtain political asylum in the 1970s after defecting from the Soviet Union. She had been refused asylum by India, Italy and Switzerland when New Zealand 'baulked' too and she was finally accepted by the United States. New Zealand declined her application because of the prevailing strong anti-communist climate.[1] Successful asylum seekers during the Cold War included some Russian seamen from freighters and fishing boats who jumped ship seeking better economic opportunities and more political freedom. Several stayed in New Zealand, marrying New Zealand women and gaining permanent resident status.[2]

Typically asylum seekers have arrived with false travel documents, temporary permits or no documents at all, because people who may be in grave danger in their own countries, or in the countries where they have sought temporary asylum, cannot acquire the required entry papers before arriving at the border. In 1980, New Zealand prepared itself to deal with possible encounters with Indo-Chinese refugee boat people. Although these did not eventuate, it is interesting to look at the policy response in the light of preparations made for mass arrivals by boat at the end of the 1990s, which also did not happen (and also in the light of preparations made in 2012 and 2013). The 1980 discussion took place during the Indo-Chinese refugee crisis, when the number of refugees fleeing Vietnam had decreased but not stopped and governments of countries bordering the South China Sea had indicated that they would not accept refugees without prior guarantees of permanent resettlement elsewhere. The planning of New Zealand's response took place in the context of media reports that some ships' masters had ignored distress signals from Vietnamese refugees and that some coastal states in the South China Sea had refused temporary asylum to those rescued at sea.

The Ministry of Defence proposed to deal with boat people first by, 'wherever practical', routing HMNZS *Canterbury* so as to 'avoid known concentrations and sea routes of the boat refugees'. But should they after all 'be unexpectedly encountered' and 'the Commanding Officer be obliged to embark them, he should immediately inform the New Zealand Government'. The ministry also noted: 'It has been assumed that, should a New Zealand warship uplift people from the sea in order to save life and those people be held to be refugees from Indo-China, New Zealand would accept full responsibility for their future.'[3]

A Ministry of Foreign Affairs briefing paper written a month later to clarify New Zealand's obligations to boat people did not make such assumptions about responsibility. As a signatory to several international conventions, for example the 1958 Convention on the High Seas (Geneva) and the 1960 Convention on the Safety of Life at Sea (London), New Zealand was obliged to assist people in distress at sea providing this would not seriously endanger the ship. However, when the various laws were drafted it was envisaged that those rescued would leave the ship at the next port, which would give temporary asylum to the persons rescued. From there they would be repatriated to their country of origin. This legislation had maritime disasters in mind, not refugee situations where the people rescued could not or did not wish to be repatriated. The international regulations gave no guidance on who was responsible for the resettlement of such people: 'In practice, however, the question of their resettlement must become a matter of negotiation between the master of the ship, the country of first port of call and the country of registration.'[4]

Academic researchers often use the term irregular migration to refer to inter-country movement that takes place in defiance of national laws and regulations.[5] Overstaying beyond the authorised period was the form of irregular migration that most frequently occurred in New Zealand until the 1980s and that occasioned much public debate. From 1974 the government clamped down on overstayers, particularly from the Pacific Islands. Since the end of the Cold War another form of irregular migration – asylum seeking – has also become the focus of considerable official and public attention.

There are links between the various types of irregular migration that many Western governments, including New Zealand, have viewed with much alarm. Many asylum seekers, who are in reality economic migrants and unlikely to qualify as refugees under the United Nations Convention of 1951 and the Protocol of 1967 relating to the status of refugees, have been exploited by people-smugglers to enter the country illegally and seek political asylum. Irregular migration, including the numbers seeking political asylum, has grown vastly since the end of the Cold War, partly because many more people see migration as the only chance to improve their lot. As sociologist Stephen Castles has observed, 'The new global economic and political elites are able to cross borders at will, while the poor are meant to stay at home. Of course many of the world's excluded also perceive that mobility brings the chance of wealth and are desperate to migrate.'[6]

Fijian Indians after 1987

In the late 1980s New Zealand was faced with an unusual situation: the need to respond to refugee status applications from one of its neighbours: Fiji. On 14 May 1987 Colonel Sitiveni Rabuka and his followers staged a military coup to overthrow the democratically elected Labour-led coalition government of Timoci Bavadra. Previous Fijian governments had been dominated by indigenous Fijians, but Bavadra filled key government positions with representatives of the Fijian Indian majority. Rabuka claimed that he intended merely to protect the interests of the indigenous Fijian minority; but in the aftermath of the coup Fijian Indians feared for their lives because they were assaulted or intimidated by Rabuka's supporters.[7]

Barbara Hill, the wife of second secretary Ian Hill at the New Zealand High Commission in Suva, recalled 'Indo-Fijians' being kicked and punched by mobs of Fijians 'on a rampage', and 'racial violence' becoming 'an almost daily occurrence'.[8] Amnesty International reported attacks on the homes and property of Fijian Indians, arrests of ministers, trade unionists, journalists and Indian shopkeepers, and the detention of people 'as a form of intimidation to deter them from engaging in non-violent political activity or exercising their right to freedom of expression'. Amnesty was particularly concerned that those arrested had been held without charge for up to four days and had not been allowed to contact family and friends.[9]

As a result, many Fijian Indians tried to seek safety overseas, including in New Zealand. Soon after a second coup on 28 September 1987 they began applying to the New Zealand authorities for admission as refugees or, if they had already entered the country on temporary visas, to be given permanent resident status. In response to six applications for refugee status from Fijian Indians already in New Zealand after the 1987 coup, all of them alleging fears of harassment and discrimination 'based primarily on the treatment that Fijian Indians in general may encounter following the coup', the Ministry of Foreign Affairs sought its minister's guidance on the general line to take.

The ministry proposed to inform refugee status applicants in Fiji that they would initially be considered by its legal division 'to determine if [the] applicant has a prima facie case'. If the applicant met 'the threshold', he or she would be interviewed by the Interdepartmental Committee on Refugees. If not, the Ministry proposed to advise them that 'the New Zealand government does not consider that the present general treatment accorded to the Indian population in Fiji amounts to persecution within the terms of the 1951 Convention and

1967 protocol on the Status of Refugees. Put simply, being a Fijian Indian is not enough by itself to base a claim to refugee status on.'[10]

The approach to Fijian Indians who were in New Zealand at the time of the coups was, however, more lenient.

> Following the recent events in Fiji, Fijian visitors to New Zealand are being granted temporary extensions to their entry permits for up to twelve months. Fijian Indians who were in New Zealand at the time of the coup and who had been here for over twelve months have had their permits extended for a further three months.[11]

The government took the view that because Fijian Indians were not generally persecuted by their government – the state had 'failed to adequately protect them from persecutions from their hostile Fijian neighbours' – they could not claim refugee status on account of the widespread ethnic violence directed against them. Rather, they needed to prove that they had been personally persecuted by the state.[12] In the view of Fijian historian Dr Brij Lal, the refugee claim was 'too hard to prove'. Fijian Indians had 'to prove victimisation and violence personally rather than generically'.[13] Instead of recognising Fijian Indians as refugees, New Zealand opted to strongly condemn the illegal change of government but, in the words of a former official, 'we did not cut off relations'.[14]

According to former senior public servant Gerald Hensley, Prime Minister David Lange had favoured a stronger response, asking for New Zealand peacekeeping troops in Lebanon to be sent to stage a counter-coup in Fiji. As Hensley recalled, some of Lange's comments following the coup were not as carefully considered as his advisers would have wished.[15] Michael Bassett, then a senior Cabinet minister, remembered Lange's 'preoccupation' with Fiji, but he 'responded to a request from Fiji's Great Council of Chiefs that New Zealand accept Fijian Indian refugees with an assurance that there would be no relaxing of normal entry rules'. The government, in Bassett's words, 'did not want to be seen as aiding a form of ethnic cleansing of the islands, although that's what was starting to take place'.[16]

In parliament, Immigration Minister Stan Rodger was evasive about how New Zealand ought to respond to refugee status applications by Fijian Indians. On 6 October 1987 in response to a question he replied, 'The normal policy guidelines relating to immigration continue to be applied to holders of Fijian passports. The position in Fiji is being closely monitored, and any adjustments will be made as appropriate.' He later added: 'Since the second coup nobody has applied for refugee status. Careful criteria are applied in such circumstances, relating to danger to life and limb and to possible injury to people as a consequence of their political views and so on. Normally, an interdepartmental committee examines such cases.' He conceded, however, that there had been 'a substantial increase in the number of applications from Fijians to come to New Zealand, to such an extent that the facilities available for the processing of such applications in the High Commission office are overloaded'.[17]

In early January 1988, Fiji solicitor Muttu Krishna was reported as claiming that Fiji's military were 'continuing to persecute and torture Fiji Indians. The victimisation extended to Indian children in schools.'[18] The New Zealand government, however, faced with numerous letters from Fijian Indians asking about applying for refugee status, chose to see an improving situation.[19] Reports between Suva and Wellington appeared to downplay human rights abuses. A report of September 1987, for example, referred to the '*short term* [my italics] detention of supporters of the deposed government and those believed to be critical of the coup'.[20] A 25 April 1988 cable read: 'No further reports of discrimination or harassment faced by Fiji Indians.'[21]

The issue of refugees from Fiji came up again in parliament five years later in relation to the acceptance of Afghan asylum seekers from the *Tampa*. In September 2002 Minister of Immigration Lianne Dalziel, in response to a question from ACT MP Richard Prebble on why the government had not given refugees from the *Tampa* temporary entry permits to avoid them applying for refugee status, as it had done in relation to refugees from Fiji, replied:

> *What the member completely overlooks is that we have an obligation to process claims that are made. In the Fiji example that was given, temporary permits were not issued to people on the basis that they had claimed refugee status; it was to prevent claims for refugee status from being lodged.*[22]

This statement highlights the differences between New Zealand's response to asylum seekers in its own back yard and those originating in distant places. Providing a safe haven for the *Tampa* asylum seekers while they applied for refugee status contributed to New Zealand's humanitarian reputation. Preventing the lodging of claims for refugee status from Fijian Indians, however, aimed to prevent an influx of asylum seekers whose emigration from Fiji would seriously destabilise that country.

The case of a Fijian Indian, 'Mr Z', whose application for political asylum in New Zealand after the 1987 Fiji coups was refused, illustrates the nature of the government's response. In 1988 Mr Z, who had fled Fiji just before the second coup, applied for refugee status in New Zealand. He had left his country 'after a series of military interrogations which included such "persuasion" techniques as forcing him to stand barefoot for hours on hot tar'. Leaving behind his wife and three young children, he had entered New Zealand on a two-week visitor's permit, claiming it was a business trip. The permit was extended while he awaited the decision on his refugee status. After a year of waiting he was told that 'because he did not have a well founded fear of persecution' the Ministers of Immigration and Foreign Affairs had declined his application. His wife, having failed to get an entry permit for New Zealand in Suva, left the children with her mother and went to Brisbane to apply for New Zealand entry. She was turned down by the Australian government too. Mr Z's lawyer regarded the length of time his client had been left dangling as 'inhumane'.[23] The New Zealand authorities may have been hoping that the situation in Fiji would improve in the interim, making it possible to decline the application. But such lengthy delays in processing refugee status applications were not uncommon in the late 1980s.

According to an article in the *Dominion*,

> Mr Z had a high profile in Fiji politics up to and during the short-lived Bavadra government ... and was regularly targeted by the military regime for intimidation. Each time he was detained soldiers arrived without warning and took him to a police station, though he was never questioned by police. While the soldiers interrogated him each time, he was made to pound kava root for hours and then serve them with drink. Sometimes they would question him about arson and bombings, sometimes about one of his friends, a member of Bavadra's government.

He was described as 'a quiet, dignified man who clearly experiences physical symptoms of fear even now as he recalls those sessions'. A close friend of Mr Z had to endure being made to drink from a cesspool and had his fingers cut by razor blades. Detainees had their arms and other parts of their bodies burned by cigarettes. Others had been forced to pound kava for long periods or had suffered sensory deprivation. 'There is no doubt that Mr Z fears persecution if he is forced to return to Fiji.' The article also quoted the response from the Ministry of External Relations and Trade: 'Applications for refugee status, including Mr Z's, are treated on their merits ... there was no ministerial directive which made it impossible for Fiji citizens to succeed in their applications.' As the article pointed out,

> The Government has consistently sent messages which imply as much. In March Foreign Affairs Minister Russell Marshall made a speech saying in effect that we shouldn't be hasty in judging Fiji because there are some responsible people there working to bring the country's troubles to a sound resolution ... [but] the moment the first Fiji Indian is granted refugee status the bubble of the government's belief in a reasonable outcome bursts, forcing it to take a stronger stand.

'Meanwhile,' the writer concluded, ' Mr Z leaves the lawyer's office and walks back to his flat. His future is bleak. Whatever happens, he won't live in Fiji again. If he's deported [from New Zealand] he'll search for asylum for his family somewhere else.'[24]

A few days after this article appeared, Bernie Kernot, of the Catholic Archdiocesan Justice, Peace and Development Commission, took up the case in a letter to Rodger. Noting that it was difficult to know why Mr Z had been refused refugee status, Kernot asked that the grounds for refusal be made public:

> *Since the two coups the Fiji Government has a record of human rights abuses and Mr Z was harassed and intimidated before leaving the country. His fears of further persecution, harassment or worse if he is forced to return to Fiji appear to be well founded. It is therefore hard to believe that Mr Z's application was treated on its merits ... the present case confirms our fears that political rather than humanitarian considerations determine the outcome of applications for political asylum and refugee status in this country.*[25]

The government declined Kernot's request. Since the UNHCR regarded the country's procedures as 'one of the most humanitarian in the world', how could there be a problem regarding Fiji?[26]

New Zealand's strategy after 1987 was to downplay human rights abuses, turn a blind eye to the potential refugee crisis and focus on stabilising Fiji. This was to be achieved by supporting the new regime to develop a non-racist constitution, by working to establish a human rights commission, by monitoring human rights issues and by doing everything possible to build greater harmony in a divided society.[27] There was no place in the strategy for the recognition of the plight of individual Fijian Indian victims of the coups and their aftermath; in fact recognising such victims as refugees might jeopardise the overall strategy.

Although the situation in Fiji 'dominated much of the year', according to the Ministry of Foreign Affairs annual report for 1988, there was no mention of refugees. The situation in Fiji 'posed a challenge to the task of enhancing the stability and prosperity of the South Pacific region'. The government's policy responses to the coups – 'downgrading the bilateral relationship with partial suspension of the aid programme' and later moving 'to restore aid' – 'were designed to encourage a return to democratic government'. New Zealand's goal was 'to support all legitimate efforts to restore civilian parliamentary government in Fiji in a way that safeguards the interests of all citizens of Fiji'.[28]

The ministry's report for the following year noted that 'business was as usual' regarding refugee status determination, but did not refer to applications for refugee status from Fijian Indians.[29] The *New Zealand Year Book* for 1988–89, however, stated that an increasing number of people from the South Pacific 'moved to take up employment opportunities absent in the Pacific Islands. Amongst these arrivals were a significant number of Fijian citizens of Indian descent who provided cultural reinforcement for the existing Indian community in New Zealand.'[30]

This statement highlights another important aspect of New Zealand's strategy regarding the crisis in Fiji. Although Fijian Indians were not recognised as refugees, a considerable number of those who had entered the country on temporary visitors' permits had their permits extended. Others, usually the better educated with English language skills who were able to meet New Zealand's immigration criteria, entered under skilled migration categories. In Brij Lal's view, 'David Lange was in fact quite generous [to refugees]. He let people in on all kinds of grounds, and many of them did not return. He was soft. So, the New Zealand government looked the other way and opened the door.'[31]

By 1990 the strategy of stabilising Fiji appeared to be working to some extent and the stream of migrants slowed, though reports of human rights violations continued to surface and Fijian Indians continued to lodge refugee status applications. According to one government report, although the coups had ushered in political and social instability and abuses of human rights had occurred for a while in 1988, 'some … quite serious in nature, though none resulted in death', the gradual 'reassertion of civilian authority and rule of law and return to limited democracy' had ended serious violations.[32]

Fiji returned to elected government in 1992 and by 1997 Prime Minister Rabuka's attitudes towards Fijian Indians seemed much more mellow. In a speech to the United Nations General Assembly he referred to 'the major challenge Fiji faces to accommodate the interests and aspirations of the newcomers' to the country and 'to reconcile them with sensibilities, perceptions and pre-eminent status of our indigenous people'.[33] In 1997–98, the New Zealand government view – that the strategy to stabilise Fiji had worked well enough and that a great deal had been achieved to bring a divided society together – appeared not unreasonable.[34]

In responding to applicants for refugee status after the two 1987 coups in Fiji, New Zealand's pursuit of national interest generally took precedence over humanitarian considerations. The plight of the coup victims had to be dealt with in a way that would not jeopardise New Zealand's relationship with the new Fijian regime. The preferred response was 'to look the other way and open the door', at least partially, rather than to recognise Fijian Indian applicants as refugees. New Zealand's special responsibility towards Pacific Island countries was seen as best discharged by stabilising Fiji and by defusing a potential refugee situation as much as circumstances allowed. This stance was thought to best serve both New Zealand's and Fiji's interests.

New Zealand also wanted to avoid a major influx of refugees from Fiji. This should be discouraged because Fiji could not afford to lose a substantial number of its better-educated population. If New Zealand had accepted all Fijian Indians who wanted to emigrate, Fiji's economy could have collapsed. New Zealand had to take account of its responsibilities towards Pacific Island migrants who were New Zealand citizens, and others from the Pacific allowed entry under various quota agreements. By the late 1980s, there was also considerable unease about the growing number of asylum seekers putting stress on the refugee status determination system. New Zealand was determined not to have a refugee situation in its own back yard.

Since 2000 there have been further coups in Fiji, casting doubt on the stability New Zealand expected to have been achieved through its efforts between 1987 and 1990. Several commentators have referred to the ongoing 'culture of coups' in Fiji, characterised by a general failure of law and order. With the sugar industry in decline, the prospect for poor people and for Fijian Indians seems bleak. Political instability and human rights violations have continued in Fiji into the twenty-first century.[35] In 2009–10 Fiji had the highest number of refugee status applications – 45 – declined by the Refugee Status Branch.[36] During 2012 there appeared to be some progress towards registering voters and establishing a constitutional commission in Fiji, with elections promised for 2014,[37] but in October 2012 Amnesty International reported that the reform process was flawed and that human rights abuses were still occurring.[38]

The response of Fijian Indians, especially the better educated, continues to be large-scale emigration. Since 1987 around 120,000 have left for Australia, the United States, Canada, New Zealand and elsewhere. Those who have already left and those who still remain understand that they have no future in Fiji.[39]

Would New Zealand respond to a new refugee situation in Fiji as it did after the 1987 coups? It might well choose, as before, not to recognise those trying to escape from Fiji as refugees but, instead, to open the back door to a certain amount of immigration. Dealing with a refugee situation close to home is a very different proposition from responding to refugee crises in distant parts of the world. The Pacific refugee situations New Zealand may have to deal with in the years ahead are discussed briefly in the final chapter.

'Unprecedented numbers' of asylum seekers, late 1980s and early 1990s

New Zealand's response to the potential refugee situation in Fiji raises the significant issue of adequate state protection. Since not all human rights abuses meet the standard of persecution required by the refugee definition, there are some abuses that people are expected to tolerate.[40] These matters came up again in relation to the growing number of asylum seeker applications from the late 1980s. New Zealand dealt with 27 refugee status applications in 1987, 145 in 1988, 330 in 1989, 600 in 1990 and 1200 in 1991. The increase was a worldwide phenomenon. Australia, for example, dealt with 1950 applications in 1989, 8700 in 1990 and 12,700 in 1991.[41]

Although the numbers were small in comparison with Australia's, the unprecedented arrivals generated considerable concern in New Zealand partly because 'the resulting pressure on the system creates delays and backlogs that affect genuine asylum seekers',[42] and partly because some of the asylum seekers came from places such as sub-Saharan Africa that had not previously been sources of refugees.[43]

Immigration reported 65 applications from 'spontaneous refugees' at Auckland airport in August, September and up to 12 October 1990, 'which represented a 342 per cent increase with the same period in the previous year'. Among the group were 12 Chinese nationals on false passports intending to travel to Canada to claim refugee status in Canada. As the Department of Labour reported, there was an increase in applications from nationals of the People's Republic of China (PRC), mainly students, following the Tiananmen Square protest in June 1989.[44] On 23 June 1994 the Minister of Immigration announced that Cabinet had approved the granting of residence to all PRC nationals who entered New Zealand on or before 31 March 1992.[45]

The panic about 'unprecedented numbers' of asylum seekers is strongly evident in two government reports of October and November 1990. The first, from a regional manager in the New Zealand Immigration Service, argued that more resources should be going into preventing the arrival of potential refugees. There was no point speeding up the process of determination, as the government proposed to do, if the number of arrivals kept increasing.[46]

> *The integrity of New Zealand's border must be in question when spontaneous refugees can arrange false documentation and gain approval to travel. If we accept that then careful consideration must be given to the fact that potential terrorists, criminals or other unwanted persons could cross our border using the same methods.*[47]

The solution proposed by Immigration came to be known as 'interception'. The government made arrangements with international airline carriers who flew direct to New Zealand from Hong Kong, Kuala Lumpur, Malaysia and Thailand to check passengers' boarding passes with travel documents. Immigration officers received training to 'correlate boarding passes with passports and travel documents'.[48]

The second government report, from the Minister of Immigration Bill Birch, referred to 'staggering' and continuing growth in numbers of asylum seekers. Birch was concerned that the system was 'being taken advantage of by migrants whose motives are principally economic, as well as by genuine fugitives from political or natural crises'. He pointed out that government policy needed to achieve a balance between conflicting claims: 'On one side are our international obligations and our desire as a nation to help the victims of political or natural crises. On the other side are the social and economic costs of accepting such refugees.'

Birch was particularly concerned that the government lacked the financial and administrative resources to deal with asylum seekers and a backlog, expected to approach 1000 by the end of 1990, had developed. This, in turn, encouraged claims for asylum: 'Asylum seekers know that a back-log means long temporary residence, which in itself encourages people to arrive and claim asylum. The number can grow dramatically and threaten wider immigration and border policy.' The system of determining refugee status needed urgent revision, while 'the longer term problem of balancing border integrity and compassion' remained.[49]

Alarm bells rang particularly loudly the following year when a group of asylum seekers came from Iran, escaping the 1991 Gulf War. The government responded with 'special provisions' that resulted in the detention of 44 people, including women and children, and the deportation of more than 30.[50] The provisions, which aimed 'to guard against the possibility that people who could pose a threat to the security of New Zealand might use the refugee process to gain access to New Zealand', were lifted on 30 April 1991.[51]

Amnesty International claimed they were in breach of the United Nations Convention and wrote to National Prime Minister Jim Bolger in March 1991, stressing its concern that 'the measures could lead to asylum seekers being returned to countries where they risked oppression, torture or execution'. Among the points emphasised by Amnesty International was one that would be made frequently by advocates for the rights of asylum seekers in the years ahead – there was no international or New Zealand evidence that the asylum procedure had been abused by terrorists: 'It has always seemed that posing as an asylum seeker (and thus focussing the attention of every official in the airport upon oneself) is an unlikely method for a terrorist to enter any country. The French terrorists of "Rainbow Warrior" notoriety chose different routes entirely.'[52]

Don McKinnon was Minister of Foreign Affairs and Trade when the numbers of applications for refugee status grew rapidly. As a new minister he found himself, along with the Immigration Minister, involved in the appellate body for all refugees whose applications had been turned down by the Refugee Status Branch. This 'incredibly time-consuming' task involved taking home 20–25 files every weekend.

> *A lot were from Fiji, many Awami League of Bangladesh, some African, some Central European. The other Minister and I were supposed to agree. If we didn't, we had a meeting to resolve an appeal – again, all very time-consuming. In one case, we both refused to compromise, so no decision was taken; months later, I asked what happened – he's still here!!! The policy then changed and this dual Ministerial Appeal Authority disappeared, which I had been encouraging, and was thankful to see achieved. I had always taken a fairly liberal view on these appeals generally. You didn't want to hear that someone had been killed in their country after deportation.*[53]

The concerns about the growing numbers of asylum seekers led to a review of the process of refugee status determination by Bill Wilson, who reported to Birch in April 1992.[54] One of his main recommendations concerned the need to prevent passengers boarding their aircraft for New Zealand unless they had the correct documentation. This could be done 'through co-operation with airlines and if necessary the enforcement of their statutory responsibilities and through stationing New Zealand Immigration Officers at points of departure to this country'. Wilson also made a number of recommendations on how to speed up the process of refugee determination 'with the aim of reaching a decision within six weeks of the lodging of the application'. He had further suggestions on how appeals to the Refugee Status Appeal Authority could be decided within two months of being lodged. If adopted, his ideas would achieve two objectives: promptly granting refugee status to those who qualified and promptly refusing applicants for refugee status who did not.[55]

On 4 August 1992 Birch announced that most of Wilson's recommendations would be implemented. The increase in refugee status applicants had been 'equally dramatic elsewhere in the world', reflecting, in part, 'the large number of economic refugees seeking back-door entry to countries like New Zealand, Australia, Canada and the United Kingdom'.[56] The Refugee Status Appeal

Authority would be enlarged to relieve pressure on the processing of appeals and there would be more interviewing officers.[57] These initiatives made some headway with reducing the backlog of asylum seeker applications. As McKinnon recalled, New Zealand 'showed a reasonable degree of generosity. We managed numbers rather than races, religious groups or ethnic groups.'[58]

The changes introduced by the government improved efficiency but they could be of only partial assistance in the complex task of determining claims for refugee status, a task that meant balancing obligations to New Zealand with giving applicants a fair hearing. A brief look at five of the 426 decisions made by the Refugee Status Appeals Authority in 1997–98 highlights these challenges. [59]

Three of the five appellants from Iran whose cases came before the authority had already appealed on another occasion. They claimed to have been imprisoned and tortured by the Iranian authorities or had family members who had been detained by the authorities, and to have endured such experiences as being 'frequently accosted by the Komiteh [the Revolutionary Committee responsible for enforcing Islamic regulations on social behaviour] for breaching Islamic dress standard' or being persecuted because they came from a pro-monarchist family. Another claimed that he would be killed if he returned to Iran because he had converted to Christianity. A hairdresser from Iran claimed to have been blindfolded, whipped and threatened with jail by the Komiteh for setting up a hairdressing business in her home, because the public display of female beauty was prohibited by the Islamic regime. A young man had got into trouble with the Islamic regime during military service because, as a moderate Muslim, he was opposed to organised and compulsory religious observances. The cases were all dismissed for failing to meet the requirements of the Refugee Convention.[60]

The threat of mass arrivals, 1997–99

Despite such measures as advanced passenger screening and information sharing with other countries, relatively large numbers of asylum seekers continued to arrive in New Zealand over 1997 and 1998. There was considerable government concern about the numbers and about the fact that most of the refugee status claims were dismissed because they had not met the correct criteria.

Of even more concern was the prospect that a large number of asylum seekers might reach New Zealand by sea. Planning for such an influx of unplanned arrivals intensified in February 1999 when 57 Chinese boat people were found heading towards New Zealand. The boat stopped in Australia. Two other boatloads of people were found drifting, possibly towards New Zealand, in early 1999, but stopped in New Caledonia.⁶¹ To deal with possible mass arrivals by sea, in 1999 Jenny Shipley's National government amended the 1987 Immigration Act, updating immigration law and policy in relation to the detention and deportation of people unlawfully in New Zealand. This major piece of legislation was intended to:

> *provide for more efficient and speedier immigration procedures especially in relation to refugee status claimants, over-stayers and potential over-stayers. In particular, it enables the granting of limited purpose visas and permits, the imposition of bond requirements and a more flexible fee structure. It also contains a special procedure for dealing with classified security information in an immigration context.*⁶²

A key feature was the introduction of faster removal procedures for those who were in New Zealand unlawfully without a permit. Passed on 1 April 1999, the Immigration Amendment Act came into force in October that year,⁶³ too late to deal with the Chinese supposedly travelling to New Zealand on a vessel called *Alexander II*. The government therefore urgently passed a second Immigration Amendment Act on 16 June 1999, opposed by Labour and the Alliance, in order to bring certain provisions of the first amendment act into force sooner.

Immigration Minister Tuariki Delamere said that the fast-track legislation would give New Zealand greater powers to deal with the possible arrival, as soon as 20 June, of more than 100 Chinese boat people seeking to enter New Zealand unlawfully.

> *Tonight's amendment will give us greater flexibility in how long we can detain these people and will also enable us to prosecute those who organise migrant trafficking. I would emphasise that it is not certain that the* Alexander 11 *genuinely intends to reach New Zealand or whether those on board intend to claim refugee status, but the government considers it prudent to be prepared should a large number of these people reach these shores.*⁶⁴

Panic about mass arrivals

Just before the introduction of the boat-people bill, there was a tone of panic in media reports about the possible arrival of the asylum seekers. The *Dominion* said that in favourable weather the *Alexander II* 'could arrive off the coast early next week'. The Chinese people, from Fujian province in the south of China, were 'understood to have paid a big amount of money to get on the boat'.⁶⁵ The *Evening Post* reported that, in addition to the *Alexander II*, two more boatloads of Chinese immigrants could be heading for New Zealand. The 98 men and four women, aged between 25 and 35, did not speak English. An Air Force Orion would 'scour the seas' in the next few days and the *Alexander II* would be 'monitored as it got near New Zealand'. The ship 'could try to land at any point on New Zealand's coast'.[66]

Prisons were reported to be ready for the arrivals – Mt Eden in Auckland for the women and Rangipo Prison near Turangi for the men. The boat people could also be held at the Refugee Resettlement Centre in South Auckland but any decision, said Immigration, would depend on who was on board.[67] Airports were reported to be on alert because another group of Chinese nationals travelling on Tongan passports as part of a 'passport racket' might arrive by air and claim refugee status, 'adding to the around 3000 refugee-seekers already waiting for claims to be determined'. The government was 'investigating reports that another two boat loads of Chinese may be on the way'.[68]

To some extent the panic resulted from the denting of New Zealand's sense that it was too far away to experience such problems. The new feeling of vulnerability was conveyed in a *New Zealand Herald* report of 17 June 1999:

> Boat people, a problem that has lapped at Asian and Australian shores for 20 years, has not touched this country before. Now it does. The news that a boatload of 102 Chinese nationals had left the Solomon Islands, New Zealand bound, has confronted us with the problem no matter whether the voyagers keep to their declared destination. It is enough to know that this country is on the radar of ventures in illegal migration and suddenly it seems naive to have supposed that distance would be a sufficient barrier to the trade. Trade appears to be the appropriate term now. The era of desperate people flinging themselves into barely seaworthy craft to flee communism in Vietnam, or troubles elsewhere, has long passed. These days the boat people are on cargo ships or seaworthy vessels of the sort said to be heading to New Zealand yesterday. Often the boat people have paid substantial amounts to shady organisations in their country of origin.[69]

The *Herald* suggested New Zealand should have been prepared but had not, like Australia, sent immigration officers to China in an attempt to prevent organised illegal migration – though even this had not prevented more and more asylum seekers from landing on remote parts of the Australian coast.

> Now we have to respond quickly. It is most important to give the message at the outset that there is no point in boat people coming this way. If one boatload is admitted, more will come. New Zealand has a shoreline easier to police than Australia's. The northern coast, closest to the current of illegal migration, is well populated but not so well that a group of new arrivals could disappear in the crowd. We patrol the coast and sea zone daily; it ought to be

possible to warn boatloads of illegal migrants that they should not approach New Zealand and that if they do they will be turned away.[70]

Delamere noted evidence that New Zealand was being targeted by migrant traffickers, escorting people who claimed refugee status on arrival. It was 'commonly known' that if you 'allowed' trafficking, 'you only encouraged it'.[71] In another press release the next day, he moved to reassure critics that while the government was 'determined to deal with illegal immigrants firmly but fairly', this was a fundamentally different issue from the arrival of refugees from Kosovo or other refugees, whom the government had actively decided to accommodate on humanitarian or other grounds. New Zealand would not compromise on 'our ability to keep our borders secure'. Illegal immigrants would be detained under the Amendment Act 1999, but 'spontaneous asylum seekers' would be able 'to present their case' and undergo a 'full determination process'.[72]

The panic about 'mass arrivals' is placed in some context when it is noted that in 1998–99 overseas visitors entering New Zealand numbered 1.555 million, with 360,200 from Asia. Permanent and long-term migration for the year ending March 1998 numbered 62,928.[73] But of course, the panic was less about numbers than lack of control.

Criticism of the boat people legislation was fairly muted, perhaps because of the speed with which it was passed and because potential critics were not quite sure whether boatloads of asylum seekers would really arrive. The Auckland Refugee Council was particularly concerned about the detention of asylum seekers, though 'with proviso of a very short stay as being possibly acceptable'. However, in a paper written in 1998, the council's lawyer David Ryken hedged his bets:

> *The concern about mass arrivals is probably ill-conceived given that New Zealand is so far away from any refugee source country that it is impossible for a ship to reach New Zealand's shores from a refugee source country without first refuelling. Nevertheless, as was reported in the media last year, a ship with a large number of asylum seekers did reach New Caledonia, apparently heading towards New Zealand.*[74]

Political opposition was also fairly low key. Matt Robson, immigration spokesman for the left-of-centre Alliance, pointed out that Delamere's stance against the Chinese was at odds with his willingness to welcome Kosovar refugees to New Zealand: 'He was happy to help those people in need, and now we have a different group of people in need and his position is suddenly very different. You have to wonder why. The best thing the New Zealand Government could do is send help to make sure these poor people don't drown.'[75] Labour MP Paul Swain was critical of the 'knee-jerk reaction' of Delamere, 'who panics at the first opportunity'. Although New Zealand had to protect its borders, it made no sense 'to rush law through in urgency about a boat when we are unsure of its whereabouts, how many people are on it, and when it's likely to arrive – if ever'. His party colleague Trevor Mallard doubted the boat people bill would have eventuated had the people on the boats been European.[76]

By 26 June 1999, nine days after the fast-tracked legislation had been passed, there was no trace of the *Alexander II* and its Chinese refugees. An Orion, which had failed to find the boat, gave up the search. The two other boatloads of refugees supposedly on their way to New Zealand had also vanished. Delamere hastened to reassure the public that though no trace of the asylum seekers had been found, the government did not regret passing urgent legislation to detain them. The legislation was prudent, not premature.

Earlier critics of the legislation were now far less muted in their opposition. According to Robson, the non-appearance of the boat people highlighted the government's 'panic reaction'. He criticised Delamere's handling of the situation, which had led to 'unfortunate racist outbursts'. Labour's immigration spokeswoman Lianne Dalziel described the legislation as 'kneejerk and an abuse of Parliament'.[77]

Dealing with the backlog

After the panic about mass arrivals by sea had died down, the focus of concern returned to arrivals at airports and the system's ability to cope with the numbers of applicants for refugee status. Further improvements were introduced when Lianne Dalziel became Minister of Immigration in Helen Clark's Labour administration in November 1999. One of her proudest achievements in the role was dealing with the backlog. In 1999 there were over 3000 refugee-status claimants awaiting the first-level determination of their claims. By 2003 the number was down to 300.[78]

As Dalziel recalled, major problems were caused by organised scams bringing people to New Zealand to make false refugee claims. These people-smugglers used the fact that people wanted to come here for a job. By making a false claim for refugee status a person could work in New Zealand while their claim was processed. 'People used to be able to stay three years in New Zealand waiting for their refugee status to be determined; then they waited more time while they appealed.' Dalziel 'poured resources' into the system to stop this happening and succeeded in reducing the backlog from three years to three months. The speedier determination was more humane, 'good for genuine refugees and good for New Zealand in case of the non-genuine refugees'.[79] 'We believe that the sooner that we can determine those who are not entitled to protection or who are abusing the determination process in order to circumvent our immigration laws, the sooner we can remove them,' she told delegates at a conference on people-smuggling held in Bali in February 2002.

> In New Zealand last year, [bogus applicants] represented over eighty per cent of those who claimed refugee status. Conversely, the sooner that we can determine that a claim is genuine, the sooner we can commence the resettlement process. We have found that lengthy delays in the determination process add to the anxiety that inhibit integration into the community, once refugee status is granted. The longer that state of limbo applies, the more difficult it is for those with genuine claims to resettle.[80]

By 2003 dealing with the backlog at primary determination level had shifted the problem more to the appeal stage; with additional resources, Dalziel expected to also improve the Refugee Status Appeal Authority's efficiency. One of the problems in dealing with asylum seekers 'without genuine claims' was the difficulty in obtaining travel documents for their country of origin. There was a need for bilateral or multilateral repatriation or readmission agreements, which would have a 'deterrent' effect and develop public confidence in the determination process.[81]

In 2007 the lack of such bilateral agreements, for example with Iran, made it difficult to deport failed asylum seekers, but other aspects of the refugee status determination process did work more efficiently after 1999. In her efforts to improve the process, Dalziel was helped by the tightening of borders around the world, especially in Australia, the United States, Europe and Canada, following the terrorist attacks of 11 September 2001, which decreased asylum seeker flows.

The *Tampa* refugees, 2001

Just before 9/11, New Zealand responded to another asylum seeker challenge. In August 2001, the Norwegian freighter *Tampa* rescued more than 400 people from a sinking boat in the Indian Ocean. They were Afghans fleeing from the Taliban. For nine days they sat on the ship's deck as Australia faced international demands to allow them ashore. The crisis harnessed support for John Howard's government and gained worldwide attention. 'We have always stood ready to take our fair share,' Howard said as he announced that the survivors would be taken to Nauru under a scheme called the Pacific Solution, which allowed Australia's refugee determination to take place on offshore islands rather than on the Australian mainland.[82] At that point New Zealand stepped in and offered to determine the status of up to 150 *Tampa* refugees. As portrayed in the media, Australia had refused to provide temporary asylum for the refugees while more compassionate New Zealand had agreed to do so. In fact the situation was somewhat more complex.

New Zealand's offer to take the *Tampa* refugees was a political decision. 'We came to the conclusion that people couldn't sit on the deck of the ship forever', Prime Minister Helen Clark recalled in a conversation with Australian journalist David Marr. 'We all walk a fine line on this issue. We cannot be seen to encourage illegal migration, but we understand that there are circumstances that force people to seek refuge somewhere else.'[83] Clark's decision originated with a UNHCR-backed request from Australia that some of those rescued by the *Tampa* be taken to New Zealand to have their claims determined. It was the first occasion that asylum seekers were brought here for this purpose.

Dalziel recalled that the government agreed because 'New Zealand felt it could be a circuit breaker. Taking refugees from the *Tampa* happened very much under the leadership of the Prime Minister … We took the family groupings or the women alone – we took them because they were the most at risk and most likely to be in need of protection. Then we put them through our determination process as quickly as possible.'[84] The decision certainly helped the Australian government. As Marr observed, 'Miss Clark saved Mr Howard's bacon in 2001. The Pacific solution would have collapsed in a heap without her.'[85]

Reflecting on the *Tampa* incident in 2007, Dalziel noted that the government appeared to have gained public support for its action, as shown by two opinion polls published in the *New Zealand Herald*. In the first, 49 per cent were in favour of the government's *Tampa* decision, 46 per cent opposed. The second poll, conducted after 9/11, showed 59 per cent in favour and 35 per cent against. Dalziel believed there were two reasons for the change.

> First there was the strong leadership of our Prime Minister, the Rt Hon Helen Clark, and second, there was the media exposure of the circumstances that drove people from Afghanistan. A level of public understanding filled the vacuum that existed before. That is why it is important that there is education about the circumstances that drive people from their homelands, so that ignorance and fear do not fuel prejudice, which is a barrier to successful resettlement. Knowledge is a powerful weapon against prejudice.[86]

There may have been public support for accepting the *Tampa* refugees, but there was also 'unrelenting' political opposition. As a senior government official recalled, 'Each intake of refugees and the arrival of their families was attacked by the National Party as a waste, profligate and as "immigration by stealth", which risked turning the country into "a soft touch" for asylum seekers.'[87]

Winston Peters, leader of New Zealand First, which had a strong anti-immigration stance, was a prominent critic of the government's position. He felt that New Zealand was already doing enough for refugees. In a debate on Afghan asylum seekers on 4 September 2001, Peters asked the Prime Minister how many United Nations signatory countries on refugees were closer to the *Tampa* than New Zealand, with the implication that New Zealand was softer on asylum seekers than other countries. He also argued that the *Tampa* refugees should not be accepted because they were jumping the queue:

> Those who have the greatest need to be refugees, resettled in our country, do not have money to hire aeroplanes and boats. They are the people whose sad faces one may see in international refugee programmes all round the Western World. Surely, if we are to have a refugee programme, then those people should be the first in line.

Why was the Prime Minister telling the country that we were obligated to fulfil a United Nations quota when 'we have twice the number of that quota – who have yet to be processed – in our country already, and when there are millions abroad, in far worthier circumstances, who are entitled to go through the United Nations protocols and procedures, who will go to the back of the queue because of this Government's decision?'

The answer, according to Peters, was that Clark wanted to be seen as having 'a soft heart', but it was 'something else to have a head to match'. The government was ignoring the needs of tax-paying New Zealanders in order 'to posture on the world stage as being great humanitarians'. Furthermore, he suggested that New Zealand taxpayers would miss out on the health care they needed in order to finance the refugees:

> I see in my clinics [people who] are unable to get an operation within six months, and whose doctors tell me: 'If they aren't given an immediate operation, they are going to die.' They will not be serviced by this sort of decision. I see other people living in tin shacks, without power or water. Even though they are New Zealanders, they will go without any attention whatsoever because of this Government's decision.

Peters defended himself, however, from accusations of racism: 'My party and I will not be told that those who raise genuine concerns are racist – they are not.' The critics, he felt, 'are concerned that we put our own people's interests first. We have always believed in the United Nations refugee quota and we have always believed in a fair go, but we do not believe that the people of New Zealand should be ripped off.'[88]

New Zealand First's attacks acquired a new edge after 9/11. On 13 September Peters asked in parliament if the government was still offering to take 145 *Tampa* asylum seekers and, if so, why? Replying on Clark's behalf, Jim Anderton answered in the affirmative:

> Refugees flee Afghanistan because they do not agree with the extreme policies being pursued by the regime in power. Five million out of seventeen million people have left Afghanistan in the last few years. They seek to come to New Zealand and similar countries because they share our belief in freedom and peace. Ours is a community of people from many parts of the world. It is intolerable, in my view, and an attack on the values that the overwhelming majority of New Zealanders hold dearest, to link someone to suspected terrorists on the basis of his or her nationality.[89]

ACT's Richard Prebble asked about the security issues involved in bringing in asylum seekers who had not been pre-screened. Although Anderton's reply brushed aside the question of security to focus on 'humanitarian considerations', measures to respond to post 9/11 security concerns were already under way, as discussed below. One hundred and thirty-one asylum seekers were eventually transferred from Nauru to New Zealand in September 2001. All gained refugee status. Seventeen *Tampa* family-linked cases also came to New Zealand, and a further 91 cases, determined either by the Australian authorities or by the UNHCR, came as mandated refugees under the annual quota.[90] A senior government official recalled 'the astronomical' phone bill when the *Tampa* boys were given mobile phones and told to find their relatives. 'But the outcome was phenomenal. Fathers, mothers, brothers and sisters began to arrive in New Zealand from all over the Middle East in March 2004.'[91]

In Dalziel's view, the *Tampa* refugees have settled well: 'They are good citizens, keen to contribute and repay New Zealand's faith in them.'[92] Looking back, she feels 'particularly proud to be a New Zealander'. The *Tampa* incident was 'a symbol of the role a small country can play when called upon to do so'.[93]

An internationally respected refugee determination process, 2000–08

The *Tampa* episode seemed to show New Zealand as more compassionate in its response to asylum seekers than Australia, whose Pacific Solution has been much criticised. The Australian government's position has been that attempts by boatloads of people to enter Australia would be unsuccessful and that Australia should determine offshore who was, and who was not, a genuine refugee.⁹⁴ In comparison, New Zealand's detention regime for asylum seekers seems benign enough, but comparison between the ways the two countries respond to asylum seekers is unfair. New Zealand's more remote location means it has yet to deal with significant numbers of asylum seekers arriving by sea.

By the beginning of the twenty-first century New Zealand had a highly developed and robust refugee determination process, seen by the UNHCR as efficient yet fair, and as an example of international best practice.⁹⁵ According to a Human Rights Commission report, in 2005 New Zealand had met international human rights standards in many respects and often surpassed them.⁹⁶

Under the 1987 Immigration Act and its amendments, claims for refugee status were assessed on the basis of 'individual merit' to determine if the applicant met the criteria of the 1951 United Nations Convention on the Status of Refugees and its 1967 protocol. The New Zealand government did not have an official policy regarding applications from any particular religious or ethnic group.⁹⁷

In brief, the process of refugee determination went as follows. The Refugee Status Branch of the New Zealand Immigration Service considered applications to determine whether the case met the requirement to show a well-founded fear of persecution for reason of the applicants' race, religion, nationality, social group, political opinions and any other criteria under the convention. Applicants were given appropriate legal representation for the initial determination hearings. Declined applicants had the right to appeal to the Refugee Status Appeal Authority against the decisions of the Refugee Status Branch. Between 1999 and 2005, the branch had dealt with around 5967 applications, with around 20 per cent of applicants gaining refugee status.⁹⁸ As discussed earlier, provisions introduced under the Immigration Amendment Act of 1999 allowed for the detention of refugee status applicants and the deportation of unsuccessful asylum seekers.⁹⁹

Tighter entry and detention regime after 9/11

Just as the refugees from the *Tampa* were being brought to New Zealand amid security concerns after 9/11, the government introduced a stricter entry and detention regime. From 19 September 2001 immigration officers had greater discretionary powers to detain asylum seekers on arrival and subsequently.¹⁰⁰ The new measures provided for different levels of detention. Most 'border asylum claimants' were, and are, initially detained at a police station or in prison 'as part of the process to refuse entry'. The vast majority were, and are, subsequently released 'on conditions or detained under warrant at the Mangere Refugee Centre'.[101]

The stronger provisions came under legal challenge from the Refugee Council and the Human Rights Commission. Opposed to what they saw as a mandatory detention regime, they argued that the pre-September 11 provisions were adequate to safeguard New Zealand's security. The new regime was 'a first step towards introducing Australian-style detention camps'. The legal challenge to the government's operational instructions was at first successful: in June 2002, the High Court ruled that the government's policy of detaining asylum seekers was unlawful. This decision was seen to open the way for claims against the government by asylum seekers seeking compensation for unlawful arrest. The government successfully appealed the decision and the operational instructions came into effect in 2004.[102]

Several months after the April 2003 Court of Appeal decision in favour of the government, Minister of Immigration Lianne Dalziel justified the tighter regime in a speech that also strongly criticised the Refugee Council's case against the government:

> September 11 was a wake-up call to us all. We have the absolute right as a nation to know who is entering our country, where they are from and why they are here. New Zealand is a country where you don't have to carry an identity or pass card just to walk down the street. Individual freedoms are valued here, but we risk jeopardising those freedoms, if we do not assert our wider responsibilities to New Zealand as a whole.

In justifying the new regulations, Dalziel pointed out that New Zealand's detention regime was humane. There was 'no comparison between detention at an open centre, such as the Mangere Refugee Resettlement Centre, and other detention centres around the world'. Furthermore, the ability to grant permits or release on conditions, where appropriate, to community hostels 'which had been funded by this government for these purposes', enabled 'the least restrictive option to be exercised when identity and level of risk had been satisfied'.[103]

Peter Cotton, the CEO (formerly Director) of RMS Refugee Resettlement, agreed with this view to some extent. Although the agency continued to oppose the detaining of asylum seekers, except in extreme circumstances, New Zealand had to be commended for so far not setting up a maximum security detention centre such as the Australians had at Port Headland and elsewhere. The level of detention at the Mangere Reception Centre was 'minimal'. 'They put back the barbed wire which was removed in the 1980s, and put in an electric fence. This turned part of the Mangere Reception Centre into a detention centre. But asylum seekers can request swipe cards. They can also be based in the community rather than at the detention centre.' Cotton felt there had to be a balance between individual rights and state security. New Zealand had the right to detain asylum seekers and some people needed to be detained. It was also relevant to note that 'around 80 per cent of people trying to claim refugee status did not meet the criteria of being a refugee in terms of the UN Convention'.[104]

The Refugee Council has continued to oppose the detention of asylum seekers. President Dr Nagalingam Rasalingam has been concerned that asylum seekers are detained together with quota refugees who have been selected by New Zealand and are undergoing orientation at Mangere.[105] Various matters of concern were identified at a Council for International Development Refugee Policy Forum held in Wellington in January 2005. Keynote speaker lawyer Deborah Manning criticised the government's policy of restricting asylum seekers entering New Zealand, detaining those who did arrive (as a deterrent) and removing failed asylum seekers. In her opinion, the effective monitoring of asylum seeker human rights was deficient. She also noted that, legally, the wholesale detention of asylum seekers remained unresolved. For detained refugee claimants, procedural safeguards remained inadequate – most significantly, there was no legal aid for habeas corpus applications or for asylum seekers to review their detention in either the District or the High Court. There was no protection for stateless persons and New Zealand was not a signatory to the relevant UN convention. Refugee determination procedures were ad hoc and there were no institutional checks to monitor those procedures. Manning also condemned the practice of New Zealand Immigration Service personnel in foreign airports interdicting those carrying suspect documentation. This was meant to stop illegal people-smuggling, but could act against the interests of genuine refugees.[106]

Workshops held at the forum identified further areas of concern. The support for those awaiting a decision about their refugee status needed improvement to a level similar to that enjoyed by quota and approved refugees, particularly in terms of access to work and to essential social services, including health and education services. There was anxiety about the detention of asylum seekers, including the length of incarceration, the time spent in isolation and the safety of asylum seekers in a prison environment. There were concerns about the Mangere Accommodation Centre – the growing numbers of refugees and asylum seekers held there and the detention of children.[107]

Sometimes New Zealand's best practice for refugee status applications falls short of the ideal. Interpreters are often from the same country as the applicant, which means that the applicant may withhold crucial information out of fear that it will be divulged to third parties. Interviewers sometimes know very little about the cultural background of the applicant, and may therefore misunderstand an answer or misread the applicant's body language, or behave in ways the applicant considers inappropriate.[108]

The refugee determination process, in New Zealand as elsewhere, is inherently difficult. Lengthy interviews – often perceived as gruelling by applicants – are necessary if, in the absence of documents, their credibility has to be assessed by checking and rechecking their statements about past events. It may also be hard for applicants to remember these events accurately without discrepancies appearing in their stories. Applicants are expected to share experiences of suffering and trauma, often through an interpreter they do not trust, in a way that will be acceptable and meaningful to immigration officials from a very different culture. The officials, in turn, have the unenviable task of trying to judge the credibility of applicants from an unfamiliar background.

Ahmed Zaoui

The case of Algerian asylum seeker Ahmed Zaoui, which aroused much debate in New Zealand between 2002 and 2008, was a test for New Zealand's refugee determination process. It highlights the difficulty of determining who is a genuine refugee and who does not meet the criteria.

Ahmed Zaoui was born in 1960 in the village of El Idrissia in Algeria. After receiving his tertiary education at Saudi University, he took up a position as Lecturer in Islamic Traditions at the University of Algiers from 1988. Around the same time, he became a sheik at a mosque. In 1991 he was elected as a member of parliament for the Front Islamique du Salut (FIS) – the Islamic Salvation Front Party.[109] When the FIS won the elections in 1991, the army intervened to stop what it saw as a religious party taking over the country. The FIS was banned in 1992 and remained so in 2007. Subsequently a civil war began between the army and the Armed Islamic Group (GIA), allegedly aligned with Osama bin Laden's al Qaeda.[110]

Zaoui, who had denied involvement with the GIA, fled Algeria in 1993 for Europe, then travelled the world seeking a haven. His search for refuge included Belgium, Switzerland, Burkina Faso and Malaysia. It was later claimed that, in these countries, he took part in the activities of criminal groups preparing terrorist acts. In 2002, he left Malaysia suddenly for Vietnam because he believed he was about to be arrested. From there he flew to New Zealand on a fake South African passport, arriving in December 2002. Before landing in Auckland, he tried to destroy his passport, then sought refugee status at the airport and was interviewed. After being processed by customs, he was detained in custody on the grounds that his identity needed to be confirmed. He was kept for some days at the Papakura police station and then transferred to the maximum security prison at Paremoremo. There he was kept in isolation for 240 days.[111]

Zaoui was interviewed by a refugee status officer on 19 December 2002. On 30 January 2003, the Refugee Status Branch declined his application for refugee status on the grounds that though he had a well-founded fear of persecution in Algeria, he was nevertheless excluded from the Refugee Convention because there were 'serious reasons' for considering that he had committed terrorist or non-political crimes. At the end of January 2003 Zaoui lodged an appeal to the Refugee Status Appeals Authority, which recognised him as a refugee in August that year.[112] However, on 20 March 2003 then SIS Director Richard Woods issued a security risk certificate stating that Zaoui's continued presence was a 'threat to national security' and 'a danger to the security of New Zealand', though without explaining why. Despite his refugee status, the government ordered Zaoui's deportation. A week later, Zaoui appealed to the Inspector-General of Intelligence and Security, Laurie Greig, for a review of the security risk certificate.[113]

In early February 2007 the Police Complaints Authority released a report on the treatment of Ahmed Zaoui based on a three-year investigation initiated by former MP Matt Robson, which showed that key agencies may have raced to quick conclusions about Zaoui. Around early 2007, after almost four years in prison, Zaoui was released on bail. While awaiting the review of the government's security risk certificate,[114] he lived with Dominican friars in Auckland, writing poetry and lecturing at Auckland University. He was required to report twice a week to police and to observe a curfew. On two occasions during this period he asked for his wife and four children, who lived in Malaysia, to be able to join him in New Zealand. He was especially concerned about his 14-year-old son with special needs, who was unable to attend school. Zaoui's request, which was supported by the UNHCR, was declined: his family was refused visas to come to New Zealand.[115]

In July 2007, nearly four years after Zaoui had appealed against the issuing of the security risk certificate against him, a four-week hearing began to review the SIS action. Amnesty International and Zaoui's lawyer Deborah Manning protested against the secrecy surrounding the hearing. Headed by Inspector-General of Intelligence and Security, Paul Neazor, it was held in the Employment Court in Auckland. One of the purposes of the review was to hear Zaoui's side of the story. Manning and Zaoui were both given summaries of classified SIS information that was used to draw up the certificate but were not allowed to view secret files.[116] Zaoui was represented at the hearing by two advocates, appointed by Neazor, who were allowed to make summaries of the classified material but were unable to give Zaoui any details.

Neazor's role was to examine the information the SIS had used in order to decide whether the certificate was justified. According to a 2005 Supreme Court ruling, the SIS needed to show that, on objectively reasonable grounds, Zaoui posed a serious and substantial threat to the security of New Zealand. If Neazor found the issue of the certificate was justified, Zaoui's deportation order would be upheld.[117]

The SIS's four-and-a-half-year effort to deport Zaoui ended on 13 September 2007 when Director Warren Tucker announced the decision to end the security risk certificate. Although the SIS had previously claimed Zaoui had links to terrorist organisations, Tucker said 'new evidence Zaoui gave to a recent hearing to review the risk certificate, along with recently received classified information, had lead the SIS to reconsider the risk'.[118] The SIS was satisfied that he no longer posed a security threat, which meant that he could stay in New Zealand and bring his family here. Perhaps another reason for the change of heart was Zaoui's high public profile, which would have made it difficult for him to carry out clandestine activities.

A key condition of the lifting of the certificate was the signing of a contract in which Zaoui promised 'good behaviour'. Swearing on the Koran, he agreed not to undertake any criminal or terrorist acts under New Zealand law. He can make contact with intelligence agents from other countries, but only if the SIS is consulted first. 'Likewise the SIS must be kept in the loop if spies make contact with him.' Tucker said the contract would 'enable him to continue to be comfortable that Mr Zaoui is no longer a risk to security'.[119]

At the end of October 2007 Ahmed Zaoui was reunited with his wife and four sons in Auckland, ending a seven-year separation. While Prime Minister Helen Clark said the decision to allow Zaoui to stay in New Zealand was Tucker's alone to make,[120] it seems likely that the final decision was a political one. Most commentators agreed that the process had taken too long and the cost – $3 million – had been too high.[121] In 2012, the man once thought a possible threat to national security was serving up hot lunches on Auckland's Karangahape Road.¹²²

The case had occasioned considerable debate, with the New Zealand community divided over what they believed to be the truth about Ahmed Zaoui. The series of allegations and counter-allegations baffled the public and called into question the judgement and credibility of the agencies involved. According to the Refugee Status Appeal Authority, Zaoui was 'a passionate advocate for peace through democracy in Algeria' and a genuine refugee, entitled to all the protections of the 1951 UN Refugee Convention.¹²³ The SIS, however, deemed him a threat to New Zealand's security. The fact that the supposedly sound reasons for this could not be revealed for security reasons did not help the government's cause.

Zaoui's own veracity became a significant consideration too. Was he a terrorist threatening New Zealand? Was he a person who had committed no offence and who faced no charge, yet had been consigned to indefinite detention? To some extent the case received so much attention because it was the first time the SIS had issued a security risk certificate against anyone in New Zealand.

There was also considerable speculation about what exactly Zaoui was suspected of doing. The Supreme Court judgement of 9 December 2004 noted that: 'The security risks identified are essentially those associated with leading and participating in criminal activities in relation to Algerian politics and encouraging the perception that New Zealand is a safe haven for those intending to undertake similar activities. The concern is with communicating and associating with others.' SIS Director Richard Wood said, 'Mr Zaoui is a foreign person ... There is good reason to believe any future activities he may undertake will be influenced by other foreign persons and/or by foreign organisations.'¹²⁴

An editorial in the *NZ Listener*, which had long supported Zaoui's release, stated: 'The right decision has finally been made in terms of Ahmed Zaoui's presence in New Zealand – pity it took so long.' It went on to speculate about Zaoui's 'remarkable transformation' into 'beloved Kiwi folk hero and Jeffersonian democrat', concluding that sympathy for 'underdogs' and Zaoui's personality and 'physical presence' – 'even critics call him an avuncular giant' – clearly played a large part in the way the country had taken Zaoui 'to its heart'. 'As much as we hate queue-jumpers, we do love underdogs – especially when they are up against faceless government agencies.'¹²⁵

Policy changes, 2006–12

In December 2006, after a review of immigration legislation, Minister of Immigration David Cunliffe proposed changes to the 1987 Immigration Act, to make it easier for desirable migrants to enter and stay in New Zealand and to improve border security against those New Zealand did not want. The government would have flexible powers to enforce immigration law and the ability to use and collect biometric information.[126] The proposed changes included merging the existing four appeal bodies into one tribunal with a single right of appeal covering all immigration and refugee categories. This move was designed to end the often lengthy process of removing failed asylum seekers and failed migrants who had several stages of appeal. It would also reduce the number of applications asylum seekers could make. Other recommendations were to give immigration officers powers to detain incoming travellers for immigration reasons for up to four hours without involving police, and additional rights to enter and search premises to serve removal orders. Employers would be able to obtain information about immigrants' immigration status.[127]

The government was responding to various criticisms from the National Opposition that it was not doing enough to stop 'dangerous terrorists entering New Zealand'. (This was despite the passing of the 2002 Terrorism Suppression Act, which made it an offence to take part in, finance or recruit for international terrorist groups.) Among the critics of government policy was Winston Peters, who did not let his role as Minister of Foreign Affairs in Helen Clark's Labour administration stop him attacking New Zealand's immigration policy on various grounds, including not dealing adequately with immigration from high-risk countries.[128]

The immigration bill also aimed to address the issues in a critical Auditor-General's report earlier in 2007, which had highlighted the 'fragility' of the immigration system, focusing on the ability of officials to detect fake identities when handling applications from refugees and skilled migrants. The report highlighted other systemic problems, such as the backlog of significant fraud cases not yet investigated; the inadequate training of immigration officers to detect migration fraud; below-standard IT systems; poor interviewing of refugee applicants before they arrived in New Zealand because of time restrictions; and 'lack of intelligence material arising from cases under investigation'.[129]

'Security risk in migrant fraud' ran the *Dominion Post* headline on 27 June 2007. In the ensuing article, Cunliffe acknowledged the existence of a 'border gap' and that 'New Zealand's security may have on occasions been compromised by lapses in the detection of immigration fraud'.[130] A cynical interpretation of the government's acknowledgement of such lapses may have been part of the government's strategy to 'talk up' New Zealand's border security and highlight the importance of the new laws to be introduced.

By mid-2007 refugee status claims in New Zealand had declined from the 'unprecedented' high levels of the late 1990s to pre-1987 levels. For the year ended June 2007, the Refugee Status Branch received 278 asylum claims, of which 66 (23 per cent) were approved. The greatest number of claims came from China, Iran, Iraq and Sri Lanka.[131]

Despite the drop in numbers, asylum seekers often made the headlines in 2007, particularly in relation to government efforts to deport those whose applications for refugee status had failed. Several continued their fight for refugee status and against deportation through the media, with community response divided over the merits of each case. One was that of Harmon Lynn Wilfred, an American, who claimed to have been persecuted by the CIA and locked in an underground prison for 120 days. Wilfred had been living in New Zealand since 2001 and had tried several channels to remain in the country. The Removal Review Authority had ordered him to leave in 2004 but he had renounced his American citizenship, saying it would be inhuman to force him to return as there was a vendetta against him by high-ranking officials. He had appealed to the High Court, which in September 2006 rejected his appeal on the grounds that Wilfred could return to Canada if he did not want to go to the United States.[132]

Two other cases which received considerable media exposure were from Iran. Both failed asylum seekers were converts to Christianity and found church support in New Zealand. Both claimed they would be persecuted as Christians if they were deported, and refused to sign the travel documents which the Iranian authorities required before they could be deported to Iran. One of the asylum seekers was Hossein Yadegary, known as Thomas after his conversion.[133] The other was Ali Panah.

Iran's requirement – that people being repatriated must sign travel documents before they departed – left Panah 'in limbo-land' after his application for refugee status failed.[134] He had applied for refugee status in New Zealand on the grounds that he had converted to Christianity and would be persecuted if he returned to Iran. When his application for refugee status failed, he went on a hunger strike at the prison where he was detained, to protest the New Zealand government's decision to deport him back to Iran.[135]

Green MP Keith Locke, who took up Panah's cause, called for his release on bail, arguing that Panah should be allowed to stay because 'if liberal New

Zealand kicks them [asylum seekers like Panah] out, there is rarely a country that will have them as permanent resident'.[136] A *Dominion Post* editorial disagreed. Locke's stance came 'close to assuming that any applicant for refugee status [was] automatically entitled to receive it'. Supporters of the 'refugee-wannabe' were 'advocating an approach to justice' that came 'perilously close to moral blackmail'.[137]

On 3 September 2007 Panah agreed to stop the hunger strike, after 53 days, and was granted bail and put in care of the Anglican church. Helen Clark said 'the government was not prepared to see Mr Panah continue his hunger strike to the point of death', and that negotiations on a memorandum of understanding with Iran to allow such deportations had not been completed.[138] Ali Panah was granted refugee status in 2009, but the problem of deporting failed asylum seekers has remained. As we have seen, then Minister of Immigration Lianne Dalziel had raised the matter in August 2003. The issue of the readmission agreements she had called for remained unresolved in 2013.

The 2009 Immigration Act, promoted by a National-led government, provided for processing group applications from asylum seekers. The legislation included reporting and residence requirements but fell short of requiring that asylum seekers be detained in a closed camp or prison.[139] It also contained 'provisions to manage potential abuses of New Zealand's asylum process' and clarified 'the process for removing refugees and protected persons who pose a risk to national security or a danger to the community'.[140] The Immigration Act recognised the limitation that arose regarding the deportation of refugees or protected persons: they could not be deported to a place where there were 'substantial grounds for believing that the person would be in danger of being subjected to torture or to arbitrary deprivation of life or cruel, inhuman or degrading treatment or punishment'.[141] In 2009–10, 688 removal orders were carried out, 45 of them on 'ex-refugees'. The meaning of 'ex-refugees' is not defined in the table but the figure of 688 included those declined refugee status. It may also have included children.[142]

In May 2012 the government announced amendments to the 2009 Immigration Act to deter a mass arrival of potentially illegal migrants and people-smugglers. Among the suggested changes were provisions to allow the detention of a group of asylum seekers (more than 10 people) in a secure facility for an initial period of up to six months.[143] Earlier provisions had allowed the detention of asylum seekers, but usually in open centres with minimal security.

The proposed legislation faced stiff opposition. Critics argued that it was not needed as New Zealand had not so far been faced with mass arrivals of asylum seekers, and also that the detention plan was a threat to the country's good reputation.[144] Prime Minister John Key believed that 'one day a boat will turn up in New Zealand' and the country needed to be prepared.[145] The Immigration Bill was passed on 14 July 2013. It defines a mass arrival as being more than 30 people, who can be detained for up to six months. In May 2013 the government had announced that the Mangere Refugee Resettlement Centre would be rebuilt to house a potential mass arrival of asylum seekers.[146]

New Zealand's response to the inconvenient obligation

A couple of days after Ali Panah was granted bail in 2007, Immigration Minister David Cunliffe said that the decision was not 'a back-down': 'We have preserved the integrity of the immigration system and lived up to the highest standards of humanity in New Zealand, for which we are internationally famous.'[147] He also referred to New Zealand's outstanding reputation for compassionate policy towards refugees and asylum seekers, commenting that 'the humanitarian strand in New Zealand policy was much stronger than in Australia'.[148]

This rosy view of New Zealand's humanitarian refugee policy has been commonly held in the community at large. Self-congratulatory perceptions aside, how has New Zealand responded to the inconvenient obligation posed by asylum seekers? Along with other countries in the West, New Zealand has been caught in a conflict between the country's 'humanitarian tradition' of meeting obligations to refugees fleeing persecution, as set out in international treaties, and addressing concerns about the influx of asylum seekers, among them refugees who have not been chosen by New Zealand. Fears of the abuse of the asylum determination system by economic migrants and, worse, by terrorists, have led to improvements in border security and to the introduction of some processes that have reduced the number of asylum seekers entering the country. Other changes, such as a faster refugee determination process, have enabled the more rapid departure of those whose claims have been unsuccessful. Improvements in border security have included the detention of asylum seekers.

In 2011–12, 364 claims were decided, with 119 approved.[149] In the same period, the Refugee Status Branch received 303 claims for refugee or protection status from 57 nationalities. Of the decisions issued in 2011–12, 32.8 per cent were recognised as refugees or protected persons under the Refugee Convention, the Convention Against Torture or Articles 6 and 7 of the International Covenant of Civil and Political Rights. The average time for decisions was approximately 130 days.[150] In 2012, 550 people were deported in the period up to 31 August, the majority of them reported to be 'overstayers' and 'convicted criminals'. There are likely to be failed asylum seekers among them.[151] The introduction in July 2013 of a tighter regime notwithstanding, the country has to some extent indeed been a model to the rest of the world in compassion, fairness and efficiency. The qualifier is warranted because New Zealand's reputation has been based on responding to only relatively small numbers of refugee status claims. A distant location has so far meant that the country's liberal tradition of dealing fairly with those seeking refuge from persecution has not been seriously challenged. On 9 February 2013, New Zealand agreed to accept 150 asylum seekers per year from Australian processing centres, Key justifying the gesture as a 'regional solution for boat people arrivals'.[152] The agreement was similar to the one struck by Helen Clark with John Howard over the *Tampa* refugees in 2001. When, in July 2013, Australia signed an agreement with Papua New Guinea to expand the Manus Island detention centre to take asylum seekers from Australia for processing and resettlement, Key said that the New Zealand agreement to take asylum seekers would not include those sent to PNG.[153]

CHAPTER NINE

'Integration takes time'

New Zealand is a country of immigration. The Maori people established themselves as the tangata whenua (people of the land) after historic voyages of migration from countries in the Pacific. Large-scale immigration from European countries, particularly the United Kingdom, over the last 200 years changed the ethnic balance and altered the cultural base of New Zealand. This in turn has been modified by more recent migratory movements from the South Pacific and immigration from countries on the Pacific rim. Immigration has moulded our national characteristics as a Pacific country.[1]

These words by Immigration Minister Kerry Burke introduced the 1986 review of immigration policy, which heralded significant changes, marking a break with the earlier emphasis on nationality and ethnic origin as the basis for admitting immigrants. The preference given to immigrants from 'traditional source' countries ended. In future, prospective migrants would be considered purely on the basis of personal merit: anyone who met specified educational, business, professional, age, or asset requirements would be admitted regardless of race or nationality.

Not everyone was pleased with the new direction. Prominent Maori voiced concerns that the multicultural emphasis would undermine the special status of New Zealand's indigenous people.[2] Other critics felt threatened by the prospect of more ethnic diversity. Nonetheless, the policy reflected a new and greater tolerance of cultural differences, and it had consequences for the refugee programme.

The annual refugee quota

During the 1970s and much of the 1980s, New Zealand's approach to settling refugees was by means of quotas, set from time to time and as the need arose, in response to specific refugee situations. In 1987, as a result of a comprehensive review of New Zealand's refugee programme, the government set an annual refugee quota of 800 for those classified as refugees by the UNHCR. This formalised New Zealand's commitment to settling refugees, replacing the earlier piecemeal approach of individual quotas.[3] New Zealand was one of a relatively small number of countries that had established refugee resettlement programmes; it 'made a clear statement about the government's support for the principle of "international responsibility sharing"'.[4]

The new system, which enabled New Zealand to respond more quickly to changes in the international refugee situation,[5] retained aspects of the old system's flexibility. Each year the Minister of Immigration determined the specific composition of the quota, after consultation with the Minister of Foreign Affairs and Trade, the UNHCR, relevant government departments and non-government organisations. Specific refugee intakes were also subject to the availability of community sponsorship.[6]

From the late 1980s until recently, the process for the setting of the annual quota followed the same basic pattern. An approach to New Zealand to accept refugees came from the UNHCR, after which New Zealand officials selected refugees, with emphasis being placed on the humanitarian aspects of each case. The ability to adapt to the New Zealand environment and working conditions was taken into account, as was 'previous association with New Zealand' and 'links with friends or relatives living in New Zealand'.[7] In consultation with the UNHCR and the other agencies, numbers have also been allocated to such categories as 'women at risk', 'medical disabled', 'UNHCR priority protection' and family reunification.[8] As the Department of Labour commented in March 2013, 'for the last few years Refugee Quota Branch has incorporated a more formal "settlement" assessment to decision making but previous association to New Zealand and adaptation to working conditions is not part of this', though family links 'are considered'.[9] From 1987 to 1997, the annual quota consisted of 800 refugees per year, then the government reduced the figure to 750 but agreed to pay the travel costs of refugees.[10] That arrangement still applies. The establishment of the quota was significant because it acknowledged that the admission of refugees was not just an occasional gesture of compassion but 'an important *on-going* [my italics] humanitarian priority in New Zealand's immigration policy'.[11]

Refugees from the Middle East and Afghanistan

Refugees from the Middle East began settling in New Zealand from the late 1970s. The first arrivals were people of Baha'i or Christian backgrounds. A group of Baha'i refugees from Iran, fleeing religious persecution and wars, arrived in 1979; between 1987 and 1989, a further 142 Iranian Baha'is came to New Zealand under the newly established refugee quota.[12] They were sponsored by the National Spiritualist Assembly of the Baha'is in New Zealand.[13]

Assyrian Christians, who had escaped from Iraq to refugee camps in Greece, started coming to New Zealand in the mid-1980s, escaping the suffering and hardship caused by the Iraq–Iran War and the Gulf War and subsequent persecution by the Muslim (Sunni) rulers.[14] Around 140 refugees came between 1985 and 1989.[15]

During the 1980s, the admission of Muslim refugees remained controversial. In 1985, in response to pressure from the UNHCR to resettle Iranian refugees, the Secretary of Labour explained that the Minister of Immigration was

> *not prepared to accept any Iranian refugees other than those members of the Baha'i faith ... As this is the third time in about eight months that the question of Iranian refugees coming to New Zealand has been raised at ministerial level and there are clearly political reasons for New Zealand not wishing to proceed in this direction, I think this is a matter which should not be pursued further at this time.*[16]

From the mid-1980s there were various approaches from individuals, churches and groups, such as Islamic Associations and the UNHCR, for New Zealand to accept refugees from Afghanistan who had registered with UNHCR offices in India or Pakistan.[17] But New Zealand was also unwilling to accept more than a very small number of the three million Afghan refugees who had sought asylum in Pakistan.[18] This was partly due to the government perception that there was lack of adequate support within New Zealand, despite the representations from churches and other organisations.[19] More important, it was considered that the refugees, who were 'devout' Muslims from rural and often nomadic backgrounds, would have difficulty fitting into New Zealand:

men and women largely live separately, with men and boys eating separately and first, and women and girls receiving leftovers; and with very low literacy rates by world standards, as low as one per cent for rural males and four per cent for urban males and almost nil for females.[20]

As the UNHCR was not considering 'resettlement in a developed country' or outside their region for Afghan refugees, the government was under comparatively little pressure to accept these people, or to change its position that the bulk of the places on the quota would remain for Indo-Chinese refugees.[21] However, a small number of refugees from Afghanistan who had connections with New Zealand and a sponsor were approved for entry on humanitarian grounds.[22]

Refugees from the Middle East arrived in significant numbers during the 1990s and in early 2000. By 2006, there were 6024 people born in Iraq and 2793 born in Iran resident in New Zealand.[23] In the 2006 census 17,514 people identified as Middle Eastern.[24] Not all the arrivals had come as refugees under the quota.

A growing number of small and diverse communities

The new emphasis of the 1987 Immigration Act, and the setting of an annual refugee quota, helped to accelerate the process of ethnic diversification that had began in the 1970s. Between 1992 and 1995, New Zealand offered 50 places to refugees from the conflict in former Yugoslavia.[25] In 1998–99 the government agreed to accept up to 600 refugees from Kosovo, though this was in addition to the annual quota.[26]

More refugees from Africa began to come to New Zealand from the 1990s. Since the first Somali arrived early in the decade, small groups of African refugees have been accepted from a range of countries, including Ethiopia, Rwanda and Somalia. They were escaping war, famine and economic collapse, which displaced millions of people.[27] In the year ended 30 June 1999, for example, New Zealand accepted 212 Somalis, 199 Ethiopians, 130 Iraqis, 47 Eritreans, 41 Afghanis, 39 Iranians, and 33 Sudanese. Smaller numbers of Congolese, Rwandans, Djboutis, Chinese and Indonesians made up the quota.[28]

In 2001, the quota comprised significant numbers of Ethiopian, Somali, Afghan, Iranian and Iraqi refugees. (Some of the Afghan arrivals were the refugees from the *Tampa*.)[29] In 2006, 1857 Somali refugees were living in New Zealand. Some had arrived as refugees, others under the 'family reunification' category. There were also 1509 Kenyans resident in 2006, 1314 Zambians and 4593 refugees from various places in sub-Saharan Africa.³⁰ Not all of the African arrivals had come as refugees.

By 2001 the RMS believed that these small, diverse communities, lacking spiritual and social support, were unsustainable. In the view of Director Peter Cotton, the 'tiny, very isolated groups' lacked the 'critical mass' to form 'viable communities or even provide adequate mutual support'. Their members were 'further isolated by a lack of potential marriage partners, lack of family or community support and seemingly impenetrable bureaucracy or policy related to family reunion matters'. The growing number of such communities was a consequence of the extension of the UNHCR's Instrument of Protection principle to New Zealand. As a result of the UNHCR's referral of an increasing number of individual protection cases 'from a broader and broader range of countries', the number of different ethnic groups in the annual refugee quota rose from seven in 1992 to over 20 in 1999.³¹ Between 1976 and 1992 the refugee programme in New Zealand had focused on a small number of nationalities – principally Cambodian, Vietnamese, Lao and Iraqi – which had made RMS planning of support services comparatively straightforward. Cross-cultural workers, for example, could be hired on long-term contracts, and reunion of extended family members was an integral part of the refugee programme, fostering support networks and the growth of viable ethnic communities.³² But from the 1990s, the proliferation of diverse and small refugee communities placed the settlement services under great pressure.

There was official concern, too, about this problem. The Immigration Service had begun to acknowledge the importance of 'critical mass' when considering the arrival of new groups, and that awareness was reflected in the composition of the quota.³³ An increase in the number of the Sudanese in Kenya from 150 to 250 was recommended for the 2003–04 quota 'on the grounds that the Sudanese have responded very well to resettlement', and because their community was still small.³⁴ In 2004–05 the focus was again on strengthening small communities. Five communities with fewer than 100 members – Burundi, Djibouti, Sudanese, Rwandan and Congolese – received a boost to their numbers under the 'Africa project'. The quota also reflected the commitment to family reunification for *Tampa* refugees and for those subsequently settled from the Asia–Pacific region.'³⁵

In 2007 the Immigration Service instigated a review of the resettlement process. The ability to settle would be considered but from the point of view of 'understanding better what New Zealand needed to do to help refugees settle well', explained Refugee Division Director Kevin Third. It was also 'a matter of maintaining a balance between New Zealand's interest and humanitarian needs'.[36] The review was timely, particularly because the existence of too many small communities required attention. 'New Zealand is a lonely country for immigrants,' a former Hungarian refugee had observed 50 years after her own arrival in New Zealand in 1956.[37] Although over 1000 refugees from Hungary were accepted for resettlement in New Zealand, that number, spread over the main centres, had been too small to form lasting and thriving ethnic communities. How intensely lonely this country must have been for members of New Zealand's newest and tiniest refugee communities.

A regional-based approach

The more 'regional based approach' to resettlement effort mentioned in the 2006–07 Immigration Service report in effect meant fewer refugees from Africa and more refugees from camps in India, Thailand and Malaysia. The UNHCR had initially been concerned at the new emphasis but was pleased to see a shift back towards UNHCR-mandated refugees and away from family reunification.[38]

This return to a regional focus had been signalled since 2002, with strategies designed to prevent countries like Indonesia from remaining 'staging platforms' for people-smugglers and 'to relieve the existing problem of the floating population of "refugees in transit" in the region'. The change of approach was expected to 'decrease the likelihood of future boat arrivals on our shores or in our territorial waters'.[39] In the government's view, the *Tampa* incident had highlighted the need for regional solutions and cooperation, especially with Indonesia. Taking even a symbolic number of refugees from camps in Indonesia or Nauru, with 'appropriate publicity', would help to reduce the demand for the services of people-smugglers.[40]

Whereas six black African refugees and immigrants were granted permanent residence in New Zealand in 1982, by 1998 the figure was around 770.[41] In 2000, two African countries were in the top six, in terms of population size, of the refugee communities settled in New Zealand, with Somalia in the top four. Somali refugee intakes, which peaked in 1999–2000, were still relatively high in 2000–01 and 2001–02 but dropped in 2002–03. That year the biggest groups resettled were 355 Iraqis, 72 Afghanis and 47 Iranians.[42]

Some in the community saw the cutback in numbers of African refugees as a reaction to settlement difficulties faced by Somali refugees, but Kevin Third denied this. The Department of Labour decided what groups of United

Nations-mandated refugees New Zealand would accept according to need for protection and the balance of communities already here. 'We have not said we are not taking any more Somalis,' Third said in relation to the composition of the 2006–07 quota. 'We assess our programme every year to see where support is most needed.'[43] He later noted that the country's policy remained open to accepting refugees from a range of areas prioritised by the UNHCR.[44]

Increased security concerns after 9/11 were reflected in immigration reports on the composition of the quota. The report on the 2004–05 quota included the comment: 'A mass arrival or significant change in country situation could make it necessary to defer or alter planned intakes.' The following year's report included the same proviso, and that for 2006–07 referred to the need to ensure that no cases posed a security risk or had 'character of concern to New Zealand'.[45]

In summary, refugee settlement under the quota between 1987 and 2007 fell into two main phases. The first was the 'mass settlement' phase of the late 1980s, when predominantly Indo-Chinese and Iraqi (Assyrian) refugees were resettled, with only a trickle from Africa. This phase ended in the early 1990s, with quota refugees henceforth selected mainly on the basis of individual protection needs as identified by UNHCR. The latter phase led to the proliferation of small and diverse ethnic communities, many of them Black African.[46] After 2002 there was a return to regional focus, with New Zealand moving away from resettling refugees from Africa and prioritising refugees in 'protracted situations'.[47]

First black African arrivals

Please don't ask me
'Why don't you go back?'
Where there is war, where there is conflict
Where I am afraid of persecution
Where there is no democracy
Where human rights are violated
I can't go back
Until then I am destined to suffer in exile
Until I go back, until my time comes
Until then I will stay.[48]

From 'If I could', Yilma Tafere Tasew

As New Zealand began to respond to the escalation of conflicts in Somalia in 1992–94, the Ethiopia–Eritrea War between 1991 and 1993 and the Rwandan genocide in 1994, how prepared was the community to embark on complex cultural encounters with more diverse groups of refugees? New Zealand was certainly more experienced in responding to cultural diversity than in earlier decades: by the late 1980s it had accepted sizable numbers of Indo-Chinese refugees, and other settlers from Asia had been entering in significant numbers.

Don McKinnon was Minister of Foreign Affairs and Trade when New Zealand began to accept increasing numbers of refugees from Africa.

> Not many New Zealanders had known African people first hand but it should not have been impossible to bring (even) more Africans to New Zealand. There was enormous pressure between 1990 and 1995 to take more and be able to show a reasonable humanitarian side. We were seen as a very empty developed country which could be more generous to the needy.[49]

RMS Director Peter Cotton recalled that New Zealand's involvement with the resettlement of refugees from Somalia began with an approach from the UNHCR. The agency was finding it difficult to resettle Somali refugees in the early 1990s – a number of countries were reluctant to accept Somalis – but New Zealand 'had virtually no referrals for the 1992–93 quota'. When Bill Birch, who was Minister of Immigration, questioned the need for a refugee quota if it remained unfilled, Cotton wrote to the UNHCR, pointing out that as New Zealand had no referrals for the current quota and as Somalis were in need of resettlement, why didn't the agency refer Somalis for New Zealand's quota? 'The next morning a fax arrived ... suggesting New Zealand take 300 Somali cases.'[50]

'New Zealand is, of course, far removed from the awful human tragedy in Somalia but we are playing our part as an active international citizen to do what we can,' said McKinnon in August 1992, confirming New Zealand's commitment to assist Somali refugees.[51] As well as meeting a humanitarian need, he saw the increasing diversity as 'investment in New Zealand's future': 'Many Hungarian and Czech refugees from the 1960s were helpful in giving us an entrée into those markets in the 1990s. A wider pool of refugees would open doors in twenty to thirty years time to areas we had never considered and may possibly find essential.'[52]

Most of the Somali refugees, who were Muslim, settled in Auckland's western suburbs, but some were also based in Hamilton, Hastings, Wellington and Christchurch. Many were women bringing up children without their fathers, who had been killed in the fighting.[53] When agreement was reached about

Somali refugees coming under the quota in 1993, there was debate about their acceptance: 'New Zealand had reservations about their coming – about their being Muslim. There was anxiety about this. What if they are fundamentalists? What about female circumcision?'[54]

As the 2002–03 RMS annual report noted, there were challenges in resettling refugees from a wide range of ethnicities, 'sometimes adding to tiny fledgling communities'. There was also a shortage of suitable accommodation to meet the needs of the high proportion of single men in the quota.[55] The report noted that 257 refugees, including non-quota family reunion and humanitarian cases, were living in Auckland, 149 in Wellington, 91 in Hamilton, 89 in Christchurch and 58 in Napier.[56]

The RMS introduced a range of support services. A weekly quilting group for women of all nationalities provided 'friendship, good self esteem and creativity', with 'friendship, laughter and warmth displayed at each workshop'. There was a variety of practical programmes to assist settlement and integration such as road code and driving lessons, and courses on nutrition, family tenancy and community law. A number of young Somalis helped with homework and language programmes which are still running.[57]

Family reunion

The ability to bring close family members to New Zealand has had a major impact on the capacity of refugees to feel at home. As we saw in Chapter Two, Jewish refugees from Nazism encountered major obstacles in bringing close family members to New Zealand, but family reunion was encouraged in the 1970s and 1980s when this was an important aspect of New Zealand's response to Indo-Chinese refugees. During this time the reunion of both immediate and family members was very much the rule rather than the exception, but attitudes and policy changed in the 1990s with the move to resettlement on the basis of greatest need for protection.[58]

In the 1990s family members entered the country under the annual quota or under the 'family reunion' or 'humanitarian' immigration categories. Although it was still accepted that refugees needed their families in order to settle well, the government and the agencies assisting refugees shared the belief that family reunion had got 'out of hand'. The perception was in part caused by the settlement of Somali refugees, which had led to 'to an unprecedented demand' for family reunion. The first group of Somali refugees, placed in Christchurch, had entered under the 'women at risk' refugee immigration category. To fit this category, they were expected to be single and without male support, but they all seemed to have male family members they wished to bring to New Zealand.

Who was to be included in family reunion? New Zealand's acceptance of 'new cultural groups' had 'sharpened the focus' on the definition of the family, 'which encompassed far more than the shrinking Western construct'. But where was the line to be drawn?[59]

In Cotton's view, differences in definition of family caused distress among refugees in New Zealand, who sought reunification with married siblings and their families, elderly parents and previously undeclared spouses, or intended spouses in culturally acceptable arranged or proxy marriages. Most were people who would not normally be included in the annual quota and did not meet the requirements of the regular New Zealand migration programme. These cultural differences also led to problems for the government: 'Once the definition of family is extended beyond the standard Western concept of the "nuclear" family, reunification requests can quickly spiral upwards, soon becoming potentially uncontainable.'[60]

Further complications arose from the variable economic and social capacity of those already in New Zealand to act as sponsors for refugee reunion. This had led to refugees believing that the government favoured some clans or ethnic groups over others when deciding who would be allowed to bring their families to New Zealand. They felt anger, frustration and disillusionment and could not 'accept that seemingly identical cases receive opposite outcomes'.[61]

In 1996, the government removed the family reunion category from the refugee quota programme, suggesting that refugees who legitimately wanted to bring relatives to New Zealand could apply through the provisions of the migration programme. This, however, was not designed with refugees in mind. In Cotton's words, 'Many refugees simply could not meet the costs and documentary requirements.' As a result they suffered from 'isolation, frustration, depression, guilt, anger and resentment', impeding 'the process of successful integration'.[62] The RMS therefore supported the use of the humanitarian category to reunite families, but the Immigration Service held that there were limits to New Zealand's capacity to respond to the family reunion needs of refugees, whatever migration category was used.[63]

When the controversial family reunion policies were reviewed in 2001, the Immigration Service ended the humanitarian category and replaced it with the refugee family quota. A ballot was introduced to control demand. The government felt something had to be done because skilled migration was getting 'swamped' by the many family members of refugees entering the country under the humanitarian stream. They were 'high need and went straight on benefits', which caused public 'disquiet'. A balance was needed.

From 2002, the RMS advocated for including in the quota a significant number of family-linked cases based on a broader definition of family adopted by the UNHCR. According to this, such cases included 'All members of a family group who are living as a family and who demonstrate a long term emotional, physical or financial dependence upon the family unit'.[64] The RMS had the support of the Refugee Council president, Dr Rasalingam.[65]

In Cotton's view, 'progress on the immensely vexed and emotive challenges posed by family reunion will require understanding and compromise from all parties'.[66] Balance was the answer: 'New Zealand can't meet all the need for family reunion – the country doesn't have the capacity. We shouldn't raise the expectations of refugees that we can provide unlimited family reunion.'[67]

Family reunion remains a thorny issue, with demand outstripping places. A limited number of family-linked cases have continued to be included in the annual quota and some refugees have been able to sponsor family members to settle in New Zealand. From 2001 the Refugee Family Reunification Trust has helped some refugees with the financial costs of bringing their families here. The trust helps with the cost of application fees and medicals required by Immigration New Zealand and with airfares.[68] By 2007, the system of refugee family reunion ballot had been replaced by a 'managed queue'.[69] In 2012 Immigration New Zealand was again dealing with family reunion as part of the refugee quota. In 2011–12, 679 UNHCR-referred refugees and individuals were reunited with families in New Zealand.[70] Many refugees, however, remained without the family support so vital for good settlement outcomes.

'Integration takes time'

In New Zealand in early 2007 Abdinasir Ahmed was studying for a business degree to add to his teaching qualifications. Back in Somalia in 1991, he had got up one morning in Mogadishu to find 25 friends, relatives and family members massacred by the government in front of their doors. 'Horrified he ran in the direction he was facing and when he went back home he found no one there.' He walked 700 km in three weeks, suffering desperate hunger, to reach Kismayo, from where he fled by boat to Kenya. Eight years later, he was chosen to come to New Zealand, a place of safety and opportunity. 'Integration,' he said, 'takes time.'[71]

In May 2007 the front page of Wellington's daily newspaper reported on a Somali refugee who had 'stabbed a man repeatedly at a party' and had two years wiped off his eight-year jail term because he suffered from post-traumatic stress caused by the violence he saw as a child in his homeland. The judgement 'infuriated' the Sensible Sentencing Trust, which said the man was just using his past as an excuse for his violence.[72]

A disproportionate number of negative media reports about refugees seem to have involved Somalis. According to anecdotal evidence, Somali refugees, like Polish and some other East European refugees in the 1980s, had acquired a reputation for not mincing words and were sometimes seen as rude, standoffish and arrogant. In the view of Abdulah Drury, a Muslim historian, part of the problem was that a 'poorly planned influx of immigrants and refugees from Africa and the Middle East in the 1990s, many of them less well educated than the Muslims already here and from different cultures', had 'overwhelmed' the earlier arrivals. There had been problems with settling the later refugees. Somalis were exposed to more racial taunts and abuse and there were cultural differences that were 'harder to bridge'.[73] Some press coverage with headlines like 'refugee stalker proving a menace – charged with indecent assault',[74] have fuelled anxieties that too many refugees are law breakers and incapable of adapting to New Zealand values.

As McKinnon noted,

> there were successes, especially when [Somali] refugees had trade rather than professional qualifications. Generally they worked hard to get jobs and to settle their children in schools. However, one act of violence, rudeness, antagonistic behaviour that was picked up by the Press sent everyone into a tailspin about the cost of these people on benefits – 'our taxes'.[75]

Peter Cotton had decided that the first group of Somali refugees would be placed in Christchurch, where they were very visible in 1993: 'Visibility is a two edged sword. It is good advertisement if refugees are settling well – it fosters support for resettlement – if it is not going well, it can be quite damaging.'[76] As he wrote in a letter to the editor of the *NZ Listener*, in response to negative reports in the media about Somali refugees, 'they're just like you and me'.

> Some of us are doing better than others. The hardest thing for many refugees is finding, or being offered, that first opportunity. Reflecting on more than a decade of resettlement, it would be my assessment that most Somalis are continuing to settle and integrate very well into their new homeland. Those of us who have changed country know that developing a sense of belonging somewhere new is always dependent upon feeling welcome and accepted.[77]

The differences, however, may simply be related to time. The earlier arrivals have had longer to adjust to life in New Zealand, and New Zealand has had longer to adjust to the refugees.

A considerable number of the media reports have been about the plight of refugees who were unable to use their previous qualifications and find suitable jobs in New Zealand. 'It's degrading driving taxis part-time and going to WINZ [Work and Income New Zealand],' said Somali refugee Hassan Adam, who had been unable, for seven years, to find a job that matched his skills. An expert in Islamic law and, with a masters degree in linguistics, Adam retrained as an English teacher and eventually found paid work. Until he did, he felt 'useless and not worth anything'. According to estimates of Auckland Somali community leader Mahad Warsame, in 2007, 60 per cent of employable Somali refugees were not in full-time work. 'They drive taxis and have seasonal agricultural contracts.' A barrier to employment had been employers' attitudes: 'You are black, you are Muslim.'[78]

'Jobless and homeless Somali lives in car,' reported the *Dominion Post* in September 2006. The article said that the man's extreme plight mirrored the difficulties of other refugees in Christchurch and elsewhere, according to a September 2006 Massey University research report on discrimination faced by migrant and refugee job seekers, especially if they were thought to be Muslim. The 22-year-old came to New Zealand as a refugee from Somalia in 2004. His parents had been killed in the Civil War when he was seven and he was taken to Kenya by his uncle. He said it was hard to find work because his English was poor, though he had been helped by the Muslim Association of Canterbury and by other Somali refugees.[79]

According to Massey University researcher Greg Clydesdale, Maori have consistently shown the most dissatisfaction with recent immigration policy, because Pacific Island migrants and refugees with similar economic profiles competed with them for resources. Many Maori on waiting lists for state housing, which was in short supply, could feel justified in saying, 'Look after us first, before you bring anyone else in.'[80]

This was not a new problem. Immigration has 'never been far from the consciousness of Maori as they grappled with successive invasions of people from Australia, Europe, Asia and the Pacific Islands seeking access to their lands, fisheries, forests and rivers'.[81] Maori academic Ranginui Walker has repeatedly expressed concern about the lack of consultation with Maori over immigration policy,[82] and has criticised the multicultural ideology, prevalent from the late 1980s, which defined Maori as just another group of immigrants, negating their first nation status as people of the land. This approach neutralised Maori claims for justice by 'disempowering Maori by flooding the country with new immigrants from Asia and other countries'.[83] And in a memoir published in 2012 Maori leader and film maker Tama Te Kapua Poata felt that the government was 'deliberately flooding' the country with new immigrants who would 'water down the renaissance of Maoridom' because they had no 'knowledge of the Treaty of Waitangi or appropriate information in regard to tangata whenua'.[84]

By 2002 the resettlement and integration into the New Zealand community of refugees from sub-Saharan African was not going well, according to research by Dr Love Chile. His investigation uncovered 'an impoverished community that is increasingly excluded from mainstream society'. Many African refugees, having been 'imported' into New Zealand 'by the goodwill of the government and people of the country', were 'shelved' on the 'fringes of society'. This disqualified them from social participation and consigned them to the 'status of underclass'.

One reason for the refugees' social exclusion was, and is, lack of literacy skills. About 70 per cent of African refugees arrive in New Zealand with little or no formal education. On arrival they are given six months of English language tuition but the success rate of these programmes in providing basic literacy skills is 'poor'. Chile was critical of the government's inaction 'in addressing the lack of literacy skills amongst African refugees [which] may in fact constitute the denial of human and political rights in terms of the capacity for freedom of expression, political participation and equality of opportunity'.

The poverty and debt burden of the refugees was a factor in the creation of an underclass, as was their exclusion from social, economic and cultural activities. Access to employment was hindered because they looked, dressed and spoke differently. This was particularly so for women. Chile described the experience of a quota refugee who came to New Zealand in 1993. She was a Muslim, a nurse, but unable to practise her profession. In 1995, when she was offered a job in a rest home on a trial basis, the supervisor told her there were three things she was required to do: she had to stop praying five times a day, she had to mix more with the other people in the home and talk to them, and she had to wear the uniform even though it had a short dress forbidden by her religion. She could not comply and lost the job.[85]

In Chile's view, although many refugees arrived in the country with a range of skills and aspirations, the focus of settlement programmes tended to be more on their deficiencies rather than 'harnessing their potentials to enhance their settlement and contribution to the community'.[86] Furthermore, 'Past traumatic experiences tend to pre-dispose refugees to more violent reaction to verbal bullying and other forms of racism and discrimination than the average person. Racism and discrimination therefore have the potential not only to cast refugees on to the fringes of society but to cast them away from society all together.'[87]

A major research project, *Refugee Voices: A journey towards resettlement*, completed by the New Zealand Immigration Service in 2004, examined the experiences of three groups of refugees – those coming through the refugee quota, those who applied for asylum and were subsequently granted refugee status, and those with refugee backgrounds who entered New Zealand through family-sponsored immigration policies. The 398 refugees interviewed, who had been in New Zealand between six months and five years, were grateful for the opportunities they had found in New Zealand, especially the chance to live in a peaceful country, and were reasonably satisfied with their lives. But the research also showed that New Zealand needed to do more to help refugees 'play a meaningful part in our society'. English language proficiency, housing, adult education, discrimination and employment were some of the matters that needed to be addressed. The report also highlighted particular difficulties for certain groups.[88] The issues raised were intended to feed into the National Immigration Strategy, which is referred to further below.

The various 2004–06 findings of Massey University's New Settlers Programme also emphasised settlement problems and underresourcing of settlement services.[89] A social work survey in 2004 suggested that immigrants, refugees and asylum seekers of various origins, not just those from Africa, had been experiencing settlement difficulties of varying degrees and constituted a new client group for New Zealand social workers: 'members of this client group often face poignant situations in which social workers feel ill-equipped to intervene appropriately because they consider they have had little or no training to deal with the new issues and problems involved.'[90]

The problems faced by African refugees and other recent arrivals are not unique – all the refugee groups discussed in this book have struggled to become re-established and have faced discrimination. Adult refugees, irrespective of their origins, rarely become in the new country what they were in the old. When they arrive aged in their thirties or older, it is usually too late for them to learn English easily or to get a prestigious and well-paid job. In a sense, they have sacrificed their own lives and success for the next generation, who have been better placed to reap the benefits and opportunities available in the new country. In 2013 Eyob Zewdie, whose parents 'left Ethiopia in search of a better life' when he was five months old, gained top marks in the national scholarship exams.[91]

If resettlement is indeed a long-term project, what counts as settlement success for the first generation of refugees? Media reports have tended to be about the experiences of earlier arrivals making good after 15 or so years in New Zealand. The Lachs from Cambodia, for example, who arrived in 1987, were reported to have 'scooped' six awards at the prestigious Bakel's Supreme Pie Awards. In the RMS annual report for 2002–03 they were pictured smiling, surrounded by the prize-winning pies at their Elite Bakery. The report also lauded the success of an Assyrian refugee from Iraq who had probably also arrived in the 1980s and who had in 2002 become a Justice of the Peace.[92]

Several press reports focused on the successful adaptation of refugees by learning new skills. Under the headline 'Refugees get reward for tech success', the *Dominion Post* of 17 May 2007 described 16 Burmese refugee families who had arrived within the last six months under the quota and who had successfully completed a computer course. 'The course helped them understand Kiwi culture and to more fully integrate into New Zealand', their interpreter was reported as saying. 'It will also help us to maintain our links with extended family and culture back in Myanmar.'[93]

'Degree caps off hard work,' reported Wellington's *City Life* newspaper in 2007. 'Despite lack of schooling', a former refugee, Mohamud Mohamed from Somalia, had graduated from Massey University with a bachelor's degree in social work. Forced by the civil war in Somalia to leave school at the age of 10, he had spent nine years in Kenya before coming to New Zealand as a refugee in 1999. It had been difficult, he said, managing work, family responsibilities and study, 'But my family is proud.'[94] In November 2007, two Somali community workers, Adam Awad and Koos Ali, won Wellingtonian of the Year Awards in the community service category. The awards were for their contribution to the ChangeMakers Refugee Forum, which represented refugee-background communities in Wellington, and the Wellington health and well-being action plan.[95] A 2012 report told of a Burmese refugee family who arrived in New Zealand in 2006 and were able to buy their own home six years later.[96]

In a special ceremony in Manukau in April 2005, the first group of 75 *Tampa* refugees received their New Zealand citizenship certificates from Prime Minister Helen Clark. In the words of Azizullah Mussa, the youngest of the young men who had come to be known as the '*Tampa* boys', 'the Prime Minister's good deed in bringing the *Tampa* group to New Zealand would be repaid by all the young men who were determined to become good citizens to show their appreciation for the opportunities New Zealand had given them.' As he said, 'Many had taken the road before us and failed, but we are the lucky ones.' When he first arrived in New Zealand, he spoke no English. By the time of the citizenship ceremony, he was one of the top science students at Selwyn College and in June 2004 had helped to represent New Zealand at a global youth conference in the United States.[97]

Specialist services

One of the urgent tasks facing the RMS refugee coordinator in 1993 was the lack of services available to help the refugees arriving in the country. 'Mainstream services didn't know how to deal with Africans, Iraqi, people with torture and trauma backgrounds. Some refugees were ending up sitting in houses behind closed curtains. Refugees needed specialist services or mainstream services needed help to provide adequate services for refugees.'

> Refugees arrived and got lost in the system. There was no recognition of their language needs, their employment needs. There was just a bit of help when they first arrived – orientation. After that everything was left to their [RMS] sponsors, who were mainly the churches. They did a good job but a limited one. The sponsors found refugees houses, beds, heaters and fridges. These things are important but were not enough. Refugees were also supposed to access mainstream services, which worked OK for some groups with their own resources such as the Assyrians. But Somali and Ethiopian refugees needed specialist help which was not available.

And, as discussed in Chapter Six, the sponsorship system had serious drawbacks. 'Sponsors felt good about helping refugees. But from the refugee point of view, they felt in debt to the sponsors.'[98]

Resettling refugees in New Zealand has always depended to a considerable extent on the work of sponsors, or volunteer support workers as they have more recently been known, with little in the way of specialist services provided by the government. In 1997 there were around 500 RMS volunteer support workers (sponsors) helping newly arrived refugees to settle into their new community. They assisted refugees with finding and furnishing new homes and with 'orientation, communication skills, advocacy and friendship'.[99]

Volunteers have often gained as much out of this work as they have put in. Alan and Muriel Lipscombe, two of the 500 volunteer support workers coordinated by the RMS, began sponsoring refugees in 1977 and 20 years later had 'lost count' of the number of refugees they had sponsored over the years. 'There have been so many, and then they've all had children – they call us Grandmum and Grandad,' said Muriel. Sponsoring started with helping the refugees 'towards independence' but the relationship changed to one of 'mutuality and friendship'. Muriel would 'gladly do it again. Helping refugees is very rewarding work, it has helped Alan and I grow as people.'[100]

RMS sponsors and volunteers were 'great people with big hearts', in the words of the former RMS Refugee Coordinator, but wanting to help and having a good heart were not enough. Until 1997 many of the sponsors were church volunteers who had received little or no training.[101] In 2002–03, when 347 new volunteers completed training with the RMS, they received New Zealand Qualification Authority (NZQA) certificates in Refugee Settlement Support. They had to complete 15 hours of training in refugee advocacy and practical resettlement support, followed by a six-month fieldwork placement helping the initial settlement of a refugee family.[102]

In the 1980s and early 1990s, the government faced considerable criticism from the community and some non-government organisations about non-existent, or poor, refugee services. The government was accused of bringing refugees to New Zealand and then doing nothing to help them settle successfully. Specialist services were needed; mainstream services did not have the capacity or capability to help refugees. Efforts made to improve the situation, such as setting up an inter-departmental working party in the late 1980s, had come to nothing (see Chapter Six).

From the mid-1990s, however, the RMS gradually obtained more resources to help refugees settle. The agency was able to increase the number of paid workers rather than leave the resettlement work almost entirely to untrained volunteers, as had happened in the past. In 1993, the RMS had two part-time refugee coordinators. By 1997, seven full-time staff were working on refugee resettlement.

The improvements were in part a response to Somali refugees who were 'outspoken about their need', and in part a result of the recognition that the African refugees were survivors of rape, torture and trauma who needed specialist help. Also the churches, dealing with growing poverty in New Zealand, had fewer resources available to assist refugees. As a consequence, the government gradually started to support some of the services refugees needed. One of the earliest improvements was the provision of more resources to help refugee children at school. Some, who had spent many years in camps, had had no formal education; schools had been struggling to cope without specialist help.[103]

These improvements gained momentum while Lianne Dalziel was Minister of Immigration from 1999 to 2004, and there were further improvements with the 2004 launch of Labour's New Zealand Settlement Strategy, with a $62 million budget.¹⁰⁴ This was a far cry from the old 'sink or swim' approach to refugee settlement. As then Minister of Immigration David Cunliffe said in May 2007:

> *Gone are the days when we accepted refugees into New Zealand but gave them little help once they had completed the basic induction into the Kiwi way of life at the Mangere centre. We recognise that many refugees and their families have high needs when they arrive here and may take more time to settle than other migrants.*¹⁰⁵

The $62 million went to support the work of agencies such as the RMS, which was able to expand its services. The funding also contributed to improvements in English language services, in refugee qualification assessment, specialist health and mental health services, employment programmes, community capacity building and advocacy.

When interviewed in 2007, Dr Rasalingam, chair of the Auckland Refugee Council and president of the Refugee Council of New Zealand since 2002, noted a great deal of improvement in post-arrival services in the last decade.¹⁰⁶ There was now a good range of mental health services, assessment centres, resource centres, language services and workshops and other services for refugee job seekers – to name just a few.¹⁰⁷ A Refugee Mobile Community Clinical Team, consisting of a multi-disciplinary group of specialist professionals including psychiatrists, psychologists, social workers, nurses and six Refugee Community Link Workers who represented the Afghan, Burmese, Kurdish, Somali and Sudanese communities, was launched in November 2007. The team's objective was to 'deliver confidential clinical mental health support for traumatised refugees living in the community as well as build capacity with mainstream health providers to increase specialist skills in becoming more accessible to refugees'.¹⁰⁸ Another service launched in August 2007 was Refugee Lifeline, which gave former refugees extensive training and supervision in telephone counselling so that refugees leaving the Mangere Refugee Reception Centre after their orientation would have a toll-free number to call for help from anywhere in the country.¹⁰⁹ There had also been improvements in communication between non-government organisations and the government. There were now regular meetings between the Refugee Council and the government and this accessibility 'helped'.¹¹⁰

But many refugee advocates considered that further improvements were needed. There were, for example, gaps or inadequate services in the areas of youth and employment.¹¹¹ Adult unemployment also remained a problem. Dr Rasalingam had a number of concerns about health services, particularly for the 12-13 per cent of refugees coming to New Zealand between 1997 and 2007 who had suffered torture and trauma. Some had post-traumatic stress disorder. In Dr Rasalingam's view, improvements were also needed in health care after refugees left the Mangere Refugee Reception Centre.[112]

Since the late 1990s, refugee resettlement had been professionalised, but by 2007 Aussie Malcolm felt there was no longer any real partnership with the community: unlike the welcoming attitude of earlier years, the current New Zealand community 'couldn't care less'. Torture and trauma victims were supposed to be helped by their own ethnic communities who were themselves struggling. As a result, refugees had decreasing contact with the wider society, and 'some ghettoisation [was] happening'.[113]

Like Malcolm, Keith Taylor, the first Director of the ICCI, thought that the New Zealand model of community sponsorship and partnership between the community and government – the system he had worked with in the 1970s and 1980s – had 'fallen away' by 2007, with regrettable consequences for some of the refugees.[114] Peter Cotton from the RMS, however, stressed that the main focus of RMS was on 'creating an interaction between the host community and refugees'.

> What is important is not the resettlement process so much as refugees feeling they belong, being helped to belong in the new country. RMS does this through enlisting community volunteers. We do this the best in the world. New Zealand does it better than Australia which is far ahead of us in terms of government funded services – interpreting, health, education and so on. Refugee belonging is fostered in New Zealand by voluntary helpers available to help a sick child get to hospital – not by a government social worker available at the office 9 to 5.[115]

During his visit in February 2009, United Nations High Commissioner for Refugees Antonio Guterres remarked on the excellent settlement services provided by New Zealand and the warm welcome its people extended to refugees.[116] Volunteers have continued to play a key role in refugee resettlement, as Brian Lynch, Chair of Refugee Services Aotearoa New Zealand, noted in December 2011. Volunteers did vital work that 'would cost many millions of dollars if the volunteers were paid'.[117]

There have since been further changes. On 10 December 2012 Refugee Services Aotearoa became part of New Zealand Red Cross, in order 'to improve the support provided to newly arrived refugees and deliver greater efficiency'. New Zealand Red Cross became the lead agency responsible for the settlement of quota refugees and Stephen Dunstan, General Manager of Immigration New Zealand, was sure that it would 'continue Refugee Services' strong community-based approach, connecting new refugees with supportive Kiwis in local communities'.[118] In July 2013 a new refugee settlement strategy came into force, with the aim of integrating refugees and allowing them to participate fully in society as soon as possible.[119]

At the time of writing, the refugee programme is in good shape. A three-year refugee quota, intended 'to assist with long-term planning and to provide more certainty for agencies resettling refugees',[120] takes six intakes a year, each of about 125 people. The various refugee branches of government within the Refugee Division of Immigration New Zealand are the Refugee Quota Branch, the Refugee Status Branch and the Immigration Risk Research Bureau. The refugee resettlement programme in 2012 was focusing on refugees in the Asia-Pacific region.[121]

Prejudice

New Zealand's small Muslim community, which had first been boosted by the arrival of Fijian Indians to work in New Zealand in the 1970s, was replenished by Fijian Indian Muslims who came as a consequence of the 1987 coups. From 1991 to 2001, the number of New Zealand residents who identified as Muslims rose from 6096 to 23,631.[122] A growing number of refugees from Africa and the Middle East after the mid-1990s meant that 36,072 people identified as Muslim in the 2006 census.[123]

There was debate about the first group of 50 Shiite Muslim refugees from Saudi Arabia who were accepted in the mid-1990s after the Gulf War. The RMS had expressed concerns to the government about the prospective arrivals on the grounds that New Zealand lacked an 'existing community of Shiite Muslims and a Mosque', but the refugees came after the United States exerted pressure on the UNHCR to find resettlement countries for the refugees.

Several non-government organisations disagreed with the RMS position, but Cotton explained that the RMS concerns were not based on religious bias: 'It is simply that some faiths will fit in better – the people will be easier to resettle. It is harder if there aren't already mosques here.' As he pointed out, 'If the challenges of resettlement are too huge – for example too many of the refugees lack literacy, or the cultural differences are too large – the community won't cope.'[124]

Refugee children can experience an often cruel lack of understanding from their peers at school and in the playground,[125] but for adults a major challenge has been job discrimination and, even worse, violence. The matter has come up in parliament on several occasions over the years. In March 1997, for example,

National MP Pansy Wong asked the Minister of Police what measures had been taken by the Christchurch police to counteract the repeated violent racist attacks on a migrant family from Somalia.[126]

Discrimination worsened after the terrorist attacks of September 2001, according to Javed Khan, president of the New Zealand Federation of Islamic Associations, speaking in 2006. When he first arrived in New Zealand in the 1980s no one cared whether he was a Muslim or not: 'The problems started after 9/11. That was the turning point. Now there is a lot of prejudice against Muslims in terms of getting employment, being accepted by the community.'[127]

A community forum held in Upper Hutt in July 2007 for groups working with refugees and migrants (including a number of refugee families from the Sudan) singled out 'community safety' as a concern and racism as 'a significant safety issue'. Racism was evident in schools and among young people, and in some housing areas. 'Current state housing in Upper Hutt was seen as an inappropriate place for some refugee families with a traumatic recent history and was unsafe for them.' After an incident in Upper Hutt in 2001, when refugees had been harassed by gangs, local kaumatua (Maori elders) had invited the Sudanese community 'for an afternoon of dialogue'. Women and children, however, had continued to experience harassment and abuse, so further action was needed. Apart from community safety, the needs of teenage refugees, barriers to employment and access to services – especially appropriate housing (state houses were often too small for large refugee families) and health care – were identified as the main issues affecting the Sudanese community and other refugees in Upper Hutt.[128]

A *New Zealand Listener* editorial in early 2007 on the theme of religious diversity contained veiled references to the cultural practices of unassimilable immigrants, practices that New Zealanders had good reason to fear. The editorial voiced disquiet that our way of life might be under threat from immigrants settling here. The sentiments expressed echoed the fear of 'alien enclaves', 'who are not at one with ourselves', that was aroused by the refugees of the 1930s, 1940s and 1950s. New Zealanders prided themselves on being welcoming and tolerant,

> but just as we bask in perceptions of our society as a clean, green environmental showpiece, the reality is sometimes only skin deep. Poor immigrants do not usually move into the same neighbourhoods as most of our community leaders and decision makers. Those who talk about tolerance are often those who don't have to practise it.

New Zealand to date had been 'mercifully free of the appalling consequences of religious intolerance and racism', but it should not be assumed *that our relative smallness and isolation insulate us against the possibility of harbouring minority groups who decline integration and who do not share what most New Zealanders would see as being essential values, such as free speech, equal rights and respect for democracy. Our distance may give us a degree of protection but it is far from failsafe ... New Zealand [will], inevitably, have to take a stand in defence of the principles and values it cherishes. We all want a society that is tolerant and inclusive, but when that comes up against a section of society that is itself intolerant, what should we do?*

The editorial concluded that New Zealanders should be talking about these issues 'without fear of being accused of racism for daring to suggest, for example, that certain cultural practices might not be welcome here'. They needed to be 'unafraid also to talk about immigration ... before the types of problems that have arisen overseas also occur here'.[129]

The two practices causing most disquiet in recent years have been female circumcision and the wearing of the burqa. In 2004 there was furore over whether a woman giving evidence in the Auckland District Court should be allowed to wear a burqa that covered her face. Concerns were also expressed about women drivers wearing a burqa.[130] In 2006 National MP Bob Clarkson said that 'Islam religion type people' who wore a burqa could be crooks hiding guns and that Muslim women should not wear the full-body veils if they wanted 'to fit into our country'. He was, he maintained, tolerant of all religions but Muslims wearing a burqa should 'go back to Islam or Iraq'. His comments came after reports that two women had been ordered to remove their veils in court.[131] In 2012 the hijab, or Muslim head scarf, was a common sight in Wellington schools. At Wellington East Girls' College, where there were more than 30 Muslim students, several of the girls said they found the school environment very welcoming. 'We are lucky to be in this school because of the way people treat us. We are treated like we are at home.'[132]

'I don't want people coming to New Zealand who repudiate our key values,' then leader of the National Party Don Brash said in 2006, identifying those values as religious and personal freedom and sexual equality. He was not interested in what people wore, provided they shared 'bedrock values'.[133] Who did he have in mind? Brash was reluctant to be explicit but was quoted in a 2006 *NZ Listener* article as saying, 'Some Muslims believe strongly in the establishment of an Islamic State and that's not consistent with bed-rock values.' Although that did not 'mean we exclude all Muslims', he felt that the ideal migrants were British, Australians and others 'who fit in very well in New Zealand'.[134]

Brash's comments were reminiscent of attitudes held before the 1970s and 1980s had ushered in greater acceptance of cultural diversity. In some ways attitudes to diversity had come full circle: from intolerance to relative acceptance, back to the disquiet that has characterised the period since 9/11. Officially the Labour government was outraged by Brash's stance, David Cunliffe telling the *NZ Listener* that it risked 'importing the stresses and tensions that many countries are finding between different religious and ethnic communities and we don't need that here'.[135] But, like Brash, Cunliffe would not name the countries from which New Zealand did not want migrants: 'We don't have a bar on any country ... [but] some countries have a higher risk profile in terms of the people they send here and the immigration profiling group within the Immigration Service ... assesses the risk of individual applicants from those countries.'

There were 23 countries on the list in September 2006 and some were Muslims, but Cunliffe could not name them for diplomatic and security reasons.[136] In February 2012, under the National-led government, the Refugee Quota Branch began collecting biometric information from quota refugees, with refugee family reunion cases finger printed at the border.[137]

Refugees with illness

New Zealand has been one of the very few countries in the world to accept refugees with HIV/Aids. Some of the around 1800 Zimbabweans who arrived in New Zealand between 2000 and 2003, fleeing government persecution,[138] were accepted initially without screening for HIV/Aids. They were subsequently required to undergo testing as part of obtaining permanent residency, and some were found to have the illness. In August 2007, the government announced that Zimbabweans could apply for permanent residency despite their HIV status and that they would not be rejected on health grounds.[139] In response to criticisms that the government had made an error 'that allowed up to 200 HIV-positive Africans into New Zealand', at a cost of $3 million a year in health care, then Minister of Immigration David Cunliffe argued that the focus had been on 'helping alleviate the humanitarian crisis in Zimbabwe'.[140] In 2007 up to 20 refugees with HIV/Aids could be accepted under the medical category of the refugee quota each year.[141]

Another concern raised from time to time in the media has been tuberculosis, with reports that most new cases of the illness were being brought to New Zealand by immigrants and refugees. Of the 344 TB cases reported in 2005, 225 were people born overseas.[142] According to research in 2006 by Dr Dilip Das at the University of Otago, 'immigrants from developing countries' accounted for most new cases of tuberculosis in New Zealand but there was 'no indication' that they were ' spreading the disease locally to any significant degree'. Das noted that the incidence rate of TB had been stable in New Zealand for the last two decades.[143]

In 2007 refugees accepted for resettlement by New Zealand were screened for TB offshore, but not declined if they had the disease. The testing was to ensure that people with active infection did not travel, putting others at risk. Health screening unrelated to HIV/Aids or TB was done after the refugees had arrived in New Zealand.[144] In 2012 the refugee quota continued to allow for the admission of refugees 'with disabilities or needing medical attention'.[145] The New Zealand government pays for the treatment, offshore, of refugees with TB, so they 'can travel when clear'.[146]

CONCLUSION
A fine record?

New Zealand's response to overseas refugees and asylum seekers has evolved as a result of varying global circumstances and the changing needs of those wishing to settle here. Has the actual record lived up to the perception that New Zealand has a long tradition of compassionate response to refugees? Although the humanitarian and compassionate impulse has not been absent, other considerations – economic, social and political – have been as important. In terms of numbers admitted the figures may seem small, but per capita, in comparison with other refugee resettlement countries, they have been relatively high. Furthermore, in accepting refugee families that included somebody with a disability in 1959, New Zealand has led the way in the adoption of a policy in which predominantly humanitarian considerations have outweighed utilitarian and pragmatic ones.

For some refugees, New Zealand has provided a haven at the time of their greatest need. Lisl Hilton arrived in Wellington from Czechoslovakia at the end of 1939. Her last memory of Europe under Nazi domination was the rudeness and arrogance of the immigration officials. When she arrived in New Zealand, she was greeted with a friendly 'How are you?' and 'Are you all right?' 'It was such a relief; it was as though a great burden like a stone, dropped from your heart.' Hilton felt like that about New Zealand for the rest of her life.[1] The good luck in reaching the safety of New Zealand has been a constant theme in refugees' recollections, regardless of their origins and their time of arrival. They have been relieved to find friendly police, helpful officials and a peaceful, pleasant country. The words 'This is a free country' are not a cliché or a point of debate for refugees, as they sometimes are for local New Zealanders. Refugees know, from their own experiences of oppressive and dictatorial regimes, the difference between a country that is free and one that is not.

Just as New Zealand cannot admit all who want to come, it cannot meet the needs of all those who do settle here. Some refugees have found adapting to New Zealand hard and unrewarding. A refugee from Chile who had not been able to adjust to an alien environment despite years of trying recalled in 1989: 'New Zealand is a good country, but it is natural for a refugee … to miss his or her home, and to be critical of what New Zealand lacks. It is not "ingratitude" if a refugee does not immediately recognise this country as paradise.'[2] Furthermore, New Zealand's record in providing services to help refugees settle has been mixed. Some refugees have felt marginalised and consider that they have been deprived of opportunities, partly because of a lack of specialist services to help them.

Once suspicious of cultural diversity, New Zealanders have come to appreciate its benefits in enlivening their society, but it cannot be assumed that this trend will continue. As the book has suggested, by early 2000 there were some signs of a withdrawal from the embrace of cultural diversity that marked the late 1980s and 1990s, with a return to the distrust of cultural differences somewhat reminiscent of attitudes of the early and mid-twentieth century.

What, if anything, has been special and unique about New Zealand's approach to refugees and asylum seekers? George Laking, reflecting on his years as senior diplomat, observed in relation to the country's foreign policy as a whole that New Zealand was eventually accepted on its 'own merits as a country having an individual viewpoint worth hearing because experience showed it was usually well informed, founded on common sense, and (with occasional lapses) reflected a not too inflated idea of our importance in the scheme of things'.[3] The comments are as applicable to refugee policy.

A key and distinctive aspect of New Zealand's refugee policy has been the role of sponsorship in settling refugees. Generally, friendly and helpful sponsors in the community have worked hard to make the newcomers feel at home. They have found houses and jobs, taken children to school and to the doctor and helped with the shopping and the numerous other adjustments to daily life in a new country. Problems have sometimes arisen in the relationship between sponsors and refugees, but the system has overall worked well to the benefit of both parties. The development of specialist services, to help torture and trauma victims, for example, has been a slow process, but the situation has improved despite occasional tension between doing more to help refugees from overseas and looking after the needy at home, particularly Maori and Pasifika.

Although the plight of indigenous people is not covered under United Nations refugee conventions, home-grown refugees are a significant aspect of the story of New Zealand and its refugees. Since 1985 efforts have been made through Waitangi Tribunal inquiries to address past injustices to Maori.

Why does New Zealand's response to refugees matter? After all, refugees comprise just a small proportion of the country's total migrant intake and refugee and asylum seeker policy is but one minor aspect of New Zealand's foreign relations and immigration policy. It matters in part because the acceptance of refugees is not a choice between narrow national self-interest and a broad internationalist outlook, but a balance between the two. Dealing with unplanned asylum seeker arrivals is an obligation that has sometimes been viewed as inconvenient, but it has also been 'a matter of morality' and a chance for New Zealand 'to stand up for human rights'.[4]

This history of New Zealand's policy regarding refugees and asylum seekers tells us that settling refugees requires effort and commitment over a long period yet is worthwhile both for the country and for refugees. It shows that New Zealanders – government and people – have wanted to help the victims of humanitarian emergencies for a complex variety of reasons: because they feel fortunate to live in a lucky country, or perhaps because they feel guilty about the past treatment of Maori. Governments have enjoyed the benefits of a worldwide reputation for independence, compassion and humanitarianism.

Although New Zealanders have had doubts in the past about the ability of some refugees to integrate, most refugees eventually became exemplary citizens. Jewish refugees from Nazi Europe struggled for acceptance in the 1930s and 1940s; and since 9/11, it has sometimes been uncomfortable being a Muslim refugee. Perhaps most importantly, history shows that resettlement is a complex and lengthy process. As Somali refugee Abdinasir Ahmed noted, 'Integration takes time.'

What of the future? Wars and violent upheavals will continue. By 2003 the number of people internally displaced by war and violence had grown to around four million. When I began this book in 2007, the emergency in Iraq was worsening, with refugees fleeing to Syria. In August 2013, when I was finishing *Refuge New Zealand*, almost 2 million people had fled from Syria.[5] Afghanistan continues to be one of the world's most dangerous places. In October 2012 the New Zealand government offered refuge to Afghan interpreters who had been working with the New Zealand Defence Force in Bamiyan.[6] In our region, human rights violations have continued, for example in Fiji and West Papua.

In the years ahead the inhabitants of small Pacific countries, such as Kiribati and Tuvalu, are particularly likely to want to migrate as they experience negative impacts of global warming on fragile atoll environments.[7] There is as yet no provision in international law for environmental refugees. According to ministerial briefing papers released to the *Dominion Post* under the Official Information Act in October 2007, the government was being advised not to treat environmental migrants as refugees.

There is every reason to suppose that New Zealanders who have responded to the needs of refugees in the past will want to help the victims of future emergencies start new lives – whether caused by war, persecution or climate change.

Notes

Introduction

1. Paul Spoonley and Richard Bedford, *Welcome to our World? Immigration and the Reshaping of New Zealand*, Dunmore Publishing, Auckland, 2012, p. 159. For major refugee groups resettled in New Zealand between 1944 and 2006 see Spoonley and Bedford, p.162, Table 6.1; for the period 1979–2009 see p. 164, Table 6.2; see also Statistics New Zealand, *NZYB*, Wellington, 2002, p. 116. For figures for arrivals since 2004, see Department of Labour, New Zealand Immigration Service (NZIS), 'Immigration Research Programme: Trends in residence approvals', www.immigration.govt.nz/migrant/General/Generalinformation/Research/GeneralResearch/TrendsStatisticsAndSummaries.htm. See also Department of Labour, Table RQ1 – Refugee Quota, April 1979 – June 2009: www.immigration.govt.nz
2. Spoonley and Bedford, *Welcome to our World?*, p. 155.
3. Jane Verbitsky, 'Refugee policy', in Raymond Miller, ed., *New Zealand Government and Politics*, 4th edn, Oxford University Press, Auckland, 2006, p. 652.
4. ANZ, ABKF, 947, W5182, Box 37, 22/1/27/24, Indo-Chinese Refugees, 1980, background paper for visit to Geneva by Secretary of Labour, June 1980, includes briefing paper from Ministry of Foreign Affairs to Minister of Foreign Affairs, filed 13 May 1980, p. 5.
5. Department of Internal Affairs, Office of Ethnic Affairs, *Ethnic Perspectives in Policy*, Wellington, 2002, pp. 37–38; Statistics New Zealand, *NZYB*, Wellington, 2000, p. 134.
6. The full definition of a refugee may be found in Article 1 of the 1951 United Nations Convention, as amended by the 1967 Protocol Relating to the Status of Refugees, New Zealand Treaty Series, 1961, No. 2; and 1973, No. 21.
7. Hannah Arendt, 'We refugees', *Menorah Journal*, Vol. 31, January 1943, p. 69.
8. Jenny Macintyre, 'Fresh start: Are Somali refugees getting a fair go in this country?', *NZ Listener*, 3 February 2007, p. 30.
9. Anton Binzegger, *New Zealand's Policy on Refugees*, New Zealand Institute of International Affairs, Wellington, 1980, pp. 5, 105.
10. Ibid., p. 10.
11. Stephen Castles, 'Towards a sociology of forced migration and social transformation', *Sociology*, Vol. 37, No. 1, 2003, pp. 13, 14.
12. Binzegger, *New Zealand's Policy on Refugees*, pp. 6–7, 8, 11, 19–21.
13. Ibid., p. 21.
14. Quoted in Binzegger, *New Zealand's Policy on Refugees*, p. 21.
15. Janet Frame, *Living in the Maniototo*, Women's Press, London, 1979, p. 148.
16. ANZ, ABHS, 950, W4627, Box 2574, 108/4/70, Part 1, Chinese refugees, Minister of Immigration Tom Shand to Alan Brash, General Secretary, National Council of Churches in New Zealand, 30 July 1962.

Chapter one: The first refugees

1. J.E. Gorst, *The Maori King*, Paul's Book Arcade, Hamilton and Auckland, 1959, 1st pub. Macmillan & Co., 1864, pp. 245, 247–48.
2. Ibid., pp. 246–47.
3. Robert Gordon Latham, *A Dictionary of the English Language*, Vol. 2, Part 2, Longmans, London, 1870, pp. 734–35.

4 *Appendix to the Journals of the House of Representatives (AJHR)* 1867, A-20, 'Papers relative to affairs at Tauranga', p. 41.
5 *AJHR*, 1910, I-3c, Native Affairs Committee, pp. 4–11.
6 For example, a report on 'Maori refugees' in 'The North', *Daily Southern Cross*, 30 November 1864, p. 7.
7 Waitangi Tribunal, *Orakei Report: Report of the Waitangi Tribunal on the Orakei claim*, Department of Justice, Wellington, 1987, p. 2.
8 Waitangi Tribunal, *Te Urewera, Pre-publication, Part 1*, Waitangi Tribunal Report, Wellington, 2009: www.waitangitribunal.govt.nz, pp. 395, 437, 448; Waitangi Tribunal, *Te Urewera, Part 2*, Waitangi Tribunal Report, Wellington, 2010, pp. 7, 21, 34, 61.
9 Waitangi Tribunal, *The Wairarapa ki Tararua Report*, Vol. 3, Legislation Direct, Wellington, 2010.
10 Waitangi Tribunal, *The Ngai Tahu Report 1991*, Waitangi Tribunal Report, Brooker and Friend, Wellington, 1991, 4.2.2; Waitangi Tribunal, *Orakei Report*, 11.4.2, 11.9.2.
11 *Guiding Principles on Internal Displacement*, developed by the United Nations between 1992 and 1998, Human Rights Education Association: www.hrea.org/erc/Library/hrdocs/refugees/guiding-principles.html
12 James Belich, *The New Zealand Wars and the Victorian Interpretation of Racial Conflict*, Penguin Books, Auckland, 1998, p. 303.
13 Belich, *The New Zealand Wars*, p. 306.
14 Michael King, *The Penguin History of New Zealand*, Penguin Books, Auckland, 2003, p. 222.
15 Mark Hickford, *Lords of the Land: Indigenous property rights and the jurisprudence of empire*, Oxford University Press, Oxford, 2011, p. 1, quoting Herman Merivale, Professor of Political Economy at Oxford from 1837 to 1842.
16 Waitangi Tribunal, *Turanga Tangata Turanga Whenua: The report on the Turanganui a Kiwa claims*, Vol. 1, Legislation Direct, 2004, pp. xvii–xviii.
17 See for example, Bronwyn Elsmore, *Like Them That Dream: The Maori and the Old Testament*, 1st pub. 1985, 3rd edn Reed, Auckland, 2011; Bronwyn Elsmore, *Mana from Heaven: A century of Maori prophets in New Zealand*, Reed, Auckland, 1999.
18 'Mr Firth's visit to the King Party', *Daily Southern Cross*, 8 June 1869, p. 4.
19 Witi Ihimaera, *The Parihaka Woman*, Vintage, Auckland, 2011, pp. 161–62.
20 Ibid., p. 196.
21 Belich, *The New Zealand Wars*, p. 310.
22 Waitangi Tribunal, *He Maunga Rongo: Report on Central North Island claims, Stage 1*, rev. edn, Vol. 1, Legislation Direct, Wellington, 2008, p. 108.
23 Ministry for Culture and Heritage, 'The musket wars': www.nzhistory.net.nz/war/new zealands-19th-century-wars/the-musket-wars; Vincent O'Malley, *The Meeting Place: Maori and Pakeha encounters, 1642–1840*, Auckland University Press, Auckland, 2012, p. 211.
24 Margaret McClure, 'Auckland region', Te Ara – the Encyclopedia of New Zealand: www.TeAra.govt.nz/en/auckland-region/6/1/1
25 Waitangi Tribunal, *The Wairarapa ki Tararua Report*, Vol. 1, Legislation Direct, Wellington, 2010, p. 10.
26 Michael King, *Moriori: A people rediscovered*, Viking, Auckland, 1989, p. 64.
27 *AJHR*, 1928, G-7, 'Confiscated native lands and other grievances: Royal Commission to inquire into confiscations of native lands and other grievances alleged by natives', pp. 7, 11, 32.
28 Waitangi Tribunal, *He Maunga Rongo*, pp. 254, 250.
29 See for example, 'Native meetings in the Thames district', *Nelson Examiner and New Zealand Chronicle*, 11 April 1867, p. 8, reporting from the *Auckland Herald* of 3 April 1867.

30 'Te Kooti – and the King native', *Daily Southern Cross*, 3 January 1870, p. 3.
31 King, *The Penguin History of New Zealand*, p. 217; Tamati Muturangi Reedy, 'Ngati Porou: Post-European conflicts and developments', Te Ara – the Encyclopedia of New Zealand: www.TeAra.govt.nz/en/ngati-porou/4
32 Waitangi Tribunal, *Turanga Tangata Turanga Whenua: The report on the Turanganui A Kiwa claims*, Vol. 1, Legislation Direct, Wellington, 2004, p. xvi.
33 Ibid., pp. xvii–xviii.
34 'Native intelligence', *Evening Post*, 2 May 1870, p. 2.
35 Tahu Potiki, 'Tame Iti's defiance deeply ingrained in Tuhoe history', *Press*, 15 June 2012, p. 17.
36 John Cousins, 'Ngati Ranginui days away from Treaty settlement', *Bay of Plenty Times*, 16 June 2012, p. 10.
37 King, *The Penguin History of New Zealand*, p. 220.
38 Buddy Mikaere, *Te Maiharoa and the Promised Land*, Reed, Auckland, 1988, pp. 117–18.
39 'New Zealand provinces: Wellington', *Wellington Independent* quoted in *Nelson Examiner and New Zealand Chronicle*, 29 August 1860, p. 3.
40 'The Taranaki relief fund', *Lyttelton Times*, 8 May 1861, p. 4.
41 'The Taranaki refugees in Nelson', *Colonist*, 16 August 1864, p. 2.
42 British Parliamentary Papers, Colonies: New Zealand, Enclosure 7, No. 67, Governor Sir G.F. Bowers to Commodore Lambert, p. 311; 'Fearful sensation at Auckland', *Wellington Independent*, 19 November 1868, p. 3.
43 'Latest telegrams', *Star*, 16 November 1868, p. 3; 'Latest from the north', *Wellington Independent*, 8 December 1868, p. 5.
44 Bryan Gilling, 'Raupatu: The punitive confiscation of Maori land in the 1860s', in Richard Boast and Richard Hill, eds, *Raupatu: The confiscation of Maori land*, Victoria University Press, Wellington, 2009, p. 24.
45 Waitangi Tribunal, *The Taranaki Report: Kaupapa Tuatahi*, GP Publications, Wellington, 1996, p. 13.
46 Waitangi Tribunal, 'Land Alienation, 1886–2006', *Tauranga Moana, 1886–2006: Report of the post-Raupatu claims*, Vol. 1, Legislation Direct, Wellington, 2010, for example, pp. 147, 150–01.
47 Waitangi Tribunal, *The Ngai Tahu Report 1991*; Belich, *The New Zealand Wars*, p. 305.
48 Waitangi Tribunal, *Orakei Report*, p. 21.
49 Waitangi Tribunal, *Muriwhenua Land Report*, GP Publications, Wellington, 1997, pp. 309–11.
50 Waitangi Tribunal, *The Ngai Tahu Report 1991*, pp. 125, 503.
51 Ibid., pp. xv, 42.
52 Waitangi Tribunal, *Manukau Report: Report of the Waitangi Tribunal on the Manukau Claim*, Department of Justice, Wellington, 1985, p. 19. Before 1947 the Maori Land Court was known as the Native Land Court.
53 Waitangi Tribunal, *Muriwhenua Land Report*, pp. 309–11, 357–58.
54 King, *The Penguin History of New Zealand*, pp. 244–45.
55 Victoria Robinson, 'Urewera Four case stumps a jury and the nation', *Dominion Post*, 21 March 2012, p. 6.
56 'Maori health, urgent problem', *Star*, 31 July 1936. The comments reported were by Rev. A.J. Seamer, former general superintendent of the Home Mission Department of the Methodist Church.
57 ANZ, ABHS, 950, W4627, Box 2574, 108/4/70, Part 1, Chinese refugees from Hong Kong, Minister of Immigration Tom Shand to Alan Brash, National Council of Churches, 30 July 1962.

Chapter two: Escaping from Europe and Asia

1. Ann Beaglehole, *A Small Price to Pay: Refugees from Hitler in New Zealand, 1936-1946*, Allen & Unwin, Wellington, 1988, p. 8.
2. Ibid., p. 23.
3. Quoted in Ann Beaglehole, 'A small price to pay: Refugees from Hitler in New Zealand 1936-1946', MA thesis, Victoria University of Wellington, Wellington, 1986, p. 149. Tapes and transcripts of Ann Beaglehole's interviews with refugees are in the Alexander Turnbull Library, Wellington.
4. Comptroller to Minister, 16 August 1937, F.A. Ponton, 'Immigration restriction in New Zealand: A study of policy, 1908-1939', University of New Zealand (Victoria) MA thesis, Wellington, 1946, p. 91, quoted in Beaglehole, *A Small Price to Pay*, p. 14.
5. New Zealand High Commissioner's Office, London, to Dr Siegfried Rothmann, 9 September 1938, quoted in Beaglehole, *A Small Price to Pay*, p. 15.
6. L.M. Goldman, *The History of the Jews in New Zealand*, Reed, Wellington, 1958, p. 229. See also Erik Olssen, *John A. Lee*, University of Otago Press, Dunedin, 1977, p. 209.
7. ANZ, IC 20/86, Part 1, 'Skilled labour and tradesmen', E.D. Good to New Zealand Trade and Tourist Commissioner, 3 March 1939, p.1, quoted in Beaglehole, *A Small Price to Pay*, pp. 15-16.
8. ANZ, Nash 1311/0616, Walter Nash to J. Thorn Esq, Religious Society of Friends, 26 April 1939, quoted in Beaglehole, *A Small Price to Pay*, p. 16.
9. ANZ, Nash 1311/0592/3, F.A. de la Mare, 'The refugee problem', p. 1, quoted in Beaglehole, *A Small Price to Pay*, p. 16.
10. ANZ, Nash 1311/0607, Walter Nash to Mrs J. Hall, 21 March 1939, quoted in Beaglehole, *A Small Price to Pay*, pp. 16-17.
11. ANZ, IC 20/86, Part 1, 'Skilled labour and tradesmen', O.H. Frankel, Christchurch Refugees' Emergency Committee, to Department of Scientific and Industrial Research, 14 March 1939, cited in Beaglehole, *A Small Price to Pay*, p. 17.
12. Beaglehole, *A Small Price to Pay*, pp. 27, 33.
13. Ibid., pp. 22, 131.
14. *Tomorrow*, 18 January 1939, p. 170, cited in Beaglehole, *A Small Price to Pay*, p. 17.
15. Ponton, 'Immigration restriction in New Zealand', p. 111; ANZ Nash 1311/0595, Walter Nash to William Gillies, Secretary International Department, Labour Party, London, 27 March 1939; R.A. Lochore, *From Europe to New Zealand: An account of our continental European settlers*, A.H. & A.W. Reed, with New Zealand Institute of International Affairs, Wellington, 1951, p. 69, summarised from Beaglehole, *A Small Price to Pay*, p. 17.
16. Beaglehole, *A Small Price to Pay*, pp. 18-19. For more information on the Christchurch Refugees Emergency Committee see Oliver Sutherland, *Paikea: The life of I.L.G. Sutherland*, Canterbury University Press, Christchurch, 2013, pp. 319-35.
17. *NZPD*, Vol. 255, 25 August 1939, pp. 585-86.
18. Beaglehole, *A Small Price to Pay*, p. 19.
19. *Dominion*, 11 July 1938, quoted in Beaglehole, *A Small Price to Pay*, p. 10.
20. *Tomorrow*, 18 January 1939, p. 170, quoted in Beaglehole, *A Small Price to Pay*, pp. 10-11. Abyssinia is now known as Ethiopia.
21. This is a summarised version of discussion in Beaglehole, *A Small Price to Pay*, pp. 8-10.
22. ANZ, PM 89/2/4, Part 2, deputation to Prime Minister, 28 August 1945, quoted in Beaglehole, *A Small Price to Pay*, p. 95.
23. *New Zealand Jewish Chronicle*, August 1945, p. 234, quoted in Beaglehole, *A Small Price to Pay*, p. 95.

24 Quoted in Beaglehole, *A Small Price to Pay*, p. 118.
25 Ibid.
26 Ibid.
27 Nancy M. Taylor, *The New Zealand People at War; the Home Front: Official history of New Zealand in the Second World War, 1939–1945*, Vol. 2, Government Printer, Wellington, 1986, pp. 1246–50.
28 James McNeish, *The Sixth Man: The extraordinary life of Paddy Costello*, Random House, Auckland, 2007, pp. 164–66; James McNeish, *Dance of the Peacocks: New Zealanders in exile in the time of Hitler and Mao Tse Tung*, Random House, Auckland, 2003, pp. 352–53.
29 *New Zealand Jewish Chronicle*, April–May 1945, p. 190.
30 *New Zealand Jewish Chronicle*, November 1945, p. 69.
31 ANZ, EA 108/4/4, Part 1, R.M. Campbell, Official Secretary, New Zealand High Commission, London, to Sir Herbert Emerson, Director, Intergovernmental Committee on Refugees, 25 January 1946, summarised from Beaglehole, *A Small Price to Pay*, pp. 119–20 and fn. 24, p. 163. Priority was also given to the dependants of servicemen who had returned to New Zealand for demobilisation.
32 ANZ, EA 108/4/4, Part 1, Sir Herbert Emerson, Director of Intergovernmental Committee on Refugees, to R.M. Campbell, Official Secretary, New Zealand High Commission, London, 14 January 1946, summarised from Beaglehole, *A Small Price to Pay*, p. 119.
33 ANZ, EA 108/4/4, Part 1, R.M. Campbell to Sir Herbert Emerson, 25 January 1946; ANZ, L1 22/1/27, Part 1, International Refugee Organization, Immigration general, from 1946, Statement by the New Zealand Delegation to the United Nations Special Committee on Refugees and Displaced Persons, 10 May 1946, summarised from Beaglehole, *A Small Price to Pay*, pp. 119–20. Also relevant to the subject of postwar immigration of relatives of refugees and of New Zealand Jews is ANZ, Nash Papers 1597/0918 and 1597/11. They refer to the period 1945–47 and are concerned with the need for a policy in order to respond to the many applications from refugees in Europe to join their relatives in New Zealand and the government's determination that servicemen must be rehabilitated before immigration could be resumed.
34 ANZ, EA 108/4/4, Part 1, R.M. Campbell to Sir Herbert Emerson, 25 January 1946, cited in Beaglehole, *A Small Price to Pay*, p. 119.
35 Goldman, *The History of the Jews in New Zealand*, p. 234. Goldman derived this figure from a report to the Interchurch Council of New Zealand by Mrs O.S. Heymann. Unfortunately no date is cited. A further 200 permits were issued some time later according to Goldman, p. 234.
36 *New Zealand Jewish Chronicle*, September–October 1945, p. 29.
37 Michael Blakeney, *Australia and the Jewish Refugees, 1933–1948*, Croom Helm, Sydney, 1985, pp. 291–93.
38 Ibid., pp. 305–08.
39 Harvey Cohen, Australian Jewish Historical Society, email, 1 August 2007. According to Michael Blakeney, the policy of allowing the entry of Holocaust survivors in the immediate postwar years aroused considerable anti-Semitism in Australia. Blakeney, *Australia and the Jewish Refugees, 1933–1948*, pp. 292–304.
40 The reasons for this trend are discussed in Department of Labour, 'Immigration', *Monthly Review of Employment*, March 1947, pp. 1–5.
41 Ibid., p. 1.
42 Jewish Communities of New Zealand, 'Memorandum to the Select Committee on Dominion Population', April 1946, quoted in Beaglehole, *A Small Price to Pay*, p. 120.
43 Ibid., pp. 120–21.

44   ANZ, Ll 22/1/27, Part 1, International Refugee Organisation, Immigration, general, from 1946, Report on data received from the Jewish communities of New Zealand regarding relatives who desire to come to this country, July 1946, enclosed with a memorandum for Acting Minister of Customs, from Permanent Head, Prime Minister's Department, 25 March 1947, quoted in Beaglehole, *A Small Price to Pay*, p. 164, fn. 39.
45   *New Zealand Jewish Chronicle*, April/May 1946, p. 157.
46   *AJHR*, Vol. 5, I-17, 1946, Report of the Select Committee on Dominion Population, p. 100.
47   Ibid., pp. 44, 99, 116, 117.
48   ANZ, LI 22/1/27, Part 1, International Refugee Organisation, Immigration, general, from 1946, Director of Employment to Acting Permanent Head, Prime Minister's Department, 25 October 1946, quoted in Beaglehole, *A Small Price to Pay*, pp. 121–22.
49   Lochore, *From Europe to New Zealand*, p. 72.
50   Ibid., p. 87.
51   Ibid., p. 88.
52   James Ng, *Windows on a Chinese Past: Larrikinism and violence: Immigration issues, 20th century assimilation: Biographies*, Vol. 3, Otago Heritage Books, Dunedin, 1993, p. 123.
53   Quoted in David Pearson, *A Dream Deferred: The origins of ethnic conflict in New Zealand*, Allen & Unwin, Wellington, 1990, p. 80.
54   Manying Ip, 'Redefining Chinese female migration: From exclusion to transnationalism', in Lyndon Fraser and Katie Pickles (eds), *Shifting Centres: Women and migration in New Zealand history*, Otago University Press, Dunedin, 2002, p. 157.
55   James Ng, *Windows on a Chinese Past: How the Cantonese goldseekers and their heirs settled in New Zealand*, Vol. 1, Otago Heritage Books, Dunedin, 1993, pp. 7–8.
56   Frank Tod, 'Terry Edward Lionel, 1873–1952, Racist, murderer', from the Dictionary of New Zealand Biography: www.TeAra.govt.nz/en/biographies/3t27/terry-edward-lionel
57   Ip, 'Redefining Chinese female migration', p. 156.
58   David McGill, *The Other New Zealanders*, Mallinson Rendel, Wellington, 1982, p. 119.
59   Ip, 'Redefining Chinese female migration', pp. 156–57.
60   Ng, *Windows on a Chinese Past: Larrikinism and violence*, p. 184.
61   Ip, 'Redefining Chinese female migration', p. 156.
62   Manying Ip, 'Chinese post-war changes', Te Ara – the Encyclopedia of New Zealand: www.TeAra.govt.nz/en/chinese/4
63   Manying Ip, *Dragons on the Long White Cloud: The making of Chinese New Zealanders*, Tandem Press, Auckland, 1996, p. 22.

Chapter three: Choosing the 'best' refugees

1   For a rough estimate of DP numbers and recent discussion on DPs, see Gerard Daniel Cohen, *In Europe's Wake: Europe's displaced persons in the post war order*, Oxford Studies in International History, Oxford, 2012.
2   ANZ, L1 22/1/27, Part 1, Statement by the New Zealand Delegation to the United Nations Special Committee on Refugees and Displaced Persons, 10 May 1946. The series L1 22/1/27, Parts 1–12, are concerned with displaced people from Europe and were consulted in 1986. Material based on the series is discussed in Ann Beaglehole, 'A small price to pay: Refugees from Hitler in New Zealand 1936–1946', MA thesis, Victoria University of Wellington, Wellington, 1986, p. 149.
3   ANZ, EA2, 1946/22b, or 108/4/1, Part 1b, Social Affairs, Refugees, 1943–46, Minister of External Affairs to New Zealand Minister, Washington, 10 June 1946.
4   ANZ, EA2, 1948/14B or 108/4/1, Part 3, External Affairs, Wellington to New Zealand

Delegation IRO, Geneva, 24 October 1947.
5   ANZ, L1 22/1/27, Part 2, Displaced persons from Europe, Acceptance of displaced persons, Report of a discussion between W.J.C. Davidge, the Director DP Centre, Senigallia and New Zealand Parliamentary Under-Secretary, H. Combs, 27 July 1948.
6   '9600 for N.Z., Immigration plan: Arrival over three years', *Evening Post*, 27 May 1947, p. 8.
7   ANZ, L1 22/1/27, Part 2, Displaced persons from Europe, Acceptance of displaced persons, notes of a deputation upon Walter Nash, Minister of Customs, Wellington, 21 June 1948. Representatives of the Presbyterian Church, Baptist Church, Church of Christ, Methodist Church, Congregational Church and Society of Friends attended.
8   ANZ, L1 22/1/27, Part 2, Displaced persons from Europe, Acceptance of displaced persons, telegram, Minister of External Affairs to High Commissioner for New Zealand, London, 24 September 1948. In addition to assistance sought by the IRO for displaced persons in Europe between 1947 and 1952, the IRO and the US Department of State urgently sought asylum for 13,000 refugees from Shanghai, considered to be in great danger in 1948. There were 13,000 refugees from Europe in China, of whom approximately 5000 were Jews and offered visas by Israel (after its foundation). The remainder were Polish or Baltic refugees and there were 8000 white Russians. New Zealand refused to accept refugees from Shanghai in 1949, citing security problems, though eventually in the 1950s a few came to New Zealand; ANZ, EA2/1956/10d, PM 108/4/77, External to IRO, 26 January 1949 and High Commissioner for New Zealand, Canberra to External Affairs, 16 February 1949.
9   ANZ, LI 22/1/27, Part 5, Displaced persons from Europe, Assistant Under-Secretary, Department of Internal Affairs to Director of Employment, Department of Labour and Employment, Immigration, 16 May 1950, p. 1, quoted in Beaglehole, 'A small price to pay', p. 125.
10 ANZ, L1 22/1/5, Post-war Immigration to New Zealand, 1941–56, Director of Employment to District Superintendent, Department of Labour and Employment, 15 October 1947, quoting a statement about Canadian policy and stating that New Zealand's views were the same as Canada's.
11 Department of Labour, 'Immigration facts and fallacies', *Labour and Employment Gazette*, Vol. I, No. 3, August 1954, p. 47.
12 ANZ, LI 22/1/27, Part 1, Displaced persons from Europe, International Refugee Organisation, Immigration, general, from 1946, Director of Employment to Minister of Employment, 23 December 1947, quoted in Beaglehole, 'A small price to pay', 1986, p. 125.
13 L.M. Goldman, *The History of the Jews in New Zealand*, Reed, Wellington, 1958, pp. 235–36.
14 ANZ, External Affairs, EA 108/4/1 Part 2, Foss Shanahan, Acting Permanent Head of Prime Minister's Department, to the Prime Minister, 20 September 1946.
15 ANZ, External Affairs, 108/4/1, Parts 3 and 4, or EA2, 1949, 15c and EA2, 1948, 14b. The UN had approved the establishment of an independent Jewish state in Palestine in November 1947 and the state of Israel was created in May 1948.
16 ANZ, LI 22/1/27, Part 1, International Refugee Organisation, Immigration, general, from 1946, Director of Employment to Minister of Immigration, 15 April 1948, summarised from Beaglehole, 'A small price to pay', p. 125.
17 ANZ, L1 22/1/27, Part 2, Displaced persons from Europe, Acceptance of displaced persons, Official Secretary, New Zealand High Commission, to Secretary of External Affairs, 17 December 1948.
18 ANZ, LI 22/1/27, Part 2, Displaced persons from Europe, Acceptance of displaced persons, Department of External Affairs to the Official Secretary, Office of the High Commissioner for New Zealand, 'Immigration: Acceptance of Displaced Persons', undated, quoted in Beaglehole, 'A small price to pay', 1986, p. 126.

19 ANZ, Department of Labour, L1 22/1/27, Part 3, Displaced persons from Europe, International Refugee Organisation, probably report of the selection team of the *Dunbalk Bay* draft, p. 2, c. April 1949.
20 This is concluded from correspondence and other documents in the International Refugee Organisation, ANZ, Department of Labour, LI 22/1/27, Part 1, Immigration, general, from 1946. For example, Director of Employment to Minister of Employment, 23 December 1947, regarding the types of displaced persons who should have priority of admission to New Zealand. Selection criteria is also discussed specifically in ANZ, Department of Labour, LI 22/1/27, Part 2, Acceptance of displaced persons, Minister of External Affairs to the Official Secretary, Office of the New Zealand High Commissioner, 'Immigration: Acceptance of Displaced Persons', undated.
21 *NZPD*, Vol. 292, 1 November 1950, p. 3906.
22 ANZ, CAB 66/1/1 Part 1, Immigration of Aliens, Minister of Immigration to Cabinet, 'Resettlement of displaced persons through International Refugee Organisation', 15 December 1950, p. 2.
23 ANZ, Department of Labour, LI 22/1/27, Part 3, Displaced persons from Europe, International Refugee Organisation, Report of the selection team of the *Dunbalk Bay* draft, c. April 1949, p. 6 and Part 4, Displaced persons from Europe, Report on *Dunbalk Bay* draft, Director of Employment to Minister of Immigration, 24 January 1950.
24 ANZ, LI 22/1/50, Resettlement of displaced medical personnel, T.R. Ritchie, Director General, Labour and Employment Department, to the Permanent Head, Prime Minister's Department, 'Resettlement of refugee medical practitioners, dentists and nurses', 27 April 1948, written in response to a request from Dr R. Coigny, Director of Health, IRO., 1 September 1947, discussed in Beaglehole, 'A small price to pay', 1986, pp. 124–25.
25 ANZ, Department of Labour and Employment, 'Immigration newsletter No. 5', 31 January 1950, p. 2.
26 ANZ, L1 22/1/27, Part 1, International Refugee Organisation, Director of Employment, to Acting Permanent Head, Prime Minister's Department, 25 October 1946, quoted in Beaglehole, 'A small price to pay', 1986, p. 123.
27 ANZ, L1, 22/1/27, Part 1, International Refugee Organisation, Immigration, general, from 1946, Director of Employment to Minister of Employment, 23 December 1947 and Department of Labour, *Monthly Review of Employment*, 'Immigration', March 1947, p. 5, summarised from Beaglehole, 'A small price to pay', 1986, p. 125.
28 Department of Labour, New Zealand Immigration Service, *Refugee Women: The New Zealand Refugee Quota Programme*, Wellington, 1994, p. 17.
29 ANZ, L1 22/1/27, Part 5, Displaced persons from Europe, Security considerations and further correspondence regarding acceptance of displaced persons, Assistant Under-Secretary Department of Internal Affairs to Director of Employment, Department of Labour and Employment, 'Immigration', 16 May 1950, p. 2.
30 ANZ, LI 22/1/27, Part 3, Displaced persons from Europe, International Refugee Organisation, Report of the selection team of the *Dunbalk Bay* draft, c. April 1949, p. 6, quoted in Beaglehole, 'A small price to pay', 1986, p. 125. The team comprised L.E. Ellison, W. Collings, and J.W. Bartrum (Medical Officer). The report was signed by Ellison.
31 ANZ, LI 22/1/27, Part 5, Displaced persons from Europe, Security considerations and further correspondence regarding acceptance of displaced persons, Assistant Under-Secretary, Department of Internal Affairs, to Director of Employment, Department of Labour and Employment, 'Immigration', 16 May 1950, p. 2. This memo was based on the conclusions of an interdepartmental meeting on immigration.

32 W.B. Sutch, *The Quest for Security in New Zealand, 1840-1966*, Oxford University Press, Wellington, 1966, p. 475.
33 ANZ, Department of Labour, L22/1/27, Part 8, Displaced persons from Europe, Immigration, general, International Refugee Organisation, Secretary for Internal Affairs to Director of Special Branch, Police Department, 4 December 1953.
34 Anthony Hubbard, 'Murderers among us?', *Listener & TV Times*, 21 May, 1990, p. 10.
35 Anthony Hubbard, 'Sanctuary: How we let in the war criminals', *Listener & TV Times*, 28 May 1990, pp. 24, 26, 28.
36 Danya Levy, 'The "Nazi Hunter" – Wayne Stringer, interviewed by Danya Levy', *Centre News*, December 2012/January 2013, p. 6.
37 ANZ, L1 22/1/27, Part 3, Displaced persons from Europe, International Refugee Organisation, Report of the selection team of the *Dunbalk Bay* draft, c. April 1949, p. 6, quoted in Beaglehole, 'A small price to pay', 1986, p. 126.
38 Michael Blakeney, *Australia and the Jewish refugees, 1933-1948*, Croom Helm, Sydney, 1985, pp. 304-06, regarding Australia's selection of displaced persons. The scramble for Balts is discussed in ANZ, L1 22/1/27, Part 1, Displaced persons from Europe, International Refugee Organisation, Immigration, general, from 1946, Acting Permanent Head, Prime Minister's Department to the Prime Minister, 'Resettlement of Refugees and Displaced Persons', 20 September 1946. The comment about competition with other British Commonwealth countries for the same kind of settler is drawn from Department of Labour, *Labour and Employment Gazette*, 'The Second Draft of Displaced Persons', Vol. 1, No. 1, 1951, p. 27. Canada's preference for Balts is discussed in I. Abella and H. Troper, *None is Too Many: Canada and the Jews of Europe 1933-1948*, Lester & Dennys, Toronto, 1982, p. 213, and in Beaglehole, 'A small price to pay', 1986, p. 126.
39 ANZ, L1 22/1/27, Part 1, International Refugee Organisation, Immigration, general, from 1946, Director of Employment to Minister of Immigration, 15 April 1948, 'Resettlement of International Refugees', quoted in Beaglehole, 'A Small Price to Pay', 1986, pp. 126-27.
40 ANZ, External Affairs, EA 103/8/4, Part 3 or EA2 1950/37c, discussion between Sir Arthur Rucker, IRO and Cabinet Committee on Immigration, 3 February 1950; telegram from External Affairs to IRO, 27 February 1950.
41 Quoted in Hubbard, 'Sanctuary', p. 28.
42 Department of Labour, *Labour and Employment Gazette*, Vol. 1, No. 1, 1951, p. 27; ANZ, L1 22/1/27, Part 2, Displaced persons from Europe, Acceptance of displaced persons, press statement by the Minister of Immigration, A. McLagan, undated, summarised from Beaglehole, 'A small price to pay', 1986, p. 127. The detailed breakdown of the nationalities of displaced persons selected for the first intake of 1949 – the *Dunbalk Bay* draft – was as follows: Balts, 503; Poles, 184; Ukranians, 70; Czechs, 53; Hungarians, 50; Nansen or stateless, 37; Yugoslavs, 36; Russians, 14; others, nine, ANZ, L1 22/1/27, Part 3, Displaced persons from Europe, Report of the selection team of the *Dunbalk Bay* draft, c. April 1949; ANZ, Department of Labour, L1 22/1/27, Part 2, Displaced persons from Europe, Acceptance of displaced persons, press statement by the Minister of Immigration A. McLagan, undated, cited in Beaglehole, 'A small price to pay', 1986, p. 127, fn. 67.
43 'Workers worried by intake of Europeans into industry', *Southland Daily News*, 23 July 1951.
44 Department of Statistics, *NZYB*, 1965, p. 75.
45 ANZ, Department of Labour, *Monthly Review of Employment*, Vol. 4, No. 8, June 1949, p. 4.
46 Ibid., p. 5.
47 Quoted in Brigitta Bönisch-Brednich, *Keeping a Low Profile: An oral history of German immigration to New Zealand*, Victoria University Press, Wellington, 2002, pp. 60–61.

48 Austin Mitchell, *The Half Gallon Quarter Acre Pavlova Paradise*, Whitcombe & Tombs, Christchurch, 1972.
49 Robert David Muldoon, *The Rise and Fall of a Young Turk*, A.H. & A.W. Reed, Wellington, 1974.
50 Department of Statistics, *NZYB*, Wellington, 1971, p. 62.
51 In 1962 there were 66,000 births. By 2001 this had dropped to 56,221. John Wilson, 'Society: Families and households', Te Ara – the Encyclopedia of New Zealand: www.TeAra.govt.nz/en/society/3
52 ANZ, Department of Labour, L1 22/1/189, Hungary, Refugees, R.M. Algie, Acting Minister of External Affairs to Cabinet, 19 November 1956.
53 Department of Statistics, *NZYB*, Wellington, 1965, p. 76.
54 Anton Binzegger, *New Zealand's Policy on Refugees*, New Zealand Institute of International Affairs, Wellington, 1980, p. 42.
55 ANZ, Department of Labour, L1 22/1/189, Box 153, Part 1, Hungary, Policy and General, 1956–57, contains PM 108/4/62, A.D. McIntosh, Secretary of External Affairs to Acting Minister of External Affairs, 8 November 1956.
56 Binzegger, *New Zealand's Policy on Refugees*, pp. 38–42; Ann Beaglehole, 'Hungarians: Immigration from 1956: refugees', Te Ara – the Encyclopedia of New Zealand: www.TeAra.govt.nz/en/hungarians/2
57 Misatauveve Melani Anae, 'Samoans: History and migration', Te Ara – the Encyclopedia of New Zealand: www.TeAra.govt.nz/en/samoans/1
58 ANZ, Department of Labour, L1 22/1/189, Hungary, Refugees, Secretary of External Affairs to Minister of Immigration, 19 November 1956.
59 ANZ, Department of Labour, L1 22/1/189, cable from Minister of External Affairs to High Commissioner, London, undated.
60 'Refugees from Hungary', *Labour and Employment Gazette*, Vol. 7, No. 2, May 1957, p. 15.
61 Statement by the Minister of Immigration, J.R. Hanan, 22 November 1956, Department of External Affairs, *External Affairs Review*, Vol. 6, No. 11, November 1956, p. 8.
62 ANZ, Department of Labour, L1 22/1/189, Report to the Secretary of Labour by the selection officer on the processing of Hungarian refugees, 16–23 December 1956.
63 Ibid., 21–29 November 1956.
64 Ibid., 16–23 December 1956.
65 ANZ, Department of Labour, L1 22/1/189, Report of the Hungarian Welfare Officer, 14 April 1958, p. 5.
66 ANZ, Department of Labour, L1 22/1/189, Report to the Secretary of Labour by the selection officer on the processing of Hungarian refugees, 21–29 November 1956.
67 Binzegger, *New Zealand's Policy on Refugees*, p. 39.
68 'The 50th anniversary of the Hungarian uprising', UNHCR, *Refugees*, No. 144, Issue 3, 2006, p. 2.
69 'A matter of the heart: How the Hungarian crisis changed the world of refugees', UNHCR, *Refugees*, No. 144, Issue 3, 2006, pp. 7–9.
70 'Refugees from Hungary', Department of Labour, *Labour and Employment Gazette*, May 1957, Vol. 7, No. 2, p. 15.
71 Rev. Ian W. Fraser, *Elderly Refugees in New Zealand: The story of Nansen Home, Lower Hutt*, Nansen Home, Lower Hutt, 1985, p. 4.
72 'Refugees from Hungary', Department of Labour, *Labour and Employment Gazette*, Vol. 7, No. 2, May 1957, p. 15.
73 Fraser, *Elderly Refugees in New Zealand*, p. 4.

74 Patricia Morrison, 'How the welfare state receives new citizens from Europe', *The NZ Social Worker*, Vol. 2, No. 3, August 1966, p. 35.
75 'Junior help for Hungary', *New Zealand Red Cross Magazine*, Vol. 5, No. 2, January 1957, p. 57; New Zealand Red Cross Society Inc., 'Annual report and financial statement', 1956–1957, p. 9.
76 ANZ, Department of Labour, L1 22/1/189, 'Immigration Policy, general – Hungary', Report to the Minister of Immigration, 29 November 1956; ANZ, Department of Labour, L1 22/1/189, 'Number of Hungarians by district, 1957 and 1958'; see also 'Magyar Millennium Park', brochure produced to coincide with opening of the park, 20 August 2003, available from the Honorary Consul of Hungary.
77 Morrison, 'How the welfare state receives new citizens', p. 35.
78 ANZ, Department of Labour, L1 22/1/189/2, 'Hungarian refugees, accommodation and jobs', October 1956; ANZ, Department of Labour, L1 22/1/189, Report of the Hungarian Welfare Officer' 14 April 1958, pp. 3–4; 'Hungarian Refugees', Report of the Department of Internal Affairs for the year ended 31 March 1957, pp. 31–32.
79 'Hungarian Refugees', Report of the Department of Internal Affairs for the year ended 31 March 1957, pp. 31–32; ANZ, Department of Labour, L22/1/189, Report of the Hungarian Welfare Officer, 14 April 1958, p. 3. The relatively large number of refugees in the young and more 'crime-prone' age groups also provides an explanation for the problem behaviours, according to sociologist Owen Hughes in 'Hungarians in New Zealand: Toward a demographic profile', paper submitted for SOSC 403: Demography, Department of Sociology, Victoria University of Wellington, 1986.
80 'Refugees inclined to act defensively', Department of Labour, *Labour and Employment Gazette*, Vol. 7, No. 2, May 1957, pp. 17–18.
81 David McGill, *The Other New Zealanders*, Mallinson Rendel, Wellington, 1982, p. 76.
82 'Eva Szegoe, 1957', in Megan Hutchings, *New Zealanders by Choice*, Identity Services, Department of Internal Affairs, Wellington, 1998, pp. 50–57.
83 ANZ, ABKF, 947, W5182, Box 165, 22/1/203/1, Part 1, Immigration – General, Czechoslovakia – Refugees, 1968–69, Secretary of Labour to Minister of Immigration, 20 September 1968. The Warsaw Pact was a military treaty signed in 1955 between the former Soviet Union and East European countries under Soviet domination during the Cold War.
84 ANZ, ABKF, 947, W5182, Box 165, 22/1/203/1, Part 1, Immigration – General, Czechoslovakia – Refugees, 1968–69, Assistant Secretary of Labour to Acting Minister of Immigration, 9 September 1968.
85 Ibid., Secretary of Labour to Minister of Immigration, 7 November 1968.
86 ANZ, ABKF, 947, W5182, Box 166, 22/1/203/1, Part 3, Immigration – General, Czechoslovakia – Refugees, Press Statement, Acting Minister of Labour, undated, probably 1970 (referring to a later group of Czech refugees).
87 ANZ, ABKF, 947, W5182, Box 165, 22/1/203/1, Part 1, Immigration – General, Czechoslovakia – Refugees, 1968–69, Assistant Secretary of Labour to Chairman Social Security Commission, 6 November 1968.
88 ANZ, ABKF, 947, W5182, Box 166, 22/1/203/1, Part 3, Immigration – General, Czechoslovakia – Refugees, Report of selection officer, Czech refugees: Recruitment from Vienna – October 1970, 11 November 1970, p. 1.
89 Ibid.
90 Ibid.
91 Ibid., pp. 2–4.
92 Ibid., Secretary of Labour to Minister of Immigration, 2 October 1970; Minister of Foreign Affairs to New Zealand High Commissioner, London, 13 October 1970.

93 Ibid., Director New Zealand Security Intelligence Service to Secretary of Labour, 22 October 1970; report of selection officer, Czech refugees: Recruitment from Vienna – October 1970, 11 November 1970, p. 3.
94 ANZ, ABKF, 22/1/27/31, Part 2, 1990–91, General Manager New Zealand Immigration Service to Minister of Immigration, 'Refugee programme 1991/92', 21 February 1991, attached paper by Department of Labour, New Zealand Immigration Service, 'Acceptance of refugees as settlers in New Zealand', June 1990, p. 1; ANZ, ABKF, 947, W5182, Box 166, 22/1/203/1, Part 3, Immigration – General, Czechoslovakia – Refugees, press statement, Acting Minister of Labour, undated, probably 1970.
95 ANZ, ABKF, 947, W5182, Box 59, 22/1/27/27, Part 1, Immigration – General, East European Refugees, 1978–81, Permanent Head of Department of Labour to All Districts, 'Polish refugees', 4 September 1981.
96 Ibid., Permanent Head of Department of Labour to District Superintendents and Immigration Staff, 'Immigration: Polish nationals', 11 January 1982.
97 Ibid.
98 Ann Beaglehole, 'Refugees: 1970s–2003: refugee groups', Te Ara – the Encyclopedia of New Zealand: www.TeAra.govt.nz/en/refugees/4
99 ANZ, ABKF, 947, W5182, Box 59, 22/1/27/27, Part 1, Immigration – General, East European Refugees, 1978–81, brief for Selection Officer, undated, probably 1981, pp. 3–4.
100 Ibid., Permanent Head of Department of Labour to all districts, 4 September 1981, pp. 2–3.
101 Ibid., brief for Selection Officer undated, probably 1981, p. 4.
102 Ibid., Secretary of Labour to Minister of Immigration, 'Polish Refugees', 9 September 1981.
103 'Anna Reutt-Marciszewski', Adrienne Jansen, *I Have in My Arms Both Ways: Stories by ten immigrant women*, Allen & Unwin, Wellington, 1990, pp. 121–37.
104 ANZ, ABKF, 947, W5182, Box 61, 22/127/28, Part 2, Inter-church Commission on Immigration and Refugee Resettlement, 'Questions that should be asked according to latest Polish group', undated, c. 1986.
105 Ibid.
106 Ibid., 'Suggestions to improve quality of intake', undated, c. 1986.
107 ANZ, ABKF, 947, W5182, Box 59, 22/1/27/27, Part 1, Immigration – General, East European Refugees, 1978–81, 'Renewal of the East European refugee quota', Minister of Immigration to Cabinet, March 1982; Department of Labour to Minister of Immigration, 28 February 1982.
108 ANZ, ABKF, 947, W5182, Box 302, 22/1/27/31, Part 2, 1990–91, General Manager New Zealand Immigration Service to Minister of Immigration, Refugee programme 1991/92, 21 February 1991, attached paper by Department of Labour, New Zealand Immigration Service, 'Acceptance of refugees as settlers in New Zealand', June 1990, pp. 2–3; Beaglehole, 'Refugees: 1970s–2003: refugee groups'.
109 ANZ, ABKF, 947, W5182, Box 302, 22/1/27/31, Part 2, 1990–91, General Manager New Zealand Immigration Service to Minister of Immigration, Refugee programme 1991/92, 21 February 1991, attached paper by Department of Labour, New Zealand Immigration Service, 'Acceptance of refugees as settlers in New Zealand', June 1990, p. 2.

Chapter four: A change of direction

1 Ann Beaglehole, 'Immigration regulation: 1946–1985: gradual change', Te Ara – the Encyclopedia of New Zealand: www.TeAra.govt.nz/en/immigration-regulation/4
2 Robin Gallienne, *'The Whole Thing was Orchestrated': New Zealand's response to the Indo-Chinese refugees exodus 1975–1985*, University of Auckland Centre for Asian Studies, Resource Papers, No. 2, 1991, p. 217. These families followed 12 families of Chinese refugees

from Indonesia admitted in 1967, New Zealand Immigration Service, *The New Zealand Refugee Quota Programme: Refugee women*, p. 19.
3   James Ng, *Windows on a Chinese Past: Larrikinism and violence: immigration issues, 20th century assimilation: Biographies*, Vol. 3, Otago Heritage Books, Dunedin, 1993, p. 150, fn. 1.
4   David Pearson, *A Dream Deferred: The origins of ethnic conflict in New Zealand*, Allen & Unwin, Wellington, 1990, pp. 84–86.
5   Ibid., p. 90.
6   Malcolm McKinnon, *Immigrants and Citizens: New Zealanders and Asian immigration in historical context*, Institute of Policy Studies, Victoria University of Wellington, Wellington, 1996, p. 27.
7   Ann Beaglehole, 'Immigration regulation: 1881–1914: restrictions on Chinese and others', Te Ara – the Encyclopedia of New Zealand: www.TeAra.govt.nz/en/immigration-regulation/2
8   McKinnon, *Immigrants and Citizens*, p. 48, fn. 21.
9   Klaus Neumann, '"Our own interests must come first": Australia's response to the expulsion of Asians from Uganda', *History Australia*, Vol. 3, No. 1, Monash University Press, 2006, pp. 10.1, 10.2.
10 Ibid., pp. 10.1–10.3.
11 Heather Benson, *A Dissolving Dream: A New Zealander in Amin's Uganda*, Bridget Williams Books, Wellington, 1992, p. 133.
12 Neumann, '"Our own interests must come first"', p. 10.1.
13 Benson, *A Dissolving Dream*, pp. 109–10.
14 Ibid., p. 134.
15 'UK "feelers" to NZ on Ugandan exodus', *Evening Post*, 22 August 1972, WPL clippings file, 'Politics – Uganda'.
16 'The international scene: Africa and the Middle East: Uganda', *New Zealand Foreign Affairs Review*, Vol. 22, No. 8, August 1972, p. 77.
17 MFAT, 251/6/1, Vol. 1, Uganda Social Affairs, general, 12 November 1962 – 30 December 1991, telex, Wellington to New Delhi, 10 August 1972; telex, Wellington to London, 10 August 1972.
18 'Asian refugees from Uganda', statement by the Minister of Foreign Affairs, 12 September 1972, *New Zealand Foreign Affairs Review*, Vol. 22, No. 9, September 1972, p. 66; ANZ, ABKF, 947, W5182, Box 180, 22/1/274, Part 3, Immigration – General Uganda, Policy and General, 1972–73, Secretary of Cabinet to Minister of Foreign Affairs, 11 September 1972 refers to Cabinet decision; ANZ, ABKF, 947, W5182, Box 180, 22/1/274, Part 3, Immigration – General Uganda, Policy and General, 1972–73, Minister of Immigration to Cabinet, 'Ugandan Asians', April 1973 refers to the need for British passports; 'British response to New Zealand government's decision to accept Asians from Uganda, statement by the Minister of Foreign Affairs', 15 September, *New Zealand Foreign Affairs Review*, Vol. 22, No. 9, September 1972, p. 67.
19 Roberto Rabel, '"The Dovish Hawk": Keith Holyoake and the Vietnam War', in Margaret Clark (ed.), *Sir Keith Holyoake: Towards a political biography*, Dunmore Press, Palmerston North, 1997, p. 174; Barry Gustafson, 'Marshall, John Ross – Biography', from the Dictionary of New Zealand Biography: www.TeAra.govt.nz/enbiographies/5m36/1; 'Displaced Asians could cause new thinking on immigration', *Evening Post*, 26 August 1972, WPL clippings file, 'Politics – Uganda'.
20 Quoted in New Zealand Immigration Service, *Refugee Women*, p. 20.
21 'More than 200 Asians may be admitted', *Dominion*, 13 September 1972, p. 1.
22 ANZ, ABKF, 947, W5182, Box 180, 22/1/274, Part 3, Immigration – General Uganda, Policy and General, 1972–73, Secretary of Labour to Minister of Immigration, 'Ugandan Asians', April and 5 March 1973.

23 'Displaced Asians could cause new thinking on immigration'.
24 'Where to with immigration?', Editorial, *Dominion*, 15 September 1972, p. 4.
25 'Maori view immigrants', *Evening Post*, 5 September 1972.
26 Karen Sutton, Letters to the Editor, *Dominion*, 16 September 1972.
27 'FOL cold on bringing Asians to NZ', Letters to the Editor, *Evening Post*, 11 August 1972.
28 'Uganda: In the name of humanity', Editorial, *Evening Post*, 13 September 1972.
29 'Possible adverse effects with Ugandan Asians', *Evening Post*, 30 August 1972.
30 Charity Begins at Home, 'Immigration of Ugandan Asians?', Letters to the Editor, *Evening Post*, 11 August 1972.
31 For example, V.R. Dimock, 'Start at home?', Letters to the Editor, *Evening Post*, 14 August 1972.
32 Mother of Two, 'People and houses', Letters to the Editor, *Evening Post*, 11 August 1972.
33 Pioneer Stock, 'Asians from Uganda', Letters to the Editor, *Evening Post*, 12 August 1972.
34 Pearson, *A Dream Deferred*, pp. 116–17, 120.
35 Ann Beaglehole, 'Immigration regulation: Controlling Pacific Island immigration', Te Ara – the Encyclopedia of New Zealand: www.TeAra.govt.nz/en/immigration-regulation/6; Pearson, *A Dream Deferred*, p. 117.
36 Department of Statistics, *NZYB*, Wellington, 1973, p. 71.
37 'Uganda: In the name of humanity', Editorial, *Evening Post*, 13 September 1972.
38 'Asian refugees from Uganda', statement by the Minister of Foreign Affairs, 12 September, *New Zealand Foreign Affairs Review*, Vol. 22, No. 9, September 1972, p. 66.
39 'Where to with immigration?', Editorial, *Dominion*, 15 September 1972, p. 4.
40 'Asian refugees from Uganda', statement by the Minister of Foreign Affairs; 'First Ugandan Asian family to arrive here is now counting its blessings', *Evening Post*, 8 November 1972.
41 ANZ, ABKF, 947, W5182, Box 180, 22/1/274, Part 3, Immigration – General Uganda, Policy and General, 1972–73, Minister of Immigration to Cabinet, 'Ugandan Asians', April 1973.
42 Ibid., Secretary of Foreign Affairs to Prime Minister, 'Ugandan Asians', 8 March 1973.
43 'First Ugandan Asian family to arrive here is now counting its blessings'.
44 ANZ, ABKF, 947, W5182, Box 180, 22/1/274, Part 3, Immigration Uganda, 1973–73, Address-in-reply Debate – Immigration, 'Ugandan Asians', undated.
45 Ibid., Secretary of Foreign Affairs and Secretary of Labour to Ministers of Foreign Affairs and Immigration, 'Ugandan Asians', 22 November 1972.
46 Ibid., Secretary of Foreign Affairs to Minister of Foreign Affairs, 'Ugandan Asians', 2 November 1972.
47 Ibid., Minister of Immigration to Cabinet, 'Ugandan Asians', April 1973; 'Government plans to ease restrictions on entry of Ugandans', *Thames Star*, 11 January 1973.
48 Quoted in ANZ, ABKF, 947, W5182, Box 180, 22/1/274, Part 3, Immigration Uganda, 1973–73, submission to the Minister of Immigration from R.M. O'Grady, Inter-Church Committee on Immigration, 22 February 1973, p. 3.
49 Ibid., p. 4.
50 Norman Kirk, *New Zealand and its Neighbours*, New Zealand Institute of International Affairs, Wellington, 1971, pp. 10–12.
51 Margaret Hayward, *Diary of the Kirk Years*, Cape Catley, Queen Charlotte Sound and Reed, Wellington, 1981, p. 319.
52 Ibid., cited p. 108.
53 ANZ, ABKF, 947, W5182, Box 180, 22/1/274, Part 3, Immigration Uganda, 1973–73, Secretary of Cabinet to Minister of Immigration, 'Ugandan Asians', 10 April 1973; Minister of Immigration to Cabinet, 'Ugandan Asians', April 1973, p. 3.
54 '"Handicapped" Ugandan Asians are to be admitted here', *Evening Post*, 17 April 1973.

55 ANZ, ABKF, 947, W5182, Box 180, 22/1/274, Part 3, Immigration Uganda, 1973–73, record of conversation between the Prime Minister Hon. Norman Kirk and Mr F. Bauman, UNDP/UNICEF/UNHCR representative for Australasia and Mr Ole Volfing, Office of the High Commissioner for Refugees, Geneva, 30 March 1973.
56 Frank Corner, phone conversation with Ann Beaglehole, Wellington, 12 March 2007. In *Diary of the Kirk Years*, Corner also recalled having a good understanding with Kirk as 'they both wanted New Zealand's foreign policy to take a more independent line', Hayward, *Diary of the Kirk Years*, p. 110.
57 Klaus Neumann, *Refuge Australia: Australia's humanitarian record*, University of New South Wales Press, Sydney, 2004, p. 47; Neumann, '"Our own interests must come first"', pp. 10.6, 10.9.
58 ANZ, ABKF, 947, W5182, Box 180, 22/1/274, Part 3, Immigration Uganda, 1973–73, for example, New Plymouth Hospital to Ministry of External Affairs, 31 October 1972.
59 'First Ugandan Asian family to arrive here is now counting its blessings'.
60 'Ugandan family finds life without servants is different', *Evening Post*, 4 December 1972.
61 Lynne Loates, 'The loneliness of the long-distance dancer: Kanan Deobhakta, expert exponent of Indian classical dance', *More*, February 1987, Issue 44, pp. 34–40.
62 Anton Binzegger, *New Zealand's Policy on Refugees*, New Zealand Institute of International Affairs, Wellington, 1980, pp. 68–69.
63 ANZ, ABKF, 947, W5182, Box 302, 22/1/27/31, Part 2, General Manager, New Zealand Immigration Service to Minister of Immigration, Refugee Programme, 1991–92, 21 February 1991, attached paper, Department of Labour, New Zealand Immigration Service, 'Acceptance of refugees as settlers in New Zealand', June 1990, p. 2.
64 The Inter-Church Committee on Immigration was established in 1969. It was the forerunner of the ICCI. Director of the Inter-Church Commission on Immigration and Refugee Resettlement, 'Inter-Church Commission on Immigration and Refugee Resettlement: A brief history', in Gallienne, *'The Whole Thing was Orchestrated'*, Appendix C, p. 235.
65 John Wilson, 'Latin Americans: Identity in New Zealand', Te Ara – the Encyclopedia of New Zealand: www.TeAra.govt.nz/en/latin-americans/2
66 ANZ, ABHS, W4627, Box 2586, 108/4/92, Part 2, Refugees from Chile, Secretary of Foreign Affairs to Prime Minister, 'Request to government to take in foreign refugees resident in Chile', 6 November 1973, p. 1.
67 Ibid., p. 2.
68 Ibid.
69 Ibid., pp. 2, 3.
70 Ministry of Foreign Affairs, 'Foreign refugees resident in Chile: Statement of the Associate Minister of Foreign Affairs', *New Zealand Foreign Affairs Review*, 23, (11), November 1973, p. 25, quoted in New Zealand Immigration Service, *Refugee Women*, p. 20.
71 Binzegger, *New Zealand's Policy on Refugees*, p. 69.
72 ANZ, ABHS, W4627, Box 2586, 108/4/92, Part 2, Refugees from Chile, Secretary of Foreign Affairs to Prime Minister, 'Chilean Refugees', 11 December 1974.
73 Ibid.
74 Ibid.
75 ANZ, ABKF, 947, W5182, Box 302, 22/1/27/31, Part 2, General Manager New Zealand Immigration Service to Minister of Immigration, Refugee Programme, 1991–92, 21 February 1991, attached paper, Department of Labour, New Zealand Immigration Service, 'Acceptance of refugees as settlers in New Zealand', June 1990, p. 2.
76 ANZ, ABHS, W4627, Box 2586, 108/4/92, Part 2, Refugees from Chile, L.J. Parton (name is hard to decipher) to R.D. Muldoon, 9 September 1974.

77 Bill Smith, 'South American refugees in New Zealand: Experiences and needs', workshop on Chilean refugees, in Max Abbott (Ed.), *Refugee Resettlement and Wellbeing*, Mental Health Foundation of New Zealand, Auckland, 1989, pp. 208, 211.
78 Wilson, 'Latin Americans: Immigration history'.
79 This was my impression when I worked with refugees from Chile as ICCI field counsellor in the 1980s; Robert Mannion, 'Refugees feel Cordillera's call', *Dominion Star Times*, 9 October 1988, p. 23.
80 Wilson, 'Latin Americans: Immigration history'.

Chapter five: Refugees from South East Asia

1 This chapter draws substantially on Robin Gallienne's excellent work, *'The Whole Thing was Orchestrated': New Zealand's response to the Indo-Chinese refugees exodus 1975–1985*, University of Auckland Centre for Asian Studies, Resource Papers, No. 2, 1991.
2 For example, Roberto Rabel, '"The Dovish Hawk": Keith Holyoake and the Vietnam War', in Margaret Clark (Ed.), *Sir Keith Holyoake: Towards a political biography*, Dunmore Press, Palmerston North, 1997, p. 173.
3 See for example, Malcolm McKinnon, *Independence and Foreign Policy: New Zealand in the world since 1935*, Auckland University Press, Auckland, 1993, p. 175.
4 *NZPD*, Vol. 397, 24 April 1975, p. 1476.
5 Anton Binzegger, *New Zealand's Policy on Refugees*, New Zealand Institute of International Affairs, Wellington, 1980, p. 60.
6 *Dominion*, 9 April 1975, quoted in Binzegger, *New Zealand's Policy on Refugees*, p. 60.
7 *NZPD*, Vol. 396, 8 April 1975, p. 263.
8 Binzegger, *New Zealand's Policy on Refugees*, p. 62.
9 Gallienne, *'The Whole Thing was Orchestrated'*, p. 19; Department of Statistics, *NZYB*, 1978, p. 73. Overall, 65,900 people migrated to New Zealand in 1974–75.
10 Gallienne, *'The Whole Thing was Orchestrated'*, p. 26.
11 'The Colombo Plan' from *An Encyclopedia of New Zealand* edited by A.H. McLintock, originally published in 1966, Te Ara – the Encyclopedia of New Zealand: www.TeAra.govt.nz/en/1966/International-Relations/4
12 Meeting between Foreign Affairs, Department of Labour and ICCI, minutes 10 June 1975, Ministry of Foreign Affairs papers, cited in Gallienne, *'The Whole Thing was Orchestrated'*, p. 27.
13 *NZPD*, 28 May 1975, Vol. 397, p. 1422.
14 Man Hau Liev and Rosa Chhun, 'Cambodians: Immigration: refugees and resettlement', Te Ara – the Encyclopedia of New Zealand: www.TeAra.govt.nz/en/cambodians/1
15 Foreign Affairs, Wellington to Permanent Representative, Geneva, telex, 5 April 1976, Ministry of Foreign Affairs papers, cited in Gallienne, *'The Whole Thing was Orchestrated'*, p. 28.
16 Prime Minister to UNHCR, 9 May 1975, Ministry of Foreign Affairs papers, quoted in Gallienne, *'The Whole Thing was Orchestrated'*, pp. 28–29.
17 Director of the ICCI, 'The Inter-Church Commission on Immigration and Refugee Resettlement: A brief history', 22 April 1977, in Gallienne, *'The Whole Thing was Orchestrated'*, Appendix C, p. 235.
18 Meeting between Foreign Affairs, Department of Labour and ICCI, 10 June 1975, Ministry of Foreign Affairs papers, cited in Gallienne, *'The Whole Thing was Orchestrated'*, p. 27.
19 Meeting between Foreign Affairs, Department of Labour and ICCI, 2 July 1975, Ministry of Foreign Affairs papers, cited in Gallienne, *'The Whole Thing was Orchestrated'*, p. 27.

20 Keith Taylor, conversation with Ann Beaglehole, 25 January 2007, Wellington. Keith Taylor was director of ICCI from its foundation in 1975 until the late 1980s. Peter Cotton took over as director in 1989.
21 Gallienne, 'The Whole Thing was Orchestrated', p. 38, fn. 64 and p. 29.
22 Meeting between UNHCR representatives Ole Volfing and G. Rizzo and Ministry of Foreign Affairs, 2 May 1977, Department of Labour papers, 1977, pp. 1–3, cited in Gallienne, 'The Whole Thing was Orchestrated', pp. 31–32.
23 Meeting between UNHCR representatives Ole Volfing and G. Rizzo and Ministry of Foreign Affairs, 2 May 1977, Department of Labour papers, 1977, p. 3, cited in Gallienne, 'The Whole Thing was Orchestrated', p. 32.
24 Gallienne, 'The Whole Thing was Orchestrated', p. 28.
25 Ann Beaglehole, 'Immigration Regulation 1946–1985: gradual change', Te Ara – the Encyclopedia of New Zealand: www.TeAra.govt.nz/en/immigration-regulation/4
26 Meeting between UNHCR representatives Ole Volfing and G. Rizzo and Ministry of Foreign Affairs, 2 May 1977, Department of Labour papers, 1977, p. 3, cited in Gallienne, 'The Whole Thing was Orchestrated', p. 33.
27 Robin Gallienne, interview with director of ICCI, 8 December 1987, Wellington, cited in Gallienne, 'The Whole Thing was Orchestrated', p. 36.
28 Gallienne, 'The Whole Thing was Orchestrated', p. 36.
29 Robin Gallienne, interview with ICCI coordinator, 25 August 1987, Auckland, quoted in Gallienne, 'The Whole Thing was Orchestrated', p. 37.
30 UNHCR statistical report, 31 December 1979, Geneva, cited in Gallienne, 'The Whole Thing was Orchestrated', p. 48.
31 ICCI to Minister of Immigration, 8 July 1977, Department of Labour papers, p. 3, cited in Gallienne, 'The Whole Thing was Orchestrated', pp. 36–37.
32 Keith Taylor, conversation with Ann Beaglehole, 25 January 2007, Wellington.
33 Past employee of Department of Labour, Immigration Division, to Robin Gallienne, 9 December 1987, Wellington, quoted in Gallienne, 'The Whole Thing was Orchestrated', p. 37.
34 Wellington to all posts, Cabinet decision and the terms of acceptance, telex, 27 July 1977, Department of Labour papers, cited in Gallienne, 'The Whole Thing was Orchestrated', p. 40.
35 Secretary of Labour to Kuala Lumpur, Bangkok, Geneva, Singapore, telex 27 July 1977, Department of Labour papers, p. 1, cited in Gallienne, 'The Whole Thing was Orchestrated', p. 44.
36 Gallienne, 'The Whole Thing was Orchestrated', pp. 49–50.
37 Ibid., pp. 39–40.
38 Ibid., p. 86.
39 Wellington to Bangkok, telex, 29 July 1977, Department of Labour papers, cited in Gallienne, 'The Whole Thing was Orchestrated', p. 46.
40 Singapore to Wellington, medical officer, Report on the selection of Vietnamese boat refugees from Malaysia and Thailand for re-settlement in New Zealand, 19 September 1977, Department of Labour papers, p. 5, quoted in Gallienne, 'The Whole Thing was Orchestrated', p. 47.
41 Singapore to Wellington, medical officer, Report on the selection of Vietnamese boat refugees from Malaysia and Thailand for resettlement in New Zealand, 19 September 1977, Department of Labour papers, pp. 1–5, quoted in Gallienne, 'The Whole Thing was Orchestrated', pp. 50–51.
42 Gallienne, 'The Whole Thing was Orchestrated', pp. 52–53.
43 Ibid., p. 53.
44 Ibid., pp. 53–54.

45 Minister of Immigration, press statement, 22 September 1977, Department of Labour papers, quoted in Gallienne, 'The Whole Thing was Orchestrated', p. 55.
46 Wellington to Kula Lumpur and Hong Kong, telex, 28 July 1977, Department of Labour papers, pp. 1–2, cited in Gallienne, 'The Whole Thing was Orchestrated' p. 56.
47 Canberra to Wellington, telex, 12 August 1977, Department of Labour papers, p. 2, cited in Gallienne, 'The Whole Thing was Orchestrated', p. 57.
48 Wellington to Kula Lumpur and Hong Kong, telex, 28 July 1977, Department of Labour papers, p. 2, quoted in Gallienne, 'The Whole Thing was Orchestrated', p. 56.
49 Gallienne, 'The Whole Thing was Orchestrated', pp. 57, 61, 69–70.
50 Ibid., pp. 61, 73.
51 Ibid., pp. 108–10.
52 Keith Taylor, conversation with Ann Beaglehole, 25 January 2007, Wellington.
53 Gallienne, 'The Whole Thing was Orchestrated', p. 108.
54 Assistant Secretary of Labour to Minister of Immigration, composite report on resettlement of Indo-Chinese refugees, 6 November 1978, Department of Labour papers, pp. 1–4, cited in Gallienne, 'The Whole Thing was Orchestrated', p. 77.
55 ANZ, ABKF, 947, W5182, Box 37, 22/1/27-24, Part 14, Immigration – General, Indo-Chinese Refugees Policy 1980, Ministry of Foreign Affairs to Minister of Foreign Affairs, briefing paper on Indo-Chinese refugees, background paper for visit to Geneva by Secretary of Labour June 1980, May 1980, p. 1.
56 Canberra to Wellington, telex, 7 December 1978, Department of Labour papers, quoted in Gallienne, 'The Whole Thing was Orchestrated', pp. 82, 84–85.
57 ANZ, ABKF, 947, W5182, Box 302, 22/1/27/31, Part 2, General Manager New Zealand Immigration Service to Minister of Immigration, Refugee Programme 1991–92, 21 February 1991, attached paper, Department of Labour, New Zealand Immigration Service, 'Acceptance of refugees as settlers in New Zealand', June 1990, p. 4.
58 Gallienne, 'The Whole Thing was Orchestrated', p. 130.
59 ANZ, ABKF, 947, Box 37, 22/1/27-24, Part 14, Immigration – General, Indo-Chinese Refugees Policy 1980, Ministry of Foreign Affairs to Minister of Foreign Affairs, background paper for visit to Geneva by Secretary of Labour, June 1980, p. 2; Gallienne, 'The Whole Thing was Orchestrated', p. 150.
60 ANZ, ABKF, 947, Box 37, 22/1/27/24, Part 14, Immigration – General, Indo-Chinese Refugees Policy 1980, Ministry of Foreign Affairs to Minister of Foreign Affairs, background paper for visit to Geneva by Secretary of Labour, June 1980, p. 4.
61 Gallienne, 'The Whole Thing was Orchestrated', p. 151.
62 Aussie Malcolm, interviewed by Ann Beaglehole, 12 April, 2007, Auckland.
63 Aussie Malcolm, email to Ann Beaglehole, 8 December 2006.
64 ANZ, ABKF, 947, Box 37, 22/1/27/24, Part 14, Immigration – General, Indo-Chinese Refugees Policy 1980, Ministry of Foreign Affairs to Minister of Foreign Affairs, background paper for visit to Geneva by Secretary of Labour, June 1980, p. 4.
65 ANZ, ABKF, 947, W5182, Box 302, 22/1/27/31, Part 2, General Manager New Zealand Immigration Service to Minister of Immigration, Report on refugee programme, 1991–92, 21 February 1991, attached paper, Department of Labour, New Zealand Immigration Service, 'Acceptance of refugees as settlers in New Zealand', June 1990, p. 4.
66 Gallienne, 'The Whole Thing was Orchestrated', pp. 86, 93.
67 New Zealand High Commission, Kuala Lumpur, to Secretary of Labour, 6 July 1979 refers to a Cabinet decision of 4 December 1978, Department of Labour papers, cited in Gallienne, 'The Whole Thing was Orchestrated', p. 93.
68 Gallienne, 'The Whole Thing was Orchestrated', pp. 92–94, 100, 101–02.

69 Robin Gallienne, interview with Private Secretary to Aussie Malcolm, 27 August 1987, quoted in Gallienne, 'The Whole Thing was Orchestrated', p. 86.
70 Aussie Malcolm, email to Ann Beaglehole, 8 December 2006.
71 Aussie Malcolm, interviewed by Ann Beaglehole, 12 April 2007, Auckland.
72 Richard Bedford, Elsie Ho and Jacqueline Lidgard, 'International migration in New Zealand: Contexts, components and policy issues', Policy Studies Centre, University of Waikato, Hamilton, No. 37, October 2000, p. 21.
73 Man Hau Liev and Rosa Chhun, 'Cambodians – Immigration: refugees and resettlement', Te Ara – the Encyclopedia of New Zealand: www.TeAra.govt.nz/en/cambodians/1
74 Borany Kanal and Adrienne Jansen, *Borany's Story*, Learning Media, Ministry of Education, Wellington, 1991, pp. 52, 74–76, 80–81, 85.
75 ANZ, ABKF, 947, W5182, Box 37, 22/1/27/24, Part 14, Indo-Chinese Refugees Policy, 1980, Ministry of Foreign Affairs to Minister of Foreign Affairs, background paper for visit to Geneva by Secretary of Labour, June 1980, Annex 3, 'Refugees in New Zealand', Labour Department pamphlet, April 1980, p. 4.
76 Department of Labour, New Zealand Immigration Service, *Refugee Women: The New Zealand refugee quota programme*, Wellington, 1994, p. 21
77 ANZ, ABKF, 947, W5182, Box 37, 22/1/27/24, Part 14, Immigration – General, Indo-Chinese Refugees Policy, 1980, Ministry of Foreign Affairs to Minister of Foreign Affairs, background paper for visit to Geneva by Secretary of Labour, June 1980, Annex 3, 'Refugees in New Zealand', Labour Department pamphlet, April 1980, pp. 4, 5.
78 ANZ, ABKF, 947, W5182, Box 302, 22/1/27/31, Part 2, General Manager New Zealand Immigration Service to Minister of Immigration, Refugee Programme 1991–92, 21 February 1991, attached paper, New Zealand Immigration Service, Department of Labour, 'Acceptance of refugees as settlers in New Zealand', June 1990, p. 5.
79 ANZ, ABKF, 947, W5182, Box 46, 22/1/27/24/3, Part 4, Immigration – General, Indo-Chinese Refugees Policy, Preparation of Cabinet Papers and Final Outcome 1982–87, Minister of Immigration, 'Indo-Chinese refugee policy continues', press release, 14 June 1984.
80 Ibid., Acting Secretary of Foreign Affairs to Acting Minister of Foreign Affairs, 'Indo-China: Refugee programme 1985/86: New Zealand intake', 4 April 1985, and Department of Labour Cabinet paper, 'Immigration: Indo-Chinese refugee policy', 6 June 1985, p. 5.
81 Ibid., Department of Labour Cabinet paper, 'Immigration: Indo-Chinese refugee policy', 6 June 1985, p. 5.
82 Gallienne, 'The Whole Thing was Orchestrated', pp. 115–22.
83 Hugo and Bill Manson to Immigration, 1 October 1979, Department of Labour papers, pp. 1–2, cited in Gallienne, 'The Whole Thing was Orchestrated', p. 121.
84 Immigration press release, 6 July 1979, Department of Labour papers, quoted in Gallienne, 'The Whole Thing was Orchestrated', p. 120.
85 Robin Gallienne, interview with Aussie Malcolm's former private secretary, 2 September 1987, quoted in Gallienne, 'The Whole Thing was Orchestrated', p. 109.
86 ANZ, ABKF, 947, W5182, Box 37, 22/1/27/24, Part 13, Immigration – General, Indo-Chinese Refugees Policy 1979–80, Minister of Immigration to P.R. Pearson, 15 November 1979.
87 Robin Gallienne, interview with immigration officer, 2 September 1987, cited in Gallienne, 'The Whole Thing was Orchestrated', pp. 109, 122.
88 ANZ, ABKF, 947, Box 37, 22/1/27-24, Indo-Chinese Refugees, 1980, survey on public opinion to refugee intakes from South East Asia, April 1980 (file stamp is 24 April 1980). The poll, conducted by the *New Zealand Herald* National Research Bureau, surveyed 2200 people throughout New Zealand; Gallienne, 'The Whole Thing was Orchestrated', p. 179.

Chapter six: From refugee to new settler

1. ANZ, ABKF, W5182, Box 302, 22/1/27/31, Part 2, Department of Labour, New Zealand Immigration Service, 'Acceptance of refugees as settlers in New Zealand', June 1990, p. 1, attached to report Refugee Programme for 1991/92 from General Manager New Zealand Immigration Service to Minister of Immigration, 21 February 1991.
2. ANZ, Department of Labour, L1 22/1/80, Prime Minister's Department, 'Assimilation of alien immigrants', 27 October 1950, p. 1.
3. ANZ, ABKF, 947, W5182, Box 180, 22/1/274, Part 3, Immigration Uganda 1973–73, minutes of meeting held on 25 September 1972, Wellington.
4. 'Churches discuss problem of Ugandan Asians with Minister', *Evening Post*, 27 January 1973.
5. 'Asian refugees from Uganda, statement by the Minister of Foreign Affairs', 12 September, *New Zealand Foreign Affairs Review*, Vol. 22, No. 9, September 1972, p. 66; ANZ, ABKF, 947, W5182, Box 180, 22/1/274, Part 3, Immigration – General, Uganda Policy and General, 1972–73, Secretary of Labour to Minister of Immigration, 'Ugandan Asians', 5 March 1973; also attached telex, Minister of Foreign Affairs to New Zealand High Commission, London, 9 March 1973.
6. Director of the ICCI, 'The Inter-Church Commission on Immigration and Refugee Resettlement: A brief history', 22 April 1977, cited in Robin Gallienne, *'The Whole Thing was Orchestrated': New Zealand's response to the Indo-Chinese refugees exodus 1975–1985*, University of Auckland Centre for Asian Studies, Resource Papers, No. 2, 1991, Appendix C, p. 235.
7. Robin Gallienne interview with Aussie Malcolm, 27 August 1987, Auckland, quoted in Gallienne, *'The Whole Thing was Orchestrated'*, p. 163.
8. 'Refugee help in NZ setting world example says UN official', *New Zealand Herald*, 12 February 1984, article reproduced in Gallienne, p. 164.
9. Aussie Malcolm, email to Ann Beaglehole, 19 March 2007.
10. Gallienne, *'The Whole Thing was Orchestrated'*, pp. 107–08.
11. Ibid., pp. 114–15, 180–82.
12. Keith Taylor quoted in Michael Alford, 'New Zealand: Sponsors are the key', *Refugees*, No. 33, September 1986, p. 29.
13. Michael Alford, 'A day to celebrate', *Refugees*, No. 21, September 1983, p. 11, published online by UNHCR as *Refugees Magazine*: www.unhcr.org
14. 'New Zealand's Refugee Sector: Perspectives and developments, 1987–2010': www.dol.govt.nz/publications/research/refugee-sector-perspectives-developments
15. Refugee Services Aotearoa New Zealand: www.refugeeservices.org.nz; see Chapter Nine about the agency combining with the New Zealand Red Cross.
16. Keith Taylor, conversation with Ann Beaglehole, 25 January 2007, Wellington.
17. Gallienne, *'The Whole Thing was Orchestrated'*, pp. 165, 173.
18. Mangere Immigration Centre to Auckland Technical Institute, report, Auckland Technical Institute, group 1, 1980, cited in Gallienne, *'The Whole Thing was Orchestrated'*, p. 173.
19. Gallienne, *'The Whole Thing was Orchestrated'*, pp. 173–75.
20. Aussie Malcolm, interviewed by Ann Beaglehole, 12 April 2007.
21. Canberra to Wellington, telex, 12 August 1977, Department of Labour papers, p. 2, cited in Gallienne, *'The Whole Thing was Orchestrated'*, p. 56.
22. Keith Taylor, conversation with Ann Beaglehole, 25 January 2007, Wellington.
23. Houmpheng Rattanong, 'Sponsorship: A refugee's point of view', in Max Abbott (ed.), *Refugee Resettlement and Wellbeing*, based on the first National Conference on Refugee Mental Health, Wellington, New Zealand, 12–15 May 1988, Mental Health Foundation of New Zealand, Auckland, 1989, p. 218.

24 ANZ, ABKF, 947, W5182, Box 302, 22/1/27/31, Part 2, General Manager New Zealand Immigration Service to Minister of Immigration, Report on Refugee Programme, 1991/92, 21 February 1991, attached paper, Department of Labour, New Zealand Immigration Service, 'Acceptance of refugees as settlers in New Zealand', June 1990, p. 7.
25 Rattanong, 'Sponsorship: A refugee's point of view', pp. 217–19.
26 'Anna Reutt-Marciszewski', in Adrienne Jansen, *I Have in My Arms Both Ways: Stories by ten immigrant women*, Allen & Unwin, Wellington, 1990, pp. 130–31.
27 Letter from refugee in Mangere to relatives in Galang camp, Indonesia, 2 April 1982, translated from Vietnamese by Vietnamese interpreter, Department of Labour papers, quoted in Gallienne, '*The Whole Thing was Orchestrated*', p. 199.
28 ANZ, ABKF, 947, W5182, Box 302, 22/1/27/31, Part 2, General Manager New Zealand Immigration Service to Minister of Immigration, Report on Refugee Programme, 1991/92, 21 February 1991, attached paper, Department of Labour, New Zealand Immigration Service, 'Acceptance of refugees as settlers in New Zealand', June 1990, p. 5.
29 Department of Labour, New Zealand Immigration Service, *Refugee Women: The New Zealand refugee quota programme*, Wellington, 1994, pp. 22–23.
30 ANZ, ABKF, 947, W5182, Box 302, 22/1/27/31, Part 2, General Manager New Zealand Immigration Service to Minister of Immigration, Report on Refugee Programme, 1991/92, 21 February 1991, attached paper, Department of Labour, New Zealand Immigration Service, 'Acceptance of refugees as settlers in New Zealand', June 1990, p. 8; New Zealand Immigration Service, *Refugee Women*, p. 23.
31 For example, there were 30 cases of tuberculosis among 623 South East Asian refugees at the Mangere Refugee Reception Centre during 1983, reported the Department of Health, *AJHR*, 1984, E. 10, Report of the Department of Health, 'Refugees', pp. 22–23.
32 Abbott, *Refugee Resettlement and Wellbeing*, p. 6.
33 ANZ, ABKF, 947, W5182, Box 177, 22/1/270/9, Part 1, Immigration – General, Settlement of Migrants in New Zealand – Refugee Settlers, 1987–89, minutes of the meeting of Cabinet Social Equity Committee, 24 May 1988.
34 Department of Labour and Employment, *Immigration Newsletter*, No. 4, 10 June 1949, p. 1.
35 ANZ, ABKF, 947, W5182, Box 33, 22/1/27/21, Part 1, Immigration – General, International Refugee Organisation – Handicapped Refugees, 1967–86, Report to the Minister of Immigration, 3 February 1971, p. 2.
36 ANZ, ABKF, 947, W5182, Box 303, 22/1/27/13, Part 1, Immigration – International Refugee Organisation – European Refugees in China 1956–62, High Commissioner for Refugees to C. Gibson Young, New Zealand Inter-Church Council on Public Affairs, Wellington, 28 February 1956.
37 Ibid.
38 Ibid.
39 *AJHR*, 1957, H 31, Report of the Director, Division of Tuberculosis, p. 81.
40 ANZ, ABKF, 947, W5182, Box 303, 22/1/27/13, Part 1, Immigration – International Refugee Organisation – European Refugees in China 1956–62, Assistant Secretary of Labour to C. Gibson Young, New Zealand Inter-Church Council on Public Affairs, 27 April 1956.
41 Ibid.
42 Ibid., file note on deputation from Inter-Church Council to the Minister of Immigration about 'hard-core refugee cases', 27 June 1956.
43 Anton Binzegger, *New Zealand's Policy on Refugees*, New Zealand Institute of International Affairs, Wellington, 1980, p. 43.
44 ANZ, ABKF, 947, W5182, Box 33, 22/1/27/21, Part 1, Immigration – General, International Refugee Organisation – Handicapped Refugees, 1967–86, UNHCR, 'The Last of the Many:

An account of the individual efforts made to resettle severely handicapped refugees', Geneva, September/October 1967, no page numbers.
45 Michael Alford, 'Sponsors are the key', *Refugees*, No. 33, September 1986, p. 28.
46 Gallienne, '*The Whole Thing was Orchestrated*', p. 216.
47 Alford, 'Sponsors are the key', p. 28.
48 New Zealand Immigration Service, *Refugee Women*, p. 18.
49 Ibid.
50 Ibid.
51 August Lindt, quoted in New Zealand Immigration Service, *Refugee Women*, p. 18, citing Alford, 'Sponsors are the key', p. 28.
52 Binzegger, *New Zealand's Policy on Refugees*, p. 49.
53 *Evening Post*, 28 September 1959, quoted in Binzegger, *New Zealand's Policy on Refugees*, p. 48.
54 Keith Sinclair, *Walter Nash*, Auckland University Press, Auckland, 1976, p. 320. In his biography, Sinclair does not mention Nash's attitude to the cause of refugees.
55 ANZ, ABKF, 947, W5182, Box 303, 22/1/27/13, Part 1, Immigration – IRO, European Refugees in China, 1956-62, Secretary of Labour to General Secretary, the National Council of Churches, 'White Russian migrants', 28 April 1961, p. 2.
56 New Zealand Immigration Service, *Refugee Women*, p. 18, quoting from the External Affairs report.
57 ANZ, ABHS, 950, W4627, Box 2574, 108/4/70, Part 1, Prime Minister Keith Holyoake to Dr E.R. Nye, Dunedin Hospital, 'Chinese refugees', 8 June 1962, p. 2.
58 New Zealand Immigration Service, *Refugee Women*, p. 18.
59 ANZ, ABKF, 947, W5182, Box 33, 22/1/27/21, Part 1, Immigration – General, IRO, Handicapped Refugees, 1967-86, Chief of Resettlement Section, Geneva, to UNHCR Office, 28 November 1967.
60 Ibid., UNHCR, 'The Last of the Many: An account of the individual efforts made to resettle severely handicapped refugees', foreword by Prince Sadruddin Aga Khan, UNHCR, Geneva, September/October 1967.
61 Rev. Ian W. Fraser, *Elderly Refugees in New Zealand: The story of Nansen Home, Lower Hutt*, Nansen Home, Lower Hutt, 1985, pp. 5-6.
62 Ibid., p. 16. One of Nansen's major achievements was the 'Nansen passport', enabling stateless refugees to travel across national borders for resettlement.
63 Ibid., pp. 8-15.
64 ANZ, ABKF, 947, W5182, Box 303, 22/1/27/13, Part 1, Immigration – General, International Refugee Organisation, European Refugees in China, 1956-62, National Council of Churches to Member Churches, 9 July 1960, sent to Prime Minister; National Council of Churches to Prime Minister, 11 July 1960.
65 Ibid., Assistant Secretary of Labour to National Council of Churches, 17 March 1958; ANZ, ABKF, 947, W5182, Box 303, 22/1/27/13, Part 1, Secretary of External Affairs to Prime Minister, 30 August 1960.
66 Ibid., Prime Minister Walter Nash to Cabinet, 'Home for White Russian refugees', 21 October 1960, p. 3.
67 Ibid., p. 2.
68 Fraser, *Elderly Refugees in New Zealand*, p. 14. Refugees were not entitled to the age benefit which had a 10-year residency requirement.
69 Ibid., p. 18.
70 Quoted in Fraser, *Elderly Refugees in New Zealand*, p. 18.
71 Rev. A. Quigley, quoted in Fraser, *Elderly Refugees in New Zealand*, p. iii.

72　Fraser, *Elderly Refugees in New Zealand*, pp. 18, 22–23. Refugees with mental health issues and other problems, now known as post-traumatic stress disorder, are helped at Refugees as Survivors (RAS) centres since their establishment in 1995 in Auckland and 1997 in Wellington. In 2013 the Wellington Centre was renamed 'Refugee Trauma Recovery'.
73　Ibid., pp. 28–29.
74　Ibid., p. 30.
75　Ibid., p. 63.
76　O'Grady, Ron, *The Old Believers: A New Zealand refugee programme*, National Council of Churches, Christchurch, 1972, pp. 6–14.
77　Ibid., p. 18.
78　Ibid., p. 21.
79　Ibid.
80　Tom Shand, quoted in O'Grady, *The Old Believers*, p. 21.
81　David McGill, *The Other New Zealanders*, Mallinson Rendel, Wellington, 1982, p. 64.
82　O'Grady, *The Old Believers*, pp. 2–4.
83　Ibid., pp. 3–4.
84　Quoted in O'Grady, *The Old Believers*, pp. 25–26, 28–29.
85　McGill, *The Other New Zealanders*, p. 64.
86　Quoted in O'Grady, *The Old Believers*, p. 23.
87　Ann Beaglehole, *A Small Price to Pay: Refugees from Hitler in New Zealand, 1936–1946*, Allen & Unwin, Wellington, 1988, especially pp. 88–114.
88　O'Grady, *The Old Believers*, p. 1.
89　Gallienne, 'The Whole Thing was Orchestrated', preface, p. v.
90　O'Grady, *The Old Believers*, p. 1.
91　Ibid., p. 41; McGill, *The Other New Zealanders*, p. 65.
92　O'Grady, *The Old Believers*, pp. 46–47, 51–52, 54.
93　ANZ, ABKF, 947, W5182, Box 302, 22/1/27/31, Part 2, General Manager New Zealand Immigration Service to Minister of Immigration, Report on Refugee Programme 1991/92, 21 February 1991, attached paper, Department of Labour, New Zealand Immigration Service, 'Acceptance of refugees as settlers in New Zealand', June 1990, p. 4.
94　Aussie Malcolm, interviewed by Ann Beaglehole, 12 April 2007, Auckland.
95　Don McKinnon, written communication to Ann Beaglehole, 19 February 2007.
96　Former Minister of Immigration Lianne Dalziel, interviewed by Ann Beaglehole, 3 May 2007, Wellington.
97　In December 1959 the population was 2.3 million: www.nzhistory.net.nz
98　Klaus Neumann, *Refuge Australia: Australia's humanitarian record*, University of New South Wales Press, Sydney, 2004, p. 38.
99　Binzegger, *New Zealand's Policy on Refugees*, p. 73. Binzegger is referring to the period up to the end of the 1970s, but his comment is also relevant to the period from the 1980s to the present day.
100　Sinclair, *Walter Nash*, pp. 360, 363.
101　Former Minister of Immigration Lianne Dalziel, interviewed by Ann Beaglehole, 3 May 2007, Wellington.

Chapter seven: 'The children are a triumph'

1　R.A. Lochore, *From Europe to New Zealand: An account of our continental European settlers*, A.H. & A.W. Reed, with New Zealand Institute of International Affairs, Wellington, 1951, p. 88.

2   'Providing for child immigrants', *New Zealand National Review*, 15 June 1944, pp. 13–14.
3   The precise figures given vary. These are cited in Adam Manterys, Stefania Zawada, Stanislaw Manterys, Jozef Zawada (eds), *New Zealand's First Refugees: Pahiatua's Polish children*, Polish Children's Reunion Committee, Wellington, 2004, p. 355.
4   Krystyna Skwarko, *The Invited: The story of 733 Polish children who grew up in New Zealand*, Millwood Press, Wellington, 1974.
5   Manterys et al., *New Zealand's First Refugees*, back cover, pp. 20–23, p. 27, p. 351.
6   Ibid., Peter Fraser quoted pp. 27–28.
7   'Polish children', *Auckland Star*, 8 August 1944, p. 2.
8   Skwarko, *The Invited*, Part 3.
9   Ibid.
10 Department of Labour, New Zealand Immigration Service, *Refugee Women: The New Zealand refugee quota programme*, Wellington, 1994, p. 16.
11 Skwarko, *The Invited*, Part 3.
12 Ibid.
13 John Roy-Wojciechowski and Allan Parker, *A Strange Outcome: The remarkable survival story of a Polish child*, Penguin Books, Auckland, 2004, pp. 113–25.
14 Ibid., p. 121.
15 Ann Beaglehole's conversation with Theresa Sawicka, 30 August 2007, Wellington, based on Theresa Sawicka-Brockie, 'Forsaken journeys: The Polish experience and identity of the Pahiatua children in New Zealand', PhD thesis, University of Auckland, Auckland, 1987.
16 Steven Sedley, *The Deckston Story: The story of Annie and Max Deckston, Jewish philanthropists, who saved twenty Polish Jewish children from the Holocaust*, Holocaust Centre of New Zealand, Wellington, 2012, p. 8.
17 Stephen Levine (ed.), *A Standard for the People*, Hazard Press, Christchurch, 1994, pp. 207–08.
18 Sedley, *The Deckston Story*, p. 21.
19 ANZ, LI 22/1/27, Part 1, Director of Employment to Minister of Employment, 23 December 1947, quoted in Ann Beaglehole, 'A small price to pay: Refugees from Hitler in New Zealand 1936–1946', MA thesis, Victoria University of Wellington, Wellington, 1986, p. 125.
20 ANZ, LI 22/1/27, International Refugee Organisation, Part 3, Report of the New Zealand selection team of the *Dunbalk Bay* draft, c. April 1949, p. 3.
21 ANZ, Department of Labour, L1 22/1/189/1, Hungarian Refugees, Children, October 1956; New Zealand Red Cross Society Inc., annual report and financial statement, 1956–1957.
22 Statement by Minister of Immigration, 22 November 1956, Department of External Affairs, *External Affairs Review*, Vol. 6, No. 11, November 1956.
23 ANZ, ABKF, 947, W5182, Box 302, 22/1/27/31, Part 2, General Manager New Zealand Immigration Service to Minister of Immigration, Report on Refugee Programme 1991/2, 21 February 1991, attached paper, Department of Labour, New Zealand Immigration Service, 'Acceptance of refugees as settlers in New Zealand', June 1990, p. 1.
24 Quoted in New Zealand Immigration Service, *Refugee Women*, p. 19.
25 Quoted in Anton Binzegger, *New Zealand's Policy on Refugees*, New Zealand Institute of International Affairs, Wellington, 1980, p. 55.
26 Lochore, *From Europe to New Zealand*, pp. 89–90.
27 Binzegger, *New Zealand's Policy on Refugees*, p. 39.
28 New Zealand Immigration Service, *Refugee Women*, p. 19.
29 Binzegger, *New Zealand's Policy on Refugees*, p. 53.
30 ANZ, PM 108/4/57, Secretary of External Affairs to Minister of External Affairs, 19 February 1958.

31　ANZ, ABHS, 950, W4627, Box 2574, 108/4/70, Part 1, Bob Strackett to Norman Kirk, 17 August 1960.
32　Ibid., Secretary of Labour to Minister of Immigration, 16 September 1960.
33　Ibid., Norman Kirk to Prime Minister, 2 January 1961.
34　Ibid., Secretary of External Affairs to Prime Minister, 24 May 1961; press statement by the Prime Minister, 12 June 1962.
35　Ibid., background notes to the Prime Minister on Chinese orphans from Hong Kong, 13 June 1962.
36　Ibid., Minister of External Affairs to High Commissioner for New Zealand, Canberra, 12 June 1962.
37　Klaus Neumann, *Refuge Australia: Australia's humanitarian record*, University of New South Wales Press, Sydney, 2004, p. 43.
38　ANZ, ABHS, 950, W4627, Box 2574, 108/4/70, Part 1, New Zealand Chinese Association to Keith Holyoake, 15 June 1962.
39　The correspondence is located at ANZ, ABHS, 950, W4627, Box 2574, 108/4/70, Part 1.
40　ANZ, ABHS, 950, W4627, Box 2574, 108/4/70, Part 1, press statement, 3 July 1962.
41　Ibid., Minister of External Affairs to New Zealand High Commissioner, Canberra, 29 June 1962.
42　Ibid., Secretary of External Affairs to Prime Minister, 19 June 1962.
43　Binzegger, *New Zealand's Policy on Refugees*, p. 57.
44　Ibid., p. 60.
45　*Evening Post*, 27 May 1975, quoted in Binzegger, *New Zealand's Policy on Refugees*, p. 60.
46　Robin Gallienne, '*The Whole Thing was Orchestrated*': New Zealand's response to the Indo-Chinese refugees exodus 1975–1985, University of Auckland Centre for Asian Studies, Resource Papers, No. 2, 1991, p. 122.
47　ANZ, ABKF, 947, W5182, Box 55, 22/1/27/24/7, Part 3, Immigration – General, Indo-Chinese Refugees, Resettlement of unaccompanied minors, 1984–89, Fred Gerbic, Parliamentary Under-Secretary to the Minister of Immigration to Clive Matthewson MP, 6 December 1989.
48　Gallienne, '*The Whole Thing was Orchestrated*', p. 159.
49　ANZ, ABKF, 947, W5182, Box 55, 22/1/27/24/7, Part 2, Immigration – General, Indo-Chinese Refugees, Resettlement of unaccompanied minors, 1983–84, Minister of Immigration to Minister of Education, 17 November 1983.
50　Gallienne, *The Whole Thing was Orchestrated*, p. 158.
51　ANZ, ABKF, 947, W5182, Box 55, 22/1/27/24/7, Part 1, Immigration – General, Indo-Chinese Refugees, Resettlement of unaccompanied minors, 1980–83, Christopher Hawley, National Coordinator of South East Asian Migrant Education, Ministry of Education to Ron Malpass, Assistant Director Special Duties, Immigration Division, Labour Department, 21 February 1983.
52　Ibid., Immigration Division, Department of Labour, Proposal to resettle a group of Khmer unaccompanied minors in …, September 1983.
53　'Australia to accept 100 young refugees', *Canberra Times*, 1 March 1983.
54　ANZ, ABKF, 947, W5182, Box 55, 22/1/27/24/7. Part 1, Immigration – General, Indo-Chinese Refugees, Resettlement of unaccompanied minors, 1980–83, Immigration Division, Department of Labour, Proposal to resettle a group of Khmer unaccompanied minors in …, September 1983.
55　Robin Gallienne, interview with Aussie Malcolm, 27 August 1987, quoted in Gallienne, '*The Whole Thing was Orchestrated*', p. 158.

56 Ann Beaglehole, interview with Aussie Malcolm, Auckland, 12 April 2007.
57 Robin Gallienne, interview with Aussie Malcolm, 27 August 1987, quoted in Gallienne, 'The Whole Thing was Orchestrated', p. 159.
58 ANZ, ABKF, 947, W5182, Box 55, 22/1/27/24/7, Part 2, Immigration – General, Indo-Chinese Refugees, Resettlement of unaccompanied minors, 1983–84, telephone call from Ron Malpass in Thailand to Wellington, Department of Labour, 17 February 1984.
59 This is my summary, based on several individual case histories of unaccompanied minors interviewed by the New Zealand selection team, ANZ, ABKF, 947, W5182, Box 55, 22/1/27/24/7, Part 2, Immigration – General, Indo-Chinese Refugees, Resettlement of unaccompanied minors, 1983–84, past and present history and assessment of unaccompanied Kampuchean children in Thailand by Catholic Relief Services.
60 ANZ, ABKF, 947, W5182, Box 55, 22/1/27/24/7, Part 3, Immigration – General, Indo-Chinese Refugees, Resettlement of Unaccompanied minors, 1984–89, Fred Gerbic, Parliamentary Under-Secretary to the Minister of Immigration to Clive Matthewson, MP, 6 December 1989.
61 Ibid., Visit to review unaccompanied minors arrangements, Ron Malpass, Assistant Director of Immigration (Special Duties), 23, 24, 25 October 1984, p. 7.
62 Ibid., Ron Malpass for Secretary of Labour to the Ambassador, New Zealand Embassy, Bangkok, 26 November 1984.
63 Ibid., Visit to review unaccompanied minors arrangements, Ron Malpass, Assistant Director of Immigration (Special Duties), 23, 24, 25 October 1984.
64 Ibid., Fred Gerbic, Parliamentary Under-Secretary to the Minister of Immigration to Clive Matthewson, MP, 6 December 1989.

Chapter eight: An inconvenient obligation?

1 Rosemary McLeod, 'Worrying signs of prejudice', *Dominion Post*, 20 September 2007, p. B4.
2 John Wilson, 'Russians, Ukrainians and Baltic peoples: Russians', Te Ara – the Encyclopedia of New Zealand: www.TeAra.govt.nz/en/Russians-Ukrainians-and-baltic-peoples/1
3 ANZ, ABKF, 947, W5182, Box 37, 22/1/27/24, Part 14, Immigration – General, Indo-Chinese Refugees Policy, 1980, draft proposals from the Ministry of Defence on Indo-Chinese Refugees – Encounter at Sea by HMNZS *Canterbury*, 1 April 1980.
4 Ibid., background paper, Ministry of Foreign Affairs to Minister of Foreign Affairs, May 1980.
5 For example, see Bimal Ghosh, *Huddled Masses and Uncertain Shores: Insights into irregular migration*, International Organisation for Migration, Martinus Nijhoff Publishers, The Hague, Boston/London, 1998, foreword by James N. Purcell Jr, Director-General, International Organisation for Migration.
6 Stephen Castles, 'Towards a sociology of forced migration and social transformation', *Sociology*, Vol. 37, No. 1, 2003, p. 16.
7 MFAT, 914/6/5, Vol. 1, Human Rights Issues, South Pacific, Fiji, Report by Amnesty International Secretariat, United Kingdom, 'Fiji: Short term detention of suspected political opponents, trade unionists and journalists', September 1987, pp. 2–8.
8 Quoted in 'Couped up in Paradise', Joanna Woods, *Diplomatic Ladies: New Zealand's unsung envoys*, Otago University Press, Dunedin, 2012, pp. 224, 226.
9 MFAT, 914/6/5, Vol. 1, Human Rights Issues, South Pacific, Fiji, Report by Amnesty International Secretariat, United Kingdom, 'Fiji: Short term detention of suspected political opponents, trade unionists and journalists', September 1987, pp. 2–8.

10 ANZ, ABKF, 947, W5182, Box 56, 22/1/27/26, Part 5, Immigration – General, Refugees – Claims for refugee status in New Zealand including interdepartmental policy and procedures, 1986–87, Secretary of Foreign Affairs to Minister of Foreign Affairs, 12 June 1987.
11 Ibid.
12 Former Ministry of Foreign Affairs and Trade official, conversation with Ann Beaglehole, 28 April 2007, Wellington.
13 Dr Brij Lal, email comment to Doug Munro, 19 October 2007.
14 Former Ministry of Foreign Affairs and Trade official, conversation with Ann Beaglehole, 28 April 2007, Wellington.
15 Gerald Hensley, *Final Approaches: A memoir*, Auckland University Press, Auckland, 2006, p. 296. Hensley headed the Prime Minister's Department under David Lange and Robert Muldoon. He was Secretary of Defence from 1991 to 1999.
16 Michael Bassett, *Working with David: Inside the Lange Cabinet*, Hodder Moa, Auckland, 2008, pp. 259–60.
17 *NZPD*, Vol. 483, 6 October 1987, p. 382.
18 'Affidavits claim torture in Fiji', *Dominion*, 23 January 1988, p. 2.
19 Government cables between Suva and Wellington in early 1988 show concern about possible human rights abuses in Fiji but also contain references to the perception of an improving situation, MFAT 701/7/9/5, Fiji, Vol. 1, cable from Suva to Wellington, 1 February 1988.
20 MFAT, 914/6/5, Human Rights Issues Fiji, General, 1/10/89 to 26/9/96, Report September 1987.
21 MFAT 701/7/9/5, Fiji, Vol. 1, cable from Suva to Wellington, 25 April 1988.
22 *NZPD*, Vol. 602, 11 September 2002, p. 439.
23 Pauline Swain, 'Fearful refugee faces return to Fiji', *Dominion*, 4 July 1989, p. 11.
24 Ibid.
25 MFAT, 701/1/9/5, Refugees: Fiji Indians, Bernie Kerot, Archdiocesan Justice, Peace and Development Commission to Stan Rodger, Minister of Immigration, 10 July 1989.
26 MFAT, 701/1/9/5, Refugees: Fiji Indians, Secretary of Foreign Affairs to Minister of Foreign Affairs, 2 August 1989.
27 MFAT, 914/6/5, Vols 1–6, South Pacific, Fiji. Numerous reports and papers in the file reflect this focus.
28 *AJHR* 1987–90, Vol. 1, A.1, Annual Report of the Ministry of Foreign Affairs and Trade for the year ended 31 March 1988, 'South Pacific', p. 29.
29 *AJHR* 1987–90, Vol. 1, A.1, Annual Report of the Ministry of Foreign Affairs and Trade for the year ended 31 March 1989, p. 35.
30 Department of Statistics, *NZYB*, 1988–89, p. 198.
31 Dr Brij Lal, email to Doug Munro, 19 October 2007.
32 MFAT, 914/6/5, Vol. 1, Human Rights Issues, South Pacific, Fiji, External Assessments Bureau, 'Fiji: Background to the human rights situation', 22 November 1990, Wellington, pp. 7–8.
33 MFAT, 914/6/5, Vol. 3, South Pacific, Fiji, General Assembly speech of Major General Rabuka, Prime Minister, p. 2, Ambassador Suzanne Blumhardt to Secretary of Foreign Affairs and Trade, 26 September 1997.
34 MFAT, 914/6/5, Vols 3 and 4, South Pacific, External Assessments Bureau report, 3 July 1998.
35 See for example Michael Field, 'An invitation no Fiji journalist can refuse', *Dominion Post*, 22 March 2007, B5.
36 New Zealand Refugee Statistics, Table 7: Five countries with the highest number of refugee status applications declined by the Refugee Status Branch during the financial years from 1992/93 to 2009/2010: www.refugee.org.nz/Stats/stats.htm

37 Morgan Tuimalealiifano, University of the South Pacific, 'Re-encountering Gordon's Fiji: Has the iTaukei Fijian caught up with rest of the world?', Abstract of paper for Pacific History Association Conference, Victoria University of Wellington, 6–8 December 2012.
38 Amnesty International reports, Annual report 2012, 'Fiji': www.amnesty.org/en/region/Fiji/report-2012
39 Bruce Connew, *Stopover: A story of migration*, Victoria University Press, Wellington, 2007.
40 Some of these issues are discussed at some depth in Savitri Taylor (Ed.), *Nationality, Refugee Status and State Protection: Exploration of the gap between man and citizen*, Federation Press, New South Wales, 2005.
41 ANZ, ABKF, 947, W5182, Box 177, 22/1/270/9, Part 2, Settlement of Migrants in New Zealand, Refugees 1988–91, Bill Wilson, Report to the Rt Hon. W.F. Birch, Minister of Immigration on the process of refugee status determination, 29 April 1992, p. 4. Wilson does not state the source for the statistics cited.
42 ANZ, ABKF, 947, W5182, Box 58, 22/1/27/26, Part 14, International Refugee Organisation – Claims for Refugee Status in New Zealand, 1992, press release Bill Birch, Minister of Immigration, 4 August 1992.
43 Love M. Chile, 'The imported underclass: Poverty and social exclusion of black African refugees in Aotearoa New Zealand', *Asia Pacific Viewpoint*, Vol. 43, No. 3, December 2002, pp. 355–66, New Zealand Immigration Service figures.
44 ANZ, ABKF, 947, W5182, Box 245, 22/1/480/9, Review of General Immigration Policy 1989 and 1990 – Refugees, 1990–92, Regional Manager Northern, New Zealand Immigration Service to Chief Executive Department of Labour, 'Spontaneous refugees at Auckland International Airport', 16 October 1990.
45 Media release by Minister of Immigration, 23 June 1994, and information circular 94/11 (24 June 1994), cited in footnote 10, R.P.G. Haines, 'Legal aid issues in the refugee determination process': www.refugee.org.nz/Reference/laid.htm
46 ANZ, ABKF, 947, W5182, Box 245, 22/1/480/9, Review of General Immigration Policy 1989 and 1990 – Refugees, 1990–92, Regional Manager Northern, New Zealand Immigration Service to Chief Executive Department of Labour, 'Spontaneous refugees at Auckland International Airport', 16 October 1990.
47 Ibid.
48 Ibid.
49 ANZ, ABKF, 947, W5182, Box 177, 22/1/270/9, Part 2, Settlement of Migrants in New Zealand, Refugees, 1988–91, Minister of Immigration Hon. W.F. Birch to Cabinet, 28 November 1990.
50 Ibid.; Steve Rizos, Review and Development, 'Spontaneous refugees at Auckland Airport', 1994; ANZ, ABKF, 947, W5182, Box 245, 22/1/480/9, Review of General Immigration Policy 1989 and 1990 – Refugees, 1990–92, Refugees, Review of immigration policy, William Smith, Refugee Coordinator Amnesty International New Zealand to Minister of Immigration Bill Birch, 24 January 1992, pp. 2–4.
51 ANZ, ABKF, 947, W5182, Box 58, 22/1/27/26, Part 14, International Refugee Organisation – Claims for refugee status in New Zealand, 1992, Bill Birch, Minister of Immigration to J. Gannon, 14 August 1991.
52 ANZ, ABKF, 947, W5182, Box 245, 22/1/480/9, Review of General Immigration Policy, Refugees, 1990–92, William Smith, Refugee Coordinator Amnesty International New Zealand to Minister of Immigration Bill Birch, 24 January 1992, pp. 2–4. Part of the Amnesty International network, Amnesty International Aotearoa New Zealand (AINZ) is one of the most important of the NGOs working to end human rights abuses, including abuses of the rights of refugees and asylum seekers. The first New Zealand Amnesty group was founded in

1965. AINZ focuses on issues within the Asia–Pacific region.
53 Don McKinnon, written communication to Ann Beaglehole, 19 February 2007.
54 ANZ, ABKF, 947, W5182, Box 177, 22/1/270/9, Part 2, Settlement of Migrants in New Zealand, Bill Wilson, Report to the Rt Hon. W.F. Birch Minister of Immigration on the process of refugee status determination, 29 April 1992.
55 Ibid., pp. 20–22.
56 ANZ, ABKF, 942, W5182, Box 58, 22/1/27/26, Part 14, International Refugee Organisation – Claims for refugee status in New Zealand, press release, Rt Hon. Bill Birch, Minister of Immigration, 4 August 1992.
57 Ibid.
58 Don McKinnon, written communication to Ann Beaglehole, 19 February 2007.
59 New Zealand Refugee Statistics, Table 13: The number and percentage of refugee status appeal applications declined and allowed by the Refugee Status Appeals Authority in the financial years from 1991/92 to 2010/11: www.refugee.org.nz/Stats./stats/htm
60 Brooker, *Immigration and Refugee Digest*, February 1999, No. 14, pp. 18–25.
61 'Authorities plan for boat people arrivals', *Evening Post*, 29 March 1999, p. 16.
62 House of Representatives, Social Services Committee, Report on the Immigration Amendment Bill, No. 183-2, 4 March 1999, p. 1; ANZ, ABGX, W5188, 16127, Box 102, SS 2/2/3, Part 1, Social Services Committee – Immigration Amendment Bill – Reports, 1998–99.
63 New Zealand Statutes, Immigration Amendment Act 1999, New Zealand Legislation: http:www.legislation.govt.nz
64 Minister of Immigration, press releases 1999, Hon. Tuariki Delamare, 'Boat people Bill to be introduced into Parliament tonight', 15 June 1999, New Zealand Executive Government News Release Archive, 15 June 1999, RefNZNews, Archives 1999: www.refugee.org.nz/news/arc1999.htm
65 Helen Bain, 'Law rushed to detain boatpeople', *Dominion*, 16 June 1999.
66 Bob Shaw, 'More boat people may be on the way', *Evening Post*, 17 June 1999.
67 Tom Cardy, 'Prisons prepare to hold Chinese boat people', *Evening Post*, 16 June 1999.
68 Katherine Hoby, 'Airport alert on passport racket', *Press*, 17 June 1999.
69 'Unwelcome by boat', *New Zealand Herald*, 17 June 1999.
70 Ibid.
71 Minister of Immigration, Hon. Tuariki Delamare, press release, 'Boat people bill passed by Parliament', 16 June 1999.
72 Minister of Immigration, Hon. Tuariki Delamare, press release, 'Boat people treatment to be firm but fair', 17 June 1999. In 1998–99, New Zealand had agreed to accept up to 600 refugees from Kosovo (part of former Yugoslavia).
73 Statistics New Zealand, *Demographic Trends 1998*: www.stats.govt.nz
74 Auckland Refugee Council, discussion paper, Vol. 1, May 1998: www.refugee.org.nz/council.htm.
75 Bain, 'Law rushed to detain boat people'.
76 'What our MPs say', *Evening Post*, 19 June 1999.
77 Helen Bain, 'No boatpeople, no regrets – rushed law change was "prudent"', *Dominion*, 26 June 1999.
78 Lianne Dalziel, speech notes for meeting, 21 August 2003, available from Lianne Dalziel.
79 Former Minister of Immigration, Lianne Dalziel, interviewed by Ann Beaglehole, Wellington, 3 May 2007.
80 Lianne Dalziel, speech to people-smuggling conference, 28 February 2002, Bali, available from Lianne Dalziel.

81 Lianne Dalziel, speech notes for meeting, 21 August 2003.
82 David Marr, 'The luck of the draw', *Dominion Post*, 26 August 2006, E1.
83 Ibid.
84 Lianne Dalziel, interviewed by Ann Beaglehole, 3 May 2007, Wellington.
85 Marr, 'The luck of the draw'.
86 From speech by Hon. Lianne Dalziel to the International Association of Refugee Law Judges, 22 October 2002, available from Lianne Dalziel.
87 Quoted in Marr, 'The luck of the draw'.
88 *NZPD*, Vol. 594, 4 September 2001, p. 11256–57.
89 *NZPD*, Vol. 595, 13 September 2001, p. 11695.
90 Lianne Dalziel, Minister of Immigration, *NZPD*, Vol. 602, 11 September 2002, p. 438.
91 Marr, 'The luck of the draw'.
92 Lianne Dalziel, interview with Ann Beaglehole, 3 May 2007, Wellington.
93 Lianne Dalziel, 'Beyond *Tampa*', speech notes, 16 May 2003.
94 Peter Cotton, Director, RMS Refugee Resettlement, interviewed by Ann Beaglehole, 26 January 2007, Wellington.
95 This is according to non-governmental sources (see next footnote) and Lianne Dalziel, *NZPD*, Vol. 602, 11 September 2002, p. 439.
96 Human Rights Commission, 'The New Zealand action plan for human rights: Priorities for Action; 2005–2010', February 2005, foreword.
97 ANZ, ABKF, 947, W5182, Box 58, 22/1/27/26, Part 14, International Refugee Organisation – claims for refugee status in New Zealand, Brendon Quirk, Operations Manager New Zealand Immigration Service, to Richard Bennet, Human Rights Commission, June 1992.
98 New Zealand Refugee Statistics, Table 4: Number of applications lodged with the Refugee Status Branch per client during the period 1 July 1999 to 30 June 2005, and Table 3: The number of refugee status applications determined, and the number of applications and people approved and declined by the Refugee Status Branch during the financial years from 1992/93 to 2009/2010, RefNZ Statistics, New Zealand Refugee Statistics: www.refugee.org.nz/Stats/stats/htm
99 Statistics New Zealand, *NZYB*, 2000, p. 135.
100 New Zealand Immigration Service, operational manual, 19 September 2001: www.immigration.govt.nz/NZIS/operations_manual
101 Summarised and quoted from Department of Labour comment to Ann Beaglehole, March 2013.
102 New Zealand Immigration Service, operational manual, 19 September 2001: www.immigration.govt.nz/NZIS/operations_manual
103 Lianne Dalziel, speech notes for meeting, 21 August 2003.
104 Peter Cotton, interviewed by Ann Beaglehole, 26 January 2007, Wellington.
105 Dr N. Rasalingam, president Refugee Council of New Zealand, interviewed by Ann Beaglehole, 26 February 2007, Wellington.
106 Refugee issues identified at Council for International Development Refugee Policy Forum in Wellington on 8 January 2005, as reported by Rod Alley who attended on behalf of the Peace Foundation, 1 February 2005.
107 Ibid.
108 Jane (not her real name) who has personal experience of the refugee determination process, was interviewed by Ann Beaglehole, 10 January 2007, Wellington.
109 Kim Ruscoe, 'Zaoui set to face secret hearing', *Dominion Post*, 7 July 2007, A10.
110 Michael Field, 'Long road to freedom', *Dominion Post* 14 July 2007, A10.

111 Ruscoe, 'Zaoui set to face secret hearing'.
112 Refugee Status Appeals Authority New Zealand, Ahmed Zaoui, Refugee Appeal No. 74540, 1 August 2003, Auckland, pp. 24–25.
113 Field, 'Long road to freedom'.
114 'Zaoui case unjust', *Dominion Post*, 19 February 2007, A11.
115 Field, 'Long road to freedom'.
116 'Zaoui gets chance to have his say', *Dominion Post*, 10 July 2007, A4.
117 Field, 'Long road to freedom'.
118 'SIS ends Zaoui's Security Risk Certificate', Parliamentary News Room, 13 September 2007.
119 Michael Field, 'Pledge of good behaviour', *Dominion Post*, 14 September 2007, A2.
120 Haydon Dewes and Michael Field, 'Zaoui free, but SIS is still watching', *Dominion Post*, 14 September 2007, front page.
121 Richard Long, 'The Long view', *Dominion Post*, 18 September 2007, B4. See Tom Scott cartoon on release: 'Zaoui ruling makes NZ a soft touch, says Foreign Minister Winston Peters', *Dominion Post*, 15 September 2007, B4.
122 Amy Maas, 'Zaoui making lunches on K Rd', www.stuff.co.nz, 5 April 2012.
123 Refugee Status Appeals Authority New Zealand, Ahmed Zaoui, Refugee Appeal No. 74540, 1 August 2003, Auckland, p. 11.
124 Quoted in Field, 'Long road to freedom'.
125 'Late entry', *NZ Listener*, editorial, 29 September 2007.
126 David Cunliffe, 'Comprehensive immigration law closer', 5 December 2006: www.beehive.govt.nz; Martin Kay, 'Returning Kiwis face scams', *Dominion Post*, 6 December 2006, A3.
127 Radio New Zealand, *Morning Report*, interview with Minister of Immigration David Cunliffe, 6 December 2006; Martin Kay, 'Immigration law faces big changes', *Dominion Post*, 5 December 2006, A2.
128 Radio New Zealand, *Morning Report*, 28 September 2007; Haydon Dewes, 'Security risk in migrant fraud', *Dominion Post*, 27 June 2007, A3.
129 Quoted in Dewes, 'Security risk in migrant fraud'.
130 Ibid.
131 *Te Punanga: Refugee Focus*, Vol. 1, No. 5, October 2007.
132 'Persecuted American seeks asylum in NZ', *Dominion Post*, 17 May, 2007, A7.
133 'Iranian in refugee row must stay in jail', *Dominion Post*, 18 November 2006, A2.
134 Martin Kay, 'Refugees stuck in limbo-land', *Dominion Post*, 15 August 2007, A2.
135 Vernon Small, 'Hunger striker in care of church', *Dominion Post*, 4 September 2007, A3.
136 Ibid.
137 'Refugee claimant found wanting', *Dominion Post*, editorial, 6 September 2007, B4.
138 Small, 'Hunger striker in care of church'.
139 Joris de Bres, 'Refugee detention plan threat to NZ's good name', *Dominion Post*, 20 June, B5.
140 Immigration New Zealand, 'Immigration Act 2009: Refugee and protection status determinations': www.immigration.govt.nz/migrant/general/general information/immigration act, Factsheets/refugees
141 Immigration New Zealand, Operational Manual, effective 29 November 2010, 'Limitation on deportation of person recognised or claiming recognition as a refugee or protected person': www.immigration.govt.nz/opsmanual/34969.htm
142 New Zealand Refugee Statistics, Table 78: The number of removal orders served, and the number of people removed as a result of removal orders executed, including those declined refugee status, and voluntary departures during the calendar years from 1993 to 1995 and financial years from 1996/97 to 2009/10, and Table 59: Child appellants at the Refugee Status Appeals Authority, including their nationality, gender and decision outcome in the 2009/2010

financial year, RefNZ Statistics: www.refugee.org.nz/stats/stats.htm, updated 25 November 2010.
143 'Submission on the Immigration Amendment Bill', 10 May 2012: www.immigration.govt.nz/migrant/general/generalinformation/news/immigamendbill.htm
144 Richard Long, 'We need balanced books, not boat people', *Dominion Post*, 11 September 2012, A7; de Bres, 'Refugee detention plan threat to NZ's good name'.
145 Danya Levy, 'More staff to deal with boat people', www.stuff.co.nz, 18 April 2012.
146 'Refugee Centre rebuild to handle mass influx', *Dominion Post*, 11 May 2013, A2.
147 Vernon Small, 'High profile Iranian may have fresh appeal grounds', *Dominion Post*, 5 September 2007.
148 Radio New Zealand, *Morning Report*, 6 December 2006.
149 Immigration New Zealand: www.immigration.govt.nz/migrant/general/generalinformation/statistics/
150 Immigration New Zealand, 'Update from Refugee Division of Immigration New Zealand': www.hrc.co.nz/newsletters/diversity-action-programme/te-punanga/2012/08/update-from-refugee-division-of-immigration-new-zealand#more-13823
151 Anna Leask, 'Samoa, India and China top deportation list', *New Zealand Herald*, 25 October 2012: www.nzherald.co.nz/news/article
152 Tracy Watkins, 'Key beats Australian drum softly', 'Key: NZ willing to take on Aussie boat-people problem', *Dominion Post,* 11 and 9 February 2013, A2.
153 Claire Trevett, 'No special deal for refugees from PNG', *New Zealand Herald*, 8 August 2013.

Chapter nine: 'Integration takes time'

1   Kerry Burke, 'Burke, 1986 Review', 'New Zealand's Immigration Policy', Department of Statistics, *NZYB*, 1988–89, p. 193.
2   Ranginui Walker, *The Walker Papers*, Penguin Books, Auckland, 1996, p. 188.
3   ANZ, ABKF, 947, W5182, Box 302, 22/1/27/31, Part 2, Department of Labour, New Zealand Immigration Service, 'Acceptance of refugees as settlers in New Zealand', June 1990, pp. 5–6, attached at back of report on refugee programme, 1991/92, to Minister of Immigration from General Manager, Department of Labour, New Zealand Immigration Service, 21 February 1991.
4   Department of Labour, New Zealand Immigration Service, Refugee quota composition 2001/02 and planning for 2002/03, Secretary of Labour and Secretary of Foreign Affairs and Trade to the Minister of Immigration and the Minister of Foreign Affairs and Trade, 22 February 2002. (Information from Refugee Quota Branch, Auckland, 2007.)
5   ANZ, ABKF, 947, W5182, Box 302, 22/1/27/31, Part 2, Department of Labour, New Zealand Immigration Service, 'Acceptance of refugees as settlers in New Zealand', June 1990, p. 6, attached at back of report on refugee programme, 1991/92, to Minister of Immigration from General Manager, Department of Labour, New Zealand Immigration Service, 21 February 1991.
6   Lianne Dalziel, interviewed by Ann Beaglehole, 3 May 2007, Wellington.
7   ANZ, ABKF, 947, W5182, Box 302, 22/1/27/31, Part 2, Department of Labour, New Zealand Immigration Service, Acceptance of refugees as settlers in New Zealand, June 1990, p. 6, attached at back of report on refugee programme, 1991/92, to Minister of Immigration from General Manager, Department of Labour, New Zealand Immigration Service, 21 February 1991; Statistics New Zealand, *NZYB*, 2000, p. 134.
8   Department of Labour, New Zealand Immigration Service, Refugee quota composition 2001/02 and planning for 2002/03, Secretary of Labour and Secretary of Foreign Affairs

and Trade to the Minister of Immigration and the Minister of Foreign Affairs and Trade, 22 February 2002. (Information provided by Refugee Quota Branch, Auckland, 2007.)
9 Department of Labour comment to Ann Beaglehole, March 2013. See later in the chapter for further discussion on the part 'family links' plays in the current process.
10 Ann Beaglehole, 'Refugees: Controlling the flow of refugees', Te Ara – the Encyclopedia of New Zealand: www.TeAra.govt.nz/en /refugees
11 ANZ, ABKF, 947, W5182, Box 302, 22/1/27/31, Part 2, Department of Labour, New Zealand Immigration Service, 'Acceptance of refugees as settlers in New Zealand', June 1990, p. 5, attached at back of report on refugee programme, 1991/92, to Minister of Immigration from General Manager, Department of Labour, New Zealand Immigration Service, 21 February 1991.
12 Ann Beaglehole, 'Refugees 1970s–2003: Refugee groups', Te Ara – the Encyclopedia of New Zealand: www.TeAra.govt.nz/en/Refugees/4.
13 ANZ, ABKF, 947, W5182, Box 302, 22/1/27/31, Part 2, Department of Labour, New Zealand Immigration Service, 'Acceptance of refugees as settlers in New Zealand', June 1990, p. 3, attached at back of report on refugee programme, 1991/92, to Minister of Immigration from General Manager, Department of Labour, New Zealand Immigration Service, 21 February 1991.
14 James Veitch and Dalia Tinawi, 'Middle Eastern peoples: Other Middle Eastern peoples', Te Ara – the Encyclopedia of New Zealand: www.TeAra.govt.nz/en/ middle-eastern-peoples/4
15 Ann Beaglehole, 'Refugees 1970s–2003: Refugee groups'.
16 ANZ, ABKF, 947, W5182, Box 217, 22/1/336, Part 1, Afghanistan Policy and General, 1980–90, R.W. Malpass for Secretary of Labour to J. Landau, Regional Representative, UNHCR, 21 March 1985.
17 See for example, ABKF, 947, W5182, Box 217, 22/1/336, Part 1, Afghanistan policy and general, 1980–90, UNHCR to Ron Malpass, Assistant Director, Immigration Division, 17 December 1984 and Eddie Isbey, Parliamentary Under-Secretary to the Minister of Immigration, to Mrs Haliburton, 16 October 1986.
18 ANZ, ABKF, 947, W5182, Box 217, 22/1/336, Part 1, Afghanistan policy and general, Minister of Immigration to Archdeacon R.J. Nicholson, Hamilton, 23 November 1984.
19 Ibid., Seclab to Rome Office, 29 April 1981.
20 Ibid., R.W. Malpass to Miss B.J. Gavan, Private Secretary to Minister of Immigration, 'Some suggested paras for your letter on Afghan refugees', 17 October 1984.
21 Ibid., Kerry Burke, Minister of Immigration to Bruce Duncan, Lower Hutt, 19 February 1985.
22 Ibid., Minister of Immigration to Archdeacon R.J. Nicholson, Hamilton, 23 November 1984; Parliamentary Under-Secretary to the Minister of Immigration to Mrs E. Haliburton, Hawke's Bay, 16 October 1986.
23 Veitch and Tinawi, 'Middle Eastern peoples: Other Middle Eastern peoples'.
24 Statistics New Zealand, 2006 Census of Population and Dwellings: www.stats.govt.nz/Census/2006. There was no census held in 2011.
25 Ann Beaglehole, 'Refugees 1970s–2003: Refugee groups', Te Ara – the Encyclopedia of New Zealand: www.TeAra.govt.nz/en/refugees/4
26 Statistics New Zealand, *NZYB*, 2000, p. 135.
27 Carl Walrond, 'Africans: Immigration', Te Ara – the Encyclopedia of New Zealand: www.TeAra.govt.nz/en/africans/2
28 Statistics New Zealand, *NZYB*, 2000, p. 134.
29 Department of Labour, New Zealand Immigration Service, Refugee quota composition 2001/02 and planning for 2002/03, Secretary of Labour and Secretary of Foreign Affairs

and Trade to the Minister of Immigration and the Minister of Foreign Affairs and Trade, 22 February 2002, p. 3. (Information provided by Refugee Quota Branch, Auckland in 2007.)
30 Statistics New Zealand, 2006 Census of Population and Dwellings: www.stats.govt.nz/Census/2006
31 Peter Cotton, Director, RMS New Zealand, 'Family reunion, an examination of family reunion issues viewed from the perspective of New Zealand', RMS submission to government and UNHCR as part of tripartite meetings in Geneva, May 2001, pp. 2, 3.
32 Peter Cotton, Director, RMS New Zealand, 'NZIS refugee quota selection', submission to NZIS, 2002, p.5.
33 Department of Labour, New Zealand Immigration Service, Refugee quota composition 2003/2004: Options, Marie Sullivan, Market Manager to General Manager, 29 January 2003, p. 1. (Information provided by Refugee Quota Branch, Auckland in 2007.)
34 Ibid.
35 Information from Kevin Third, Director of the Refugee Division, Department of Labour, interviewed by Ann Beaglehole, 26 November 2007, Wellington; and also from Department of Labour, New Zealand Immigration Service, ref. 04/38374, Refugee quota composition 2004/05, Secretary of Labour and Secretary of Foreign Affairs and Trade to Minister of Immigration and Minister of Foreign Affairs and Trade, 19 July 2004, pp. 1, 6. (Information provided by Refugee Quota Branch, Auckland in 2007.)
36 Kevin Third, Director Refugee Division, interviewed by Ann Beaglehole, 26 November 2007, Wellington.
37 Former Hungarian refugee, conversation with Ann Beaglehole, September 2007, Wellington.
38 Department of Labour, New Zealand Immigration Service, Refugee quota composition 2006/07, Secretary of Labour and Secretary of Foreign Affairs and Trade to Minister of Immigration and Minister of Foreign Affairs and Trade, 9 May 2006, pp. 5-6. (Information provided by Refugee Quota Branch, Auckland in 2007.)
39 Peter Cotton, RMS, 'NZIS Refugee quota selection', submission to NZIS, 2002, p. 4.
40 Department of Labour, New Zealand Immigration Service, Refugee quota composition 2001/02 and planning for 2002/03, Secretary of Labour and Secretary of Foreign Affairs and Trade to the Minister of Immigration and the Minister of Foreign Affairs and Trade, 22 February 2002, pp. 4, 6. (Information provided by Refugee Quota Branch, Auckland in 2007.)
41 Love M. Chile, 'The imported underclass: Poverty and social exclusion of black African refugees in Aotearoa New Zealand', *Asia Pacific Viewpoint*, Vol. 43, No. 3, December 2002, Abstract, p. 355.
42 RMS, Refugee and Migrant Service Annual Report 2002-03. The other groups were: Sri Lankan, 21; Cambodian, 9; Palestinian, 13; Ethiopian, 12; Somali, 25; Sudanese, 11; Burundi, six; Rwandan, five. There were also tiny numbers of Congolese, Syrian, Eritrean and Indonesian refugees.
43 Quoted in Jenny Macintyre, 'Fresh start: Are Somali refugees getting a fair go in this country?', *NZ Listener*, 3 February 2007, p. 31.
44 Simon Collins, 'African exiles giving way to Asians', *New Zealand Herald*, 9 November 2007, A11.
45 Department of Labour, New Zealand Immigration Service, ref 04/38374, Refugee quota composition 2004/05, Secretary of Labour and Secretary of Foreign Affairs and Trade to Minister of Immigration and Minister of Foreign Affairs and Trade, 19 July 2004, p. 5; New Zealand Immigration Service, ref 05/45242, Proposed refugee quota composition 2005/06, Secretary of Labour and Secretary of Foreign Affairs and Trade to Minister of Immigration and Minister of Foreign Affairs and Trade, 25 February 2005, p. 5; Refugee

quota composition 2006/07, Secretary of Labour and Secretary of Foreign Affairs and Trade to Minister of Immigration and Minister of Foreign Affairs and Trade, 9 May 2006, p. 2. (Information from Refugee Quota Branch, Auckland, 2007.)
46 Peter Cotton, Director, RMS New Zealand, 'Family reunion, an examination of family reunion issues viewed from the perspective of New Zealand', RMS submission to government and UNHCR as part of tripartite meetings in Geneva, May 2001, p. 3. The sub-Saharan region of Africa, that is, areas that lie south of the Sahara, is sometimes referred to as 'Black Africa'.
47 Kevin Third, Director of Refugee Division, Department of Labour, interviewed by Ann Beaglehole, 26 November 2007, Wellington.
48 From 'If I could', Yilma Tafere Tasew, 'Agonizing wounds', quoted in Department of Labour, New Zealand Immigration Service, *Refugee Voices: A journey towards resettlement*, Wellington, June 2004, p. 7.
49 Former Foreign Affairs Minister Don McKinnon, written communication to Ann Beaglehole, 19 February 2007.
50 Peter Cotton, CEO, RMS Refugee Resettlement, interviewed by Ann Beaglehole, 26 January 2007, Wellington.
51 Statement by Don McKinnon, Deputy Prime Minister, quoted in Department of Labour, New Zealand Immigration Service, *Refugee Women: The New Zealand Refugee Quota Programme*, Wellington, 1994, p. 23.
52 Former Foreign Affairs Minister Don McKinnon, written communication to Ann Beaglehole, 19 February 2007.
53 Walrond, 'Africans – Immigration'.
54 Former RMS Refugee Coordinator, interviewed by Ann Beaglehole, 10 and 11 April 2007 in Auckland and 15 April 2007 in Wellington.
55 Refugee and Migrant Service, Annual Report, 2002–2003, 'Regional roundup' and Peter Cotton, 'A "singularly" challenging year for RMS'.
56 Refugee and Migrant Service, Annual Report, 2002–2003, 'Regional roundup'.
57 Ibid.
58 Peter Cotton, 'Family reunion, an examination of family reunion issues viewed from the perspective of RMS New Zealand', RMS submission to government and UNHCR as part of tripartite meetings in Geneva, May 2001, p. 2.
59 Peter Cotton, CEO, RMS Refugee Resettlement, interviewed by Ann Beaglehole, 26 January 2007, Wellington.
60 Cotton, 'Family reunion, an examination of family reunion issues viewed from the perspective of New Zealand', p. 1.
61 Ibid., p. 3.
62 Ibid., p. 2.
63 Peter Cotton, CEO, RMS Refugee Resettlement, interviewed by Ann Beaglehole, 26 January 2007, Wellington.
64 RMS Director Peter Cotton, NZIS refugee quota selection, submission to NZIS, 2002, p. 4.
65 Dr N. Rasalingam, president, New Zealand Refugee Council, interviewed by Ann Beaglehole, 26 February 2007, Wellington.
66 Cotton, 'Family reunion, an examination of family reunion issues viewed from the perspective of New Zealand', p. 4.
67 Peter Cotton, CEO, RMS Refugee Resettlement, interviewed by Ann Beaglehole, 26 January 2007, Wellington.
68 *Refugee Family Reunification Trust Newsletter*, No. 11, November 2012, 'Trust helps more than 200 refugee families'.

69　Kevin Third, Director, Refugee Division, interviewed by Ann Beaglehole, 26 November 2007.
70　Human Rights Commission, 'Update from Refugee Division of Immigration New Zealand', August 2012: www.hrc.co.nz/newsletter/diversity-action-programme/te-punanga/2012/08/update-from-refugee-division-of-immigration-new-zealand#more-13823
71　Quoted in Macintyre, 'Fresh start', p. 31.
72　Adam Ray, 'Refugee's jail term cut for "trauma"', *Dominion Post*, 5 May 2007, p. 1.
73　Bruce Ansley, 'Who's moving in next door?', *NZ Listener*, 2 September 2006, p. 19.
74　'Refugee stalker proving a menace', *Dominion Post*, 9 December 2006.
75　Former Foreign Minister Don McKinnon, written communication to Ann Beaglehole, 19 February 2007.
76　Peter Cotton, Director, RMS Refugee Resettlement, interviewed by Ann Beaglehole, 26 January 2007, Wellington.
77　Peter Cotton, CEO, RMS Refugee Resettlement, letter to the editor of *NZ Listener*, 17 February 2007, p. 7.
78　Quoted in Macintyre, 'Fresh start', p. 30.
79　'Jobless and homeless Somali lives in a car', *Dominion Post*, 18 September 2006, A10.
80　Greg Clydesdale, 'Maori concern at migrants justified', *Dominion Post*, 5 September 2007, A13.
81　Richard Bedford, Elsie Ho and Jacqueline Lidgard, 'International migration in New Zealand: Contexts, components and policy issues', Population Studies Centre, University of Waikato, Hamilton, No. 37, October 2000, p. 5.
82　Ranginui Walker, 'Immigration policy and the political economy of New Zealand', in S.W. Greif (ed.), *Immigration and National Identity in New Zealand: One people, two peoples, many peoples?* Dunmore Press, Palmerston North, 1995, pp. 282–302.
83　Walker, *The Walker Papers*, p. 187.
84　Prue Poata (ed.), *Poata: Seeing beyond the horizon: Tama Te Kapua Poata*, Steele Roberts, Wellington, 2012, p. 176.
85　Chile, 'The imported underclass', pp. 355–66.
86　Love M. Chile, 'Refugee Development Centre: A discussion paper', Institute of Public Policy, Auckland University of Technology, undated, p. 2.
87　Chile, 'The imported underclass', p. 364.
88　Department of Labour, New Zealand Immigration Service, *Refugee Voices: A journey towards resettlement*, Wellington, June 2004, foreword by Paul Swain, Minister of Immigration, p. 5.
89　Mary Nash, John Wong and Andrew Trlin, 'Civic and social integration: A new field of social work practice with immigrants, refugees and asylum seekers', *International Social Work*, 2006, Vol. 49, p. 345; Mary Nash and Andrew Trlin, *Social Work with Immigrants, Refugees and Asylum Seekers in New Zealand*, New Settlers Programme, Massey University, Palmerston North, 2004.
90　Nash and Trlin, *Social Work*, p. 346.
91　Alex Fensome, 'Top pupils' marks "outstanding"', *Dominion Post*, 13 February 2013, A5.
92　'Some of the best pies in Tawa' and 'New Justice of the Peace', Refugee and Migrant Service, Annual Report, 2002–03.
93　Dave Burgess, 'Refugees get award for tech success', *Dominion Post*, 17 May 2007, A11.
94　Priyanka Bhonsule, 'Degree caps off hard work', *City Life*, 21 June 2007, p. 6.
95　Ann Beaglehole's conversation with Rachel Kidd, senior staff member, New Zealand Red Cross Refugee Services, 18 January 2013; *Te Punanga: Refugee Focus*, November 2007: www.hrc.co.nz/newsletters. Electronic issues of *Te Punanga: Refugee Focus* before 2009 are hard to access. (Some hardcopies are available from Ann Beaglehole.)
96　Gabriel Humphries, 'Dream of having own home comes true for refugees', *Dominion Post*, 31 March 2012, A20.

97 'Citizenship for *Tampa* refugees', RMS Refugee Resettlement, Annual Report, 2004–05.
98 Former RMS Refugee Coordinator, interviewed by Ann Beaglehole, 10 and 11 April 2007 in Auckland and 15 April 2007, Wellington.
99 RMS, Annual Report, 1997–98, p. 7.
100 Ibid.
101 Former RMS Refugee Coordinator, interviewed by Ann Beaglehole, 10 and 11 April 2007 in Auckland and 15 April 2007, Wellington.
102 'Volunteer Programme: NZQA recognition', Refugee and Migrant Service, Annual Report, 2002–2003.
103 Former RMS Refugee Coordinator, interviewed by Ann Beaglehole, 10 and 11 April 2007 in Auckland and 15 April 2007, Wellington.
104 Speech by Hon. David Cunliffe, Minister of Immigration at the National Refugee Settlement Forum in Hamilton, 29 May 2007, 'Minister's speech at National Resettlement Forum', Human Rights Commission, *Te Punanga: Refugee focus*, Vol. 1, No. 1, June 2007: www.hrc.co.nz/newsletters.
105 Ibid.
106 Dr N. Rasalingam, interviewed by Ann Beaglehole, 26 February 2007, Wellington. Dr Arif Saeid is the current president of the Refugee Council: www.rc.org.nz
107 Former RMS Refugee Coordinator, interviewed by Ann Beaglehole, 10 and 11 April 2007 in Auckland and 15 April 2007, Wellington; information about services was also obtained from various community newsletters.
108 'Refugee mobile community clinical team', *Te Punanga: Refugee Focus*, Vol. 1, No. 5, October 2007.
109 'Refugee lifeline goes operational', *Te Punanga: Refugee Focus*, Vol. 1, No. 5, October 2007.
110 Dr N. Rasalingam, interviewed by Ann Beaglehole, 26 February 2007, Wellington.
111 Former RMS Refugee Coordinator, interviewed by Ann Beaglehole, 10 and 11 April 2007 in Auckland and 15 April 2007, Wellington.
112 Dr N. Rasalingam, interviewed by Ann Beaglehole, 26 February 2007, Wellington.
113 Former Minister of Immigration Aussie Malcolm, interviewed by Ann Beaglehole, 12 April 2007, Auckland.
114 Former ICCI Director Keith Taylor, conversation with Ann Beaglehole, 25 January 2007, Wellington.
115 Peter Cotton, RMS Refugee Resettlement Director, interviewed by Ann Beaglehole, 26 January 2007, Wellington.
116 Richard Towle, 'Message from UNHCR', Refugee Family Reunification Trust newsletter, No. 8, November 2009.
117 Refugee Services Aotearoa New Zealand, 'Report of Board Chairman Brian Lynch', Annual General Meeting of Refugee Services Aotearoa New Zealand, 1 December 2011: www.refugeeservices.org.nz/about_us/rms_board
118 New Zealand Red Cross Refugee Services, 'New Zealand Red Cross to lead the delivery of refugee services', media release, 6 December 2012.
119 Human Rights Commission, 'Refugee resettlement strategy', *Race Relations in 2012*: www.hrc.co.nz
120 Immigration New Zealand, Refugee resettlement factsheet: www.immigration.govt.nz/migrant/general/general information/media/refugeefactsheet.htm
121 Ibid. The bulk of the refugee quota for 2011–12 was made up of refugees from Myanmar (351); followed by Iraq (113); and Bhutan (89), Human Rights Commission, 'Update from Refugee Division of Immigration New Zealand': www.hrc.co.nz/newsletter/diversity-action-

programme/te-punanga/2012/08/update; New Zealand Red Cross Refugee Services, 'New Zealand Red Cross to lead the delivery of refugee services'.
122 Statistics New Zealand, *NZYB*, 2006, p. 104.
123 Statistics New Zealand, 2006 Census of Population and Dwellings, cited in Statistics New Zealand, *NZYB*, 2010, p. 106: www.stats.govt.nz/Census/2006
124 Peter Cotton, RMS Refugee Resettlement Director, interviewed by Ann Beaglehole, 26 January 2007, Wellington.
125 Some of these issues are explored in a story for young people: Adrienne Jansen, *Asli's Story*, Learning Media, Wellington, 2000.
126 *NZPD*, Vol. 559, 11 March 1997, p. 751.
127 Ansley, 'Who's moving in next door?', p. 17.
128 Settlement Support New Zealand, Community Services, Upper Hutt City Council, 'Report: Upper Hutt community forum for groups working with refugees and migrants', 20 July 2007.
129 Joanne Black, 'Time to talk', editorial, *NZ Listener*, 13 January 2007, p. 5.
130 Rebecca Thomson, 'Prof rewarded for peaceful dialogue', *The Wellingtonian*, 30 August 2007, p. 5.
131 Martin Kay, 'Unveil or leave, MP tells Muslims', *Dominion Post*, 26/27 August 2006, p. 1.
132 Jim Chipp, 'Muslim girls: Not so different', *The Wellingtonian*, 12 April 2012, p. 3.
133 Kay, 'Unveil or leave, MP tells Muslims'. Don Brash is the son of Alan Brash, chairperson of the National Council of Churches and mid-twentieth-century refugee advocate.
134 Ansley, 'Who's moving in next door?', p. 18.
135 Ibid., p. 16.
136 Ibid., p. 19.
137 Human Rights Commission, 'Update from Refugee Division of Immigration New Zealand', August 2012: www.hrc.co.nz/newsletter/diversity-action-programme/te-punanga/2012/08/update-from-refugee-division-of-immigration-new-zealand#more-13823
138 Walrond, 'Africans: Immigration'.
139 Kim Ruscoe, 'Refugees test positive for HIV', *Dominion Post*, 2 December 2006, A6; '930 from Zimbabwe apply for residency', *Dominion Post*, 2 March 2007, A8. Figures for the number of Zimbabweans with HIV/AIDS have varied in different news reports.
140 Keri Welham and Haydon Dewes, '$3m Aids error on refugees', *Dominion Post*, 31 August 2006, front page.
141 Former Minister of Immigration Lianne Dalziel, interviewed by Ann Beaglehole, 3 May 2007, Wellington; Kevin Third, Director Refugee Division, interviewed by Ann Beaglehole, 26 November 2007, Wellington.
142 Sarah Barnett, 'Hard to swallow', *NZ Listener*, 29 September 2007, p. 21, report on findings of Dr Andrea Forde, senior adviser for public health medicine.
143 'New frontiers: TB stable in NZ', *NZ Listener*, 4 November 2006, p. 35.
144 Kevin Third, Director Refugee Division, interviewed by Ann Beaglehole, 26 November 2007, Wellington.
145 Immigration New Zealand, Refugee resettlement factsheet: www.immigration.govt.nz/migrant/general/generalinformation/media/refugeefactsheet.htm
146 Department of Labour comment on draft 'Refuge New Zealand', March 2013.

Conclusion: A fine record?

1 Beaglehole, Ann, *A Small Price to Pay: Refugees from Hitler in New Zealand, 1936–1946*, Allen & Unwin, Wellington, 1988, pp. 32–33, quoting from Ann Beaglehole's interviews with

refugees, tapes and transcripts in the Alexander Turnbull Library, Wellington.
2   Quoted in Bill Smith, 'South American Refugees in New Zealand: Experiences and needs', Interview with Chilean Refugee, in Max Abbott (ed.), *Refugee Resettlement and Wellbeing*, based on the first National Conference on Refugee Mental Health, Wellington, New Zealand, 12–15 May 1988, Mental Health Foundation of New Zealand, Auckland, 1989, p. 212.
3   Quoted in Sir George Laking, 'Stranger in the House: A view of Holyoake', Margaret Clark (ed.), *Sir Keith Holyoake: Towards a political biography*, Dunmore Press, Palmerston North, 1997, p. 151.
4   Conrad Wright, Manager, Refugee Status Determination, conversation with Ann Beaglehole, Wellington, 3 April 2013.
5   Martin Chulov and Mark Rice-Oxley, 'A refugee crisis for the world', *Guardian Weekly*, 2–8 August 2013.
6   'Afghan interpreters cannot be left to die', *Dominion Post*, 29 October 2012, A10.
7   Richard Bedford, Elsie Ho and Jacqueline Lidgard, 'International Migration in New Zealand: Contexts, components and policy issues', Policy Studies Centre, the University of Waikato, Hamilton, No. 37, October 2000, p. 28.

Bibliography

Books

Abbott, Max (ed.), *Refugee Resettlement and Wellbeing*, based on the first National Conference on Refugee Mental Health, Wellington, New Zealand, 12–15 May 1988, Mental Health Foundation of New Zealand, Auckland, 1989

Abella, I. and H. Troper, *None is Too Many: Canada and the Jews of Europe 1933–1948*, Lester & Dennys, Toronto, 1982

Apse, Andris and Ron Crosby, *Odyssey and Images: An illustrated biography*, Reed, Auckland, 2006

Bandyopadhyay, Sekhar (ed.), *India in New Zealand: Local identities, global relations*, Otago University Press, Dunedin, 2010

Bassett, Michael, *Working with David: Inside the Lange Cabinet*, Hodder Moa, Auckland, 2008

Beaglehole, Ann and Hal Levine, *Far from the Promised Land: Being Jewish in New Zealand*, Pacific Press, Wellington, 1995

Beaglehole, Ann, *Facing the Past: Looking back at refugee childhood in New Zealand, 1940s–1960s*, Allen & Unwin, Wellington, 1990

Beaglehole, Ann, *A Small Price to Pay: Refugees from Hitler in New Zealand, 1936–1946*, Allen & Unwin, Wellington, 1988

Belich, James, *The New Zealand Wars and the Victorian Interpretation of Racial Conflict*, Penguin Books, Auckland, 1998

Benson, Heather, *A Dissolving Dream: A New Zealander in Amin's Uganda*, Bridget Williams Books, Wellington, 1992

Binzegger, Anton, *New Zealand's Policy on Refugees*, New Zealand Institute of International Affairs, Wellington, 1980

Blakeney, Michael, *Australia and the Jewish Refugees, 1933–1948*, Croom Helm, Sydney, 1985

Boast, Richard, *Buying the Land, Selling the Land: Governments and Maori land in the North Island 1865–1921*, Victoria University Press, Wellington, 2008

Boast, Richard and Richard Hill (eds), *Raupatu: The confiscation of Maori land*, Victoria University Press, Wellington, 2009

Bönisch-Brednich, Brigitta, *Keeping a Low Profile: An oral history of German immigration to New Zealand*, Victoria University Press, Wellington, 2002

Clark, Margaret (ed.), *Sir Keith Holyoake: Towards a political biography*, Dunmore Press, Palmerston North, 1997

Cohen, Gerard Daniel, *In Europe's Wake: Europe's displaced persons in the postwar order*, Oxford Studies in International History, Oxford, 2012

Connew, Bruce, *Stopover: A story of migration*, Victoria University Press, Wellington, 2007

Crosby, R.D., *The Musket Wars: A history of inter-iwi conflict 1806–1845*, Libro International, Auckland, 2012

du Fresne, Yvonne, *The Bear from the North: Tales of a New Zealand childhood*, Women's Press, London, 1989

Elder, Chris, *New Zealand's China Experience: Its genesis, triumphs, and occasional moments of less than complete success*, Victoria Unversity Press, Wellington, 2012

Eggers, David, *What is the What*, Hamish Hamilton, London, 2006

Elsmore, Bronwyn, *Like them that Dream: The Maori and the Old Testament*, 1st pub. 1985, 3rd edn, Reed Books, Auckland, 2011

Elsmore, Bronwyn, *Mana from Heaven: A century of Maori prophets in New Zealand*, Reed Books, Auckland, 1999

Frame, Janet, *Living in the Maniototo*, Women's Press, London, 1981
Fraser, Rev. Ian W., *Elderly Refugees in New Zealand: The story of Nansen Home, Lower Hutt*, Nansen Home, Lower Hutt, 1985
Gallienne, Robin, *'The Whole Thing was Orchestrated': New Zealand's response to the Indo-Chinese refugees exodus 1975-1985*, University of Auckland Centre for Asian Studies, Resource Papers, No. 2, Auckland, 1991
Ghosh, Bimal, *Huddled Masses and Uncertain Shores: Insights into irregular migration*, International Organisation for Migration, Martinus Nijhoff Publishers, The Hague, Boston/London, 1998
Goldman, L.M., *The History of the Jews in New Zealand*, A.H. & A.W. Reed, Wellington, 1958
Gorst, J.E., *The Maori King*, Paul's Book Arcade, Hamilton and Auckland, 1959, 1st pub. Macmillan & Co., 1864
Greif, Stuart William (ed.), *Immigration and National Identity in New Zealand: One people, two peoples, many peoples?*, Dunmore Press, Palmerston North, 1995
Hayward, Margaret, *Diary of the Kirk Years*, Cape Catley Ltd, Queen Charlotte Sound and Reed, Wellington, 1981
Hensley, Gerald, *Final Approaches: A memoir*, Auckland University Press, Auckland, 2006
Hickford, Mark, *Lords of the Land: Indigenous property rights and the jurisprudence of empire*, Oxford University Press, Oxford, 2011
Hunt, Graeme, *Spies and Revolutionaries: A history of New Zealand subversion*, Reed Publishing (NZ) Ltd., Auckland, 2007
Ihimaera, Witi, *The Parihaka Woman*, Vintage, Auckland, 2011
Ip, Manying and Nigel Murphy, *Aliens at my Table: Asians as New Zealanders see them*, Penguin, Auckland, 2005
Ip, Manying, *Dragons on the Long White Cloud: The making of Chinese New Zealanders*, Tandem Press, Auckland, 1996
Jansen, Adrienne, *Asli's Story*, Learning Media, Wellington, 2000
Jansen, Adrienne, *I Have in My Arms Both Ways: Stories by ten immigrant women*, Allen & Unwin, Wellington, 1990
Kanal, Borany and Adrienne Jansen, *Borany's Story*, Learning Media, Ministry of Education, Wellington, 1991
King, Michael, *Moriori: A people rediscovered*, Viking, Auckland, 1989
King, Michael, *The Penguin History of New Zealand*, Penguin Books, Auckland, 2003
Levine, Stephen (ed.), *A Standard for the People: The 150th anniversary of the Wellington Hebrew Congregation 1843-1993*, Hazard Press, Christchurch, 1994
Latham, Robert Gordon, *A Dictionary of the English Language*, Vol. 2, Part 2, Longmans, London, 1870
Lochore, R.A., *From Europe to New Zealand: An account of our continental European settlers*, A.H. & A.W. Reed, with New Zealand Institute of International Affairs, Wellington, 1951
Manning, Selwyn, *I Almost Forgot the Moon: The disinformation campaign against Ahmed Zaoui*, Multimedia Investments, 2004
Manterys, Adam, Stefania Zawada, Stanislaw Manterys, Jozef Zawada (eds), *New Zealand's First Refugees: Pahiatua's Polish children*, Polish Children's Reunion Committee, Wellington, 2004
McGill, David, *The Other New Zealanders*, Mallinson Rendel, Wellington, 1982
McKinnon, Malcolm, *Immigrants and Citizens: New Zealanders and Asian immigration in historical context*, Institute of Policy Studies, Victoria University of Wellington, Wellington, 1996
McKinnon, Malcolm, *Independence and Foreign Policy; New Zealand in the world since 1935*, Auckland University Press, Auckland, 1993

McNeish, James, *The Sixth Man: The extraordinary life of Paddy Costello*, Random House, Auckland, 2007

McNeish, James, *Dance of the Peacocks: New Zealanders in exile in the time of Hitler and Mao Tse-Tung*, Random House, Auckland, 2003

Mikaere, Buddy, *Te Maiharoa and the Promised Land*, Reed, Auckland, 1988

Ng, James, *Windows on a Chinese Past: How the Cantonese goldseekers and their heirs settled in New Zealand*, Vol. 1, Otago Heritage Books, Dunedin, 1993

Ng, James, *Windows on a Chinese Past: Larrikinism and Violence: Immigration Issues, 20th Century Assimilation: Biographies*, Vol. 3, Otago Heritage Books, Dunedin, 1993

Miller, Raymond (ed.), *New Zealand Government and Politics*, 4th edn, Oxford University Press, Auckland, 2006

Mitchell, Austin, *The Half Gallon Quarter Acre Pavlova Paradise*, Whitcombe &Tombs, Christchurch, 1972

Muldoon, Robert David, *The Rise and Fall of a Young Turk*, A.H. & A.W. Reed, Wellington, 1974

Nash, Mary and Andrew Trlin, *Social Work with Immigrants, Refugees and Asylum Seekers in New Zealand*, New Settlers Programme, Massey University, Palmerston North, 2004

Neumann, Klaus, *Refuge Australia: Australia's humanitarian record*, University of New South Wales Press, Sydney, 2004

O'Grady, Ron, *The Old Believers: A New Zealand refugee programme*, National Council of Churches, Christchurch, 1972

Oliver, W.H., *Claims to the Waitangi Tribunal*, Waitangi Tribunal Division, Department of Justice, Wellington, 1991

Olssen, Erik, *John A. Lee*, University of Otago Press, Dunedin, 1977

O'Malley, Vincent, *The Meeting Place: Maori and Pakeha encounters, 1642–1840*, Auckland University Press, Auckland, 2012

Pearson, David, *A Dream Deferred: The origins of ethnic conflict in New Zealand*, Allen & Unwin, Wellington, 1990

Poata, Prue (ed.), *Poata: Seeing beyond the horizon, a memoir: Tama Te Kapua Poata*, Steele Roberts, Wellington, 2012

Sandoval, Jorge, *Surviving Pinochet*, as told to Peter Bidwell, Steele Roberts, Wellington, 2008

Sedley, Steven, *The Deckston Story: The story of Annie and Max Deckston, Jewish philanthropists who saved twenty Polish Jewish children from the Holocaust*, Holocaust Centre of New Zealand, Wellington, 2012

Sinclair, Keith, *Walter Nash*, Auckland University Press, Auckland, 1976

Skwarko, Krystyna, *The Invited: The story of 733 Polish children who grew up in New Zealand*, Millwood Press, Wellington, 1974

Spoonley, Paul and Richard Bedford, *Welcome to Our World? Immigration and the reshaping of New Zealand*, Dunmore Publishing, Auckland, 2012

Suchanski, Alina, *Alone*, Alina Suchanski, Te Anau, 2012

Sutch, W.B., *The Quest for Security in New Zealand, 1840–1966*, Oxford University Press, Wellington, 1966

Sutherland, Oliver, *Paikea: The life of I.L.G Sutherland*, Canterbury University Press, Christchurch, 2013.

Taylor, Nancy M., *The New Zealand People at War; the Home Front: Official history of New Zealand in the Second World War, 1939–1945*, Government Printer, Wellington, 1986, Vols 1 & 2

Taylor, Savitri (ed.), *Nationality, Refugee Status and State Protection: Explorations of the gap between man and citizen*, Federation Press, Annandale, New South Wales, 2005

Templeton, Hugh (ed.), *Mr Ambassador: Memoirs of Sir Carl Berendsen*, Victoria University Press, Wellington, 2009

Wellington Refugees' Survivors Trust, *Beyond the Dark Journey: Short stories and poems by young refugees in New Zealand*, Wellington Refugees' Survivors Trust, Wellington, 2008

Walker, Ranginui, *The Walker Papers*, Penguin Books, Auckland, 1996

Wojciechowski, John Roy and Allan Parker, *A Strange Outcome: The remarkable survival story of a Polish child*, Penguin Books, Auckland, 2004

Woods, Joanna, *Diplomatic Ladies: New Zealand's unsung envoys*, Otago University Press, Dunedin, 2012

Wyman, Mark, *DPs: Europe's displaced persons, 1945–1951*, Cornell University Press, Ithaca and London, 1998

Articles and chapters

Adison, Rob, 'The powers that be: The story of Ali Panah', *Salient*, 3 September 2007

Alford, Michael, 'Sponsors are the key', *Refugees*, No. 33, September 1986

Alford, Michael, 'A day to celebrate', *Refugees*, No. 21, September 1983, p. 11, published online by UNHCR as *Refugees Magazine*: www.unhcr.org

Arendt, Hannah, 'We refugees', *Menorah Journal*, Vol. 31, January 1943, p. 69

Ansley, Bruce, 'Who's moving in next door?', *NZ Listener*, 2 September 2006, pp. 14, 16

Bargh, Maria, 'Te Tiriti o Waitangi in international relations and trade', in Veronica M.H. Tawhai and Katarina Gray-Sharp (eds), *'Always Speaking': The Treaty of Waitangi and public policy*, Huia, Wellington, 2011

Bedford, Richard, Elsie Ho and Jacqueline Lidgard, 'International migration in New Zealand: Contexts, components and policy issues', Policy Studies Centre, University of Waikato, Hamilton, No. 37, October 2000, pp. 5, 10–20, 21, 28

Castles, Stephen, 'Towards a sociology of forced migration and social transformation', *Sociology*, Vol. 37, No. 1, 2003, pp. 13–14

Chile, Love M., 'The imported underclass: Poverty and social exclusion of Black African refugees in Aotearoa New Zealand', *Asia Pacific Viewpoint*, Vol. 43, No. 3, December 2002, pp. 355–66

Davidson, Graeme, 'Interfaith conference call for religious education could backfire', *Dominion Post*, 9 June 2007

Dewe, Nicky, 'Welcome home', *AA Directions*, Winter, 2007, pp. 24–25

Durie, Mason, 'Foreword', in Veronica M.H. Tawhai and Katarina Gray-Sharp (eds), *'Always Speaking': The Treaty of Waitangi and public policy*, Huia, Wellington, 2011

Field, Michael, 'The dying days of Fiji's cane fields', a review of Bruce Connew, *Stopover, A Story of Migration*, Victoria University Press, Wellington, 2007, *Dominion Post*, 25 August 2007, E8

Griffiths, David, 'Somali refugees in tower hamlets: Clanship and new identities', *New Community*, Vol. 23, No. 1, pp. 5–24, January 1997

Guerin, Bernard, Pauline B. Guerin, Roda Omar Diiriye, 'Somali refugee communities as a window on New Zealand society', Migration Research Group, the University of Waikato, Hamilton

Hubbard, Anthony, 'Murderers among us?', *Listener & TV Times*, 21 May 1990, pp. 10–13

Hubbard, Anthony, 'Sanctuary: How we let in the war criminals', *Listener & TV Times*, 28 May 1990, pp. 24–28

Ip, Manying, 'Redefining Chinese female migration: From exclusion to transnationalism', in Lyndon Fraser and Katie Pickles (eds), *Shifting Centres: Women and migration in New Zealand history*, Otago University Press, Dunedin, 2002

Iqbel, Alimohamed, UNHCR Regional Representative, 'A global perspective on refugees and asylum seekers,' in Max Abbott (ed.), *Refugee Resettlement and Wellbeing*, based on the first

National Conference on Refugee Mental Health, Wellington, New Zealand, 12–15 May 1988, Mental Health Foundation of New Zealand, Auckland, 1989

Laking, George, 'A stranger in the House: A view of K.J. Holyoake' in Margaret Clark (ed.), *Sir Keith Holyoake: Towards a political biography*, Dunmore Press, Palmerston North, 1997

Leckie, Jacqueline, 'They sleep standing up', in Stuart William Greif (ed.), *Immigration and National Identity in New Zealand: One people, two peoples, many peoples?*, Dunmore Press, Palmerston North, 1995

Levy, Danya, 'The "Nazi Hunter" – Wayne Stringer interviewed by Danya Levy', *Centre News*, December 2012/January 2013

Macintyre, Jenny, 'Fresh start: Are Somali refugees getting a fair go in this country?', *NZ Listener*, 3 February 2007, p. 30

McLeod, Rosemary, 'Worrying signs of prejudice', *Dominion Post*, 20 September 2007, B4

Mannion, Robert, 'Refugees feel Cordillera's call', *Dominion Star Times*, 9 October 1988, p. 23

Marr, David, 'The luck of the draw', *Dominion Post*, 26 August 2006, E2

Morrison, Patricia, 'How the welfare state receives new citizens from Europe', *The NZ Social Worker*, Vol. 2, No. 3, August 1966, p. 35

Nash, Mary, John Wong and Andrew Trlin, 'Civic and social integration: A new field of social work practice with immigrants, refugees and asylum seekers', *International Social Work*, Vol. 49, 2006, p. 345

Neumann, Klaus, '"Our own interests must come first": Australia's response to the expulsion of Asians from Uganda', *History Australia*, Vol. 3, No. 1, Monash University Press, 2006, pp. 10.1, 10.2, 10.6, 10.9

Pangerl, Markus, 'Notions of insecurity among contemporary Indo-Fijian communities', *The Asia Pacific Journal of Anthropology*, Vol. 8, No. 3, September 2007, p. 252

Rabel, Roberto, 'The Dovish Hawk: Keith Holyoake and the Vietnam War', in Margaret Clark, (ed.), *Sir Keith Holyoake: Towards a political biography*, Dunmore Press, Palmerston North, 1997

Rattanong, Houmpheng, 'Sponsorship: A refugee's point of view', in Max Abbott (ed.), *Refugee Resettlement and Wellbeing*, based on the first National Conference on Refugee Mental Health, Wellington, New Zealand, 12–15 May 1988, Mental Health Foundation of New Zealand, Auckland, 1989

Smith, Bill, 'South American refugees in New Zealand: Experiences and needs: Interview with a Chilean refugee', in Max Abbott, (ed.), *Refugee Resettlement and Wellbeing*, based on the first National Conference on Refugee Mental Health, Wellington, New Zealand, 12–15 May 1988, Mental Health Foundation of New Zealand, Auckland, 1989

Swain, Pauline, 'Fearful refugee faces return to Fiji', *Dominion*, 4 July 1989, p. 11

Ventnor, Nick, 'Kiwi Keith a "can do" conservative', review of Barry Gustafson, *Kiwi Keith*, Auckland University Press, Auckland, 2007, *Dominion Post*, 13 November 2007, B5

Verbitsky, Jane, 'Refugee policy', in Raymond Miller (ed.), *New Zealand Government and Politics*, 4th edn, Oxford University Press, Melbourne, 2006

Walker, Ranginui, 'Immigration policy and the political economy of New Zealand', in Stuart William Greif (ed.), *Immigration and National Identity in New Zealand: One people, two peoples, many peoples?*, Dunmore Press, Palmerston North, 1995

Official publications

Appendix to the Journals of the House of Representatives (AJHR), 1867, A-20, Papers relative to affairs at Tauranga

AJHR, 1869, A-12, Papers Relative to Mr Firth's Visit to the Waikato

AJHR, 1910, I-3c, Native Affairs Committee
AJHR, 1928, G-7, Confiscated Native Lands and Other Grievances: Royal Commission to Inquire into Confiscations of Native Lands and Other Grievances Alleged by Natives
AJHR, 1946, Vol. 5, I-17, Report of the Select Committee on Dominion Population
AJHR, 1957, H-31, Report of the Director, Division of Tuberculosis
AJHR, 1984–5, E-10, Report of the Department of Health, 'Refugees'
AJHR, 1987–1990, Vol. 1, Annual Report of the Ministry of Foreign Affairs and Trade for the year ended 31 March 1989
AJHR, 1987–1990, Vol. 1, Annual Report of the Ministry of Foreign Affairs and Trade for the year ended 31 March 1988, 'South Pacific'
British Parliamentary Papers, Colonies: New Zealand, Enclosure 7, No. 67, Governor Sir G.F. Bowers to Commodore Lambert
Department of External Affairs, *External Affairs Review*, Vol. 6, No. 11, November 1956, statement by the Minister of Immigration, Mr J.R. Hanan, 22 November 1956
Department of Internal Affairs, Report for the year ended 31 March 1957, 'Hungarian refugees'
Department of Internal Affairs, Office of Ethnic Affairs, *Ethnic Perspectives in Policy*, Wellington, 2002
Department of Labour, *Monthly Review of Employment*, 'Immigration', March 1947
Department of Labour, *Labour and Employment Gazette*, Vol. I, No 3, 'Immigration facts and fallacies', 1947
Department of Labour, *Labour and Employment Gazette*, 'The assimilation and naturalization of alien immigrants', undated, probably early 1950s, p. 21, article contributed by the Naturalisation Branch of the Department of Internal Affairs
Department of Labour, *Monthly Review of Employment*, Vol. 4, No. 8, June 1949
Department of Labour and Employment newsletter, No. 4, 10 June 1949
Department of Labour and Employment, *Immigration Newsletter No. 5*, 31 January 1950
Department of Labour, *Labour and Employment Gazette*, Vol. 1, No. 1, p. 27, 1951, 'The second draft of displaced persons'
Department of Labour, *Labour and Employment Gazette*, Vol. 7, No 2, May 1957, 'Refugees from Hungary'
Department of Labour, *Labour and Employment Gazette*, Vol. 7, No. 2, May 1957, 'Refugees inclined to act defensively'
Department of Labour and Employment, *Immigration Newsletter No. 5*, 31 January 1950
Department of Labour, New Zealand Immigration Service, *Refugee Voices: A journey towards resettlement*, Wellington, June 2004
Department of Labour, New Zealand Immigration Service, *Refugee Women: The New Zealand refugee quota programme*, Wellington, 1994
Department of Labour, New Zealand Immigration Service Fact Pack, July 2002
Hutchings, Megan, *New Zealanders by Choice*, Identity Services, Department of Internal Affairs, Wellington, 1998
Ministry of Foreign Affairs, *New Zealand Foreign Affairs Review*, Vol. 22, No. 9, September 1972, p. 66, 'Asian refugees from Uganda', statement by the Minister of Foreign Affairs, 12 September 1972
Ministry of Foreign Affairs, *New Zealand Foreign Affairs Review*, Vol. 22, No. 8, August 1972, 'Uganda'
Ministry of Foreign Affairs, *New Zealand Foreign Affairs Review*, Vol. 22, No. 9, September 1972, p. 67, 'British response to New Zealand government's decision to accept Asians from Uganda', statement by the Minister of Foreign Affairs, 15 September 1972

Ministry of Foreign Affairs, *New Zealand Foreign Affairs Review*, Vol. 23, No. 11, November 1973, 'Foreign refugees resident in Chile', statement of the Associate Minister of Foreign Affairs
Ministry of Foreign Affairs, New Zealand Treaty Series, 1961, No. 2; and 1973, No. 21
Te Puni Kokiri/Ministry of Maori Development, *He Tironga Okawa Ki te Tiriti o Waitangi*, Wellington, 2001
New Zealand Parliamentary Debates *(NZPD)*, including 1920, 1939, 1950, 1975, 1987–1988, 1997, 2001, 2002
Department of Statistics and Statistics New Zealand, *New Zealand Official Yearbook*, Wellington, 1947–1949, 1965, 1971, 1973, 1988–1989, 1993–1998, 2000, 2002, 2006
Statistics New Zealand, *Demographic Trends*, 1998
Statistics New Zealand, 2006 Census of Population and Dwellings: www.stats.govt.nz/census/2006census homepage
Tables of New Zealand, *Acts and Ordinances and Statutory Regulations in Force*, up to January 2007, Parliamentary Counsel Office, Wellington

Waitangi Tribunal Reports

Waitangi Tribunal, *Manukau Report: Report of the Waitangi Tribunal on the Manukau claim*, Department of Justice, Wellington, 1985
Waitangi Tribunal, *Orakei Report: Report of the Waitangi Tribunal on the Orakei claim*, Department of Justice, Wellington, 1987
Waitangi Tribunal, *The Ngai Tahu Report 1991*, Brooker and Friend, Wellington, 1991
Waitangi Tribunal, *The Taranaki Report: Kaupapa tuatahi*, GP Publications, Wellington, 1996
Waitangi Tribunal, *Muriwhenua Land Report*, GP Publications, Wellington, 1997
Waitangi Tribunal, *Turanga Tangata Turanga Whenua: The report on the Turanganui a Kiwa claims*, Vol. 1, Legislation Direct, Wellington, 2004
Waitangi Tribunal, *He Maunga Rongo: Report on Central North Island claims, Stage One*, rev. edn, Vol. 1, Legislation Direct, Wellington, 2008
Waitangi Tribunal, *Te Urewera, Pre-publication, Part 1*, Waitangi Tribunal Report, Wellington, 2009: www.waitangitribunal.govt.nz
Waitangi Tribunal, *Te Urewera, Part 2*, Waitangi Tribunal Report, Wellington, 2010
Waitangi Tribunal, *Tauranga Moana, 1886–2006: Report of the post-Raupatu claims*, Vol. 1, Legislation Direct, Wellington, 2010
Waitangi Tribunal, *The Wairarapa ki Tararua Report*, Vol. 3, Legislation Direct, Wellington, 2010
Waitangi Tribunal, *The Wairarapa ki Tararua Report*, Vol. 1, Legislation Direct, Wellington, 2010

Newspapers, periodicals, magazines and newsletters

Auckland Herald
Bay of Plenty Times, 2012
Brooker's, *Immigration and Refugee Digest*, 1999
Centre News, 2012
City Life, 2007
Colonist, 1864
Connecting Cultures, Journal of ESOL Home Tutors, Issue 8, 2006
Daily Southern Cross, 1864, 1869, 1870
Dominion Post, 2006, 2007, 2012, 2013
Dominion, 1972, 1975, 1988, 1989, 1999
Dominion Sunday Times, 1990

Evening Post 1944, 1947, 1959, 1972, 1973, 1975, 1978, 1999, (also WPL clippings, Uganda – Politics, 1972–73)
Guardian Weekly, August 2013
NZ Listener, 2006, 2007
Lyttelton Times, 1861
More, February 1987
Nelson Examiner, 1860, 1867
New Zealand Chronicle
New Zealand Herald
New Zealand Jewish Chronicle, 1945, 1946
New Zealand National Review, 1944
New Zealand Radio Record, 1939
New Zealand Red Cross Magazine, Vol. 5, No. 2, January 1957
New Zealand Social Worker, Vol. 2, No. 3, August 1966
Press, 1999
Refugee Family Reunification Trust Newsletter, No. 6, November 2007
Refugee Family Reunification Trust Newsletter, No. 7, November 2008
Refugee Family Reunification Trust Newsletter, No. 8, November 2009
Refugee Family Reunification Trust Newsletter, No. 9, November 2010
Refugee Family Reunification Trust Newsletter, No. 11, November 2012
Southland Daily News, 1951
Star, 1868, 1936
Te Punanga: Refugee Focus, June–November 2007 (contact Human Rights Commission to access online issues)
UNHCR, *Refugees*, No. 144, Issue 3, 2006
Wellingtonian
Wellington Independent, 1868

Theses

Beaglehole, Ann, 'A small price to pay: Refugees from Hitler in New Zealand 1936–1946', MA thesis, Victoria University of Wellington, Wellington, 1986
Beaglehole, Ann, 'Facing the past: Looking back at refugee childhood in New Zealand', PhD thesis, Victoria University of Wellington, Wellington, 1990
Bihi, Abdi, 'Cultural identity, adaptation and wellbeing of Somali refugees in New Zealand', MA thesis, Victoria University of Wellington, Wellington, 1999
Dunsford, Deborah Ann, 'Seeking the prize of eradication: A social history of tuberculosis in New Zealand from World War Two to the 1970s', PhD thesis, University of Auckland, Auckland, 2008
Hughes, O.R., 'Hungarians in New Zealand: Toward a demographic profile', paper submitted for SOSC 403: Demography, Department of Sociology, Victoria University of Wellington, Wellington, 1986
Mortensen, A., 'Refugees as "Others": Social and cultural citizenship rights for refugees in New Zealand health services', PhD thesis, Massey University, Albany, 2008
Pheng, Sokeary, 'La politique d'accueil des réfugiés de la Nouvelle-Zélande: Entre obligations internationals et intérêts nationaux 1944–2006', PhD thesis, University of Avignon, Avignon, 2006
Sawicka-Brockie, Theresa, 'Forsaken journeys: The Polish experience and identity of the Pahiatua children', PhD thesis, University of Auckland, 1987

Reports (published)

Amnesty International reports, Annual report 2012, 'Fiji': www.amnesty.org/en/region/Fiji/report-2012

Campbell, Gordon, *The Intergenerational Settlement of Refugee Children in New Zealand: A report on the findings of a survey conducted for the New Zealand Refugee and Migrant Service*, Royal Society of New Zealand, 2003

Human Rights Commission, *The New Zealand Action Plan for Human Rights: Priorities for Action, 2005–2010*, Human Rights Commission, February 2005

Kirk, Norman, *New Zealand and its Neighbours*, New Zealand Institute of International Affairs, Wellington, 1971

New Zealand Red Cross Society Inc., *Annual Report and Financial Statement, 1956–1957*

Refugee and Migrant Service, Annual Reports, 1996–97, 1997–98, 1998–99, 2002–03, 2004–05

Refugee Services Aotearoa New Zealand, 'Report of Board Chairman Brian Lynch, Annual General Meeting of Refugee Services Aotearoa, New Zealand', 1 December 2011: www.refugeeservices.org.nz/about_us/rms_board

Refugee Status Appeals Authority New Zealand, *Ahmed Zaoui*, Refugee Appeal No. 74540, 1 August 2003, Auckland

Websites and web-based sources

Ann Beaglehole, 'Refugees', Te Ara – the Encyclopedia of New Zealand: www.TeAra.govt.nz/en/refugees

Ann Beaglehole, 'Refugees: New Zealand as a haven', Te Ara – the Encyclopedia of New Zealand: www.TeAra.govt.nz/en/refugees/1

Ann Beaglehole, 'Refugees 1870s–1940s: Refugee groups', Te Ara – the Encyclopedia of New Zealand: www.TeAra.govt.nz/en/refugees/2

Ann Beaglehole, 'Refugees 1950s–1970s: Refugee groups', Te Ara – the Encyclopedia of New Zealand: www.TeAra.govt.nz/en/refugees/3

Ann Beaglehole, 'Refugees 1970s–2003: Refugee groups', Te Ara – the Encyclopedia of New Zealand: www.TeAra.govt.nz/en/refugees/4

Ann Beaglehole, 'Immigration regulation', Te Ara – the Encyclopedia of New Zealand: www.TeAra.govt.nz/en/immigration-regulation/2/3

Ann Beaglehole, 'Immigration regulation 1881–1914: Restrictions on Chinese and others', Te Ara – the Encyclopedia of New Zealand: www.TeAra.govt.nz/en/immigration-regulation/2

Ann Beaglehole, 'Immigration regulation 1946–1985: Gradual change', Te Ara – the Encyclopedia of New Zealand: www.TeAra.govt.nz/en/immigration-regulation/4

Ann Beaglehole, 'Immigration regulation: Controlling Pacific Island immigration', Te Ara – the Encyclopedia of New Zealand: www.TeAra.govt.nz/en/immigration-regulation/6

Ann Beaglehole, 'Hungarians: Immigration from 1956: Refugees', Te Ara – the Encyclopedia of New Zealand: www.TeAra.govt.nz/en/hungarians/2

Auckland Refugee Council, Discussion Paper, Vol. 1, May 1998: www.refugee.org.nz/council.htm

Barry Gustafson, 'Marshall, John Ross – Biography', from the Dictionary of New Zealand Biography, Te Ara – the Encyclopedia of New Zealand: www.TeAra.govt.nz/en/biographies/5m36/1

Carl Walrond, 'Africans', Te Ara – the Encyclopedia of New Zealand: www.TeAra.govt.nz/en/africans

Carl Walrond, 'Africans: Immigration', Te Ara – the Encyclopedia of New Zealand: www.TeAra.govt.nz/en/africans/2

Carl Walrond, 'Africans: Assimilation and culture', Te Ara – the Encyclopedia of New Zealand: www.TeAra.govt.nz/en/africans/3

Carl Walrond, 'Africans: Facts and figures', Te Ara – the Encyclopedia of New Zealand: www.TeAra.govt.nz/en/africans/4

David Cunliffe, 'Comprehensive immigration law closer', 5 December 2008: www.beehive.govt.nz

Department of Labour, 'Migration Trends': www.immigration.govt.nz/migrant/general/generalInformation/research/general research/TrendsStatisticsAndSummaries.htm

Department of Labour, New Zealand Immigration Service, 'Immigration research programme: Trends in residence approvals': www.immigration.govt.nz/migrant/General/Generalinformation/Research/GeneralResearch/TrendsStatisticsAndSummaries.htm

Department of Labour, New Zealand Immigration Service, 'Operational manual': www.immigration.govt.nz/NZIS/operational_manual

Frank Tod, 'Terry Edward Lionel, 1873–1952, Racist, murderer', from the Dictionary of New Zealand Biography: www.TeAra.govt.nz/en/biographies/3t27/terry-edward-lionel

Guiding Principles on Internal Displacement, developed by the United Nations between 1992 and 1998, Human Rights Education Association: www.hrea.org/erc/Library/hrdocs/refugees/guiding-principles.html

Human Rights Commission, Annual Review of Race Relations, (2012), 'Refugee Resettlement Strategy': www.hrc.co.nz

Immigration information: www.immigration.govt.nz/workshop/hist.htm

Immigration New Zealand, 'Operational manual', effective 29 November 2010: www.immigration.govt.nz/opsmanual/34930.htm

Immigration New Zealand, 'Immigration Act 2009: Refugee and protection status determinations': www.immigration.govt.nz/migrant/general/generalinformation/immigrationact

Immigration New Zealand, 'Refugee resettlement factsheet': www.immigration.govt.nz/migrant /general/general information/media/refugeefact

Immigration New Zealand, 'Update from Refugee Division of Immigration New Zealand': www.hrc.co.nz/newsletters/diversity-action-programme/te-punanga/2012/08/update

James Veitch and Dalia Tinawi, 'Middle Eastern peoples', Te Ara – the Encyclopedia of New Zealand: www.TeAra.govt.nz/en/middle-eastern-peoples

James Veitch and Dalia Tinawi, 'Middle Eastern peoples: Other Middle Eastern peoples', Te Ara – the Encyclopedia of New Zealand: www.TeAra.govt.nz/en/middle-eastern-peoples/4

John Wilson, 'Society: Families and households', Te Ara – the Encyclopedia of New Zealand: www.TeAra.govt.nz/en/society/3

John Wilson, 'Latin Americans: Immigration history', Te Ara – the Encyclopedia of New Zealand: www.TeAra.govt.nz/en/latin-americans/1

John Wilson, 'Latin Americans: Identity in New Zealand', Te Ara – the Encyclopedia of New Zealand: www.TeAra.govt.nz/en/latin-americans/2

John Wilson, 'Russians, Ukrainians and Baltic peoples: Russians', Te Ara – the Encyclopedia of New Zealand: www.TeAra.govt.nz/en/russians-ukrainians-and-baltic peoples/1

Man Hau Liev and Rosa Chhun, 'Cambodians: Immigration: Refugees and resettlement', Te Ara – the Encyclopedia of New Zealand: www.TeAra.govt.nz/en/cambodians/1

Manying Ip, 'Chinese: Post-war changes', Te Ara – the Encyclopedia of New Zealand: www.TeAra.govt.nz/en/chinese/4

Manying Ip, 'Dinkum aliens: Chinese New Zealanders in World War Two': www.stevenyoung.co.nz/chinesevoice/misc.dinkum.htm

Margaret McClure, 'Auckland region', Te Ara – the Encyclopedia of New Zealand: www.TeAra.govt.nz/en/auckland-region/6/1/1

Ministry of Culture and Heritage, NZ history online, 'The Musket Wars': www.nzhistory.net.nz/war/newzealands-19th-century-wars/themusket-wars

Minister of Immigration, Tuariki Delamare, Press Releases, 1999, New Zealand Executive Government News Release Archive, RefNZnews, Archives 1999: www.refugee.org.nz/news/arc1999.htm

Misatauveve Melani Anae, 'Samoans: History and migration', Te Ara – the Encyclopedia of New Zealand: www.TeAra.govt.nz/en/samoans/1

New Zealand Book Council: www.bookcouncil.org.nz

New Zealand Statutes, Immigration Amendment Act 1999: www.legislation.govt.nz

New Zealand Statutes, Immigration Amendment Act (No. 2) 1999: www.legislation.govt.nz

'New Zealand's refugee sector: Perspectives and developments, 1987–2010': www.dol.govt.nz/publications/research/refugee-sector-perspectives-developments/summary.asp

RefNZ Statistics (New Zealand Refugee Statistics): www.refugee.org.nz/Stats/stats.htm

Refugee Services Aotearoa New Zealand: www.refugeeservices.org.nz/about_us/rms_board

Richard Boast, 'Te Tango whenua – Maori land alienation'; 'Raupatu – confiscations', Te Ara – the Encyclopedia of New Zealand: www.TeAra.govt.nz/en/te-tango-whenua-maori-land-alienation/4

R.P.G. Haines, 'Legal aid issues in the refugee determination process': www.refugee.org.nz/Reference/laid.htm

'The Colombo Plan' from *An Encyclopedia of New Zealand*, A.H. McLintock (ed.), originally published in 1966, Te Ara – the Encyclopedia of New Zealand: www.TeAra.govt.nz/en/1966/International-Relations/4

Steven Young, 'A guide to the law and policies relating to the Chinese in New Zealand': www.stevenyoung.co.nz/The Chinese-in-New-Zealand/Current-historical-Research/Laws-and-policies-relating-to-the-Chinese-in-New-Zealand.html

Interviews and conversations with and emails to author

Interview with Lianne Dalziel, former Minister of Immigration, 3 May 2007, Wellington

Conversation with former Senior Department of Labour official, 5 April 2007, Wellington

Interview with former Refugee and Migrant Service Coordinator, 10 and 11 April 2007 in Auckland and 15 April 2007, Wellington

Interview with former Minister of Foreign Affairs and Trade, Don McKinnon (communication in writing), 19 February 2007

Interview with Kevin Third, Director Refugee Division, 26 November 2007, Wellington

Interview with Dr N. Rasalingam, Chairperson Refugee Council of New Zealand, 26 February 2007, Wellington

Interview with Peter Cotton, Director/CEO RMS Refugee Resettlement, 26 January 2007, Wellington

Email messages from former Minister of Immigration, Aussie Malcolm, 8 December 2006 and 19 March 2007

Interview with former Minister of Immigration, Aussie Malcolm, 12 April 2007, Auckland

Conversation with former senior official from the Ministry of Foreign Affairs and Trade, 28 April 2007, Wellington

Conversation with Theresa Sawicka-Brockie, 30 August 2007, Wellington

Conversation with Keith Taylor, former director of the Interchurch Commission on Immigration and Refugee Resettlement, 25 January 2007, Wellington

Conversation with Brian Easton, 7 May 2007, Wellington

Conversation with former Hungarian refugee, September 2007, Wellington
Conversation with Rachel Kidd, Red Cross Refugee Services, 18 January 2013
Email from Dr Brij Lal to Doug Munro, 19 October 2007
Conversation with Frank Corner, 12 March 2007, Wellington
Email from Harvey Cohen, webmaster and author of the website of the Australian Jewish Historical Society, 1 August 2007
Conversation with refugee status applicant support person, 10 January 2007, Wellington
Conversation with Conrad Wright, Manager Refugee Status Determination, 3 April 2013

Archival sources

Department of Labour files

Postwar immigration and displaced persons from Europe

(The files on postwar immigration and displaced persons from Europe were consulted in 1983–84)

ANZ, L1 22/1/27, Part 1, Statement by the New Zealand Delegation to the United Nations Special Committee on Refugees and Displaced Persons, 10 May 1946

ANZ, L1 22/1/27, Part 1, Acting Permanent Head, Prime Minister's Department to the Prime Minister, 20 September 1946

ANZ, L1 22/1/27, Part 1, Director of Employment to Acting Permanent Head, Prime Minister's Department, 25 October 1946

ANZ, L1 22/1/27, 'Notes of Discussion with Wing Commander Robert Innes, Director of Resettlement, International Refugee Organisation', c. 1946–47

ANZ, L1 22/1/27, Part 2, Minister of External Affairs to the Official Secretary, Office of the New Zealand High Commissioner, 'Immigration: Acceptance of displaced persons', undated

ANZ, L1, 22/1/27, Part 1, 'Report on data received from the Jewish communities of New Zealand regarding relatives who desire to come to this country', July 1946. This report was enclosed with a memorandum for Acting Minister of Customs, from Permanent Head, Prime Minister's Department, 25 March 1947

ANZ, L1 22/1/50, T.R. Ritchie, Director General, Labour and Employment Department to the Permanent Head, Prime Minister's Department, 'Resettlement of refugee medical practitioners, dentists and nurses', 27 April 1948, written in response to a request from Dr R. Coigny, Director of Health, IRO., 1 September 1947

ANZ, L1 22/1/5, Comptroller of Customs, Customs Department to Director of Employment, Department of Labour and Employment, 14 October 1947

ANZ, L1 22/1/5, Director of Employment to District Superintendent, Department of Labour and Employment, 15 October 1947

ANZ, L1 22/1/27, Part 1, International Refugee Organisation, Director of Employment to Minister of Employment, 23 December 1947

ANZ, L1 22/1/27, Part 2, Report entitled 'Immigration: Acceptance of displaced persons' from the Department of External Affairs to the Official Secretary, Office of the High Commissioner for New Zealand, undated

ANZ, L1 22/1/27, Part 1, Director of Employment to Minister of Immigration, 15 April 1948

ANZ, L1 22/1/27, Part 2, Notes of a deputation upon Walter Nash, Minister of Customs, Wellington, 21 June 1948

ANZ, L1 22/1/27, Part 2, Report of a discussion between the Director DP Centre, Senigallia and New Zealand Parliamentary Under-Secretary, H. Combs, 27 July 1948

ANZ, L1 22/1/27, Part 2, New Zealand delegate to IRO to Minister of External Affairs, 19 September 1948

ANZ, L1 22/1/27, Part 2, telegram, Minister of External Affairs to High Commissioner for New Zealand, London, 24 September 1948
ANZ, L1 22/1/27, Part 2, Official Secretary, New Zealand High Commission to Secretary of External Affairs, 17 December 1948
ANZ, L1 22/1/27, Part 2, undated, press statement by the Minister of Immigration, A. McLagan, c. 1946–49
ANZ, L1 22/1/27, Part 3, International Refugee Organisation, Report of the selection team of the *Dunbalk Bay* draft, c. early 1949
ANZ, L1 22/1/27, Part 4, Director of Employment to Minister of Immigration, 24 January 1950
ANZ, L1 22/1/27, Part 5, Assistant Under-Secretary, Department of Internal Affairs to Director of Employment, Department of Labour and Employment, 'Immigration', 16 May 1950
ANZ, L1 22/1/80, Prime Minister's Department, 'Assimilation of alien immigrants', 27 October 1950
ANZ, L1 22/1/80, Branch Secretary, New Zealand Labour Party, Palmerston North Branch, to Minister of Labour, 30 June 1951
ANZ, L1 22/1/27, Immigration, General, Part 8, International Refugee Organisation, Secretary for Internal Affairs to Director of Special Branch, Police Department, 4 December 1953
ANZ, Department of Labour, L1, 22/1/80, 'Present policy regarding admission of aliens', c. 1955

International Refugee Organisation, European refugees in China
ANZ, ABKF, 947, W5182, Box 303, 22/1/27/13, Part 1, High Commissioner for Refugees to C. Gibson Young, New Zealand Inter-church Council on Public Affairs, Wellington, 28 February 1956
ANZ, ABKF, 947, W5182, Box 303, 22/1/27/13, Part 1, Assistant Secretary of Labour to C. Gibson Young, New Zealand Inter-church Council on Public Affairs, 27 April 1956
ANZ, ABKF, 947, W5182, Box 303, 22/1/27/13, Part 1, File note on Deputation from Inter-Church Council to the Minister of Immigration about 'hard core' refugee cases, 27 June 1956
ANZ, ABKF, 947, W5182, Box 303, 22/1/27/13, Part 1, Assistant Secretary of Labour to National Council of Churches, 17 March 1958
ANZ, ABKF, 947, W5182, Box 303, 22/1/27/13, Part 1, National Council of Churches to Member Churches, 9 July 1960, sent to Prime Minister; National Council of Churches to Prime Minister, 11 July 1960
ANZ, ABKF, 947, W5182, Box 303, 22/1/27/13, Part 1, Secretary of External Affairs to Prime Minister, 30 August 1960
ANZ, ABKF, 947, W5182, Box 303, 22/1/27/13, Part 1, Prime Minister Walter Nash to Cabinet, 'Home for White Russian refugees', 21 October 1960
ANZ, ABKF, 947, W5182, Box 303, 22/1/27/13, Part 1, Secretary of Labour to General Secretary, the National Council of Churches, 28 April 1961

Refugees from Hungary
(The files on refugees from Hungary were consulted in the late 1980s)
ANZ, L1 22/1/189/2, 'Hungarian refugees: Accommodation and jobs', October 1956
ANZ, L1 22/1/189, R.M. Algie, Acting Minister of External Affairs to Cabinet, 19 November 1956
ANZ, L1 22/1/189, Department of Labour, Secretary of External Affairs to Minister of Immigration, 19 November 1956
ANZ, L1 22/1/189/1, Hungarian Refugees, Children, October 1956; New Zealand Red Cross Society Inc, Annual report and financial statement, 1956–57
ANZ, L1 22/1/189, 'Report to the Secretary of Labour by the selection officer on the processing of Hungarian refugees', 21 November 1956–29 November 1956

ANZ, L1 22/1/189, 'Immigration policy, general – Hungary', Report to the Minister of Immigration, 29 November 1956

ANZ, L1 22/1/189, 'Report to the Secretary of Labour by the selection officer on the processing of Hungarian refugees', 16 December–23 December 1956

ANZ, L1 22/1/189, 'Report of the Hungarian Welfare Officer', 14 April 1958

ANZ, L1 22/1/189, Cable from Minister of External Affairs to High Commissioner, London, no date

ANZ, L1 22/1/189, Number of Hungarians by district, 1957 and 1958

International Refugee Organisation, handicapped refugees

ANZ, ABKF, 947, W5182, Box 33, 22/1/27/21, Part 1, Chief of Resettlement Section, Geneva, to UNHCR Office, 28 November 1967

ANZ, ABKF, 947, W5182, Box 33, 22/1/27/21, Part 1, UHHCR, 'The last of the many: An account of the individual efforts made to resettle severely handicapped refugees', foreword by Prince Sadruddin Aga Khan, Geneva, September/October 1967

ANZ, ABKF, 947, W5182, Box 33, 22/1/27/21, Part 1, Report to the Minister of Immigration, 3 February 1971

ANZ, ABKF, 947, W5182, Box 33, 22/1/27/21, Part 1, Indo-Chinese refugees handicapped quota, 1984

Immigration – General, Czechoslovakia refugees

ANZ, ABKF, 947, W5182, Box 165, 22/1/203/1, Part 1, Czechoslovakia refugees, 1968–69, Assistant Secretary of Labour to Acting Minister of Immigration, 9 September 1968

ANZ, ABKF, 947, W5182, Box 165, 22/1/203/1, Part 1, Czechoslovakia refugees, 1968–69, Secretary of Labour to Minister of Immigration, 20 September 1968

ANZ, ABKF, 947, W5182, Box 165, 22/1/203/1, Part 1, Czechoslovakia refugees, 1968–69, Assistant Secretary of Labour to Chairman Social Security Commission, 6 November 1968

ANZ, ABKF, 947, W5182, Box 165, 22/1/203/1, Part 1, Czechoslovakia refugees, 1968–69, Secretary of Labour to Minister of Immigration, 7 November 1968

ANZ, ABKF, 947, W5182, Box 166, 22/1/203/1, Part 3, Czechoslovakia refugees, press statement, Acting Minister of Labour, undated, probably 1970

ANZ, ABKF, 947, W5182, Box 166, 22/1/203/1, Part 3, Czechoslovakia refugees, press statement, Acting Minister of Labour, undated, probably early 1970s

ANZ, ABKF, 947, W5182, Box 166, 22/1/203/1, Part 3, Czechoslovakia refugees, Secretary of Labour to Minister of Immigration, 2 October 1970

ANZ, ABKF, 947, W5182, Box 166, 22/1/203/1, Part 3, Minister of Foreign Affairs to New Zealand High Commissioner, London, 13 October 1970

ANZ, ABKF, 947, W5182, Box 166, 22/1/203/1, Part 3, Czechoslovakia refugees, Director New Zealand Security Intelligence Service to Secretary of Labour, 22 October 1970

ANZ, ABKF, 947, W5182, Box 166, 22/1/203/1, Part 3, Czechoslovakia refugees, Report of selection officer, Czech refugees: Recruitment from Vienna, 11 November 1970

Asian refugees from Uganda

ANZ, ABKF, 947, W5182, Box 180, 22/1/274, Part 3, Secretary of Cabinet to Minister of Foreign Affairs, 11 September 1972

ANZ, ABKF, 947, W5182, Box 180, 22/1/274, Part 3, Immigration Uganda, 1973–73, minutes of meeting held on 25 September 1972, Wellington

ANZ, ABKF, 947, W5182, Box 180, 22/1/274, Part 3, Immigration Uganda, 1973–73, New Plymouth Hospital to Ministry of External Affairs, 31 October 1972

ANZ, ABKF, 947, W5182, Box 180, 22/1/274, Part 3, Secretary of Foreign Affairs to Minister of Foreign Affairs, 2 November 1972

ANZ, ABKF, 947, W5182, Box 180, 22/1/274, Part 3, Secretary of Foreign Affairs and Secretary of Labour to Ministers of Foreign Affairs and Labour, 22 November 1972

ANZ, ABKF, 947, W5182, Box 180, 22/1/274, Part 3, Submission to the Minister of Immigration from R.M. O'Grady, Inter-Church Committee on Immigration, 22 February 1973

ANZ, ABKF, 947, W5182, Box 180, 22/1/274, Part 3, Immigration – General Uganda, policy and general, 1972–73, Secretary of Labour to Minister of Immigration, 5 March 1973

ANZ, ABKF, 947, W5182, Box 180, 22/1/274, Part 3, Immigration – General Uganda, policy and general, 1972–73, Secretary of Foreign Affairs to Prime Minister, 8 March 1973

ANZ, ABKF, 947, W5182, Box 180, 22/1/274, Part 3, Record of a conversation between the Prime Minister, Hon. Norman Kirk, F. Bauman, UNDP/UNICEF/UNHCR representative for Australasia and Ole Volfing, Office of the High Commissioner for Refugees, Geneva, 30 March 1973

ANZ, ABKF, 947, W5182, Box 180, 22/1/274, Part 3, Minister of Immigration to Cabinet, April 1973

ANZ, ABKF, 947, W5182, Box 180, 22/1/274, Part 3, Secretary of Cabinet to Minister of Immigration, 17 April 1973

ANZ, ABKF, 947, W5182, Box 180, 22/1/274, Part 3, Immigration Uganda, 1973–73, Address-in-reply Debate, Immigration, Ugandan Asians, undated.

Indo-Chinese refugees
ANZ, ABKF, 947, W5182, Box 37, 22/1/27/24, Part 13, Indo-Chinese refugees, policy, 1979–80, Minister of Immigration to P.R. Pearson, 15 November 1979

ANZ, ABKF, 947, W5182, Box 37, 22/1/27-24, Part 14, Indo-Chinese refugees policy, 1980, draft proposals from the Ministry of Defence on Indo-Chinese refugees: Encounter at sea by HMNZS *Canterbury*, 1 April 1980

ANZ, ABKF, 947, W5182, Box 37, 22/1/27/24, Indo-Chinese refugees, 1980, briefing paper from Ministry of Foreign Affairs to Minister of Foreign Affairs, 13 May 1980

ANZ, ABKF, 947, W5182, Box 37, 22/1/27-24, Part 14, Indo-Chinese refugees policy 1980, Ministry of Foreign Affairs to Minister of Foreign Affairs, briefing paper on Indo-Chinese refugees, May 1980, includes Annex 11, Meeting on refugees and displaced persons in South East Asia: Geneva, 21 July 1979, statement made by A.G. Malcolm MP, Parliamentary Under-Secretary to the Minister of Immigration

ANZ, ABKF, 947, W5182, Box 37, 22/1/27-24, Indo-Chinese refugees, 1980, survey on public opinion to refugee intakes from South East Asia, April 1980

ANZ, ABKF, 947, W5182, Box 46, 22/1/27/24/3, Part 4, 1982–87, Minister of Immigration, press release, 14 June 1984

ANZ, ABKF, 947, W5182, Box 46, 22/1/27/24/3, Part 4, 1982–87, Acting Secretary of Foreign Affairs to Acting Minister of Foreign Affairs, 4 April 1985

ANZ, ABKF, 947, W5182, Box 46, 22/1/27/24/3, Part 4, 1982–87, Department of Labour Cabinet paper, 6 June 1985

East European refugees
ANZ, ABKF, 947, W5182, Box 59, 22/1/27/27, Part 1, East European refugees, 1978–1981, brief for Selection Officer, undated, probably 1981

ANZ, ABKF, 947, W5182, Box 59, 22/1/27/27, Part 1, East European refugees, 1978–81, Permanent Head of Department of Labour to All Districts, 4 September 1981

ANZ, ABKF, 947, W5182, Box 59, 22/1/27/27, Part 1, East European refugees, 1978–81, Secretary of Labour to Minister of Immigration, 9 September 1981

ANZ, ABKF, 947, W5182, Box 59, 22/1/27/27, Part 1, East European refugees, 1978–81, Permanent Head of Department of Labour to District Superintendents and Immigration Staff, 11 January 1982

ANZ, ABKF, 947, W5182, Box 59, 22/1/27/27, Part 1, East European refugees, 1978–81, Department of Labour to Minister of Immigration, 28 February 1982

ANZ, ABKF, 947, W5182, Box 59, 22/1/27/27, Part 1, East European refugees, 1978–81, Minister of Immigration to Cabinet, March 1982

ANZ, ABKF, 947, W5182, Box 61, 22/127/28, Part 2, Interchurch Commission on Immigration and Refugee Resettlement, 'Questions that should be asked according to latest Polish group', undated, circa 1986

ANZ, ABKF, 947, W5182, Box 61, 22/127/28, Part 2, Interchurch Commission on Immigration and Refugee Resettlement, 'Suggestions to improve quality of intake', undated, circa 1986

Refugees from Afghanistan

ANZ, ABKF, 947, W5182, Box 217, 22/1/336, Part 1, Afghanistan – policy and general, 1980–90, Seclab to Rome Office, 29 April 1981

ANZ, ABKF, 947, W5182, Box 217, 22/1/336, Part 1, Afghanistan – policy and general, 1980–90, Department of Labour, telex, Canberra to Wellington, 15 July 1982

ANZ, ABKF, 947, W5182, Box 217, 22/1/336, Part 1, Afghanistan – policy and general, 1980–90, R.W. Malpass to Miss B.J. Gavan, Private Secretary to Minister of Immigration, 'some suggested paras for your letter on Afghan refugees', 17 October 1984.

ANZ, ABKF, 947, W5182, Box 217, 22/1/336, Part 1, Afghanistan – policy and general, 1980–90, Minister of Immigration to Archdeacon R.J. Nicholson, Hamilton, 23 November 1984.

ANZ, ABKF, 947, W5182, Box 217, 22/1/336, Part 1, Afghanistan – policy and general, 1980–90, UNHCR to Ron Malpass, Assistant Director, Immigration Division, 17 December 1984

ANZ, ABKF, 947, W5182, Box 217, 22/1/336, Part 1, Afghanistan – policy and general, 1980–90, Kerry Burke, Minister of Immigration to Bruce Duncan, Lower Hutt, 19 February 1985.

ANZ, ABKF, 947, W5182, Box 217, 22/1/336, Part 1, Afghanistan – policy and general, 1980–90, R.W. Malpass for Secretary of Labour to J. Landau, Regional Representative, UNHCR, 21 March 1985.

ANZ, ABKF, 947, W5182, Box 217, 22/1/336, Part 1, Afghanistan – policy and general, 1980–90, Parliamentary Under-Secretary to the Minister of Immigration to Mrs E. Haliburton, Hawke's Bay, 16 October 1986

Immigration of Indo-Chinese refugees, unaccompanied minors

ANZ, ABKF, 947, W5182, Box 55, 22/1/27/24/7, Part 1, Immigration – Indo-Chinese refugees, resettlement of unaccompanied minors, 1980–83, Christopher Hawley, National Coordinator of South East Asian Migrant Education, Ministry of Education, to Ron Malpass, Assistant Director of Immigration (Special Duties), Department of Labour, 21 February 1983

ANZ, ABKF, 947, W5182, Box 55, 22/1/27/24/7, Part 3, Immigration – General, Indo-Chinese refugees, resettlement of unaccompanied minors, 1984–89, 'Australia to accept 100 young refugees', *Canberra Times*, 1 March 1983

ANZ, ABKF, 947, W5182, Box 55, 22/1/27/24/7, Part 1, Immigration – General, Indo-Chinese refugees, resettlement of unaccompanied minors, 1980–83, Immigration Division, Department of Labour, Proposal to resettle a group of Khmer unaccompanied minors, ICCI involvement, September 1983

ANZ, ABKF, 947, W5182, Box 55, 22/1/27/24/7, Part 2, Immigration – General, Indo-Chinese refugees, resettlement of unaccompanied minors, 1983–84, Minister of Immigration to Minister of Education, 17 November 1983

ANZ, ABKF, 947, W5182, Box 55, 22/1/27/24/7, Part 2, Immigration – General, Indo-Chinese refugees, resettlement of unaccompanied minors, 1983–84, telephone call from Ron Malpass in Thailand to Department of Labour, 17 February 1984

ANZ, ABKF, 947, W5182, Box 55, 22/1/27/24/7, Part 3, Immigration – General, Indo-Chinese refugees, resettlement of unaccompanied minors, 1984–89, report of visit 21–25 September 1984

ANZ, ABKF, 947, W5182, Box 55, 22/1/27/24/7, Part 3, Immigration – Genera, Indo-Chinese refugees, resettlement of unaccompanied minors, 1984–89, visit to review unaccompanied minors arrangements, Ron Malpass, Assistant Director of Immigration (Special Duties), 23–25 October 1984

ANZ, ABKF, 947, W5182, Box 55, 22/1/27/24/7, Part 3, Immigration – General, Indo-Chinese refugees, resettlement of unaccompanied minors, 1984–89, Ron Malpass for Secretary of Labour to the Ambassador, New Zealand Embassy, Bangkok, 26 November 1984

ANZ, ABKF, 947, W5182, Box 55, 22/1/27/24/7, Part 3, Immigration – General, Indo-Chinese refugees, resettlement of unaccompanied minors, 1984–89, R.W. Malpass, for Secretary of Labour to J. Landau, Regional Representative, UNHCR, 21 March 1985

ANZ, ABKF, 947, W5182, Box 55, 22/1/27/24/7, Part 3, Immigration – General, Indo-Chinese refugees, resettlement of unaccompanied minors, 1984–89, Secretary of Labour to New Zealand Embassy, Bangkok, 17 December 1986

ANZ, ABKF, 947, W5182, Box 55, 22/1/27/24/7, Part 3, Immigration – General, Indo-Chinese refugees, resettlement of unaccompanied minors, 1984–89, Parliamentary Under-Secretary to the Minister of Immigration to Clive Matthewson, MP, 6 December 1989

Iraqi Christian refugees
ANZ, ABKF, 947, W5182, Box 61, 22/1/27/28, Part 2, Refugees Iraqi Christian 1987–89, Secretary of Labour to Rev K.J. Taylor, 19 October 1987
ANZ, ABKF, 947, W5182, Box 61, 22/1/27/28, Part 2, Refugees Iraqi Christian 1987–89, Secretary of Labour to Minister of Immigration, 10 May 1988

Refugee quota and settlement
ANZ, ABKF, 947, Box 177, 22/270/9, Part 1, Settlement of refugees, 1987–89, minutes of the meeting of Cabinet Social Equity Committee, 24 May 1988
ANZ, ABKF, 947, W5182, Box 302, 22/1/27/31, Part 2, General Manager, New Zealand Immigration Service to Minister of Immigration, 21 February 1991, Report on refugee programme, 1991–92, attached paper, Department of Labour, New Zealand Immigration Service, 'Acceptance of refugees as settlers in New Zealand', June 1990

Refugee status
ANZ, ABKF, 947, W5182, Box 56, 22/1/27/26, Part 5, Refugees claim for refugee status 1986–87, Secretary of Foreign Affairs to Minister of Foreign Affairs, 12 June 1987
ANZ, ABKF, 947, W5182, Box 245, 22/1/480/9, Spontaneous refugees at Auckland International Airport, Regional Manager New Zealand Immigration Service, Northern, to C.J. McKenzie, Chief Executive Department of Labour, 16 October 1990
ANZ, ABKF, 947, W5182, Box 177, 22/1/270/9, Part 2, Settlement of migrants in New Zealand, Minister of Immigration Hon W.F. Birch to Cabinet, 28 November 1990
ANZ, ABKF, 947, W5182, Box 177, 22/1/270/9, Part 2, Settlement of migrants in New Zealand, Steve Rizos, Review and Development, Spontaneous refugees at Auckland Airport, November 1990

ANZ, ABKF, 947, W5182, Box 58, 22/1/27/26, Part 14, International Refugee Organisation, claims for refugee status in New Zealand, 1992, Bill Birch, Minister of Immigration to J. Gannon, 14 August 1991

ANZ, ABKF, 947, W5182, Box 245, 22/1/480/9, Refugees, review of immigration policy, Amnesty International to Minister of Immigration 13 September 1991

ANZ, ABKF, 947, W5182, Box 245, 22/1/480/9, Refugees, review of immigration policy, William Smith, Refugee Coordinator Amnesty International New Zealand to Minister of Immigration Bill Birch, 24 January 1992

ANZ, ABKF, 947, W5182, Box 177, 22/1/270/9, Part 2, Settlement of migrants in New Zealand, Bill Wilson, 'Report to the Rt. Hon. W.F. Birch, Minister of Immigration, on the process of refugee status determination', final report, 29 April 1992

ANZ, ABKF, 947, W5182, Box 58, 22/1/27/26, Part 14, International Refugee Organisation, claims for refugee status in New Zealand, 1992, Brendon Quirk, Operations Manager New Zealand Immigration Service, to Richard Bennett, Human Rights Commission, June 1992

ANZ, ABKF, 942, W5182, Box 58, 22/1/27/26, Part 14, International Refugee Organisation, claims for refugee status in New Zealand, 1992, press release, Rt. Hon. Bill Birch, Minister of Immigration, 4 August 1992

Department of Labour files (obtained from Refugee Quota Branch in 2007)

Department of Labour, New Zealand Immigration Service, Refugee quota composition 2001/02 and planning for 2002/03, Secretary of Labour and Secretary of Foreign Affairs and Trade to the Minister of Immigration and the Minister of Foreign Affairs and Trade, 22 February 2002

Department of Labour, New Zealand Immigration Service, Refugee quota composition 2003/2004: Options, Marie Sullivan, Market Manager to General Manager, 29 January 2003

Department of Labour, New Zealand Immigration Service, 04/38374, Refugee quota composition 2004/05, Secretary of Labour and Secretary of Foreign Affairs and Trade to Minister of Immigration and Minister of Foreign Affairs and Trade, 19 July 2004

Department of Labour, New Zealand Immigration Service, 05/45242, Proposed refugee quota Composition 2005/06, Secretary of Labour and Secretary of Foreign Affairs and Trade to Minister of Immigration and Minister of Foreign Affairs and Trade, 25 February 2005

Department of Labour, New Zealand Immigration Service, Refugee quota composition 2006/07, Secretary of Labour and Secretary of Foreign Affairs and Trade to Minister of Immigration and Minister of Foreign Affairs and Trade, 9 May 2006

Department of Labour, New Zealand Immigration Service, 97/005363, The composition of the 1997/98 quota, Chris Hampton, General Manager, New Zealand Immigration Service, to Minister of Immigration, 12 September 2007

External Affairs and Foreign Affairs files (Archives NZ)

Postwar immigration

(Files on postwar immigration consulted 1983–84)

ANZ, EA 108/4/4, Part 1, Sir Herbert Emerson, Director of Intergovernmental Committee on Refugees to R.M. Campbell, Official Secretary, New Zealand High Commission, London, 14 January 1946

ANZ, EA 108/4/4, Part 1, R.M. Campbell, Official Secretary , New Zealand High Commission, London to Sir Herbert Emerson, Director, Intergovernmental Committee on Refugees, 25 January 1946

ANZ, EA 108/4/4, Part 1, R.M. Campbell to Sir Herbert Emerson, 25 January 1946

ANZ, 22/1/27, Part 1, Statement by the New Zealand delegation to the United Nations Special Committee on Refugees and Displaced Persons, 10 May 1946

ANZ, EA2, 1946/22b, or 108/4/1, Part 1b, Social affairs, refugees, 1943–46, Minister of External Affairs to New Zealand Minister, Washington, 10 June 1946

ANZ, EA 108/4/1 Part 2, Foss Shanahan, Acting Permanent Head of the Prime Minister's Department, to Prime Minister, 20 September 1946

ANZ, EA2, 1948/14B or 108/4/1, Part 3, External Affairs, Wellington to New Zealand delegation IRO, Geneva, 24 October 1947

ANZ, EA 108/4/1, Parts 3 and 4, c. 1946–48

ANZ, EA2, 14b, 1948

ANZ, EA2, 15c, 1949

ANZ, EA2/10d, 1956 and PM 108/4/77, External to IRO, 26 January 1949 and High Commissioner for New Zealand, Canberra to External Affairs, 16 February 1949

ANZ, EA 103/8/4 or EA2 1950/37c, A.D. McIntosh, Secretary External Affairs, to High Commissioner for New Zealand, 18 October 1949

ANZ, EA 103/8/4, Part 3 or EA2 1950/37c, discussion between Sir Arthur Rucker, IRO and Cabinet Committee on Immigration, 3 February 1950

ANZ, EA 103/8/4, Part 3 or EA2 1950/37c, telegram from External Affairs to IRO, 27 February 1950

Chinese refugees

ANZ, ABHS, 950, W4627, Box 2574, 108/4/70, Part 1, Bob Strackett to Norman Kirk, 17 August 1960

ANZ, ABHS, 950, W4627, Box 2574, 108/4/70, Part 1, Secretary of Labour to Minister of Immigration, 16 September 1960

ANZ, ABHS, 950, W4627, Box 2574, 108/4/70, Part 1, Norman Kirk to Prime Minister, 2 January 1961

ANZ, ABHS, 950, W4627, Box 2574, 108/4/70, Part 1, Secretary of External Affairs to Prime Minister, 24 May 1961

ANZ, ABHS, 950, W4627, Box 2574, 108/4/70, Part 1, Minister of External Affairs to High Commissioner for New Zealand, Canberra, 29 May 1962

ANZ, ABHS, 950, W4627, Box 2574, 108/4/70, Part 1, National Council of Churches, Christchurch Branch, to Keith Holyoake, 31 May 1962

ANZ, ABHS, 950, W4627, Box 2574, 108/4/70, Part 1, Owen S. Robinson, Presbyterian Church of New Zealand to the Prime Minister, 4 June 1962

ANZ, ABHS, 950, W4627, Box 2574, 108/4/70, Part 1, New Zealand Chinese Association to Prime Minister, 6 June 1962

ANZ, ABHS, 950, W4627, Box 2574, 108/4/70, Part 1, Prime Minister to Dr and Mrs McKenzie, 6 June 1962

ANZ, ABHS, 950, W4627, Box 2574, 108/4/70, Part 1, External Affairs to Prime Minister, 8 June 1962

ANZ, ABHS, 950, W4627, Box 2574, 108/4/70, Part 1, Prime Minister Keith Holyoake to Dr E.R. Nye, Dunedin Hospital, 8 June 1962

ANZ, ABHS, 950, W4627, Box 2574, 108/4/70, Part 1, Minister of External Affairs, Wellington to High Commissioner for New Zealand, Canberra, 12 June 1962

ANZ, ABHS, 950, W4627, Box 2574, 108/4/70, Part 1, press statement by the Prime Minister, 12 June 1962

ANZ, ABHS, 950, W4627, Box 2574, 108/4/70, Part 1, background notes to the Prime Minister on Chinese Orphans from Hong Kong, 13 June 1962

ANZ, ABHS, 950, W4627, Box 2574, 108/4/70, Part 1, New Zealand Chinese Association to Keith Holyoake, 15 June 1962

ANZ, ABHS, 950, W4627, Box 2574, 108/4/70, Part 1, Secretary of External Affairs to Prime Minister, 19 June 1962

ANZ, ABHS, 950, W4627, Box 2574, 108/4/70, Part 1, Minister of External Affairs, Wellington to New Zealand High Commissioner, Canberra, 29 June 1962

ANZ, ABHS, 950, W4627, Box 2574, 108/4/70, Part 1, press statement, 3 July 1962

ANZ, ABHS, 950, W4627, Box 2574, 108/4/70, Part 1, Minister of Immigration Tom Shand to Alan Brash, National Council of Churches, 30 July 1962

Refugees from Uganda
ANZ, Ministry of Foreign Affairs, 251/6/1, Vol. 1, Uganda social affairs, General, cable, Wellington to New Delhi, 10 August 1972; cable, Wellington to London, 10 August 1972

Refugees from Chile
ANZ, ABHS, W4627, Box 2586, 108/4/92, Refugees from Chile, Part 2, Secretary of Labour to Deputy Secretary of Foreign Affairs, 1 November 1973

ANZ, ABHS, W4627, Box 2586, 108/4/92, Refugees from Chile, Part 2, Secretary of Foreign Affairs to Prime Minister, 6 November 1973

ANZ, ABHS, W4627, Box 2586, 108/4/92, Refugees from Chile, Part 2, L.J. Parton (name is hard to decipher) to R.D. Muldoon, 9 September 1974

ANZ, ABHS, W4627, Box 2586, 108/4/92, Refugees from Chile, Part 2, Secretary of Foreign Affairs to the Prime Minister, 11 December 1974

Ministry of Foreign Affairs files (at the Ministry of Foreign Affairs, not Archives New Zealand)

Asian Refugees from Uganda
MFAT, 251/6/1, Vol. 1, Uganda social affairs, General, 1962–1991

Fijian Indians
MFAT, 701/7/9/5, Fiji, Vol. 1, Secretary of Foreign Affairs to applicant, 30 June 1987

MFAT, 914/6/5, Vol. 1, Human rights issues, South Pacific, Fiji, General, 1/10/89 to 29/6/96, Report by Amnesty International Secretariat, United Kingdom, 'Fiji: Short term detention of suspected political opponents, trade unionists and journalists', September 1987

MFAT, 701/7/9/5, Fiji, Vol. 1, cable from Suva to Wellington, 1 February 1988

MFAT, 701/7/9/5, Fiji, Vol. 1, cable from Suva to Wellington, 25 April 1988

MFAT, 701/1/9/5, Refugees: Fiji Indians, Bernie Kerot, Archdiocesan, Justice, Peace and Development Commission to Stan Rodger, Minister of Immigration, 10 July 1989

MFAT, 701/1/9/5, Refugees: Fiji Indians, Secretary of Foreign Affairs to Minister of Foreign Affairs, 2 August 1989

MFAT, 914/6/5, Vol. 1, Human rights issues, South Pacific – Fiji, External Assessments Bureau, 'Fiji: Background to the human rights situation', 22 November 1990

MFAT, 701/7/9/5, Fiji, Vol. 1, cable, Ministry of Foreign Affairs, Suva to New Zealand Immigration Service, Christchurch, 10 August, year not given, but file refers to period 1/5/87 to 31/10/90

MFAT, 914/6/5, Vol. 3, South Pacific, Fiji, General Assembly speech of Major General Rabuka, Prime Minister, 1997

MFAT, 914/6/5, Vols. 3 and 4, South Pacific, External Assessments Bureau Report, 3 July 1998

Industries and Commerce
(Consulted in 1983–84)
ANZ, IC/20/86, Part 1, Skilled labour and tradesmen, 1939

Prime Ministers series
(Consulted in 1983–84)
ANZ, PM 108/4/62, A.D. McIntosh, Secretary of External Affairs to Minister of External Affairs, 8 November 1956
ANZ, PM 108/4/57, Secretary of External Affairs to Minister of External Affairs, 19 February 1958

Nash papers
(Consulted in 1983–84)
ANZ, Nash Papers 1597/0918; 1597/11; 1311/0592/3; 1311/0607; 1311/0595 (Concerning the entry of Jewish refugees in the 1930s)

Report to Cabinet
(Consulted in 1983–84, the file was contained within the EA series)
ANZ, CAB 66/1/1, Part 1, Individual immigration of aliens: Report of the Cabinet Committee, 4 September 1950

Social Services Committee
House of Representatives, Social Services Committee, Report on the Immigration Amendment Bill, No. 183-2, 4 March 1999, p. 1, ANZ, ABGX, W5188, 16127, Box 102, SS 2/2/3, Part 1, Social Services Committee – Immigration Amendment Bill – Reports, 1998–99

Unpublished reports, papers and documents in possession of the author

Department of Labour, Immigration Division, 'Acceptance of refugees as settlers in New Zealand', June 1982
Former Minister of Immigration Lianne Dalziel: speech to people-smuggling conference, 28 February 2002, Bali; speech to the International Association of Refugee Law Judges, 22 October 2002; 'Beyond *Tampa*', speech notes, 16 May, 2003; speech notes for meeting, 21 August 2003, available from Lianne Dalziel or Ann Beaglehole
Papers on Hungarians in New Zealand, collected by Owen Hughes and Ann Beaglehole
'Magyar Millennium Park', brochure produced to coincide with opening of the park, 20 August 2003, available from the Honorary Consul of Hungary
Peter Cotton, RMS, NZIS refugee quota selection, submission to NZIS, 2002, available from Peter Cotton or Ann Beaglehole
Peter Cotton, Director, RMS New Zealand, 'Family reunion, an examination of family reunion issues viewed from the perspective of New Zealand', RMS submission to government and UNHCR as part of tripartite meetings in Geneva, May 2001, available from Peter Cotton or Ann Beaglehole
Notes of speech by Hon David Cunliffe, Minister of Immigration at the National Refugee Settlement Forum in Hamilton, 29 May 2007, Human Rights Commission, *Te Punanga: Refugee Focus*, Vol. 1, No. 1, June 2007

Chile, Love M., 'Refugee development centre: A discussion paper', Institute of Public Policy, Auckland University of Technology, undated
Nash M., and Trlin, A., 'Social work with immigrants, refugees and asylum seekers in New Zealand', Palmerston North, New Zealand, New Settlers Programme, Massey University
Settlement Support New Zealand, Community Services, Upper Hutt City Council, 'Report: Upper Hutt community forum for groups working with refugees and migrants', 20 July 2007
Settlement Support New Zealand, Community Services, Upper Hutt City Council, 'Report: Meet the Mayor; Orientation event for newcomers', 15 June 2008

Seminar presentations, Radio New Zealand National interviews and miscellaneous sources

Giselle Byrnes, 'Reframing New Zealand history: The Oxford History of New Zealand', presentation at Victoria University of Wellington History Department seminar, 11 May 2007
Human Rights Education Association website, 'Guiding principles on internal displacement', developed by the United Nations between 1992 and 1998
Jewish Communities of New Zealand, 'Memorandum to the Select Committee on Dominion population', April 1946
Morgan Tuimalealiifano, University of the South Pacific, 'Re-encountering Gordon's Fiji: Has the iTaukei Fijian caught up with rest of the world?', Abstract of paper for Pacific History Association Conference, Victoria University of Wellington, 6–8 December 2012
New Zealand Red Cross Refugee Services, 'New Zealand Red Cross to lead the delivery of refugee services', media release, 6 December 2012
Refugee and Migrant Service (RMS), Submission on the Immigration Act Review, June 2006
Theresa Sawicka, presentation on the Polish children as one of the panellists on Victoria University of Wellington Stout Research Centre presentation on 4 April 2007, Series: Watching the Kiwis: how anthropologists look at New Zealand: 'First and second sights: the English eye on New Zealand'
Report of refugee issues identified at the Council for International Development Refugee Policy Forum held in Wellington on 8 January 2005, as reported by Rod Alley who attended on behalf of the Peace Foundation, 1 February 2005
Radio New Zealand, *Morning Report*, interview with Minister of Immigration David Cunliffe, 6 December 2006
Radio New Zealand, *Morning Report*, interview with Paul Rogers, Oxford Research Group, August 2007
Radio New Zealand, *Morning Report*, interview with Dr Andrew Ladley, Policy Studies, Victoria University of Wellington, 14 September 2007
Radio New Zealand, *Morning Report*, Terrorism Suppression Amendment Bill 2007, 27 September 2007
Radio New Zealand, *Morning Report*, Terrorism Suppression Amendment Bill 2007, 28 September 2007
Wellington City Public Library, *Evening Post* clipping, Politics – Uganda, 1972–73

Index

Abyssinian crisis 35
Adam, Hassan 11, 175
adjustment of refugees to NZ life: Cambodian children 126–28; children and young people 40, 53, 127–28; Chilean refugees 78, 189; Hungarian refugees 55–57, 168; Indo-Chinese refugees 93, 102; Jewish refugees 39–40; Polish children 127; Polish refugees 61–62, 174; small ethnic communities 166–69; Somali refugees 168–69, 173–75; Ugandan Asian refugees 74–75; well-educated refugees 74–75, 96; White Russian refugees 109
adoption of orphaned children 119, 121; Chinese orphans 122, 123; Hungarian orphans 53
advocacy 16, 34, 41, 179, 180, 181
Afghan asylum seekers and refugees 115, 134, 147–50, 165–66, 168, 181, 191, 246–47
Africa 12, 68, 93, 139, 166–67, 168, 169–71, 174, 176, 183; *see also* refugees from specific African countries, e.g. Ugandan Asian refugees
Aga Khan, Sadruddin 107
Agenda for Protection 2002 10
Ahmed, Abdinasir 173
Albanian refugees 49–50
Alexander II 143–44, 146
Algie, Ronald 52
Ali, Koos 178
'alien enclaves' 15, 45, 99, 111, 120, 184
Allende, Salvador 75–76
Amin, Idi 64, 65–66
Amnesty International 16, 132, 138, 140, 156
Arendt, Hannah 11
Armenian refugees 11–12
ASEAN (Association of South East Asian Nations) countries 94
Asia 12, 63, 68, 72, 80, 105, 107, 121, 170
Asiatic Restriction Bill 1896 64
assimilation of new settlers *see* integration of new settlers
Assyrian Christians 165, 169, 178, 179, 248
asylum seekers 10, 12, 17, 129–31, 150–51,
177, 190; Ahmed Zaoui 17, 154–57;
Chinese 139; deportation 140, 141, 143, 147, 151, 156, 159–60, 161–62; definition of 10; detention regime 140, 143, 145, 151–54, 159–61; differentiated from refugees 10, 11; Fijian Indians 132–38; late 1980s and early 1990s 139–42; policy changes, 2006–12 158–61; refugee determination process 139, 141–42, 146–47, 148, 153, 154–57, 158, 159, 161–62; *Tampa* asylum seekers 115, 134, 147–50, 162, 167, 178–79; threat of mass arrivals, 1997–99 142–46; Vietnamese 81–82, 102–03, 130–31
Auckland 54–55, 60, 74, 100, 101, 170, 171
Auckland Refugee Council 145, 181
Australia: asylum seekers 139, 141, 142, 144, 150–51, 152, 161, 162; Chilean refugees 78; Czech and Slovak refugees 58; disabled refugees 114; displaced persons from World War II 44, 46; Fijian Indian asylum seekers 135, 138; Hong Kong refugees 123; Indo-Chinese refugees 83, 85, 86, 88, 89, 91, 100, 125, 126; Jewish refugees 35, 38, 56; migration of refugees from NZ to Australia 78, 100; Old Believers 111; Pacific Solution scheme 148; selection of refugees in labour-market terms 113; specialist services for immigrants and refugees 15, 182; *Tampa* refugees 115, 147–48; Ugandan Asian refugees 71, 73
Austria 30, 33, 35, 43, 52, 53, 57, 58–59, 61, 121
Awad, Adam 178

Baha'i refugees 165
Baltic States, refugees 46, 48; *see also* Estonian refugees; Latvian refugees; Lithuanian refugees
Bassett, Michael 80, 133
Bavadra, Timoci 132, 135
Bay of Plenty 27
Beaglehole, John 34
Belich, James 20, 22

253

Benson, Heather 65–66
Binney, Judith 21
Binzegger, Anton 76, 114–15
biometric information 158, 186
Birch, Bill 140, 141–42, 170
Bloodworth, Thomas 34
'boat people' 83, 84, 85, 86, 88, 95, 130–31, 142–46, 150–51, 161, 162
Bobic, Lore 51
Bockett, Herbert Leslie 44–45
Bolger, Jim 140
border security 139–40, 145, 146, 147, 158–59, 161
Brash, Alan 29, 108, 115
Brash, Don 185
Britain 30, 34; asylum seekers 141; disapproval of NZ racist immigration legislation 64; emigrants to NZ 30, 39, 44, 47, 63, 64, 80, 81, 84, 122; NZ anglophilia 40; pressure on NZ to accept Ugandan Asian refugees 65
British Medical Association, Otago Division 35
Bulgarian refugees 49–50
Burdekin, Cyril 34–35
Burke, Kerry 163
Burmese refugees 178, 181
Burundian refugees 12, 167

Calwell, Arthur 38
Cambodian refugees 12, 83, 85, 91, 92–93, 94, 167, 178; Colombo Plan and Ford Foundation scholarship students 82; unaccompanied minors 14, 124–27, 247
Cameron, Clive 48
Campbell, R.M. 37
Canada 44, 58, 71, 92, 113, 138, 139, 141, 147, 159
Castles, Stephen 131
Catholic Church 71, 97, 120
ChangeMakers Refugee Forum 178
Chatham Islands 21, 23, 25
Chifley, Ben 38
child refugees: adjustment and integration 40, 53, 120, 121, 124, 127–28; Cambodian 14, 124–27, 247; Chinese 41–42, 121–24; detention 154; first priority 14, 40, 47; Hungarian 53, 121; Jewish 40, 117,
120; Polish 114, 117–21, 127; school support 180; Vietnamese 124; see also orphan refugees
Chile, Love 176
Chilean refugees 75–78, 97, 189, 250
China 16, 68, 99, 100, 108, 109, 110–11, 139; European refugees from 121
Chinese asylum seekers 139, 159; boat people 142–46; Tiananmen Square protest 139
Chinese Immigrants Act 1881 40
Chinese refugees 12, 29, 30, 40–42, 63, 64, 77, 87, 166, 249–50; children 41–42, 121–24
Christchurch 55, 113, 170, 171, 174, 175, 184
Christchurch Refugees Emergency Committee 33, 34
churches' response to refugees: advocacy 16, 34, 41; Asian refugees 67; Cambodian unaccompanied minors 125, 126; Chilean refugees 75, 76, 97; Chinese orphans 123, 124; Cold War refugees 97; disabled refugees 106; Indo-Chinese refugees 82, 83, 84–86, 98, 100–01, 126; influence on government policy 15, 44; Iranian asylum seekers 159, 160; Jewish refugees 34; Middle East and Afghan refugees escaping religious persecution 165; Old Believers 111, 112, 113; refugees with tuberculosis 104, 105; sponsorship 179, 180; Ugandan Asian refugees 68, 71–72, 97
Clark, Helen 115, 146, 148, 156, 160, 162, 178
Clarkson, Bob 185
Clydesdale, Greg 175
Cold War 12; asylum seekers 130; refugees 51–62, 97, 106
Coleman, Fraser 81
Colombo plan students, granting of asylum 81–82
Combs, Harry 44
communism 12, 47, 48, 48, 51, 52, 53–54, 59, 77, 80, 92, 121, 129, 130; see also Cold War
community acceptance and support 16, 182–83; Cambodian minors 125, 126–27; capacity building 181; Chilean refugees 76–77; Chinese refugees 96; Department of Labour's role in generating support 98; ethnic community workers 101, 103; Hungarian refugees 55;

Indo-Chinese refugees 82–83, 84, 86, 92, 94–95, 99; Jewish refugees 34, 39, 96, 190; Old Believers 112–13; Polish refugees 60, 101–02; Somali refugees 174; Ugandan Asian refugees 64, 74, 100; see also integration of new settlers; public opinion on immigration and refugee policy; sponsorship of refugees
confiscation of Maori land 27
Congolese refugees 167
Corner, Frank 73, 77
CORSO (Council of Organisations for Relief Service Overseas) 109
Costello, Paddy 37
Cotton, Peter 152–53, 167, 170, 172, 173, 174, 182, 183
Council for International Development Refugee Policy Forum 153–54
Cunliffe, David 158, 161, 181, 186
Customs Department 36, 88
Czechoslovak refugees 12, 31, 36, 50, 57–59, 65, 121, 170, 188, 244–45

Dalziel, Lianne 134, 146–47, 148, 152, 160, 180–81
Danes 11, 129, 130
Das, Dilip 186–87
De la Mare, F.A. 32
Deckston, Max and Annie 120
Delamere, Tuariki 143, 145, 146
Deobhakta, Avinash Ganesh and Kanan 74–75
Department of Agriculture 112
Department of Education 125
Department of External Affairs 37, 46, 97, 106–07, 122, 124
Department of Health 86
Department of Industries and Commerce 33
Department of Internal Affairs 48, 55, 122
Department of Labour 15, 45, 50, 59, 60, 61, 86, 91, 95, 97, 98, 104, 106, 108, 119, 121, 122, 123, 124, 139, 168–69, 242–43; Employment and Immigration Division 55–56; Immigration Division 82–83, 84, 85; settlement services 62, 96
Department of Labour and Employment 47
Department of Social Welfare 86, 103

deportation of asylum seekers 140, 141, 143, 147, 151, 156, 159–60, 161–62
Depression, 1920s–early 1930s 32, 33
detention of asylum seekers 140, 143, 145, 151–54, 159–61
disabled refugees 9, 14, 32, 73, 83, 105–07, 113, 115–16, 187, 244
discrimination against refugees 175–76, 177; employment 175, 183; ethnic bias in selection 44–46; Muslims 175, 183–86; selection of refugees 46, 72, 80
displaced persons 11, 12, 14; from World War II 43–51, 77, 80, 96, 99, 103–06, 107, 121, 249
Djibouti refugees 166, 167
Dominion Settlement Association 34
Drury, Abdulah 174
Dunstan, Stephen 182–83

East Coast 21, 24
economic benefits of refugees 13, 114–15, 188; Chinese refugees 42; Czech and Slovak refugees 57–58, 59, 170; disabled refugees 107; Hungarian refugees 52, 170; Indo-Chinese refugees 94; Jewish refugees 33, 34, 38–39; Polish refugees 59; Somali refugees 170; see also occupational criteria for entry
Einhorn, Helmut 36
elderly refugees: Chinese 38; displaced persons from World War II 44, 50; Hungarian 52, 53; Kirk's views 73; Nansen Home 55, 107–10, 115
Ellison, L.E. (Ted) 49–50
Elsmore, Bronwyn 21
emergency protection cases 9
employment: Department of Labour's role 98; displaced persons from World War II 50; Hungarian refugees 55; Indo-Chinese refugees 88, 95, 102; Muslims 176, 184; need for guaranteed employment 31; New Zealand Settlement Strategy 181; Old Believers 113; Polish refugees 60; skilled professionals 39, 47; in small communities 100; Somali refugees 174, 175; sponsors' role 15, 98, 189; Ugandan Asian refugees 74, 97; see also occupational criteria for entry

Index 255

entry permits *see* selection of refugees
environmental refugees 191
Estonian refugees 46
Ethiopia-Eritrea War 1991-93 170
Ethiopian refugees 12, 166, 167, 170, 177, 179
ethnic groups 166-69
Europe 10, 12, 35, 36, 38, 105, 107, 147; refugee camps 12
Evian Conference 34, 35

Fagan, Mark 32
family groups, refugee 44, 47, 49, 52, 53, 124; with disabled members 105, 106, 114, 115-16, 188
family reunion: Ahmed Zaoui 155, 156; annual refugee quota 164, 167, 171-73; biometric information from refugees 186; Chinese refugees 41-42; Indo-Chinese refugees 90-91, 92, 93-94, 171; Jewish refugees 36-37, 38-39, 93-94, 171; Somali refugees 166, 171-72; *Tampa* refugees 150, 167; Ugandan Asian refugees 73
Federation of Labour (FOL) 33-34, 68-69, 76
Fiji 64, 69, 132-33, 136, 137-38, 191
Fijian Indian asylum seekers 132-38, 183
Fijian Indian refugees 132-38, 183, 251
Five Million Club 34
foreign policy, links to refugee policy 14, 72-73, 77, 80-81, 115, 189
Fraser, Ian W. 54-55, 107-08, 109, 115
Fraser, Janet 118
Fraser, Peter 37, 43, 118
Fuchs, Klaus 48

Gallienne, Robin 84, 86, 87, 89, 113
General Randal 118-19
Germany 11, 12, 30-31, 34, 35, 36, 43, 58, 118
Gilbert, Gerty 31
Gill, Frank 88
Gisborne 24
gold miners, Chinese 40
Good, Edwin Dudley 32
Gore 113
Gorst, John 19
government policy *see* immigration policy; refugee policy
Greek Roumanian refugees 49-50
Green Party 159-60

Greig, Laurie 155
Gulf War 1991 140, 183
Guterres, Antonio 182

Hamilton 170, 171
Hanan, Ralph 52-53, 55, 105, 121
'hard core' refugees 103-07, 114
Harrison, R.J. 81
Hartling, Paul 98, 126
Hastings 170
Hawke's Bay 27
Hayward, Margaret 72
health criteria for entry 85, 113, 114; tuberculosis 85, 104-05, 186-87
health needs and services 9, 103, 104-05, 113-14, 126, 164, 181-82, 184, 186-87
Hebrew Immigrants' Aid Society / United Hebrew Immigration Society (HIAS) 16, 62, 97
Hensley, Gerald 90, 133
High Commissioner for Refugees *see* League of Nations High Commissioner for Refugees; United Nations – High Commissioner for Refugees
Hill, Barbara 132
Hilton, Lisl 188
HIV/Aids 114, 186
Holocaust, Holocaust survivors 37, 38, 94, 196, 215, 234
Holyoake, Keith 57, 65-66, 68, 70, 79, 111, 123
Hong Kong 110, 111, 112
Hong Kong refugees 29, 121, 122-24, 140
Hongi Hika 22
housing 39, 47, 51, 55, 58, 93, 97, 98, 100, 171, 177, 179, 184, 189
Howard, John 147, 148, 162
Hubbard, Anthony 48-49
Hughes, Gladstone 44
Human Rights Commission 151, 152
humanitarianism, NZ 13, 14, 190; and annual refugee quota 165, 171, 172; Asian refugees 67, 68; asylum seekers 134-38, 147-51, 161-62; Cambodian unaccompanied minors 127-28; Chilean refugees 77; Czech refugees 57, 58; disabled refugees 73, 103, 105-07, 114-16; displaced persons from World

War II 50, 62; elderly refugees 50, 103, 108, 109, 115; family reunion 171–73; Hungarian refugees 52; Indo-Chinese refugees 88, 93, 95; Old Believers 112–13; outweighing utilitarian and pragmatic considerations 188; Polish orphans 120; refugees with special health 103–04, 113–14; traumatised refugee children 127–28
Hungarian refugees 12–14, 35, 50, 51–57, 65, 80, 99, 105, 106, 121, 170, 244

Ihimaera, Witi 21
Immigration Act 1974 84
Immigration Act 1987 143, 151, 158, 166
Immigration Act 2009 and amendments 160–61
Immigration Amendment Act 1961 65
Immigration Amendment Act 1999 143, 145, 146, 151
Immigration New Zealand 173, 182–83; *see also* Immigration Risk Research Bureau; New Zealand Immigration Service; Refugee Quota Branch; Refugee Status Branch
immigration policy: Asian immigrants 81, 121–22, 124, 129; European bias 63, 80, 84, 122; Germans 129; links to refugee policy 14, 31–32, 121–22, 166, 177; National Immigration Strategy 177; and NZ race relations 67; non-British subjects 31–32, 39, 41, 45, 65, 81; preference for British immigrants 30, 39, 44, 47, 63, 64, 80, 81, 84, 122; removal of ethnic bias 63, 65, 67–68, 72–73, 81, 87, 163–64, 166; restrictions on people with communist, socialist or radical nationalist beliefs 129; review, 1987 163; 'white' New Zealand 41, 52, 57, 64; *see also* public opinion on immigration and refugee policy; refugee policy
Immigration Restriction Act 1899 64
Immigration Restriction Act 1920 and amendments 31, 37, 41, 64
Immigration Risk Research Bureau 183
Indian Association 97
Indian refugees 64–65; Fijian Indians 132–38, 183, 251; Ugandan Asians 64–75, 97, 100, 245, 251

Indo-Chinese boat people 83, 84, 85, 86, 88, 95, 130–31
Indo-Chinese refugees 16, 79–95, 98, 99, 100, 102–03, 113, 124, 166, 169, 170, 171, 245–46; Comprehensive Plan of Action (CPA) 102–03; Orderly Departure Programme (ODP) 90; *see also* Cambodian refugees; Laotian refugees; Vietnamese refugees
Indonesia 83, 121, 168; refugees 166
information services for refugees 61, 62, 96, 171
integration of new settlers 96, 183, 190; African refugees 176, 177; Asian refugees 67; Balts 46, 48, 49; children 53, 120, 121, 124, 127–28; dispersed throughout country (pepper-potting) 15, 89, 99–100; and ethnicity 45, 46, 49, 62, 67, 84, 89; Indo-Chinese refugees 84, 88, 89; Jewish refugees 45, 46, 49, 62; and job skills 39, 47; Muslims 165–66, 174, 175, 176; Somali refugees 174–75; *see also* adjustment of refugees to NZ life; community acceptance and support
'interception' of potential refugees 139–40
Inter-Church Commission on Immigration and Refugee Resettlement (ICCI) 16, 75, 82, 83, 84–86, 89, 97–99, 100–01, 125, 126, 182; *see also* Inter-Church Committee on Immigration; Refugee and Migrant Service (RMS); Refugee Services Aotearoa New Zealand; RMS Refugee Resettlement
Inter-Church Committee on Immigration 71–72, 75, 76, 97
Inter-Church Council on Public Affairs 104, 105
Interdepartmental Committee on Refugees 132
Intergovernmental Committee on Political Refugees 34
Inter-governmental Committee on Refugees (IGCR) 12–13, 37
internally displaced persons 11, 12, 20, 23, 190
International Covenant of Civil and Political Rights 161
International Refugee Organisation (IRO) 13, 44, 46, 49, 50, 104
Invercargill 16, 111, 112–13

Index 257

Ip, Manying 42
Iran (Persia) 118, 119; asylum seekers 140, 142, 147, 159–60; refugees 12, 165, 166, 168, 178
Iraqi refugees 159, 165, 166, 167, 168, 169, 190, 248
irregular migration 131; *see also* asylum seekers
Islamic Association 16
Israel 45–46
Italy 12, 35, 43, 107, 130

Japan 41, 42
Jewish asylum seekers 129–30
Jewish refugees 11, 12, 16, 30–40, 44, 45–46, 49, 50, 62, 77, 93–94, 171, 190; children 40, 117, 120
Jewish Relief and Welfare Organisation 97
Jewish Welfare Society 37

Kampuchean refugees *see* Cambodian refugees
Kanal, Borany 92–93
Kernot, Bernie 136
Key, John 161, 162
Khan, Javed 184
Khmer Rouge 92, 124
King Country 20–21
Kingi, Wiremu 23
Kingitanga (King Movement) 20–21, 24
Kiribati 191
Kirk, Norman 15, 63, 68, 71, 72–74, 75, 80, 122, 123
Kosovar refugees 145, 166
Kozutina, Natalia 110
Krishna, Muttu 134
Kruger, Tamati 29

Labour and Labour-led governments 13, 32, 44, 67–68, 71, 72–74, 75, 80, 81–83, 94, 106, 108, 115, 133–37, 146–50, 156, 158–60, 180–81, 186
Laking, George 13, 189
Lal, Brij 133, 137
Lange, David 94, 133, 137
language issues 36, 55, 56, 60, 61, 64, 71, 82, 91, 96, 98, 99, 109, 112, 117, 120, 126, 127, 137, 171, 175, 176, 177
Laotian refugees 12, 85, 91, 100–01, 167

Latin American refugees 77–78; *see also* Chilean refugees
Latvian refugees 46, 50
League of Nations High Commissioner for Refugees 12
League of Nations Union 34
Lindt, August 106, 114
Lipscombe, Alan and Muriel 179–80
Lithuanian refugees 46
Lochore, Reuel 39–40, 117, 121–22, 127
Locke, Keith 159–60
Lynch, Brian 182

Malaysia 83, 85, 87, 89, 140, 154, 155, 168
Malcolm, Aussie 90, 91, 92, 94–95, 98, 100, 113, 114, 115, 125–26, 182
Mallard, Trevor 146
Mangere Reception / Refugee Resettlement Centre 55, 100, 103, 126, 152, 153, 154, 161, 181, 182
Manning, Deborah 153, 155
Manson, Hugo and Bill 94
Maori: attitudes to immigration and refugees 29, 68, 163–64, 175–76, 184; inter-tribal warfare 11, 22–23; land loss 11, 19, 21, 22, 25, 27–28, 29; and New Zealand Wars 19–21, 23–25, 27; population 51; as refugees 11, 19–22, 29, 190
Maori Land Court 28
Marshall, John 66
Marshall, Russell 135
Massey University 175; New Settlers Programme 177
Massey, William 41
McDowell, David 73
McIntosh, Alistair 52
McKinnon, Don 114, 141, 142, 170, 174
medical practitioners 35, 47, 53, 74
mental health services 103, 181, 182
Middle East 12, 93, 105, 107, 150, 165–66, 174, 183
migrants, differentiated from refugees 10
Mikaere, Buddy 25
Ministry of Agriculture and Fisheries 88
Ministry of Defence 130
Ministry of External Relations and Trade 135
Ministry of Foreign Affairs 81, 83, 84, 91, 94, 131, 132, 135, 136–37

Mitchell, Austin 51
Mohamed, Fowzia 11
Mohamed, Mohamud 178
Moriori 23
Muldoon, Robert 51, 83
Musket Wars 22–23
Muslim Association of Canterbury 175
Muslims, prejudice against 176, 183–86, 190
Mussa, Azizullah 178–79

Nansen, Fridtjof 12
Nansen Home 54, 107–10, 115
Napier 171
Nash, Walter 32, 44, 106, 108, 115
National and National-led governments 66, 68, 71, 79, 80, 83, 90, 94, 107, 111, 114, 115, 125, 139–46, 160–61, 162, 170, 186
National Council of Churches 16, 29, 68, 71, 76, 86, 97, 106, 108, 111, 115, 124
National Immigration Strategy 177
Nauru 148, 150, 168
Nazism 11, 12, 30–31, 32, 35, 36–37, 38, 45, 77, 188; war criminals 47–49
Neazor, Paul 156
Nelson 26
New Zealand Chinese Association 123
New Zealand First Party 149–50
New Zealand Immigration Service 139–40, 144, 153, 167–69, 172, 177, 186; see also Immigration New Zealand; Refugee Quota Branch; Refugee Status Branch
New Zealand Institute of International Affairs 121
New Zealand League of Rights 69
New Zealand Migration Office, London 52
New Zealand planning for response to boat people 130–31
New Zealand Qualification Authority, certificates in Refugee Settlement Support 180
New Zealand Settlement Strategy 180–81
New Zealand Settlements Act 1863 27
New Zealand Wars: displaced Maori 19–21, 23–25, 27; displaced Pakeha 25–26
Ng, James 41, 64
Ngai Tahu 25, 28
Ngai Te Rangi 27
Ngapuhi 22

Ngati Awa 27
Ngati Maniapoto 24
Ngati Maru 22
Ngati Paoa 22
Ngati Porou 24
Ngati Ranginui 25
Ngati Tuwharetoa 23
Ngati Whatua 20, 22

Obote, Milton 65
occupational criteria for entry 32–33, 39, 47, 53, 71, 85; education and qualifications 91; Occupational Priority List 59; skilled workers 32, 33, 39, 47, 52, 57–58, 59, 68, 74, 94; unskilled workers 32, 39, 46–47, 52, 71; see also employment
Oestreicher, Paul 36
O'Grady, Ron 111–12, 113, 115
Old Believers 16, 99, 100, 110–13
Operation Babylift 81, 124
Orderly Departure Programme (ODP) 90
orphan refugees 14, 40, 44, 53, 127; Chinese 121–24; displaced after World War II 47, 121; Polish 117–18, 119–20, 127; Vietnamese 81, 124
Otago 40
Ottoman Empire 11–12

Pacific Islands 63, 68, 80
Pacific Islands immigrants 52, 67, 69, 70, 90, 131, 138, 175
Pacific Solution scheme 148
Pahiatua Reception and Training Centre 50–51, 96, 119, 120, 127
Pai Marire 21, 23, 24, 26
Palestine 34, 45–46
Palestinian refugees 13
Panah, Ali 159–60, 161
Papua New Guinea 162
Parihaka 21, 23, 25
Peace Pledge Union 34
people smugglers 131, 146, 147, 153, 160, 168
People's Republic of China see China
pepper-potting system 15, 93, 99–100
Persia see Iran
Peters, Winston 149–50, 158
Pinochet, Augusto 75

Index 259

Poata, Tama Te Kapua 176
Pol Pot 92, 94, 95, 125, 126, 127
Poland 11, 118
Police Complaints Authority 155
Polish Association 16
Polish Children's Camp 119, 120, 127
Polish refugees 12, 16, 50, 59–62, 80, 101–02, 114, 174; children 114, 117–21
poll tax 40–41, 42, 64
population, NZ 51; Maori 51; Pacific Island peoples 70; population needs, and refugees 38, 44
Poverty Bay 26, 27
Prebble, Richard 134
Presbyterian Church 41, 44, 54–55
Presbyterian Support Services (PSSA) 110
prisons, detention of asylum seekers 144, 152, 153, 155, 159–60
Protocol Relating to the Status of Refugees 1967 10, 131, 132, 151
public opinion on immigration and refugee policy 16, 98, 99; Asian settlers 81; asylum seekers 143–46, 148; displaced persons from World War II 50; ethnic diversity 185–86, 189; Indian settlers 64; Indo-Chinese refugees 82, 83, 84, 85, 86, 88, 89, 95; Jewish refugees 35–36, 39–40, 112–13; Somali refugees 174–75, 184; *Tampa* refugees 148; Ugandan Asian refugees 67, 68–70; *see also* community acceptance and support
Pukas, Jonas 49

Quigley, A. 109
quotas *see* refugee quotas

Rabuka, Sitiveni 132, 137
Rasalingam, Nagalingam 153, 173, 181–82
Ratana religious movement 21
Rattanong, Houmpheng 100–01
reception centres 55, 57; Mangere Reception / Refugee Resettlement Centre 55, 100, 103, 126, 152, 153, 154, 161, 181, 182; Pahiatua Reception and Training Centre 50–51, 96, 119, 120, 127
Red Cross 16, 36, 118, 125; NZ Red Cross 16, 55, 86, 99, 119, 121, 182–83
Refugee and Migrant Service (RMS) 99, 167, 170, 171, 172, 173, 179, 180, 181, 183; *see also* Inter-Church Commission on Immigration and Refugee Resettlement; Inter-Church Committee on Immigration; Refugee Services Aotearoa New Zealand; RMS Refugee Resettlement
Refugee Council of New Zealand 152, 153, 173, 181
Refugee Day 99
Refugee Family Reunification Trust 173
Refugee Lifeline 181
Refugee Mobile Community Clinical Team 181
refugee policy 13–14, 55; changes, 2006–12 158–61; links to foreign policy 14, 72–73, 77, 80–81, 115, 189; links to immigration policy 14, 31–32, 121–22, 166, 177; past policies used to justify current practice 66–67, 77, 90, 111; refugee needs rather than labour market requirements 14, 72, 91, 103–04, 106, 107, 113; *see also* asylum seekers; family reunion; immigration policy; public opinion on immigration and refugee policy; selection of refugees; settlement of refugees
Refugee Quota Branch 164, 183, 186
refugee quotas 99, 138, 153, 182, 248–49; annual quota 114, 150, 164–65, 166, 170, 171, 172, 173, 177, 186; Chilean refugees 75; displaced persons after World War II 49, 50; Eastern European refugees 58, 62; ethnic groups 49, 166–67, 168–69, 170–71; family members 171, 172, 173; Indo-Chinese refugees 89, 90, 93, 94, 102–03; Jewish refugees 62; refugees with disabilities or needing medical attention 187; security concerns 169; single women 49; Somali refugees 170, 171; *Tampa* refugees 149–50; three-year quota 183; Ugandan Asian refugees 71, 74; UNHR individual protection cases 167, 169
Refugee Services Aotearoa New Zealand 16, 99, 182–83; *see also* Inter-Church Commission on Immigration and Refugee Resettlement; Inter-Church Committee on Immigration; Refugee and Migrant Service (RMS); RMS Refugee Resettlement

Refugee Status Appeal Authority 141–42, 147, 151, 157
Refugee Status Branch 138, 140, 151, 155, 159, 161–62, 183
refugee status determination process 134–38, 139, 141–42, 146–47, 148, 150–51, 153, 154–57, 158, 159, 161–62, 248
Refugee Voices: A journey towards resettlement 177
refugees: definition 10; differentiated from migrants and asylum seekers 10–11
Refugees as Survivors (RAS) 15
refugees, NZ, statistics 9, 166
Returned Servicemen's Association (RSA) 35–36, 39
Reutt-Marciszewski, Anna 60–61, 101–02
Ringatu religious movement 21, 25
Rizzo, Gilbert 83
RMS Refugee Resettlement 99, 152; *see also* Refugee and Migrant Service (RMS)
Robson, Matt 145, 155
Rodger, Stan 133–34, 136
Roosevelt, Franklin D. 34
Roumanian refugees 49–50
Rowling, Wallace (Bill) 74, 80, 82
Ruatahuna 20
Russia 11; Revolution, 1917 11, 107, 110
Russian asylum seekers 130; *see also* Soviet Union
Russian refugees 50, 62, 99, 100, 107–13
Rwandan genocide 1994 170
Rwandan refugees 12, 166, 167, 170
Ryken, David 145

Samoan immigrants 89
Scandinavian immigrants 46
security, border 139–40, 145, 146, 147, 158–59, 161
Security Intelligence Service (SIS) 59, 76, 155–56, 157
security screening of refugees 47–48, 53–54, 59, 76
Seddon, Richard 41, 64
selection of refugees 31–35; Czech and Slovak refugees 57–59; displaced persons from World War II 44–50, 99; financial considerations 33, 36; Hungarian refugees 13–14, 52–54, 99; Indo-Chinese refugees 85, 86–87, 91–92, 93, 94–95, 99; and personal contacts 33, 36; Polish refugees 59–60, 61, 62; Ugandan Asian refugees 70–71; *see also* family reunion; health criteria for entry; occupational criteria for entry; refugee quotas; special needs refugees
Semple, Bob 47
settlement of refugees 15, 97–103, 176–79; Cambodian children 126–27; dispersal throughout NZ (pepper-potting) 15, 42, 55, 93, 99–100; Hungarian refugees 55–56, 57; Indo-Chinese refugees 85–86, 88, 89, 91–92, 93–94, 100, 126–27; information and education 61, 62, 96, 171; main phases 169; New Zealand Settlement Strategy 180–81; Old Believers 111–12; Polish children 119–20, 127; refugees from wide range of ethnicities 171; regional-based approach 168–69; specialist services 15, 179–83, 189, 190; success stories 177–79; *see also* adjustment of refugees to NZ life; community acceptance and support; employment; health needs; housing; integration of new settlers; language issues; sponsorship of refugees
Shanahan, Foss 45–46
Shand, Tom 17, 29, 111
Shipley, Jenny 143
Sim Commission 23
Simon Wiesenthal Center, Los Angeles 48, 49
Sinclair, Keith 115
Sino-Japanese War 41
Skinner, Tom 68–69
Skwarko, Krystina 118, 119
Slavic refugees 44, 45, 49, 62
Slovakian refugees 12, 57–59
smugglers of people 131, 146, 147, 153, 160, 168
Society of Friends (Quakers) 34
Somali refugees 11, 166, 167, 168, 170–72, 178, 179, 180, 181, 184
Somalian conflicts 1992–94 170
South Auckland 27
South East Asia Treaty Organisation (SEATO) 79
Southland Trades Council 50
Soviet Union 62, 107, 118, 129, 130

Spanish Civil War 12
special needs refugees: 'hard core'
    refugees 103-07, 114; since 1970s 113-
    16; *see also* disabled refugees; elderly
    refugees; health needs
sponsorship of refugees 16, 33, 37, 60, 86, 88,
    93, 95, 97, 98, 99, 100-02, 105, 112, 164,
    172, 179-80, 189-90
Sprackett, Bob 122, 123
Sri Lanka 159
St Vincent de Paul Society 86
Stalin, Svetlana 130
statistics on refugee numbers 9
stigma 11
Stringer, Wayne 49
Sudanese refugees 12, 166, 167, 181, 184
Sudetenland 34
Sutch, Bill 48
Swain, Paul 146
Syria 190
Szegoe, Eva 56-57

Tai Tokerau District Maori Council 68
Tainui 27
Tampa asylum seekers 115, 134, 147-50, 162,
    167, 178-79
Taranaki 23, 24, 26, 27; *see also* individual
    place names
Tauranga 25, 27
Taylor, Keith 82-83, 85, 86, 89, 98, 125, 182
Te Aroha, Reihana 21
Te Kooti Arikirangi Te Turuki 21, 25
Te Maiharoa, Hipa 25
Te Urewera 20, 25
Terrorism Suppression Act 2002 158
terrorist attacks, 11 September 2001 147, 152,
    169, 186
terrorists, no evidence of abuse of asylum
    procedures to gain entry 140-41
Terry, Lionel 41
Thailand 83, 85, 87, 89, 92-93, 125, 126, 140,
    168
Third, Kevin 167, 168-69
Thomson, David 57, 80
Toth, Louis 56
Traiskirchen Camp, Austria 58-59, 61
travel costs 58, 86, 88, 97, 165, 173
Trentham reception centre 55, 57

tuberculosis 85, 104-05, 186-87
Tucker, Warren 156
Tuhoe 25, 27, 29
Turanga 24-25
Turnovsky, Fred 36-37
Tuvalu 191

Ugandan Asian refugees 16, 63-75, 97, 100,
    245, 251
unemployment 32, 33, 61, 69, 181
unions 32, 33-34
United Hebrew Immigration Society / Hebrew
    Immigrants' Aid Society (HIAS) 16, 62,
    97
United Nations: Convention Against
    Torture 161; Convention Relating to
    the Status of Refugees 1951 10, 54, 131,
    151, 155, 157, 161; High Commissioner
    for Refugees (UNHCR) 10, 13, 44, 54,
    66, 73, 76, 82, 83, 85, 86, 87, 95, 98, 104,
    106, 107, 121, 124-26, 164, 165, 167,
    170, 173, 182; Protocol Relating to the
    Status of Refugees 1967 10, 131, 132, 151;
    Relief and Rehabilitation Administration
    (UNRRA) 13; Relief and Works Agency
    for Palestinian Refugees (UNRWA) 13;
    Special Committee on Refugees and
    Displaced Persons 37, 43
United Nations Association 106
United States 36, 58, 59, 80, 83, 87, 89, 92, 130,
    138, 147, 159
Upper Hutt 184

Vanteeva, Irina 109-10
Vietnam War 12, 68, 79-80, 94
Vietnamese refugees 12, 80-83, 85, 87, 88,
    90-91, 95, 102-03, 124, 167
Volfing, Ole 73, 83, 89
volunteer support services 15, 84, 98, 99,
    100-02, 125, 179-80, 182

Waerenga-a-Hika 24
Waikato 19-20, 21, 23-24, 27
Wairoa 26
Waitaki Valley 25
Waitangi Tribunal 190; reports describing
    Maori as refugees 20, 23
Waldensian Church 107

Walding, Joe 76
Walker, Ranginui 175
war and violence 190-91; *see also* Cold War; Ethiopia-Eritrea Wars; Gulf War 1991; New Zealand Wars; Rwandan genocide; Sino-Japanese War; Somalian conflicts; Spanish Civil War; Vietnam War; World War I; World War II
Warsame, Mahad 175
welfare benefits 98, 101, 105, 108, 172
Wellington 21, 26, 51, 55, 56, 93, 119, 170, 178, 185
Wellington Indian Association 97
Wellington Polytechnic School of Languages 86
West Papua 191
Whakatohea 27
'white' New Zealand 41, 52, 57
White Russian refugees 100, 107-10
Wilfred, Harmon Lynn 159
Wilson, Bill 141-42
Woburn reception centre 55
Wodzicka, Countess 118
Wodzicki, Count Kamimierz 118
Wojciechowski, Jan 119
women, refugees: Chinese 41-42; displaced persons from World War II 44; Hungarian 52; Muslim, wearing of burqa 185; wearing of hijab 185; at risk 9, 164, 171-72; single women preferred over men 47, 49; Somali 170, 171-72
Wong, Pansy 184
Wood, Sidney 69
Woods, Richard 155, 157
World Council of Churches 83
World Refugee Year (WRY) 105, 106, 107, 108, 115
World War I 11
World War II 10, 11, 12, 13, 35-37, 42, 117-18; displaced persons 43-51, 77, 80, 96, 99, 103-06, 107, 121, 249; war criminals 47-49

Yadegary, Hossein (Thomas) 159
Yugoslavian refugees 50, 166
YWCA 86

Zambian refugees 166
Zaoui, Ahmed 17, 154-57
Zewdie, Eyob 177
Zimbabwean refugees 186